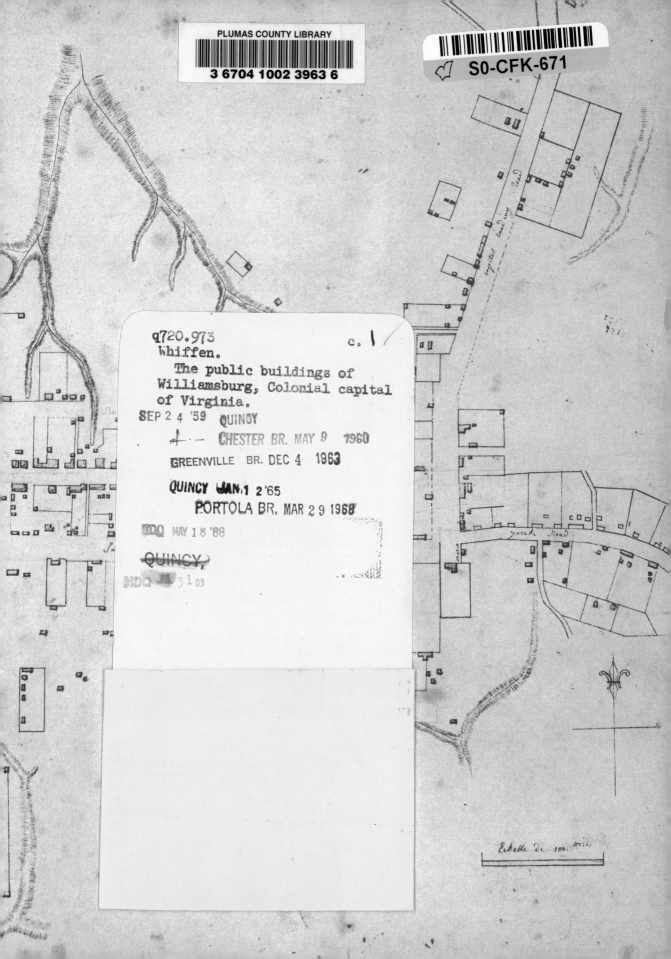

Echelle de 100 toises

York Road

THE PUBLIC BUILDINGS
OF WILLIAMSBURG

WILLIAMSBURG ARCHITECTURAL STUDIES

VOLUME ONE

THE PUBLIC BUILDINGS
OF WILLIAMSBURG

Colonial Capital of Virginia

AN ARCHITECTURAL HISTORY

by Marcus Whiffen

ARCHITECTURAL HISTORIAN, COLONIAL WILLIAMSBURG

COLONIAL WILLIAMSBURG
WILLIAMSBURG, VIRGINIA

ACKNOWLEDGMENT

This is the first volume of a projected series on the architecture of Williamsburg that will be written in the Architects' Office of Colonial Williamsburg. It is based upon work done by and for the architects of Colonial Williamsburg over the years since 1928. To the many who had a part in that work, and thereby contributed to this study, grateful acknowledgment is made.

Printed in the United States of America

Foreword

THOSE OF US who have worked over the years with the colonial architecture of Williamsburg, which is to say of Tidewater Virginia, have come to feel the greatest respect for the perfection of its style and the manner in which it was disposed on a notable city plan. To see it honored by publication has long been our sincere hope, both because a knowledge of the architectural history of the public buildings is necessary for their proper interpretation and because the great wealth of the research material available may form a real contribution to architectural scholarship. Furthermore, the account of how the architects proceeded to restore and reconstruct the buildings is in itself a fascinating story.

A brief word about the scope of the physical recreation of Williamsburg is important, first, because it forms the background against which the public buildings are placed and, second, because it is of considerable size. Colonial Williamsburg represents the first attempt on a large scale to recover the form and atmosphere of a colonial town. The restored area, as it has come to be known, embraces the most significant portions of the colonial city and contains 130 acres, eighty of which are now landscaped gardens and greens. To accomplish the restoration, 731 modern buildings were taken down or moved from the historic section. Eighty-one existing, original buildings were restored, and 413 buildings were reconstructed on their original foundations.

That the original city plan had been left practically intact was indeed a most fortunate circumstance. This original layout of the principal streets, public greens and squares, along with the eighty-one existing colonial structures, formed a true gauge of the architecture of the place.

However, a staggering amount of research had to be done to support the restoration factually and to solve problems of all kinds. Researchers examined many sources in America and abroad, digging through libraries and archives, probing old deeds, letters, wills, inventories, insurance policies, and other material. From the foundations in the restored area archaeologists sifted over 100 tons of artifacts which provided numerous clues to the life and customs of the eighteenth-century city. A wealth of information about history, government, institutions, economics, manners, and crafts, indeed all fields affecting colonial life, was thus assembled and indexed.

But, though this material was of immense help, the design groups were still faced with a surprising lack of published material on the architecture and gardens. The architects then turned to the surviving examples of colonial buildings and gardens in Williamsburg, Tidewater Virginia and the neighboring colonies. This meant arduous but exciting journeys into the field to discover and study the examples in detail in order to learn the Virginia manner in design. At the same time, archaeology played its patient, but indispensable, part—particularly where the public buildings were concerned.

As the work in the restored area moved ahead, the need for a series of architectural studies was increasingly recognized and was made more compelling by expressions passed on to us by laymen and scholars alike. Despite the desire to commence the studies, the preparation of working drawings and the construction itself under ever-expanding programs absorbed every minute of the time of those engaged on the project. With restoration and the reconstruction work nearing completion, it is now possible to make a start on a program of publications. Perhaps it is just as well that the work in all its phases has been largely concluded before publication began. The deepened perspective affords the opportunity for sounder judgment and wiser appraisal since the author has readily available all of the material to work with.

In this first volume of what will be called the *Williamsburg Architectural Studies,* we are fortunate in having an author possessing a thorough knowledge of the architecture of England, a great sensitivity to Virginia's architectural history, and a lively talent for expression.

It is our hope that this volume will contribute to a deeper understanding, not only of the public buildings of eighteenth century Williamsburg, but of the people who produced them and expressed in them a great faith in liberty, justice and representative government.

A. EDWIN KENDREW, F.A.I.A.
Senior Vice President, Director of
Architecture, Construction and Maintenance,
Colonial Williamsburg

Author's Preface

THERE have been two kinds of books about American colonial architecture: histories and books of record. The latter have been far the more numerous. Indeed, one might think that there was not a moulding, let alone a building, surviving from colonial times that had not been measured, drawn, photographed and published. Of course that is not really so; yet the appreciation of America's heritage of colonial architecture that may be said to have begun with the famous trip along the New England shore made by McKim, Mead, White and Bigelow in 1877 has resulted in its having been recorded and published as fully as any other comparable body of buildings.

Histories of colonial architecture are less numerous, though some of them have been of fine quality. (Among the more general histories one thinks of the late Fiske Kimball's still unrivalled *Domestic Architecture of the American Colonies and Early Republic;* among histories of specific areas, of Anthony Garvan's *Architecture and Town Planning in Colonial Connecticut.*) But then architectural history, if not precisely a new kind of writing, is a kind of writing that has only recently come into full flower. And the even tenor of colonial architecture has seemed to many architectural historians less attractive than the architecture of the nineteenth century with its heights and depths.

This book is a history, a history of the public buildings of the colonial period at Williamsburg. It is an attempt to tell how and why and through whom those buildings came to be what they were, to relate them to the architecture of contemporary England, and to show how they influenced the architecture of the rest of Virginia. It is first of all a book about the buildings as they existed in the eighteenth century: it is not a description of them as restored or reconstructed in the twentieth. However, both to round off the tale and to help the visitor to Williamsburg, the final chapter traces their history from 1780, when Richmond succeeded Williamsburg as capital of Virginia, down to the present.

During the past quarter-century or more, the Department of Research of Colonial Williamsburg has brought together a very large collection of source material concerning Williamsburg's colonial buildings. Material concerning the public buildings has been assembled in typescript volumes of two kinds: "Historical Notes," consisting of chronologically arranged extracts from documents, papers and printed sources, and (in the cases of the Courthouse and the Public Hospital) "Research Reports," in which the available evidence is both set down and interpreted. The first and greatest obligation that I have to acknowledge is to the research workers who thus laid the foundations of the present book. If the fabric that I have raised upon those foundations should be found wanting it will be no fault of theirs.

It gives me pleasure to record my gratitude to present members of Colonial Williamsburg. In the Architects' Office, Mr. A. Edwin Kendrew, Resident Architect, Mr. Mario E. Campioli, Mr. Howard Dearstyne, Mr. Orin M. Bullock, Mr. Ernest M. Frank, Mr. Albert Koch and Mr. Paul Buchanan have been helpful. To Mr. Singleton P. Moorehead special thanks are due, not only for his exquisite renderings of the plans and elevations, which adorn as well as illustrate the book, but also for his readiness to impart his detailed knowledge of the colonial architecture of Virginia (probably unequalled by that of anyone alive) at what cannot always have been the most convenient moments. In the Department of Research, Dr. Edward M. Riley, Dr. Jane Carson and Miss Mary Stephenson have been kind. Mrs. Rose Belk, Research Librarian, has shown in arranging inter-library loans for me even more than the usual patience and pertinacity of her profession. Mrs. Mary R. M. Goodwin, through her familiarity with sources both primary and secondary, has saved me trouble on countless occasions, and in undertaking the compilation of the index has relieved me of a task as important as it is laborious.

People outside Colonial Williamsburg to whom I am especially indebted include Professor Carroll L. V. Meeks and Mr. T. Rutherfoord Goodwin, both of whom read the manuscript and made valuable suggestions, the Librarian of the College of William and Mary and his staff, who have been most hospitable at all times, Professor Bruce T. McCully, who told me of the engravings of Codrington College, Mr. A. Lawrence Kocher, who lent me his copies of Rubens' *Palazzi di Genova* and of Serlio, and Mr. Stephen T. Riley, Librarian of the Massachusetts Historical Society, who both granted me facilities for examining Jefferson's Palace drawings and was good enough to arrange for their photography. In England, Mr. Raymond Smith, Librarian of the Guildhall of the City of London, had search made for plans

and views of Doctors' Commons; Mr. Geoffrey W. Beard gave me information about
Edial Hall, and Mr. J. R. Lindley, Honorary Literary Secretary of the Johnson So-
ciety of Lichfield, supplied photographs of the drawing of that house; Mr. Anthony
D. C. Hyland drew Jefferson's octagonal chapel from the original notes and plan.
Other English correspondents who have been helpful include Mr. Howard Colvin,
of St. John's College, Oxford, Mr. Cecil Farthing, Deputy Director of the National
Buildings Record, Mr. R. Romilly Fedden, Secretary of the Historic Buildings Com-
mittee of the National Trust, Mr. John Summerson, Curator of Sir John Soane's
Museum, and Mr. Rupert Gunnis.

Finally, I extend my thanks to all those individuals and institutions named in
the list of illustrations, for permitting the reproduction of drawings or photographs
in their possession.

Marcus Whiffen

Contents

	PAGE
Foreword by A. Edwin Kendrew	v
Author's Preface	vii
Illustrations	xii
Abbreviations	xvi
I. The Scene is Set	1
II. William and Mary: The First Building	18
III. The Capitol and the Gaol	34
IV. The Palace Before 1710	53
V. 1710–1726: Church and State	67
VI. 1710–1726: Learning and the Stage	96
VII. The Reign of George II	118
VIII. 1760–1780: Steeple, Courthouse, and Hospital	149
IX. Jefferson at Williamsburg	172
X. Since 1780	188
Notes	209
Appendix I. Governors of Virginia, 1689–1781	225
Appendix II. Specifications for the Capitol in the Acts of the Assembly	227
Appendix III. Robert Smith's "Description" of the Public Hospital	229
Appendix IV. Agreement Between Benjamin Powell and the Directors of the Public Hospital	231
Appendix V. Jefferson's Octagonal Chapel	232
Bibliography	235
Index	243

ILLUSTRATIONS

PAGE

1 JAMES BLAIR. Portrait. (College of William and Mary. Photograph: Colonial Williamsburg.) 3

2 WILLIAMSBURG AND THE PUBLIC BUILDINGS. Map. (Library of Congress.) . 13

3 THE COLLEGE OF WILLIAM AND MARY. Plan from the Bland survey. (Public Record Office, London.) 19

4 THE COLLEGE OF WILLIAM AND MARY. Drawing by F. L. Michel. (Stadtbibliothek, Berne, Switzerland. Photograph: College of William and Mary.) . 27

5 HERIOT'S HOSPITAL, EDINBURGH. Plan. (W. Adam, *Vitruvius Scoticus*.) . 28

6 A CITY HOUSE BY SERLIO. Plan. (S. Serlio, *Architettura*.) 29

7 PALAZZO ANTONIO DORIA, GENOA. Plan. (P. P. Rubens, *Palazzi di Genova*.) . 29

8 THE CAPITOL. Excerpt from Jefferson manuscripts. (Library of Congress.) . 38

9 THE CAPITOL. Plan from the Bland survey. (Public Record Office, London.) . 39

10 THE CAPITOL. Plan of ground floor. (Drawing by S. P. Moorehead.) . . 44

11 THE CAPITOL. Plan of upper floor. (Drawing by S. P. Moorehead.) . . 45

12 THE CAPITOL. Plan of excavated foundations. (Drawing by S. P. Moorehead.) 47

13 THE CAPITOL. From the "Bodleian plate." (Colonial Williamsburg.) . . 49

14 THE PALACE. From the "Bodleian plate." (Colonial Williamsburg.) . . 58

15 THE PALACE. Plan of excavated foundations. (Drawing by S. P. Moorehead.) . 59

16 THE PALACE. Measured plan by Thomas Jefferson. (Massachusetts Historical Society.) 60

17 CHEVENING HOUSE, KENT. Elevation. (C. Campbell, *Vitruvius Britannicus*.) . 61

18 HOUSE BY SERLIO. Elevation. (S. Serlio, *Architettura*.) 61

19 EDIAL HALL, STAFFORDSHIRE, ENGLAND. Water-color by Paul Braddon. (Johnson Society of Lichfield.) 62

20 NETHER LYPIATT MANOR, GLOUCESTERSHIRE. Exterior. (Photograph: National Buildings Record.) 63

21 ALEXANDER SPOTSWOOD. Portrait by Charles Bridges. (Commonwealth of Virginia. Photograph: Colonial Williamsburg.) 69

22 FLAT ROOFS BY WILLIAM POPE. (G. Richards' edition of Palladio.) . . 71

23 FLAT FLOOR OR FLAT ROOF BY SERLIO. (S. Serlio, *Architettura*.) . . 71

24 TRABES COMPACTILES. (D. Barbaro's edition of Vitruvius.) 72

25 ROOF OF THE SHELDONIAN THEATRE, OXFORD. (C. Wren, *Parentalia*.) . . 72

26 FLAT ROOFS AND "A ROOF PARTLY FLAT." (W. Salmon, *Palladio Londinensis*.) 73

27 THE GAOL. Plan. (Drawing by S. P. Moorehead.) 74

PAGE

28 THE FIRST BRICK CHURCH OF BRUTON PARISH. Plan. (Drawing by
    S. P. Moorehead.)   76

29 THE FIRST BRICK CHURCH OF BRUTON PARISH. Drawing by F. L. Michel.
    (Stadtbibliothek, Berne, Switzerland.)   78

30 BRUTON PARISH CHURCH. Diagrammatic elevation. (Author. Redrawn
    by A. Koch.)   81

31 BRUTON PARISH CHURCH. Diagrammatic plan. (Author. Redrawn
    by A. Koch.)   81

32 THE MAGAZINE. Plan. (Drawing by S. P. Moorehead.)   .   .   .   85

33 THE MAGAZINE. Elevation. (Drawing by S. P. Moorehead.)   .   .   .   87

34 THE COLLEGE OF WILLIAM AND MARY. From the "Bodleian plate." (Colonial
    Williamsburg.)   97

35 THE COLLEGE OF WILLIAM AND MARY. Daguerreotype. (Photographic copy:
    Colonial Williamsburg.)   98

36 THE COLLEGE OF WILLIAM AND MARY. Plan by Thomas Jefferson. (Henry
    E. Huntington Library.)   99

37 THE COLLEGE OF WILLIAM AND MARY. Plan of main building. (Drawing by
    S. P. Moorehead.)   101

38 THE COLLEGE OF WILLIAM AND MARY. East elevation of main building.
    (Drawing by S. P. Moorehead.)   102

39 CODRINGTON COLLEGE, BARBADOS. Elevations engraved for Society for the
    Propagation of the Gospel. (Houghton Library, Harvard University.)   .   104

40 CODRINGTON COLLEGE, BARBADOS. Plan engraved for Society for the
    Propagation of the Gospel. (Houghton Library, Harvard University.)   .   105

41 THE BRAFFERTON. Plan. (Drawing by S. P. Moorehead.)   .   .   .   108

42 THE BRAFFERTON. Elevation. (Drawing by S. P. Moorehead.)   .   .   109

43 THE BRAFFERTON. Exterior. (Photograph: Colonial Williamsburg.)   .   .   110

44 THE OLD RECTORY, SUTTON COLDFIELD, WARWICKSHIRE. Exterior. (Photograph:
    National Buildings Record.)   111

45 THE PLAYHOUSE. Plan of excavated foundations. (Drawing by
    S. P. Moorehead.)   115

46 THE PRESIDENT'S HOUSE. Exterior. (Photograph: Colonial Williamsburg.)   .   124

47 THE PRESIDENT'S HOUSE. Elevation. (Drawing by S. P. Moorehead.)   .   .   126

48 THE PRESIDENT'S HOUSE. Plan. (Drawing by S. P. Moorehead.)   .   .   127

49 THE SECRETARY'S OFFICE. Plan. (Drawing by S. P. Moorehead.)   .   .   131

50 THE SECRETARY'S OFFICE. Elevation. (Drawing by S. P. Moorehead.)   .   .   132

51 THE SECRETARY'S OFFICE. Exterior. (Photograph: Colonial Williamsburg.)   .   133

52 ABINGDON CHURCH. Doorway. (Photograph: author.)   135

53 CARTER'S GROVE. Doorway. (Photograph: Colonial Williamsburg.)   .   .   135

54 BRUTON PARISH CHURCHYARD. Nott tomb. (Photograph: author.)   .   . 144

55 BRUTON PARISH CHURCHYARD. Bray tomb. (Photograph: author.).   .   . 145

56 BRUTON PARISH CHURCHYARD. Barradall tomb. (Photograph: author.).   . 147

57 BRUTON PARISH CHURCH. Steeple. (Photograph: Colonial Williamsburg.)   . 151

58 BRUTON PARISH CHURCH. Exterior. (Photograph: Colonial Williamsburg.)   . 153

59 BRUTON PARISH CHURCH. Plan. (Drawing by S. P. Moorehead.)   .   .   . 154

60 BRUTON PARISH CHURCH. Elevation. (Drawing by S. P. Moorehead.)   .   . 155

61 THE COURTHOUSE. Exterior. (Photograph: Colonial Williamsburg.)   .   . 156

62 THE COURTHOUSE. Plan. (Drawing by S. P. Moorehead.)   158

63 THE COURTHOUSE. Elevation. (Drawing by S. P. Moorehead.)   .   .   . 159

64 THE PUBLIC HOSPITAL. Plan. (Restoration by A. L. Kocher and
        H. Dearstyne.)   163

65 THE PUBLIC HOSPITAL. Drawing of *circa* 1825. (W. B. Blanton,
        Medicine in Virginia in the Eighteenth Century.)   .   .   . 165

66 THE BOTETOURT STATUE. General view. (Photograph: author.)   .   .   . 169

67 THE BOTETOURT STATUE. Relief on pedestal. (Photograph: author.)   .   . 170

68 THOMAS JEFFERSON. Portrait by Mather Brown. (Charles F. Adams, Jr.
        Photograph: Frick Art Reference Library.)   173

69 THE PALACE. Plan. (Drawing by S. P. Moorehead.)   175

70 THE PALACE. Mantelpiece. (Photograph: Colonial Williamsburg.)   .   . 176

71 THE PALACE. Plan by Thomas Jefferson. (Massachusetts Historical Society.) . 178

72 THE PALACE. Plan by Thomas Jefferson. (Massachusetts Historical Society.) . 178

73 THE PALACE. Plan by Thomas Jefferson. (Massachusetts Historical Society.) . 180

74 THE PALACE. Plan by Thomas Jefferson. (Massachusetts Historical Society.) . 180

75 THE PALACE. Plan by Thomas Jefferson. (Massachusetts Historical Society.) . 180

76 DESIGN FOR A CHAPEL. Plan by Thomas Jefferson. (Henry E. Huntington
        Library.)   183

77 DESIGN FOR A CHAPEL. Notes by Thomas Jefferson. (Henry E. Huntington
        Library.)   184

78 OCTAGONAL CHAPEL. Plan by Robert Morris. (R. Morris, *Select Archi-
        tecture.*)   185

79 CHAPEL DESIGN BY JEFFERSON. Elevation-cum-section. (Drawing by
        A. D. C. Hyland.)   186

80 THE MAGAZINE. View of 1848. (B. J. Lossington, *The Pictorial Field-Book
        of the Revolution.*)   190

81 THE MAGAZINE. Water-color by L. J. Cranston. (Formerly in the
        possession of Colonial Williamsburg.)   191

82 DUKE OF GLOUCESTER STREET. Water-color by T. C. Millington. (College of
        William and Mary.)   192

PAGE

83   THE PUBLIC HOSPITAL. Engraving. (Colonial Williamsburg.)   .   .   .   193

84   THE COLLEGE OF WILLIAM AND MARY. The main building in its third state.
      (Colonial Williamsburg.)   194

85   THE PALACE. East fore-building from water-color by L. J. Cranston.
      (Colonial Williamsburg.)   194

86   THE COLLEGE OF WILLIAM AND MARY. The main building in its fourth
      state. (Colonial Williamsburg.)   197

87   THE COLLEGE OF WILLIAM AND MARY. Main building from east. (Photograph:
      Colonial Williamsburg.)   198

88   THE COLLEGE OF WILLIAM AND MARY. Main building from west. (Photograph:
      Colonial Williamsburg.)   199

89   THE CAPITOL. Exterior. (Photograph: Colonial Williamsburg.)   .   .   200

90.   THE PALACE. Exterior. (Photograph: Colonial Williamsburg.)   .   .   201

91   THE MAGAZINE AND GUARDHOUSE. Exterior. (Photograph: Colonial
      Williamsburg.)   202

92   THE GAOL. Exterior from south-east. (Photograph: Colonial Williamsburg.)   .   203

93   THE GAOL. Exterior from south-west. (Photograph: Colonial Williamsburg.)   .   204

94   BRUTON PARISH CHURCH. Interior, looking east. (Photograph: Colonial
      Williamsburg.)   206

95   BRUTON PARISH CHURCH. Nave, looking west. (Photograph: Colonial
      Williamsburg.)   207

Endpapers
      "THE FRENCHMAN'S MAP." Billeting map of the French Army, 1782.
      (College of William and Mary.)

ABBREVIATIONS

D. A. B.	:	*Dictionary of American Biography*
D. N. B.	:	*Dictionary of National Biography*
O. E. D.	:	*Oxford English Dictionary*
P. R. O.	:	*Public Record Office, London*
V. M. H. B.	:	*Virginia Magazine of History and Biography*
W. & M. Q.	:	*William and Mary Quarterly*

In accordance with the general practice in colonial Virginia, the resident representative of the crown is called the Governor even when he was strictly speaking the Lieutenant Governor. The official titles of the successive "Governors" are given in full in Appendix I.

THE NOTES

Exceptions to the general practice of citing authorities in the notes are made in cases of information or excerpts from the following:

W. W. Hening, ed., *The Statutes at Large; being a Collection of All the Laws of Virginia,* 13 volumes (Richmond, 1810–1823).

H. R. McIlwaine, ed., *Journals of the House of Burgesses of Virginia,* 8 volumes (Richmond, 1909–1915).

H. R. McIlwaine, ed., *Legislative Journals of the Council of Colonial Virginia,* 3 volumes (Richmond, 1918–1919).

H. R. McIlwaine and W. L. Hall, eds., *Executive Journals of the Council of Colonial Virginia,* 5 volumes to date (Richmond, 1925–).

To have given every reference to these works would have resulted in a vast increase in the number of notes without a corresponding increase in their usefulness: every student of the period will be aware that they are the chief sources of knowledge of debates, legislation and executive action affecting the public buildings of the colony.

THE PUBLIC BUILDINGS
OF WILLIAMSBURG

The Scene Is Set

IF COMMEMORATIVE ZEAL should ever bring about the setting up in Virginia of a statue of Opechancanough—after all, Boadicea rides in bronze in London, which she sacked—surely the most suitable site would be the campus of the College of William and Mary at Williamsburg. For had not that Indian king, whose "motiones of religion" so encouraged the Virginia Company's Deputy George Thorpe, given the word for the massacre of the English colonists on Good Friday morning in 1622, there would almost certainly have been no need for the establishment of "a certaine Place of universal Study" seventy years later. One would have already existed, forty miles further up the James River on what we know as Farrar's Island; and it would have been the oldest college not only in the South, but in all British America.

The story of Henrico College may be said to begin in 1617,[1] when James I commanded that the English clergy make two special collections a year for two years, the proceeds to be devoted to assisting the Virginia Company in a programme of building schools and churches for the Indians. The King's interest in the conversion and enlightenment of the Indians had doubtless been increased if not aroused by the example of Pocahontas, who died that year after enjoying a *succès d'estime* both at court and in London at large. When George Yeardley was appointed Governor late in 1618 he was instructed "that a convenient place be chosen and set out for the planting of a University at the said Henrico in time to come and that in the meantime preparation be there made for the building of the said College for the children of the Infidels."

Next year, in 1619, the land granted for the support of the college, something over 10,000 acres along the James, was laid out, and in July we find the General Assembly of the colony beseeching "the Treasurer, Counsell and Company that, towards the erecting of the University and Colledge, they will sende, when they shall thinke it most convenient, workmen of all sortes, fitt for that purpose." In November the fifty men who were to settle the college lands and hand over half their profits to the College arrived in Virginia in the *Bona Nova.* They had had "a wonderful & miraculous passage," but one guesses that it was the last time they had cause to feel that the hand of the Almighty was with them. No sooner had they landed than it was discovered that the supplies of food and clothing sent with them were much less than promised and quite insufficient to keep them through the winter—which turned out "extreame Cold." Most of them were hired out to established planters for a year for their own preservation; seventeen were to perish in the Massacre of 1622.

It is not our business, in a book about architecture, to follow the story of Henrico College in detail. The college never came to architecture, even though after the Massacre the Virginia Company took steps to ensure that the contracts which had been made with brick-makers should not lapse. Nor, though again we read of "men sent for the buildings," did the East India School, planned for Charles City (now City Point) as a preparatory school for Henrico College. The most active mover in this project was Patrick Copland, "Preacher to the Navy and Fleet of the East India Company," who had been led to interest himself in the affairs of Virginia by Sir Thomas Dale, the founder of Henrico, when they were thrown together in Japan. A philanthropist with a gift for fund-raising that would qualify him for high academic position today, Copland was a graduate of Marischal College, Aberdeen, and had already endowed a chair of divinity there. In his work for the East India School he may, it has been pointed out,[2] have been thinking of his old university, where also an attached preparatory school (unknown in English universities) was provided for from the first. As part of his reward, the Virginia Company made him Rector—the title is significantly Scottish—of "the intended Colledge of Virginia" at Henrico.

A quarter of a century had gone by since the Massacre. Patrick Copland, now living in Bermuda, was troubled about the fate of his Aberdeen endowments. A fellow Scot, Robert Smyth, was returning to their homeland, and Copland seized the opportunity to write for news to a clergyman whom Mr. Smyth had heard preach in Ireland and who had since moved to Aberdeen.[3] The clergyman was Robert Blair, father of that James Blair who was to become the founder and first President of the College of William and Mary.

Figure 1. JAMES BLAIR. Portrait by an unknown artist, painted between 1720 and 1730; the second College building is in the background.

THE FOUNDING OF WILLIAM AND MARY

The Virginia Company never abandoned the "intended Colledge" altogether. But after the revocation of the company's charter in 1624, when the colony became a royal province, nothing was done for higher education in Virginia until 1660. In that year the idea of a college with an attached preparatory school was revived, and reached the statute books in no less than three acts of the General Assembly. The emphasis had shifted, however: no longer was the benefit of "the children of the Infidels" the first consideration; the objects were stated to be "the advance of learning, education of youth; supply of the ministry and promotion of piety."

Another thirty years, and the first steps towards the founding of William and Mary were taken by the son of Copland's Aberdeen correspondent, the Rev. James Blair. Born in 1656 and educated at Marischal College and the University of Edinburgh, Blair was persuaded to go to Virginia by Henry Compton, Bishop of London, with whom he became acquainted when working in the office of the Master of the Rolls in London. Virginia was in the diocese of the Bishop of London, and Blair obtained the living of Varina (later known as Henrico). That was in 1685; in 1689 the Bishop showed his appreciation of Blair's abilities by creating a new post for him, that of Commissary. In this capacity Blair had authority to exercise a general supervision over the clergy in the colony, and it was in this capacity that, at a convention called by him at Jamestown in 1690, he urged the clergy to action in the matter of the so long deferred college. It was hardly to be expected that the exhortations of the Bishop of London's deputy would go unheeded. The result was the "severall Propositions to be humbly P'sented to the Consideration of the next Generall Assembly, for the better incouragement of Learning By the founding a Colledge in this Country." [4] In this document it was "proposed that the Gen^ll Assembly would humbly address their sacred Maj^ties to grant their Lysence and Royall Charter to the Colledge"; means of maintaining it were suggested, and the salaries of the President and Professors, and of the Master and Usher of the grammer school that was to form part of the foundation, were named. Clearly Blair was the author.

The Governor of the colony at the time of the convention was Francis Nicholson, very recently arrived from England. In later years, during Nicholson's second tenure of the Governorship, Blair was to quarrel with him and even be instrumental in getting him recalled. At this early stage, however, all was harmony be-

tween them; indeed, Nicholson's share in the promotion of the scheme for a
college was second only to Blair's. In less than a month he and his Council had
examined and approved the proposals, and soon the machinery for collecting
subscriptions was once more set in motion. The matter was taken up by the
General Assembly in the spring of 1691; by the end of June, Blair was on the
high seas with an Address of the Assembly to be presented to William III, and
with written instructions which, while detailed, left much to his discretion. His
departure had been only slightly delayed by a resolution of the House of Burgesses
that it was not safe for him to take passage to England with a certain Captain John
Jennings, "for that it hath plainly appeared to this gen[ll] Assembly how maliciously
and disdainfully he hath contemned the Govern[mt] & abused the inhabitants
thereof."

Blair was in England for most of two years, the charter for the College not
being finally signed until February 1693. We know something of how he spent
his time from his letters to Nicholson. Things went swimmingly whenever he
came face to face with the dignitaries whose aid he sought; but it was not always
easy to achieve that degree of proximity. His patience was, as he put it, "sufficiently
exercised."

> When I came first to London, which was the first day of September, there were
> many things concurred to hinder my sudden presenting of the address about
> the College, for Mr. Jeoffreys was in Wales, & did not come to Town to present
> the address upon their majesties' accession to the crown; the Bishop of London
> thought it not so proper to present an address about business; then the King was
> in Flanders; my friend the Bishop of Salisbury was at Salisbury; the Bishop of
> St. Asaph at his diocese in Wales, and before Mr. Jeoffreys came to Town the
> Bishop of London was taken very sick. . . .[5]

Then later in the winter

> There was another reason too why my business was delayed & that was that my
> Lord Archbishop of Canterbury, who is the person I depend upon for managing
> of it with the King & Queen, was for five weeks frozen up at Lambeth so that
> he could neither get to Court nor Parliament but by coming round by the bridge,
> which he found to be so long and so bad a way that he chose for the most part
> to stay at home.[6]

However, Blair was not idle. He solicited and obtained subscriptions, and he in-
terviewed possible masters and ushers; these were not easily found, for "in England
their masters of their colleges have a much easier life than is designed for the masters
& professors of our college in Virginia."[7] It must have been a gratifying moment

when he could at last assure himself that the charter made "our well-beloved in Christ, James Blair, Clerk . . . first President of the said College during his natural Life."

For the building and maintenance of the College the charter granted four sources of income: £11,985 out of Virginia quit-rents, the proceeds of a tax of a penny a pound on all tobacco exported from Virginia and Maryland to other countries than England, the fees from the office of Surveyor-General of the Virginia Colony, and 20,000 acres of land on Blackwater Swamp and at Pamunkey Neck in Virginia—the land to be held for the quit-rent of two copies of Latin verses delivered to the Governor at his house every November 5. Besides the charter, Blair brought back with him the College seal. Whether he also brought, as a writer of 1724 implies,[8] designs for the College building by the Surveyor-General of the King's Works, Sir Christopher Wren, is a question to which we must return later.

MIDDLE PLANTATION BECOMES WILLIAMSBURG

The site of the College still remained to be decided. The Virginia clergy had proposed that it should be built "as near as may be to the Centre of the Country," but the peculiar geography of the Tidewater, and its lack of any town that could be thought to provide a centre in an other than geographical sense, laid the proposal open to interpretations that differed according to the interests of the interpreter. At first there were those who favoured a site on the north side of York River, in Gloucester County, and this faction did indeed win the opening round in the House of Burgesses. But after the Council had delivered its views the House changed its mind, and it was resolved that the College should be built on the south side of York River near Yorktown. This site was mentioned in the instructions Blair took with him to England. However, the charter left liberty of choice in the matter to the Assembly, and in October 1693 the discussion was renewed. On the second day of the debate Blair, who had been invited to attend, presented a report on four places that had been suggested: Yorktown, York Old Fields, "Green's land in Gloucester County" (the site first approved by the Burgesses back in 1691), and Middle Plantation. Someone advocated a site on the newly granted land a Pamunkey Neck. Upon the question being put it was

> Resolved that it was the Opinion of the house that Middle-plantation is the most convenient & fit place to erect the Colledge upon & that a byll be prepared for erecting the Same at that place, as near the Church as convenience will permit.

It was an historic decision. Though they could not know it, the Burgesses had
settled, with the site of the College, the location of the next capital of Virginia.
Five years later, in October 1698, the Statehouse at Jamestown where they met,
which had been built in 1685, went up in flames. In 1699 a May Day celebration was held at the College. Francis Nicholson, who had returned to the colony
for his second term of office as Governor a few weeks after the Statehouse blaze,
sponsored it. And it may be supposed that he inspired at least the third of the five
speeches made on the occasion. In this were set forth "the advantages which arise
from the mutual relation between a Town"—as yet there was nothing at Middle
Plantation that could have been called a town even in seventeenth-century Virginia
—"and the College":

> First that the Colledge will help to make the Town . . . The very numbers of the
> Colledge who will be obliged to reside at this place viz. the president and
> Masters with all their Servants and attendants, the Scholars, with such servants
> as will be necessary for the kitchin, Buttery, Gardens, wooding, and all other
> uses will make up about 100 persons to be constantly supply'd at this market . . .
> Besides the College being not yet finish'd will employ in builders and Labourers
> a very considerable number; and it is easily to be foreseen that the prime Youth
> of the Country being here, it will occasion a great resort hither of parents and
> other friends.[9]

Later in the month, on May 18, this speech was read in the House of Burgesses,
immediately after a message from the Governor recommending the placing of the
new Statehouse at Middle Plantation; on the same day the House resolved "that
the said State house be built at the Middle Plantation." *An Act directing the building the Capitoll and the City of Williamsburgh* became law on June 7.

"The Capitoll and the City": the order of the words is significant. For some time
past the lack of towns in Virginia had been deplored both by legislators in the colony
and by the authorities in England, and there had been enactments designed to
remedy the situation. But the tyranny of tobacco, in conjunction with the abundance of navigable waterways and the self-sufficiency of the plantations, rendered
inoperative the usual economic factors making for the growth of towns: where every
man cultivated the same staple for sale overseas there was little call for markets, and
where sea-going vessels could both load that staple and unload European goods
within a mile or two of most men's homes there was no need for ports. The kind of
decentralization that resulted did not fit into the pattern of the Baroque age, of which
Francis Nicholson's conception of a new city serving the needs of those who attended
the legislature and the courts is so thoroughly characteristic. For the Act of 1699

makes it clear that this was to be the main function of Williamsburg, stating as it does that "the general assemblies, and general courts, of this his majesty's colony and dominion, cannot possibly be held and kept at the said capitol, unless a good town be built and settled adjacent to the said capitol, suitable for the accommodation and entertainment of a considerable number of persons, that of necessity must resort thither."

FRANCIS NICHOLSON AND THE PLANNING OF WILLIAMSBURG

These then are the conditions to which Williamsburg owes its existence: if the fourth Statehouse at Jamestown had not burned there would have been no absolute necessity for a new one when Nicholson returned to govern Virginia a second time; if there had been no College at Middle Plantation he might not have been able to effect the removal of the capital. And without detracting from James Blair's part in the proceedings one may suggest that without Nicholson there might have been no College.

For a man of whom it has been said that he was "almost the only Englishman of his time who might be called a professional colonial governor" [10]—in 35 years of service abroad he governed Maryland, Nova Scotia and South Carolina as well as Virginia—Nicholson is a surprisingly obscure figure. His parentage is in doubt, there is no record of his physical appearance, and the accounts of his character that have come down to us are more than usually prejudiced. It is clear that he had exceptional energy; he also had a violent temper, and the remark of the Indian who said that he was "born drunk" is probably as descriptive as it is succinct. Of his public actions outside Virginia there is only one that need concern us here, and that is his founding, four years before the founding of Williamsburg, of Annapolis as the new capital of Maryland.

Maryland had ceased to be a proprietary colony and become a royal province in 1691; Nicholson was the second royal Governor. The ostensible reason for the removal of the Assembly and Courts from St. Mary's City was its inaccessibility; the real reason was the strength of the Roman Catholics there. The plan of the new capital departed radically from the normal colonial town plan. Instead of the checkerboard or gridiron, which had been adopted for Kingston, Jamaica, in the same decade and for Charleston and Philadelphia in the previous one, Annapolis was given a layout which, with its *ronds-points* or "circles" and its diagonal streets, must have been inspired by the plans of Christopher Wren and John Evelyn for the rebuilding of London after the Great Fire of 1666; it thus became the first British town actually to be built to a Baroque plan.[11] To whom was this due? The Surveyor of Anne Arundel County, Richard Beard, was responsible for the technical part of laying out Annapolis; in 1696 his "mapp and platt" of the town, "drawn up and presented" to the Assembly "by order and Direction of his Excellency" the Governor, was "carefully Examined and Sealed with the Greate Seale of the Province att the four Sides thereof and upon the backside thereof Sealed with his Excellencys Seale att Armes on a red Cross with red Tape"[12]—measures which signally failed to impress the rats, owing to whose attentions "several parts" of it had to be amended and fairly transcribed" two years later.[13] Perhaps Beard was responsible for the character of the layout too. But it would seem more likely that Nicholson was.

For Williamsburg Nicholson proposed a plan which employed Baroque diagonals to produce something with rather the character of a sixteenth-century "conceit." Robert Beverley tells us that he "mark'd out the Streets in many Places, so that they might represent the Figure of a *W*, in Memory of his late Majesty King *William*, after whose Name the Town was call'd Williamsburg";[14] according to Hugh Jones the streets were to be "in the Form of a Cypher, made of *W*. and *M*."[15] It is not too easy to see how the thing could have been done. But no matter: in the event Williamsburg got a plan that combined Baroque principles in the placing of the principal buildings with the traditional gridiron in the street layout. The change was due to Alexander Spotswood, Governor in 1710–1722.[16]

The use of the gridiron plan for colonial towns has a history that goes back to Greek antiquity. Although it is in fact a primitive type, the ancients considered that its inventor was Hippodamus of Miletus, who laid out the colony of Thurii in South Italy for Pericles in 443 B.C. The Roman variety was distinguished from the Greek by its possession of two main axial streets, the *decumanus* running east and west and the *cardo* running north and south; the origin of these features is doubtless to be found in the planning of the Roman military camp. By the sixteenth century Roman practice was well enough known—from literary sources, for there was no direct knowledge of Roman town plans before the archaeological excavations of the nineteenth century—to inspire Francis I's rebuilding of Vitry-le-François; in his *Theorike and Practike of Moderne Warres* of 1598 Robert Barret shows a military camp which is "very close indeed to the popular conception of Caesar's encampments in the Gallic wars."[17] And in the second decade of the seventeenth century the town of Londonderry in Ulster was laid out along unmistakably Roman lines.

Unlike Roman towns, Williamsburg was never fortified. The *decumanus* is still represented by Duke of Gloucester Street plainly enough. But the *cardo*? On a present-day plan it is not immediately evident, owing to the modern street system in Market Square. In colonial times, however, Market Square was not a green cut up by streets, but an open space into which the streets debouched. Once one reads it as such, England Street may be seen as the central north-south axis, the *cardo*.

Although the resemblance of Williamsburg's plan to that of a Roman town— whether intentional or not—dates only from the second decade of the eighteenth century, it may be that classical learning played a considerable part from the very beginning. When Annapolis was founded as the new capital of Maryland its accessibility was given as the reason; the reasons given for the choice of Middle Plantation were its healthfulness and the ease of provisioning that the site offered—

> forasmuch as the place commonly called and known by the name of the *Middle Plantation,* hath been found by constant experience to be healthy, and agreeable to the constitutions of the inhabitants of this his majesty's colony and dominion having the naturall advantage of a Serene and temperate aire dry and champaign land and plentifully stored with wholesom Springs and the conveniency of two navigable and Pleasant Creeks that Run out of James and York River's, necessary for the supplying the place with provisions and other things of necessity. . . .[18]

Now it has been argued that the planners of New Haven in 1635 "were fully aware of Vitruvius (the Roman writer on architecture whose manuscripts were discovered in the fifteenth century) and his maxims for town planning." [19] It is at least as likely that the founders of Williamsburg knew their Vitruvius in 1699, and therefore it may be no accident that the foregoing passage should recall the Roman author's instructions concerning the site of a city:

> First comes the choice of a very healthy site. Such a site will be high, neither misty nor frosty, and in a climate neither hot nor cold, but temperate; further, without marshes in the neighbourhood. For when the morning breezes blow toward the town at sunrise, if they bring with them mists from marshes and, mingled with the mist, the poisonous breath of the creatures of the marshes to be wafted into the bodies of the inhabitants, they will make the site unhealthy. Again if the town is on the coast with a southern or western exposure, it will not be healthy, because in summer the southern sky grows hot at sunrise and is fiery at noon, while a western exposure grows warm after sunrise, is hot at noon, and at evening all aglow.[20]

Vitruvius later mentions as the second consideration, "after insuring . . . the healthfulness of the future city," the necessity of "selecting a neighborhood that can supply plenty of food stuffs to maintain the community, with good roads or else convenient rivers or seaports affording easy means of transport to the city." [21]

Illustrating the undesirability of marshy sites, Vitruvius writes:

> A case of a town built in such a spot was Old Salpia in Apulia . . . Year after year there was sickness, until finally the suffering inhabitants came with a public petition to Marcus Hostilius and got him to agree to seek and find them a proper place to remove their city. Without delay he made the most skilful investigations, and at once purchased an estate near the sea in a healthy place, and asked the Senate and Roman people for permission to remove the town. He constructed the walls and laid out the house lots, granting one to each citizen for a mere trifle. This done, he cut an opening from a lake into the sea, and thus made of the lake a harbour for the town. The result is that now the people of Salpia live on a healthy site and at a distance of only four miles from the old town. [22]

Did Nicholson see himself as a second Marcus Hostilius? According to Robert Beverley, he "flatter'd himself with the fond Imagination, of being the Founder of a new City," [23] and although the story of Old and New Salpia does not resemble that of Jamestown and Williamsburg in every particular the resemblance is close enough for it to have ministered to his vanity.

Finally—and here at least the classicizing tendency cannot be denied—there is the name given to the new statehouse by the Act of 1699, when it laid down "that the sd building shall for ever hereafter be caled and knowne by the name of the Capitoll." This was the first time the term Capitol was applied to a statehouse in America; moreover, it appears that the Williamsburg building may have been the only one to which it was ever applied before the Revolution. [24]

In one respect Nicholson could outdo Ancient Rome. To judge from library inventories and booksellers' advertisements, many Virginians must at least have looked into Basil Kennett's *Romae Antiquae Notitia*, [25] or *Roman Antiquities* as the inventories generally have it—a book dedicated, incidentally, to the little boy for whom Duke of Gloucester Street was named. If Nicholson did so too he could have read, of "the *Capitol*, or Temple of *Jupiter Capitolinus*": "The Structure stood on a high Ridge, taking in four Acres of Ground." Capitol Square covers five acres.

THE TOWN AND ITS ARCHITECTURE

The total area acquired for the new town was 283 acres. Some of this was accounted for by the ports or landings on the creeks of the York and James rivers and the roads leading to them: the town proper was assigned 220 acres. The land was surveyed by Theodorick Bland; his "platt" still exists, in the Public Record Office in London. The course and the name of Duke of Gloucester Street was settled by the Act, which ordered that "the other streets and lanes" should be "built in such manner, and according to such rules and orders as shall be given and made by the directors," who were appointed by the Act and at whose head was Nicholson. The town was laid out in half-acre lots, which were sold to private individuals who forfeited them unless they built houses conforming to certain minimum specifications within two years of the date of sale. These requirements, and the modifications of them that were introduced when the Act was re-enacted with additions in 1705, do not concern us as they would if our subject were the domestic architecture of Williamsburg. But one point worth notice here is that the dimensions of the statutory houses—as also of the Capitol—are given in multiples of five and ten instead of numbers deriving from the traditional house-bay, whose length of sixteen feet had been standardized in very early times as the space required for four oxen in the stall.[26] This innovation was due to contemporary London practice, for ten feet was the length of the London carpenter's measuring rod.[27]

Williamsburg has the more charm in our eyes today because it never "went" as its founders presumably hoped it would. It remained a "greene country towne" (as Penn had described his ideal for Philadelphia) with a population that never in colonial times exceeded 1,800. Yet for all its openness it had a regularity which was ensured by the framers of the Act when they wrote into it: " . . . the front of each house [on Duke of Gloucester Street] shall come within six foot of the street, and not nearer; and . . . the houses in the several lots in the said main street shall front alike." The feature that from the first distinguished it from other colonial towns was the termination of the main axial street by two dominant public buildings, the College and the Capitol; later, an important secondary axis was created with the Governor's Palace as its climax (Fig. 2). This axial placing of the public buildings also distinguished Williamsburg from existing English towns; for these, to use Lavedan's antithesis, were *villes spontanées* rather than *villes créées*, and in the *ville spontanée* public buildings have to take their chance. The *ville créée* was out of tune with English political and mercantile ideas—as the fate of Wren's plan to impose order on the emphatically spontaneous City of London demonstrated. Even if one moves forward into the great age of English town planning, the late eighteenth century and the early nineteenth, it remains difficult, if not impossible, to find close parallels to the Williamsburg plan: the English town planner, in lay-

Figure 2. WILLIAMSBURG AND THE PUBLIC BUILDINGS. A French army map of 1781.

39.ᵉ Camp à **William's burg** le 26 Septembre 7 milles de Arches'hupe

Le 27 Séjour

Chemin d'habitation

Chemin d'York

Chemin de Burwells-ferry

M.ᵈᵉ d'habitation particulier

Queen's Creek

Capitole Landing

Chemin d'habitation particulier

William's burg

Capitole

Gouvernement

Maison des fous

College

College Landing

College - Creek

Chemin d'habitation

Richr mill's

Chemin de Richmond

Chemin d'habitation

Chemin d'habitation particulier

Chemin d'habitation James' Town &c.

ing out and designing his streets and squares and crescents and terraces, was thinking in residential terms and was rarely concerned with the setting off of public buildings. For axial town planning of the kind we see at Williamsburg we should look rather to the France of Louis XIV, and it is likely enough that both Nicholson and Spotswood knew something of French town planning. In any case the axial placing of the chief buildings at Williamsburg was in the spirit of the age—the age of the Baroque.

The adjective Baroque can be applied to those buildings themselves only in the most general sense. The College, the Capitol, the Palace and Bruton Parish Church were built when England was developing a Baroque architecture of her own; but they belonged, as many buildings of their time in the English provinces belonged, to an older tradition. Nevertheless, it would be hard to exaggerate their importance in the history of American colonial architecture. A slight effort of the historical imagination is enough to enable one to understand how deeply impressed eighteenth-century travellers must have been by buildings so substantial and indubitably modern (even if not *avant-garde*) on these distant shores, and with what pride the inhabitants of the place must have regarded them. No wonder "magnificent" was an epithet that occurred readily to the early writers: "There are two fine Publick Buildings in this Country, which are the most Magnificent of any in America," wrote Beverley of the College and the capitol.[28] "The Palace, or governor's house, is a magnificent structure," wrote Hugh Jones, and added: "These buildings are justly reputed the best in all *English America,* and are exceeded by few of their kind in *England.*"[29] Beverley described the Gaol as "large and convenient" and Jones found Bruton Parish Church "nicely regular and convenient, and adorned as the best Churches in *London.*"[30] Even the anonymous and dyspeptic writer of 1736 who thought Williamsburg "a most wretched contriv'd Affair for the Capital of a Country" allowed that the College and the Palace were "no bad Piles";[31] three decades later the more appreciative Lord Adam Gordon thought the second Capitol "very handsome," the College "very large and handsome," and the Palace "handsome and commodious."[32] It was left to Thomas Jefferson, who believed with Alberti that "the principal Ornament in all architecture certainly lies in Columns,"[33] to damn the College, bell, book and candle: to him it and the Public Hospital seemed "rude, mis-shapen piles, which but that they have roofs, would be taken for brick-kilns." How could elegance be expected when "a workman could

scarcely be found here capable of drawing an order"? Still, Jefferson perceived capabilities in the Palace—capabilities which he was not destined to develop, though
as we shall see he gave the subject much thought—and he had a high enough opinion of the second Capitol ("on the whole . . . the most pleasing piece of architecture we have") to do it the compliment of criticising its portico in detail.[34]

It will be part of our purpose in the following chapters to place the public buildings at Williamsburg in relation to what had gone before and what came after. In
architecture, as in other spheres, the tiny capital of Virginia had an importance quite
disproportionate to its size. We shall see how both the College and the Capitol
were first examples in the American colonies of new building types, replacing
(though in the case of the Capitol clearly based upon) the domestic type that had
hitherto been adapted to their respective functions; how the Palace set a new standard for the larger plantation houses in Virginia and how it might have become a
leading monument of Neo-Classicism in Jefferson's hands; how Bruton Parish
Church introduced the cruciform plan into the ecclesiastical architecture of
Virginia; how the Magazine was prescribed as a model as much as sixty years after it
was built; how the Playhouse on Palace Green was the first theatre in the colonies;
how the Courthouse of 1770 was the forerunner of the porticoed courthouses
which still ornament so many of Virginia's county seats, and how the Public
Hospital not only had its own importance in medical and sociological history but
was the elder brother of America's first model prison.

BUILDERS AND ARCHITECTS

Another topic that will concern us is the arrangements made for the erection
of these buildings, the business side of building. "There are 3 ways of working,"
wrote Wren: [35] "by the Day, by Measure, by Great"—that is to say, by day-work,
by piece-work, and by general contract. Wren was writing in 1681, but the situation remained unaltered in England throughout our period, and in fact until the
rise of the building contractor in the nineteenth century. For it should be remembered that in seventeenth and eighteenth-century England there were no "builders"
with men skilled in all the crafts necessary for the erection of buildings on their
payrolls: although a carpenter or a bricklayer might contract to erect a whole
building for a fixed sum, when he was called the "undertaker," his competence
and that of his journeymen extended only to the carpentry or the brickwork, as the

case might be; all those parts of the work which involved the other crafts had to be let out by him to sub-contractors. It was, generally speaking, the same in Virginia, although sometimes a wealthy planter would undertake whole buildings with his own slaves and indentured servants—the advantage to the building owner, in a society chronically short of cash, no doubt being that such a man could afford to give credit when the craftsman-contractor could not. The history of the second College building supplies an early instance of the general contract in Virginia; direct labor was commonplace; piece-work was resorted to at the Palace and for finishing the first Capitol. It is only recently that building methods in eighteenth-century England have been submitted to historical scrutiny; building methods in the colonies are still the subject of broad generalizations which may be true but would certainly be safer for a solid foundation of fact. Some of the material for that foundation may be quarried from the history of the public buildings at Williamsburg.

Last, but by no means least, there is the question of the designers of the buildings. Here again it is necessary to remember that just as the eighteenth-century master-builder differed from the building contractor of later times, so the eighteenth-century architect was a very different sort of person from the registered architect of the nineteen-fifties. The colonial architect was most frequently a craftsman bred up in one or other of the building trades; occasionally he might be a wealthy amateur without technical training but with some book-learning and a talent—or at least a *penchant*—for design. In England in the earlier part of the eighteenth century there were also the men trained in the royal Office of Works, such as Nicholas Hawksmoor, the placemen with talents adapted to places in the Works, such as Sir John Vanbrugh, and the men who had been to Italy and become pupils of Italian architects, such as James Gibbs; and there were land surveyors who took on the measurement and supervision of building work.[36] None of the former three categories existed in colonial America, and the land surveyors were as a rule sufficiently occupied in surveying land.

It was not possible to enter a private architect's office in England for the avowed purpose of receiving professional training until the second half of the eighteenth century, when Sir Robert Taylor initiated the practice of taking on pupil-assistants with the status of articled clerks; in America, Benjamin Henry Latrobe was the first architect to take pupils, early in the nineteenth century. What the few and short-lived "schools of architectural drawing" that were started in the colonies[37] offered could hardly be considered professional training. Then in colonial America the architect's remuneration was never, so far as we know, calculated as a percentage of the cost of the building, although the practice was well established in London by 1730.[38] If the architect was the builder too—a state of affairs as opposed to the modern rules of the profession as were the newspaper advertisements of his services to which he sometimes resorted—he got his profit; if he supplied the design but did not contract for the construction he might be paid a cash sum for the design; if he was employed as surveyor or overseer he received a salary; if he was an amateur he looked for the approval of men of taste as his only reward.

II

William and Mary:
The First Building

WHILE JAMES BLAIR was in England negotiating for the College charter, Virginia had a change of Governors. So it was not Francis Nicholson but Sir Edmund Andros who headed the Council at the laying of the foundation of the College building on August 8, 1695. We learn from a contemporary observer that it was done "with the best Solemnity we were capeable,"[1] but we have no details. The same writer said that he feared that the building would not be finished "in the tyme was hoped and desired" on account of the shortage of good workmen. In fact it was never finished, if by finished is meant the execution of the whole of the original design. Only two ranges of what was planned as a square building with a central courtyard were built (Fig. 3).[2] Shortage of money proved an even more serious handicap than shortage of workmen.

In President Blair's anything but humble opinion it was all the new Governor's fault. As early as January 2, 1693/4—less than two months after the Assembly had passed an *Act Laying an Imposition upon Skins and Furs for the Better Support of the College*—he told Nicholson in Maryland: "As to the College tho nothing was done for its encouragement in comparison of what might have been expected had you been here, yet we reckon it is well that it is no worse."[3] On May 8, 1695 he wrote:

> May it please your Excellency, we have been taken up three days at James Town about the College business which now looks with as bad an appearance as ever; Collo. Ludwell seeing how matters are like to be governed, will not be perswaded on any Acc't to undertake the work. The reason he gives out Publickly is his age & unwillingness to leave his son entangled; But he sticks not to say among his Friends, that he sees no possibility of carrying it on in this Governors time.[4]

18

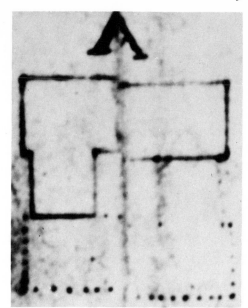

Figure 3. THE COLLEGE OF WILLIAM AND MARY. Plan of the first building from the Bland survey; dotted, or "pricked," lines show those parts of the original design which had not been executed at the date of the survey.

Other charges against Andros which no doubt originated with Blair are set forth in a manuscript in the Bodleian Library.[5] This alleges that he had shown himself "an enemy to the College of W & M in Virginia":

> By seducing some of the workmen that were gone from England to Virginia upon the account of the College: Money was given to Pocock to relinquish the work of the College, & was afterwards entertained & work given him by Sir. E. A. Mr. Park when agreed with, to burn the bricks for the College was desired by the Governour to make & burn some 30,000 for him.

And it repeats the information that Blair gave Nicholson about Philip Ludwell's refusal to sign the contract for the building, adding that it was due to "fear of Sir A. as appears by his own Letter written to Mr. Blair on that subject which Letter may be produced if there be Occasion."

In May 1695 Blair was smarting from the indignity of having been suspended by Andros from the Council, to which he had been appointed by the King in the spring of the previous year. His biographer in the *Dictionary of American Biography* tells us that he was suspended "for purely personal reasons"—an explanation which one can accept without necessarily accepting the same writer's belief in Blair's invariable rectitude. Andros' account of the matter was given in a letter to the Duke of Shrewsbury, dated June 4.[6] He had, he said, done all in his power to advance the College, but Blair "could not be obliged by all Endeavors nor containe himself within bounds."

> His restless Comport I ever passed by till the whole Councill for his Demeanor before them faulting him as unfitt to be in Councill I thought it my Duty . . . to suspend him . . . till further Order.

When the further order came, on August 12, 1696, it was for Blair's reinstatement. Nobody ever got the better of James Blair for long.

Although Andros' public actions with regard to the College were correct enough —besides attending the foundation-laying ceremony he joined its board of Governors and he passed on to the Assembly the Crown's instructions relating to it—he certainly was guilty of some private indiscretions that might be held to betray his real feelings. Two witnesses of such indiscretions appeared before Francis Nicholson, sitting in Council at Annapolis. The first was a Colonel Coursey (or Courcey), who related how he had made some remark to Andros about the educational benefits that would accrue from the College, "to which the said Sir Edmond made answer, pish, it will come to nothing." The other was a Mr. Clarke, to whom Sir Edmund had said: "I will go and shew you the Colledge, but you'l expect I should shew you the ffree schole first, but I suppose this Colledge is to teach Children their A; B; C." Clarke added that he had been told "that the reason why Sir Edmond was angry with Mr. Blaire was for his preaching a Sermon wherein he did say, that they who withdrew back & did not put forward their helping hand towards the Building of the Colledge would be damned." [7]

Whether or not Nicholson shared Blair's view that Andros was their leader, he agreed that the College had enemies. In a letter of March 18, 1695/6,[8] probably to the Bishop of London, he wrote: "Now that the enemys of the Coll. dare not attack it publickly, they endeavour to undermine it by insinuating into the people that the setting up the Coll. will be introducing Tiths &c. as it is in England." Rightly or wrongly, he and Blair thought that subscriptions were not coming as they might be expected to, other things being equal. In October 1696 Blair, back in the Council, tried to put through an *Act for facilitating the payment of the Donations already made to the College of William and Mary in Virginia*; it never reached the House of Burgesses. However, Blair had his revenge. In 1697 he was sent to England again to raise more funds. At the end of the year he appeared before the Archbishop of Canterbury at Lambeth to press his charges against the Governor, which by then included one to the effect that Andros had promised a gift of bricks for the College chapel and then denied having done so. William Byrd represented Andros at the hearing, of which a full account has been printed.[9] It would not be quite fair to describe the proceedings as an expression of ecclesiastical solidarity: if the clergyman out-talked the planter that was not altogether the Archbishop's fault. But the result was the recall of Andros.

THE SURVEYOR AND THE WORKMEN

On Philip Ludwell's refusal to undertake the building of the College, as we learn from Blair's same letter to Nicholson, another prominent member of the Council, Edmund Jenings, came forward. He was given fifteen days to think it over, and evidently thought better of it; for in the event the College was built by direct labour, perhaps with some of the carpentry contracted for. General supervision was exercised by a building committee, consisting of the Rector of the College, Miles Cary, and five or six of its Governors; [10] this committee met once a month. In direct charge of the building operations for the first sixteen months or so was Thomas Hadley, whom Blair had engaged in England. His title was surveyor (though Blair called him "overseer" in one letter [11]) and in addition to supervising the craftsmen and labourers he would have measured any work done on a piece-work or contractual basis and passed the accounts for it.

A copy of the College accounts from 1694 down to April 16, 1697—by which date the walls were up and the roof nearly finished, "Collo. Ludwell haveing promised to Shingle it upon Creditt" [12]—was forwarded to the Board of Trade by Andros and exists in the Public Record Office in London.[13] It shows that a total of £3,889 . 1s. 10d. had been spent on the building. The bricks were made on the spot by Daniel Parke, a member of the Council, for 14s. a thousand.[14] Shells for lime cost £169 . 3s. 9½d.; [15] paving stone £115 . 14s. 7d. Timber cost nothing, since it came off the College land, but sawyers' work added up to the considerable sum of £408 . 1s. 7¾d. It is noticeable that while bricklayers were simply "paid," on several occasions cash was "advanced" to the carpenter Robert Harrison, which may be thought to indicate that he had contracted for his part of the work—especially as he built the Gaol at Yorktown under contract in 1698.[16]

Two of the chief carpenters, as we learn from another source,[17] were James Blair's servants; the hiring out of slaves and indentured servants for whom the master had no immediate employment was a common practice in the colonies, and obviously a profitable one. "Several" workmen came from England. One of them, Pocock, has already been named as a pawn in Andros' alleged machinations, and the names of two others, George Cryer and Samuel Baker, both bricklayers, are given in the accounts, together with the information that they were advanced £22 before they set sail and that their passages cost £14 . 5s. It is of Thomas Hadley that one would like to know more. He was advanced £40 in England; it is not easy to determine his salary as surveyor, but it seems to have been £100 per annum. Soon after arriving in Virginia he married a lady with the formidable name of Dionysia Savage Ravens-croft; she was daughter of a Thomas Savage and widow of a Captain Samuel Ravenscroft.[18] Blair told the Archbishop at Lambeth that at the time of the episode of the Governor's bricks Hadley was "pretty well in favor" with Andros. On January 21, 1697/8, according to a letter from Blair to the Bishop of London,[19] he had been "out of the Service of the Coll. about two months." And that is the last we hear of him. Did he return to England? If he did, he left his wife behind, for it was recorded in the quit-rent rolls of James City County in 1704 that Dionysia Hadley owned 100 acres of land,[20] and in 1705 she was granted a licence to keep an ordinary in her new dwelling house in Williamsburg;[21] she died, intestate, in 1714.[22]

THE BUILDING FINISHED

When Blair was sent to England again in April 1697 the available funds had been overspent by a matter of £170 odd. For 1698, in the December of which year Francis Nicholson returned to Virginia as Governor for the second time, we have no records relating to the progress of the building. In 1699 there was held at the College that May Day celebration which was instrumental in promoting Middle Plantation as the site for the new capital of the colony. The year 1700, as befitted the first year of a new century, was something of an *annus mirabilis*. In February, Blair could tell the Archbishop of Canterbury: "The subscriptions that were made to our College do now come in apace, so that we are in hopes of having it quite finished before next Winter." [23] In March *The London Post Boy* [24] announced to the world: "Some letters from Virginia tell us, that the University which has been lately founded there by the Government of that Province, is so crowded with Students, that they begin to think of enlarging the College." It may be that it was during this year that a move was made towards the completion of the quadrangle, with the building, or at least the beginning, of a lobby at the west end of the hall.[25] In May the Archbishop of Canterbury succeeded the Bishop of London as Chancellor.[26] In June (presumably) the first Commencement was held; on this occasion, according to one authority, "it being a new thing in *America* to hear Graduates perform their Academical Exercises, the *Indians* themselves had the Curiosity to come to *Williamsburgh* . . . and the whole Country rejoiced as if they had some Relish of Learning."[27] (In picturing the scene one should realize that this was only a grammar school graduation, and that the graduates were but young boys.) And October 10, 1700 is the date of an account containing the item: "His Excellency Sir *Edm. Andros* paid for Sashing the College, £56 . 7s. 6d."[28]

But the College was not so "crowded with Students" that it could not be made to serve purposes which, though honorable, were not those for which it was designed. Under the date April 24, 1700 the Journals of the Council record:

> The Trustees and Governours of the College of William and Mary in Virginia having made an offer to His Excellency and the Councill of whatsoever Roomes within the said Colledge shall be wanted for the use of the Country to hold their Generall Meetings and Assemblyes till the Capitoll be built and fitted for that purpose, it is thereupon resolved and accordingly ordered, that the present Generall Court (at the end thereof) shall be adjourned to sitt at the said Colledge in October next.

The Council sat in the College for the first time on October 17, the House of Burgesses on December 5, and they continued to sit there until they moved into the Capitol in October 1703 and April 1704 respectively. As a matter of cold fact, in 1702—the first year for which we have exact figures—the roll of the College comprised the Chancellor, President, Rector, School Master, Usher, Writing Master and Registrar, and twenty-nine students.[29]

CHARACTER OF THE BUILDING

What was this first College building like? The evidence on which any answer must be based is not plentiful. But it is not negligible; moreover, it is of all the three kinds desirable in the case of a destroyed building—documentary, archaeological, pictorial. For documentary evidence we have, in addition to what is provided by the building account and letters already quoted, depositions and letters relating to the building's destruction by fire in 1705. The archaeological evidence was brought to light and recorded in 1929–1930, in connection with the restoration of the building to its second form. The pictorial evidence consists of an early copy of a drawing made by a Swiss traveller in 1702.

William Byrd, when the second building was under consideration, recorded that it was resolved to use not merely the foundations but the actual walls of the first, and archaeological investigation has confirmed that the resolution was carried out.[30] The main range was 138 ft. long by 46 ft. wide; that is to say, it covered three squares of 46 ft. The hall was 64 ft. long by 32 ft. wide externally—a double square on plan. Now 32 ft. is the length (to the nearest foot) of the side of a square of which the diagonal is 46 ft.; or to put it another way, 32:46 is the ratio of the so-called Golden Section. We shall meet with further instances of this kind of system of proportion.

The interior planning of the first building must have been substantially the same as that of the second, for which we have the valuable authority of a plan drawn by Thomas Jefferson. The chief difference was probably in the position of the main stairs. In the second building these were placed in a separate stair-hall, to the south of the entry. However, there is no wall in the basement to support the southern partition of the stair-hall, and this strongly suggests that it was not a feature of the first building. In guessing where the stairs were in the first building we are perhaps aided by a phrase in a letter written by the first School Master, Mongo Ingles, to Francis Nicholson.[31] He is discussing the question of the source of the fire and says that it could not have started at the north end of the building:

> for then must the stairs have been wholy burnt (standing as your Excy: well knowes) in the Middle of the Pile before it could have melted the lead which dropt on Mr Thacker at the South end.

It may be suggested that "the Middle of the Pile" is to be taken literally, to mean that the stairs went straight up from the central entry—and incidentally that the arrangement was abandoned in the second building because it provided a too efficient "chimney" in case of fire. Poor Mr. Thacker's ordeal by molten lead was due to another difference between the two buildings: the first had gutters. Several particulars in which the first building resembled the second are established by the testimony of the witnesses of the fire; for instance, it shows that the school room was the large room north of the entry, that there was a stair that ascended from the gallery at the east end of the hall to the upper floor, and that there was an outside stair at the south end of the main range of the building.

Anyone who cares to examine the fabric of the College today may see for himself that the pavilion in the centre of the east front was a feature introduced in the second building, for its foundations are not bonded into the older wall, part of which was demolished to make way for it. The absence of any central projection on this front is confirmed by the plan in Theodorick Bland's survey and also by the only known drawing of the first College building, which we must now consider.

MICHEL'S DRAWING

In April 1702 there landed at Yorktown a Swiss, Franz Ludwig Michel, who had come from Berne, via Rotterdam and London, to investigate the possibility of planting a Swiss settlement in America. About the middle of the following month a French frigate arrived with the news (some two months old) of the death of William III, soon to be followed by an English warship with a letter instructing the Governor to proclaim Queen Anne. Nicholson made the most of the opportunity for ceremonial display, and by a stroke of luck Michel, who wrote an account of his travels,[32] was at Williamsburg to watch and record the proceedings:

> . . . On the appointed day a large number of people appeared with as well as without arms. Three theatres [grand-stands] were erected before the college where the fireworks were to be set off. The celebration began on a Thursday morning. The armed contingents, on foot as well as on horse, were drawn up in line. Two batteries were also mounted and a tent was pitched, where the bishop [Commissary Blair] delivered an oration on the King's death. The armed men were then drawn up before the college in a threefold formation, in such a way that the college building formed one side. . . . I have already given their number as about 2,000. As can be seen from the drawing, the college has three balconies. On the uppermost were the buglers from the warships, on the second, oboes and on the lowest violinists, so that when the ones stopped the others began. Sometimes they all played together. When the proclamation of the King's death was to be made they played very movingly and mournfully. Then the constable appeared with the scepter. It was like the English standards, which were woven with gold, covered with crape. Likewise those who carried them were dressed in mourning. Then followed the Governor in mourning as also his white horse, whose harness was draped with black. The death of King William was then announced by the Secretary. Afterwards the Governor ordered the rifles reversed under the arms and with mournful music they marched with the clergy to the above named tent, where a touching oration was delivered which caused many people to shed tears . . . It was now noon. The musicians began to play a lively tune. Then the constable appeared in a green suit, the scepter no longer draped. The Governor, who had retired, appeared in blue uniform, covered with braid. He had also exchanged his horse. The Secretary then read publicly, while heads were uncovered everywhere, the royal letter and edict, that the second daughter of departed and late King James had been chosen and crowned Queen. . . . Then everybody shouted three times Hurrah! . . . Then the Governor caused most of those present, i.e., the most prominent people, to be entertained right royally; the ordinary persons received each a glass of rum or brandy with sugar. . . .

In the evening there were fireworks, set off with an inexpertness which roused Michel's scorn:

> . . . nothing was successful, the rockets also refused to fly up, but fell down archlike, so that it was not worth seeing. Most of the people, however, . . . praised them highly. . . . I had taken my place in the highest part of the tower of the college building, whence the best outlook was to be had by day and night. As it was eleven o'clock at night and my lodging place was two miles away . . . I stayed up there over night. . . . When day dawned I left the building, without anybody noticing. . . .

There followed a second day of celebration, with more marching and eating and giving of toasts and a shooting match for Indians and Virginia-born colonists.

Michel's diary, as we have it, is one of at least three copies made by his brother, Johan.[33] It may be that Franz was a more skilful draftsman than Johan's copies of his drawings would lead one to believe, but it seems safe to assume that the copies were as faithful as Johan's abilities allowed. Perhaps the crudity of the drawings may even be considered some warrant of their essential veracity. In any case, a reading of Franz Ludwig Michel's diary makes it clear that he was in general a careful and intelligent observer.

His drawing of the College (Fig. 4) shows a front ten windows wide and three full storeys and a basement high, with a half-storey in the roof. In fact the first College building, as the surviving wall shows, was thirteen windows wide. But the error is intelligible, for even the trained observer can be hard put to it to remember the number of windows in quite familiar façades. Michel is less likely to have been mistaken about the number of storeys, especially as he had climbed the stairs to the top of the lantern or cupola and spent the night there. And it can be taken as certain that the horizontal division of the front was essentially as he depicts it. In 1929–1930 the archaeologists discovered that the grade to the east of the building had at one time been about three feet lower than it is today. So the arrangement of the main entrance shown by Michel, with its threshold approached by five or six steps and level with the basement window sills, and with the crown of the arch below the sills of the first floor windows, would have been perfectly possible. Probably there was an inside stair leading from the entrance lobby up to the first floor, which would account for the placing of the doors to the school room and (present) stair hall, and of the corresponding doorways in the basement, at the extreme west end of the partition walls. As for there being three full storeys below the eaves, supporting evidence is provided by the west wall of the second building;

Figure 4. THE COLLEGE OF WILLIAM AND MARY. The east front of the first building from an early copy
of a drawing made by Franz Ludwig Michel in 1702.

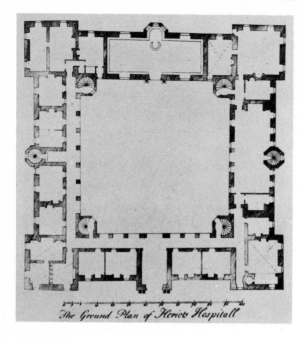

Figure 5. HERIOT'S HOSPITAL, EDINBURGH.
Plan, from *Vitruvius Scoticus.*

this also had three full storeys below the eaves and was perhaps the only wall of the first building to be sound for its full height after the fire, protected as it was from the greatest heat by the longitudinal wall between the loggia and the main rooms. In the second building as restored its height is 41 ft. If one adds 2 ft. for the entablature drawn by Michel and 3 ft. for basement wall buried when the yard was regraded, the result is 46 ft. for the height to the cornice in the first building. The fact that the main range was 46 ft. wide—so that a height of 46 ft. with its known length of 138 ft. would give it a volume of three 46 ft. cubes—increases the probability of this figure being correct.

THE WREN PROBLEM

Had the College been completed as designed, it would have been the first quadrangular building in British America. Of the earlier and contemporary buildings at Harvard, the Old College was built in 1638–1642 on the traditional E-plan of the Elizabethan and Jacobean manor house, while Harvard Hall and Stoughton Hall, built in 1674–1677 and 1698–1699 respectively, were plain rectangular blocks.[34]

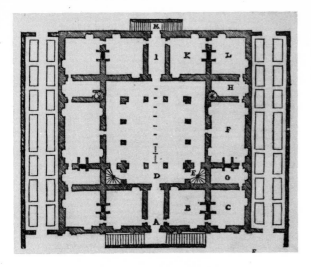

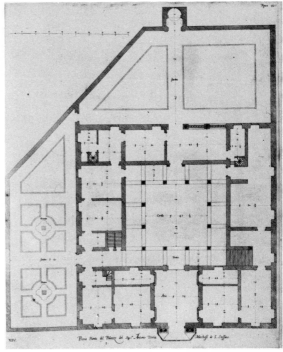

Figure 6. PLAN OF A CITY HOUSE BY SERLIO.
Plan, from *Architettura,* Book VII.

Figure 7. PALAZZO ANTONIO DORIA, GENOA.
Plan, from Rubens, *Palazzi di Genova.*

Yet it would not have resembled any of the quadrangular colleges of Oxford or Cambridge as closely as one might have expected. On plan—and it is always the plan that reveals fundamental relationships—the building in Britain that it would have most nearly resembled, had the quadrangle been completed, was Heriot's Hospital, Edinburgh, which was built as a school for orphans in 1628-1650. (Fig. 5.) Now Blair, as we have seen, went to Edinburgh University; and, like the projected Henrico College, William and Mary, with its Rector and its attached grammar school, had more in common with Scottish than with English foundations. Was the building also based on a Scottish prototype, perhaps—and here one remembers Blair's alleged prejudice in favour of his own countrymen—even designed by a Scottish architect, such as Sir William Bruce, the Surveyor-General for Scotland, or Robert Mylne, the Principal Master Mason to the King in Scotland who added a cupola to Heriot's Hospital in 1693?

It is not inconceivable. However, it can be shown that the resemblances between the College and Heriot's Hospital may be due to a common source of inspiration rather than to any more direct connection. Until the elevation of Palladio to the status of supreme authority in the eighteenth century, the sixteenth-century architectural treatise that was most influential in Britain was the *Architettura* of Sebastiano Serlio. The plan of Heriot's Hospital clearly was suggested by page 225 of Book VII of this treatise. The College plan might have had much in common with the plan for a city house on page 41 of the same Book (Fig. 6)—though if we are looking for prototypes the plan of the Palazzo Antonio Doria as given in Rubens' *Palazzi di Genova* (published in 1622 and also influential in seventeenth-century Britain) is a possible alternative (Fig. 7).[35]

And then there is the statement made by the Rev. Hugh Jones, in *The Present State of Virginia*, that the architect of the College was Wren:

> The Building is beautiful and commodious, being first modelled by Sir *Christopher Wren*, adapted to the Nature of the Country by the Gentlemen there; and since it was burnt down, it has been rebuilt and nicely contrived, altered and adorned by the ingenious Direction of Governor Spotswood; and is not altogether unlike Chelsea Hospital.

Hugh Jones had spent five years in Virginia, and had been Professor of Mathematics at William and Mary for four of them; it is reasonable to suppose that he knew what he was talking about. However, false attributions to Wren have been so numerous that the architectural historian must take the risk of seeming to impugn a clergyman's honor by setting down the reasons that he sees for doubting Jones's statement. The first is the total absence of any corroborative evidence, at least of a documentary nature. This is not to say that one would expect Wren's name to appear in the building accounts: one would not. It is to say that it would be reassuring if some sign of Thomas Hadley having worked for Wren appeared in the length and breadth of the twenty volumes of the Wren Society—which it does not. Secondly, there is the consideration that Jones's book, for all its admirable qualities, was patently written to "sell" Virginia; indeed, there is an element of sales talk in the likening of the (second) College building to Chelsea Hospital. Thirdly, the book was published in 1724; Jones had returned to England in 1721 and it is probable enough that he witnessed Wren's great and solemn funeral at St. Paul's Cathedral in 1723. In the eighteenth century even the avowed connoisseur was apt to be easy-going in matters of attribution: when he said that a painting was by Raphael or a building by Inigo Jones or Wren he might be expressing a judgment of value rather than making a statement of fact. That understood, we see that a misstatement about the authorship of the College building by Hugh Jones, however unfortunate from our point of view, would have been but a venial sin in him; and we need not be unduly shocked even by the observation that it is just possible that Jones brought Wren into the picture because he too was a mathematician.

Nor can it be held that there was anything about the building itself, as far as our knowledge of it goes, to suggest Wren's hand. Early in his architectural career, when asked to design a quadrangle for Trinity College, Oxford, Wren insisted that it should be "a lame one, somewhat like a three-legged table" [36]—that is, with one side left open—and this would seem to tell against the attribution of the William and Mary quadrangle to him, though admittedly his objection may have been to a closed quadrangle in the particular instance rather than to the scheme in general. The Michel drawing is too crude for any assessment of quality to be made from it. It does, however, show two features that have a bearing on the question of attribution. One is the treatment of the basement storey, which appears to be faced, up to window sill level, with faceted blocks of stone; the other is what appears to be a frieze ornamented with a smaller version of the same motif under the eaves, although it is possible to see this, alternatively, as an ordinary cornice, by reading the "blocks" as the spaces between the modillions—that is, as concave rather than convex elements. [37] While the frieze was doubtless of wood, the basement presents a problem, for in view of the shortage of funds and the fact that all stone had to be imported it would be surprising indeed if it had actually been faced with stone; in Ireland, however, there exists to this day a custom, of uncertain age and origin, of *painting* just such rustication as this on a plaster rendering.[38] The motif of the faceted block originated in Italy, where it was employed for rusticating expanses of wall from the middle of the fifteenth century (e.g., Palazzo Bevilacqua, Bologna) till late in the seventeenth (e.g., Palazzo Pesaro, Venice), and rather more frequently around arches and on pilasters (e.g., Porta Camollia, Siena, and the entrance to the Citadel, Parma) during the same period; it is given by Serlio in his fourth Book. In Britain it became a not too common motif in the style that Summerson has named Artisan Mannerism. It is by no means the kind of thing one would expect from Wren in the 1690's, when he was helping to create the English Baroque; its use on a frieze would have offended his strong feeling for the classical proprieties at any time.

Yet when all has been said against Hugh Jones's attribution, there remains much to be said for it. The evident unsuitability of the original design for the conditions obtaining in the colony makes one the more willing to believe that it came from the other side of the Atlantic. The College was a royal foundation, and the Surveyor-General of the King's Works might well have been asked to produce a design for such. Even if Wren did not supply the design in that capacity, there were other circumstances that might have led to his doing so. When in England, James Blair had business in high ecclesiastical circles in which Wren had always been at home. And had not Wren, after all, designed the cathedral of the bishop of whose diocese Virginia was then a part, and whom the royal charter appointed first Chancellor of the College?

Moreover there is the qualifying phrase in Jones's statement: the building, he says, was "first modelled" by Wren, and *adapted to the Nature of the Country by the Gentlemen there."* That is, Wren's design was altered. And here we may note that Wren's designs did not have to cross the Atlantic to be altered. His style was so much purer than that generally current in England at the time that when they got into the hands of any except his few chosen craftsmen the results were apt to be quite different from what he intended. As it happens, we have an example of what occurred in such a case that is precisely contemporary with the College, and concerns an educational building too. In 1693 Wren supplied a design for Sir John Moore's School, to be built at Appleby in Leicestershire. Thomas Woodstock, one of his favourite carpenters, was to supervise the work. But Woodstock died before things had progressed far, and a Midland mason, Sir William Wilson, took over. The school, as completed by Wilson in 1697, and Wren's design for it both exist. [39] That there is any connection between them is not, at first glance, obvious.

So those who like to call the main building of the College of William and Mary "the Wren Building" perhaps need not deny themselves that pleasure, although they would do well to remember that it is only the *first* form of the building for which Wren may have supplied a design. The more historically-minded will recognize that the question whether Wren did supply a design for it is as open as any such question can be, and will be content to rest in uncertainty until some new evidence turns up to settle the question one way or the other.

THE FIRE

Sometime between Christmas 1702 and late October, 1705, Francis Nicholson wrote a "Memorandum of Several faults in the Building of William & Mary Colledge which have proved dangerous & prejudicial to the said Building": [40]

> All the chimneys in the 2d Story are scarce big enough for a Grate whereas the only firing in this Country being wood, a fire cant be made in them without running the hazard of its falling on the floor, as it once happened in the room where the Sectys office was kept, a log tumbling out of the Chimney sett the

floor on fire & had it not been timely discovered might have burnt down the building the Chimney in the School hath some Joysts laid into the very hearth so that one of the said Joists took fire; but being timely discovered the danger was prevented

The chimney over the Hall hath one of the principal Girders running through the middle of the hearth whereby no use can be made of it

The hearth in the Councill chamber had Some plank laid just under it insomuch that at Christmas 1702, a Constant fire being kept there, the wood under the hearth took fire & was almost all consumed before it was discovered . . . .

Nicholson, at least, cannot have been surprised by what happened at about 11 p.m. on Monday, October 29, 1705.[41]

That fateful night William Eddings, James Blair's overseer, had gone to bed, when he heard the dogs bark. His wife got up to see what the matter was, and told him that there were horses in the corn field. So Mr. Eddings, though he was very lame, got up himself. As he went out of the house he became aware of a great light in the air and a great smoke, and then he saw that the College was on fire. Owing to his lameness he did not go to the scene. If he had, he might have been overtaken on the way by the hurrying figures of some gentlemen who had been in John Marot's ordinary, followed by Mr. Marot himself, by John Young, another ordinary keeper, by George Burton, a painter, and doubtless by many more. Once at the College, he might have seen Mr. Wheatly, who had been reading before a very small fire in his own room when the conflagration began, Mr. Reedwood, who had been prevented by the flames from saving the map of the world from the school room, Colonel Hill, busy removing his chest and portmanteau and a saddle and a silver tankard from the building by way of the south door, Mr. Lightfoot helping Colonel Hill with the chest, Mr. Thacker, his clothes spoilt by molten lead, rushing to and fro to carry things thrown from the windows out of harm's way; he would certainly have witnessed the happy escape of Harry Randolph and two other boys who emerged from the hall, having saved themselves by the small stair that descended into the gallery from the upper floor, long after their friends and relations had given them up for dead.

If Mr. Eddings later observed what Mongo Ingles called "the singular and Notorious blackness" of the outside of the chimney of President Blair's chamber,[42] which Blair (who was away at the time) had lent to Colonel Hill, no doubt he kept his thoughts to himself.

The Capitol and the Gaol

A s WE HAVE SEEN, it was on May 18, 1699, that the House of Burgesses resolved that the new statehouse, to fulfil the functions of the Jamestown building burnt in October 1698, should be located at Middle Plantation. On the following day the Governor's Council concurred with the resolution, *nemine contradicente*. On May 24 the Burgesses asked for a conference with the Council, "to Consider of a Modell for the Statehouse, and what quantity of land will Necessarily be required for that purpose, and also what will be the most proper Methods of Carrying on the Said building." The conference was held the same afternoon, and at it the Council produced "a Plott or Draught of the building."

There being no attribution to Wren at stake, the identity of the designer of the Capitol has aroused less interest than that of the designer of the College, though some strange guesses have been made.[1] The fact that the plan was produced by the Council may incline one to think that it was procured by Nicholson. If it was, it may have come from England. But even if one could assume that it came from England, its authorship would still be a matter for conjecture. For there was no official whose business, strictly speaking, it would have been to design such a building—the Office of Works at that time being concerned exclusively with the maintenance of the royal palaces and other buildings on Crown lands.

It seems likely that the design, whatever its provenance, had been procured before or soon after the opening of the spring session of the Assembly in 1699. In a message to the Burgesses on May 3—three weeks before it was produced in conference—Nicholson wrote: "I doe recommend to you to have such a Pile of Buildings Erected so soon as possible as may not be only larger, but more conveniently serve the publick Uses than that which was unfortunately burnt the last ffall." The fourth Statehouse at Jamestown could scarcely be called "a Pile of Buildings." The plural does however fit the Capitol, for this can be regarded as two buildings of identical design joined together by a third (whose original form we shall have to consider presently). Indeed, there is evidence that it was so regarded by the Burgesses when the plan was laid before them. The Journal of the House for May 25 records agreement upon a number of points of detail that were later incorporated in the *Act directing the building the Capitoll and the City of Williamsburgh*. The projected building was still called the Statehouse, and for four paragraphs the singular is maintained, so that we read that it was agreed

> That the ffoundation of the building be four Brick thick up to the Surface of the Ground, three brick and a half thick to the Water Table to the Top of the first Story three Brick thick and from there to the Top of the Second Story two Brick and half thick.

In the fifth paragraph, however, we find that the building has become plural, a pile of buildings in fact:

> The Gallary between the two buildings to be raised upon Piazos and built as high as the other Building, and the Walls to be of the same thickness, and a Cupulo to be in the middle of the Cross building And that there be an Iron Balcony upon the first floor in Each ffront.

After a clause specifying the treatment of the windows and roof, it is laid down

> That one Building be appropriated to the Use of the Genll Court and Council and the offices thereto belonging.
> That the other building be appropriated to the Use of the House of Burgesses and the Offices thereof.
> That the Great Roomes below of each building be laid with fflagg stone.

We then find ourselves back with the building in the singular for a paragraph, only to be confronted with the plural again when we are told that it was agreed

> That the Committee appointed for the Revisall of the Laws be required and impowered to Article with Undertakers or other waies for carrying on and finishing the buildings according to the Dimensions aforesaid.

Finally, we read that it was

> Ordered That the Committee of Proposicons and Greivances do prepare and bring in a Bill directing the building of a State House.

The confusion in the minds of the Burgesses was not wholly due to their being unaccustomed to such complex buildings. For what they saw in the plan, and what we also may see easily enough if we turn it with the east to the top, is essen-

tially the plan of the fourth Statehouse at Jamestown *doubled;* even the dimensions on plan of each of the wings are very close to the dimensions of the Statehouse.[2]

Does this prove that the Capitol was actually designed in the colony? It is certainly a piece of circumstantial evidence tending to suggest that it was. Yet it should
be remembered that the fourth Jamestown Statehouse, like its predecessor on the
site, followed one of the standard Elizabethan symmetrizations of the medieval
house plan, with the doorway placed centrally and yet with the *hall,* the principal
public room, still placed with its longer axis parallel to the front and entered at
the "lower" end. A statehouse was after all but a house—a house for affairs of
state:[3] the seventeenth century knew no great specialization of building types. In
London itself many public and semi-public functions were still held in *halls*—the
greatest of them all, Westminster Hall, medieval in structure, and the majority,
such as the halls of the City Companies, rebuilt more or less to the traditional medieval plan after the Great Fire; in the provinces there were the guildhalls of country
towns.

The semicircular terminations of the wings of the Capitol constitute the most important difference between them and the Jamestown Statehouse. There was no
precedent for this feature in any house in the colonies or in English houses with
halls of the traditional kind, and bow windows in such halls are always placed laterally. At first the effect seems rather ecclesiastical, and one is reminded that the first
Assembly of the colony had sat in the church at Jamestown, while the House of
Commons had been sitting in a college chapel since 1547. But St. Stephen's Chapel
at Westminster had no apse; nor had any of the early churches at Jamestown. There
were probably less than half-a-dozen seventeenth-century churches built with apses
in England and almost certainly none in the American colonies—for all the evidence
suggests that Trinity Church in Dorchester County, Maryland, which does have
an apse and which has been ascribed to the 1680's, is of eighteenth-century date.
There was, however, a possible London prototype, an interior which was both a
hall and a court-room: the hall of Doctors' Commons near St. Paul's. Doctors' Commons was a College of Doctors of Civil Law, founded in the sixteenth century. Its
second home was destroyed by the Fire, and rebuilt in 1672; in the hall, one end
of which was semicircular, were held the High Court of the Admiralty and four
ecclesiastical courts—the Court of Arches, the Prerogative Court, the Court of Fac-
ulties and Dispensations, and the Consistory Court of the Bishop of London. The
hall apart, Doctors' Commons, which was planned round two quadrangles, bore no

resemblance to the Capitol.[4] The possibility remains that the form of the main halls of the Capitol was due to the conscious classicism that gave the building its name: at least in the General Court the semicircular termination corresponds to the tribune of a Roman basilica in function as well as in form.

THE CROSS GALLERY

After the first reference to a "Modell" the design for the Capitol is called the "Plott or Draught." The absence of any mention of an "upright," as an elevation was then called, may be due to the inadequacy of the Burgesses' technical vocabulary. Or it may mean that no elevation was provided; this explanation is perhaps supported by the fact that the entry in the Journal for May 25 begins by stating that it was agreed "that the House be built according to the forme and dimentions of the Plott or Draught" and says later that it was agreed that "the Gallary between the two buildings . . . be raised upon Piazos[5] and built as high as the other Building" —for if there had been an elevation the latter clause would have been either superfluous, or contradictory of the agreement to build according to the draught. In any case we may be sure that the draught was not a very detailed affair: it is noteworthy that in the Act, which is printed in so far as it describes the projected building in Appendix I, there is no mention of it, although there are references to the plot of the town.

The "Bill for the building a State house" was put through with a dispatch that did not always mark the proceedings of the Assembly. It was read in the House of Burgesses for the first time on May 27, the second (when the word Capitol first appears) on May 30, the third on June 6, and it was passed on June 7. During its passage certain amendments were made in it; whether they related to the design of the building we have no means of telling. There is, however, evidence that the original design differed in an important respect from the Capitol as built.

A manuscript copy of the Act of 1699 shows that the building was to be "made in the forme and figure," not of an H, but Ⱨ (Fig. 8)[6]. Any inclination to ignore this as a mere clerk's whim must be put aside when we observe that the block plan of the building given in Bland's survey (Fig. 9) is of similar form.[7] Moreover, there is a phrase in the Act which is very hard to explain unless we grant that both the clerk and Theodorick Bland meant what they drew. The passage containing it runs: ". . . that the two parts of the building shall be joyned by a Cross Gallery of thirty foot long and fifteen foot wide each way according to the figure herein

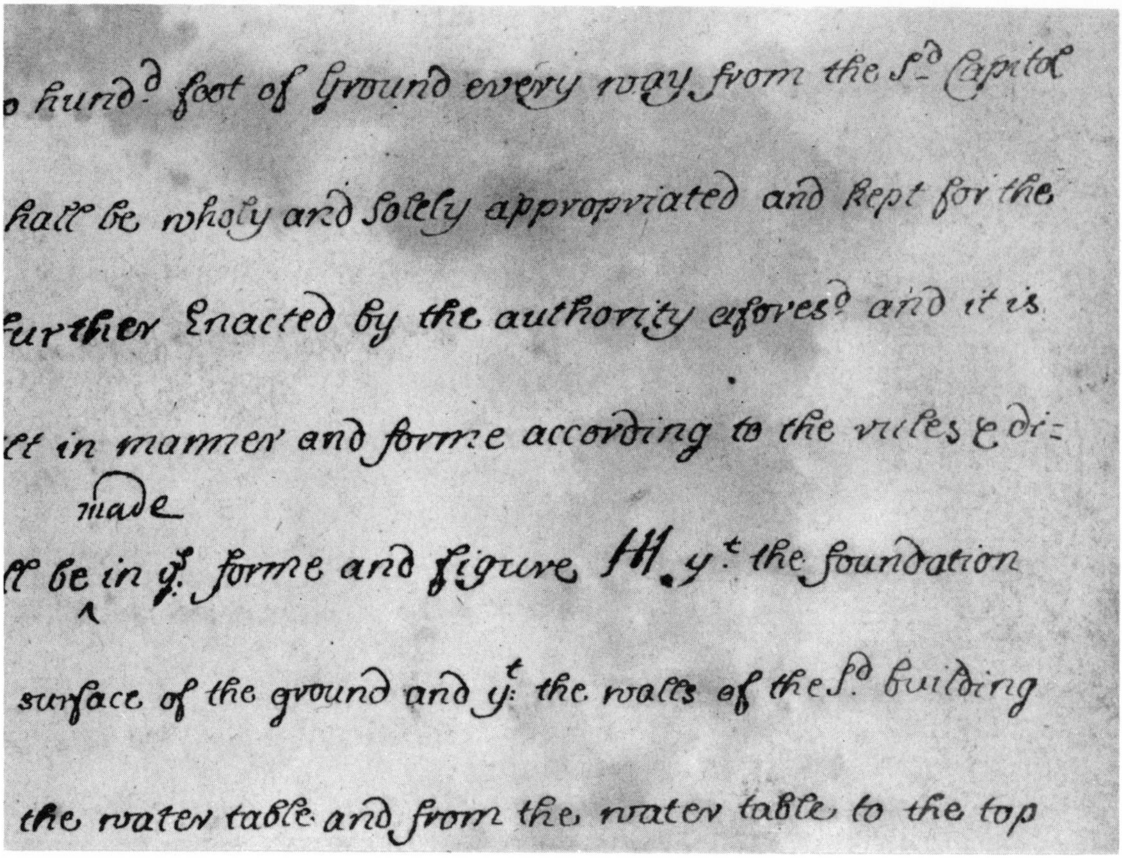

o hund.d foot of Ground every way from the Sd Capitol
hall be wholy and Solely appropriated and kept for the
urther Enacted by the authority aforesd and it is
et in manner and forme according to the rules & di-
made
l be in ye forme and figure H. yt the foundation
surface of the ground and yt the walls of the Sd building
the water table and from the water table to the top

Figure 8. THE CAPITOL. Excerpt from the manuscript copy of *An Act directing the building the Capitoll and the City of Williamsburgh* among the Jefferson manuscripts in the Library of Congress, showing the "forme and figure" of the Capitol.

before specified. . ." It is the phrase "each way" that must give pause to the attentive reader. How can an ordinary gallery be thirty feet long and fifteen foot wide *each way?* The answer surely is that this was not an ordinary gallery, but a *cross* gallery—a gallery planned as a cross. If it was not something out of the ordinary there would seem to be no good reason for the Act directing that it was to be built "according to the figure herein before specified": the verbal description would have been enough.

Twenty-six months later, in August 1701, a committee of the Council and Burgesses proposed that "the Cross Gallery be built of the same breadth the main buildings is." The House at first disagreed, but came round to the Committee's way of thinking, and the *Act giving further directions in building the Capitol,* passed in the same session, laid down that "the cross building betwixt the two main buildings be of the same breadth with the maine buildings." The effect of this change was to

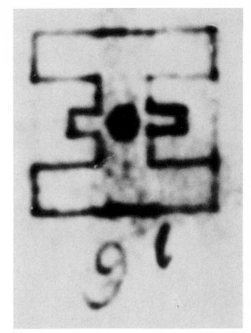

Figure 9. THE CAPITOL. Plan from the Bland survey, showing a "cross building" of the form indicated in the manuscript copy of the Act of 1699.

fill in the square spaces in the angles of the cross, thus turning the building as a whole into a simple H.[8] There are no further references to the room over the loggia as a gallery, and when the parts of the building were appropriated to their respective uses it was described as "the Chamber between the two great buildings over the Pe'ach" and became the Conference Room—by which name it was subsequently always known.

The cross gallery would have been an awkward thing to execute. Since its arms were only half the breadth of the wings of the building, its roofs would have had to differ from theirs either in height or in rake. Perhaps that was why it was abandoned. It is more difficult to account for its having been designed in the first place, unless we are prepared to see in it another reminiscence of the Jamestown Statehouse, which was an example of that type of cruciform building (represented near Williamsburg by Bacon's Castle also) in which front and back porches—the back porch containing the stairs—supply the shorter arms of the cross. In this connection it may be noted as possibly significant that the first Statehouse at Annapolis, built in 1695–1698 with Francis Nicholson (then Governor of Maryland) taking a lively interest in the work, was of that same type.[9]

MEN AND MATERIALS

The design being settled by the Act, the question of "the most proper Methods of Carrying on the Said building" remained. On the day following the passing of the Act the Committee for the Revisal of the Laws, which had been put in charge of the building, asked the Governor "to give notice that all manner of persons that should be desirous to be concerned in all or any part of the Work of the Capitol either as Undertaker Overseer or Workman might repair to James City where the said Com^tee would be to treat with them." [10] Nicholson accordingly issued a proclamation, naming four days in September when the Committee would be "ready to receive the proposal of any person concerning what of the sd building he is willing to undertake either in the quality of an Undertaker, Overseer or Workman, and to make such contract or agreement with any person or persons that shall then and there apply themselves to them as shall be reasonable and necessary."

We have no record of what happened on those days. It would not be surprising if nobody had turned up to tender for the whole building—to offer (in the phrase of the time) to "take it by the great": the magnitude of the project (by Virginian standards) would have made this very risky. In any case, the committee reached no decision concerning the question of supervision, for it is not until November that we find the first mention of the eventual "overseer," which goes as follows:

> A Petition of Mr. Henry Cary to his Excll^cy to be Imployed to Oversee the building of the Capitol and by his Ex^cell refer'd to the Consideration of the Committee, being considered The next day being the 10th of the sd Instant 9ber The Com^tee desired the said Henry Cary to agree with any Capeable pson to make 500000 bricks for the Capitol at 18s. per *M* and at the same time promised to pay him for all Such Trouble as he should be at in makeing bargains for the Com^tee as they directed according to the Merit of his Service.[11]

This Henry Cary was an elder brother of Miles Cary, who besides being Rector of the College was Burgess for Warwick County and Clerk of the Committee for the Revisal of the Laws, and who became a member of the building committee appointed in 1701. Their father was Miles Cary senior, who was son of a Bristol draper and had emigrated to Virginia in 1646, soon becoming prominent in the colony.[12] Henry was born in 1650. His home was The Forest, in Warwick County—the house has gone—and in 1704 he owned a comfortable 670 acres (as against the 600 of his brother Miles).[13] We first hear of him engaged in building works in 1697, when he built the first Courthouse at Yorktown [14] and was paid for a platform at the fort there. [15]

In England the term overseer, which we have already met at the College, was rarely used in connection with building works. [16] In the plantations it had of course a special meaning, but it was probably applied to Hadley and to Cary as a translation, so to speak, of the term surveyor: "the name of a surveyor is a frenche name, and is as moche as to say in Englysshe as an overseer," wrote John Fitsherbert in 1523. [17] It should be understood that Henry Cary was not the "undertaker" of the Capitol. His position was rather that of the modern supervising architect, with authority to enter into contracts on behalf of his client. At first, as the passage quoted above shows, he was on trial; in April 1701 he was given £50 "for his particular attendance and service upon the business of the Capitol til that time," and in July that year he agreed with the building committee for a salary of £100 per annum. [18]

But this is to anticipate. The year 1700 and the first seven months of 1701 were taken up with the collection of materials and workmen. The committee was over-optimistic in hoping to get bricks at 18s. a thousand; in April 1700 the price was raised to 20s. and even then it was not until August that John Tullitt, owner of the house at Jamestown that served as the Assembly's temporary quarters between the Statehouse fire and its move to the College, agreed to make 600,000 at that price. Other materials purchased included oyster-shells, whose carriage from Queen's Creek on the York River cost 1s. 3d. per hogshead, and the Governor sent to England for "several particulars" to the value of £104. 11s. 2d. In September 1700 Cary was instructed "to get fit scantlins sawd of high land white Oak for the Capitol doore Cases and windowe frames so as the same might be in a readiness to be wrought up the next Summer, and also to provide pine plank Inch thick for scaffolding and Inch and quarter thick for floors and to buy twenty Barrels of Porke one hundred and fifty bushels of Corne and twenty Bushels of pease for diet for the Workmen."

Six of these workmen, three bricklayers and three carpenters, were brought from England, and two houses were built for their reception. One pities them the more for having to eat their way through twenty barrels of salt pork when one reads the order of the Assembly of 1701 "prohibiting all Ordinary keepers from Entertaining any of them or selling them any drink" without a special licence.

The foundation of the Capitol was laid on August 8, 1701—six years to the day after the laying of the foundation of the College. Committees were appointed thick and fast during that month; their exact composition and terms of reference need not detain us. The most interesting entries in the journals of the Burgesses and Council are concerned with a somewhat belated offer to contract for the entire building. On the day of the laying of the foundation the first building committee reported: "We find Mr. Henry Cary to have been Imployed . . . as overseer of the building and workmen, and know not of a fitter person or better method." However, on August 21 a certain Robert Snead successfully petitioned the House for leave to lay before it "proposalls to undertake the building of the Capitoll," and appeared in person with them. The proposals were tabled, but the House voted against seeing the drawings mentioned in them. Eight days later the proposals were debated at some length, the result being the appointment of a new committee "to inquire into the proceedings of the Committee appointed to inspect and oversee the building the Capitoll." When this committee reported, on September 5, Snead's proposals were put to the vote and rejected. What they were cannot be told, although there is a reference to Snead in an estimate of costs drawn up in December:

> To Timber Carpenters &c. more according to
> Mr. Snead's Proposition - - - - £1100 : 00 : 0 [19]

It is tempting to think that this had to do with the cross building, and that Snead did in fact leave his mark on the Capitol as built.

I have not been able to identify this Robert Snead. Someone of the name, whose father also was Robert, turns up in the York County Records with some frequency in the early years of the eighteenth century, and the rent rolls show that in 1704 he owned fifty acres in the county; there is nothing to show that he undertook buildings. Another Robert Snead was Clerk of Accomack County from 1703 until 1712; one of his grandsons, John Snead, began the building of Pongoteague church (which could have owed its apse to the example of the Capitol) in the 1730's.[20]

THE CAPITOL GOES UP

The Act "giveing further directions in building the Capitoll and for building a Public Prison" became law in October 1701; the part relating to the Capitol is printed in Appendix II, where it will be seen that in addition to changing the design of the cross building it directed that the ground floor windows and all the main doors should be arched. Sash windows had been specified by the Act of 1699; in this respect the Capitol resembled the College and differed from its exact contemporary, the second City Hall at New York,[21] which was given casement windows of the kind that has a central mullion and a single transom.

No news is good news when buildings are going up, and the scarcity of references to the Capitol in the official records of 1702 presumably means that the main structural work went on steadily through the year. Steadily, but perhaps slowly too— at least in the opinion of Francis Nicholson, among whose virtues patience was not to be numbered. In his message to the Assembly at the opening of the fall session in August he proposed that a committee should be appointed to decide the functions of the various rooms, and asked whether it was convenient that the General Courts should be held in the building that October. The House of Burgesses answered next day: it was not convenient. The committee for appropriating the rooms was appointed and allocated them as in the accompanying plans of the reconstructed building (Figs. 10, 11). The Governor had asked "particularly that the House of Burgesses may choose whether they will Sitt in the great Roome below, or above." No doubt this was because at Jamestown, as we know, the Burgesses sat upstairs.

On Lady Day in 1703 Nicholson returned to the attack, pointing out that the finishing of the Capitol before the next winter would "save at least two hundred pounds to the Country." In April the Assembly approved the building committee's recommendations concerning the finishing and furnishing of the building—for instance

> That that part of the ffloor without the Barr of of the Assembly Room and from the ffootsteps within be pav'd with Stone, and from the Barr to the Setting off of the Circle on each side of the House a platform a foot from the ffloor four foot and a half broad with a Seat next the Wall of a Suteable highth, and the Wall to be wainscotted three foot above that, and one other seat within the Barr round the room of a Suitable hight above the ffloor, and that a break to pass through next the barr, and in the middle of the Lower Side Seats, be left open, and that the Queens Arm's be provided to be Set up in the Assembly room

and

> That all the Seats in the Genrall Court and Assembly room be cover'd with Green Serge and Stuft with hair, and that there be provided Serge hair red tape and brass burnished nails sufficient for doing the same.

In the same month of April 1703 the Court first sat in the new building, as we learn from a report signed by Cary which Nicholson sent to England;[22] the paragraph containing the information and the one following it are worth quoting because they show the state of the works in July that year:

> That parte that the Corte sitts in is Compleatly finnished on the outside except the balcony over the Grate doore Comming in on the west side & the lower flower are finished for that the Corte sate there in Aprill last.

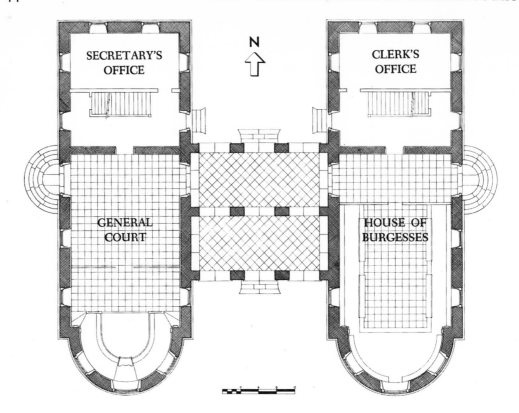

Figure 10. THE CAPITOL. Plan of the ground floor of the reconstructed building.

> The other parte is Covered & wants onley Glaseing and painting to be Compleatly finnished on the outside. The Middle building is Covered & the lower floor paved and the steps made & wants onley the Cupolow to be finnished the Dorment windows to be Closed on the sides Glased & Painted which will be performed in a month or six weeks & then there remain onley the inside worke to be finnished butt what time that will take to performe I am not able to determin butt doe hope itt will not be above Eight or ten months.

An account transmitted with this report shows that between April 4, 1700 and July 20, 1703 a total of £3,822 . 2s . 6¾d. had been spent on the building. The account is not itemized as fully as one could wish, so that it is not possible to make out exactly what the workmen's wages amounted to, for instance. Four negroes were bought from Miles Cary for £120—Henry Cary bought three of them at cost when their services were no longer required—and a carter for £18. Shingles for the Capitol and Gaol cost £200. Bringing the six workmen from England cost £60; "necessaryes"

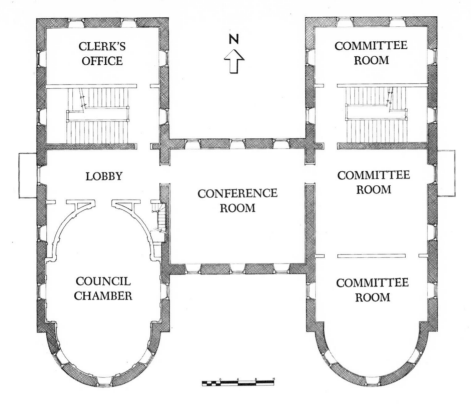

Figure 11. THE CAPITOL. Plan of the upper floor of the reconstructed building.

from England, which meant hardware, glass, paint and stone, accounted for a further £450 beyond the cost of the things that the Governor had sent for.

Cary was disappointed in his hope that the building would be completely finished in eight or ten months from July 1703. Although the first Council was held in it on October 20 and the Burgesses sat in it for the first time on April 21 the following year, in May 1705—more than a year after the latter event—the Assembly resolved, *inter alia,*

> That the Wainscot & other wooden work on the first & second floor in that part of the Building where the Genll Court is, be painted like marble, & the wainscot & other wooden work on the two first floors in the other part of the Building shal be painted like Wainscot . . .

Another resolution of the same date was

> That the roof of the Capitol & prison be tarr'd again this Summer as often as the overseer of the Building shal think fitt.

Tarred shingles may not be to our taste today,[23] but the Assembly recognized a need unchanged by the years when it resolved

> That there be a privy House built convenient to the Capitol upon the Hillside Eight foot wide and sixteen foot long with a lock upon every door.

The original workmen, who had been lodged and boarded in the country houses (as they were called), were dismissed in the fall of 1704, and the building committee and overseer were instructed to "enter into Contract with such workmen as they think most proper. . . and . . . agree with them at the easiest Prices they can, the sd workmen to furnish themselves Provisions." So while the Capitol was begun and its main structure built by direct labour, some of the interior work was completed by a system of contracts with individual craftsmen. We have the names of three of the workmen employed in the earlier period, John Newman, Daniel Westertoun and Thomas Whitby, while in 1705 we meet James Minge, a surveyor who calculated and drew eight sundials. John Newman was a servant of James Blair and had worked at the College. Of Daniel Westertoun we know only that he and the other workmen—evidently he was their leader—petitioned the Assembly about something or other in March 1704. Of Thomas Whitby, who in April 1704 prayed allowance for his care and diligence, and a year later payment "after the Rate of Fifty pounds per Annum for Three Months & Seventeen Days which he was to have by Agreement with the Committee," a little more is discoverable.[24] He was a carpenter and joiner and in 1711 he took an orphan, Owen Morris, as his apprentice. Young Owen, who could not sign his name when the indenture was made, was to receive at the end of his apprenticeship the sum of money appointed by law and carpenter's tools to the value of £6. However, Whitby died early the next year, leaving his estate to his wife; the inventory shows that his personal property, which included a negro man, two negro wenches, and two negro children, was worth £233 . 2s . 5d. It would be pleasant to report that he remembered Owen Morris in his will; but it would not be true.

COMPLETION AND EMBELLISHMENT

As a rule the "finishing" of public buildings is an indeterminate affair, and the Capitol provides no exception. If one must have a date to answer August 8, 1701, when the foundation was laid, one might choose November 30, 1705; on that day the four master keys that had been in the keeping of Cary and others concerned with the work of construction were broken in the presence of the Speaker of the

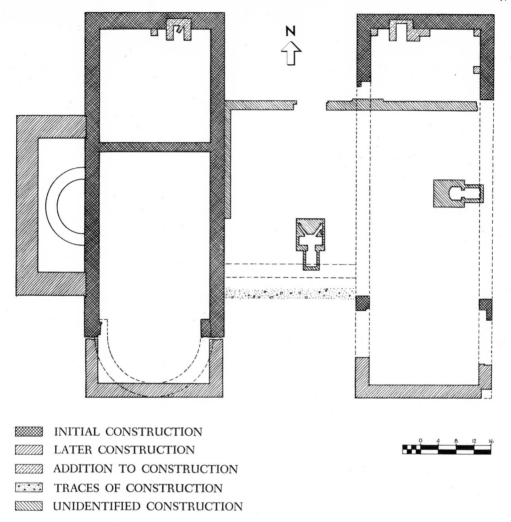

INITIAL CONSTRUCTION
LATER CONSTRUCTION
ADDITION TO CONSTRUCTION
TRACES OF CONSTRUCTION
UNIDENTIFIED CONSTRUCTION

Figure 12. THE CAPITOL. Plan of excavated foundations.

House of Burgesses. On December 5 Cary was officially discharged from the position of overseer. (Nevertheless he continued to be employed about the building from time to time during the period in which he was chiefly engaged on the Palace, carrying out some alterations of an unspecified nature as late as 1710.)

Three and a half months earlier, in August 1705, a more imposing personage had made his exit when Governor Nicholson was recalled, to be succeeded by Edward Nott. For this James Blair was largely responsible. Among the many grievances harboured by Blair against Nicholson was one that may be described in the latter's own words:

> He [Blair] had the Assurance (to give it no worse name) to reflect upon
> what I had order^d to be put upon the Capitoll which was done in cutt bricks,
> & first showed on the day that (according to my duty) I proclaimed her
> Ma[jes]ty, at top there was cut the Sun, Moon, and the planet Jupiter, and un-
> derneath thus HER MAJESTY QUEEN ANNE HER ROYALL CAPITOLL.
>
> He s^d that in Chelsea College it was mentioned that it was begun in King
> Charles the 2d time, continued in King James's and finished in King Williams:
> in whose time there was nothing of the Capitoll done but the foundation; he
> taxed me with flattery that I did it to make my court to her Majesty, as if
> I had never done it before.[25]

What Blair objected to was the failure to give William III any of the credit for the
building rather than the device of the sun and moon and the planet Jupiter. The
meaning of this was unexceptionable. The sun—as the presence of Nicholson's
motto, *"Deus mihi sol,"* under his arms elsewhere on the building made clear—was
God;[26] the moon was Diana, the virgin goddess and therefore Virginia—just as poets
had apotheosized Queen Elizabeth as Diana;[27] Jupiter was Jupiter Capitolinus and
therefore stood for the Capitol. Thus the whole device symbolized the light of God
shining upon Virginia and her Courts and Assembly.

Other external embellishments of the Capitol due to Nicholson (or perhaps to
James Minge the gnomonist) were easily removed. Soon after he left the colony it
was

> Ordered that the Boards or Dial Plates with the Inscriptions thereon set up
> on the East & West fronts of the Capitol be pulled down, the Inscriptions
> being improper, and set up there without any publick authority, and that the
> Overseer of the work of the Capitol see that same forthwith performed, and
> that the Overseer take care that no other Inscriptions be put up any where else
> about the Capitol.

And in July 1706 the Assembly passed a resolution which must have given Blair a
certain bitter satisfaction:

> That the Queens Arms be painted in the same place where Collo Nicholsons arms
> are now painted.

THE ARCHITECTURAL CHARACTER OF THE CAPITOL
AND ITS INFLUENCE

Only one contemporary view of the first Capitol is known. On a copper plate
engraved in the 1730's,[28] it is a perspective of the north side, showing the building
with chimneys (Fig. 13). As a precaution against the kind of fate that had overtaken the Jamestown Statehouse, the Capitol was originally built without fireplaces.

Figure 13. THE CAPITOL. The north side of the first building, from a copper plate (the "Bodleian Plate") probably engraved in 1737 or shortly after.

However, the passage of a quarter of a century was enough to make the risk of fire seem less formidable than the actuality of cold and damp, and in June 1723 the Council empowered a committee of three "to agree with Workmen to build two stacks of Chimneys with two fire places in each Chimney, at the North End of the Capitol."

The architectural style of the building is a visual equivalent of the good plain English in which the doings of those who met in it were written down. The only touch of fantasy is supplied by the tall cupola. On plan this is a hexagon, a figure which the Baroque preferred to the octagon for such a feature because a hexagon set upon a rectangle gives a sense of direction, as an octagon does not; it is placed so that two of its sides are parallel with the ridge of the roof on which it rides—the only aesthetically satisfactory arrangement—and therefore may be said to face north and south. Its lower stage bears a marked resemblance to the cupola of the first College building (as drawn by Michel), which for a few months answered it at the other end of Duke of Gloucester Street. Perhaps it was modeled upon it.

To appreciate the originality of the Capitol, and incidentally to understand why it turns what might seem to be its flank rather than its front to Duke of Gloucester Street, one must remember that it was not descended from the Elizabethan H-plan house, in which the hall was always in the cross-bar of the H. As we have seen, its plan seems rather to have been arrived at by doubling that of the Jamestown State-house, which itself derived from a simpler dwelling house type. In assessing the influence of the Capitol on the architecture of the colony, one must bear the same considerations in mind. It will then be seen that Tuckahoe in Henrico County, as Waterman pointed out,[29] is a clear case of a house with a plan inspired by it; as completed after 1730, Tuckahoe is indeed the result of a process of duplication in a literal sense, the two wings belonging to different building periods. Significantly, the principal entrance remained in one of the uprights of the H. But Stratford, Westmoreland County, where the principal entrance (as the outbuildings establish) is in the cross-bar of the H, is another matter.[30]

Two features of the first Capitol were much borrowed by designers of county courthouses in Virginia. Its "piazza," a feature that it had in common with many town-halls and market-halls in England and with New York City Hall, as well as with the College, re-appeared as an arcaded front porch in the 1730's in the Charles City, Hanover and King William Courthouses, in that order; at mid-century it was employed in the Richmond County Courthouse at Warsaw, and as late as 1803 in the Caroline County Courthouse at Bowling Green. The other feature, the apsidal end or tribune, was adopted in the Lancaster County Courthouse in 1740—the specification calls it a "compas End"[31]—and in the Isle of Wight Courthouse at Smithfield about 1750. In 1767 it was adopted outside Virginia in the handsome Chowan County Courthouse at Edenton, North Carolina; the architect, Thomas Leigh, is said to have been a Williamsburg man.[32] It continued to be employed in Virginia long after the colonial period—for instance in the Doric-porticoed Goochland Courthouse of 1826, to whose architect its classical ancestry may have been as strong a recommendation as the local tradition of its use.

THE GAOL

In 1702–1703 there was going up, a hundred yards to the north of the rising Capitol, a building of less architectural consequence and no amiable purpose, yet none the less necessary for the functioning of the law in the colony—the Gaol. The need for a gaol at Williamsburg to confine defendants in General Court cases was first mentioned in the official records in April 1700, when the Council recommended that the Committee for the Revisal of the Laws should "consider of the most proper method for the building a Publick Prison." In September 1701 the committee preparing the bill that authorized changes in the design of the Capitol was instructed to "consider of a Suitable prison and to direct the modell." The result was the section in the Act of October 1701 that gave specifications for a "substantiall Brick Prison, thirty foot long in the clear and twenty foot wide in the clear."

These dimensions were familiar in Williamsburg. The building of "one good dwelling house, containing twenty foot in width, and thirty foot in length" was the minimum requirement under the Act of 1699 for "saving" the grant of a lot on Duke of Gloucester Street. Nor did the Gaol differ conspicuously in plan and general appearance from the ordinary house of the period. In seventeenth-century Virginia prisons had in fact been neither more nor less than ordinary houses. An Act of 1647 noted that "the poverty of the Country and want of necessaries here, will not admitt a possibility to erect [as prisons] other than such houses as we frequently inhabite," and went on to regularize the situation by directing that "such houses provided for that purpose shall bee accounted sufficient prisons, as are built according to the ordinary forme of Virginia houses."

As a special measure of security the Gaol was "underlaid with timbers under ground to the foundations to prevent undermining." Its roof was shingled. The accommodation comprised three rooms on the first floor—a large one for the gaoler and two smaller for male and female prisoners respectively—and "chambers" in the roof for the gaoler's use and the confinement of petty-offenders. At the west end was a yard, twenty feet square and surrounded by a wall ten feet high, "for the prisoners to be let into to aire them as occasion shall require for preservation of their life and health till tryall."

"Till tryall"—the phrase serves as a reminder of the radical difference of function between the colonial gaol and a prison of today. In colonial days "imprisonment was reserved almost entirely and solely for the purpose of detaining prisoners until the time of their trials, as distinguished from depriving them of freedom for a stated period as punishment for their derelictions." [33] Debtors were the only class of offender liable to suffer long periods of imprisonment; for them an addition was made to the Williamsburg Gaol in 1711, but discussion of that belongs to a later chapter.

The building accounts of the Gaol were combined with those of the Capitol and Henry Cary supervised the work. On July 20, 1703 he reported that the walls were up and the roof was "this day raising"; he was confident that the building would be finished in September. The first prisoners arrived in May 1704. They were James Mash and Coscohunk, two Chickahominy Indians.

The Palace Before 1710

IN THE SEVENTEENTH CENTURY royal governors of Virginia occupied at Jamestown two successive official residences. The first was a frame house built between 1611 and 1614 by Sir Thomas Gates. The second was a brick house, of
unknown date. This was sold by the Assembly in 1660 (and probably destroyed in
Bacon's Rebellion in 1676).[1] Sir William Berkeley, Governor in 1660–1677, lived
in his own house at Green Spring. Thereafter, the governors had to make shift with
rented quarters, an allowance for rent of £150 a year being granted them by the
Treasury.

Naturally enough, seeing that the cost of a new house for the governors would
fall on the colony, the authorities in England were not satisfied with this state of
affairs. In 1684 Lord Howard of Effingham was instructed to remedy it, but on being asked by the House of Burgesses to choose a site, he replied that as a new comer
to the country he needed time to consider; and there the matter was allowed to rest.
When Nicholson arrived for his first term as Governor he carried instructions to the
same effect, and "the building a house for the Govr" was a matter referred by the
Council to the Assembly in 1691. When he returned to Virginia in 1698 Nicholson was told that it was not "reasonable that his Majestye should alwaies continue
to allow . . . House Rent, whilst no advance is made on the other side towards the
building of the said House"; he was therefore

> to consider of the fittest place for building the same, which you are to propose
> the Councill and Assembly there in order to the raiseing money for that pur-
> pose. As also to send over the Draught of such an house to his Majestye and
> the Commis^{ars} for Trade and Plantations with the propositions that shall be
> made for the building thereof in order to his Majestys Determination thereupon
> & his further Directions about the aforementioned allowance for House Rent.

A committee of the House of Burgesses considered the matter in May 1699. It expressed the opinion "that in regard there are many Publick Debts and other Charges and particularly that of Building a Statehouse which lyes on the Country, the Country is not in a capacity to undertake so great a work at this time." Nicholson evidently shared this view. But the Board of Trade was not to be put off easily: another letter mentioning the subject was dispatched in June, and in January 1700 Nicholson was exhorted to use his utmost endeavors to get a "convenient house" built.[2] He replied that he had hopes of being able to do so "in a year or two," hopes which the Board found "very acceptable." [3] In December the Burgesses drew up an Address to the King representing that his "most antient Colony and Dominion" was "und' very low and needy Circumstances being ingaged in many Publick Debts and Charges" and asking for alleviation in the form of a grant out of the quit-rents.

And so it went on, with the Board of Trade prodding Nicholson and Nicholson prodding the Assembly and the Assembly giving its "continued answer . . . that the Country at this time is not in a condition to sustain so great a charge." [4] Sixty-three acres of land, however, were purchased by order of the Council; the question whether this was a "Country charge"—that is, payable out of the treasury of the colony—or whether the Governor should foot the bill out of the funds at his immediate disposal led to a sharp dispute between Nicholson and the Burgesses.

By the time of Edward Nott's arrival for his brief term of office the Capitol was to all intents and purposes finished; moreover, the new Governor's mildness must have seemed to the Burgesses a pleasant change after Nicholson's high-handed behavior. In his first message to the Assembly, in October 1705, Nott told them that he was "by the Royal Command to Recommend Earnestly to you Gentlemen . . . the Building a house fit for the Reception of your Governor." A month later the Burgesses resolved that it was necessary to build such a house but, as Nott told the Board of Trade in December, could not settle how it should be paid for. The solution of the problem, reached the following spring, was a new duty on slaves and liquor imported into the colony.

The plan of the Capitol, as we have seen, had come from the Council—and probably to the Council from the Governor, Nicholson. So on May 1, 1706 Robert Beverley and some other members waited on Nott and requested him "to cause a draught of such a house as by him shal be thought most convenient to be laid before the House of Burgesses." Nott, feeling no doubt that the mere decision to build represented an achievement for him, and perhaps sensing that he would soon be beyond the shelter of earthly architecture, replied in writing:

Gentlemen

Y^{or} hearty and ready compliance with what her Maty commanded me to recommend to you in relation to the building of a house for your Governour, is such a testimony to y^{or} loyalty and duty to so Gracious a Queen, as will undoubtedly be very acceptable to her Maty . . . I have considered y^{or} message, whereby you desire me to send a draught of such a house, as I shall think convenient, but Gentlemen, I leave it wholy to you to give such directions therein, as you think proper . . .

The appropriate committee was accordingly told to prepare a bill and *An Act directing the building an house for the Governor of this Colony and dominion* was passed late in June 1706.

THE ACT OF 1706

The Act begins by stating that her majesty's most dutiful and loyal subjects had cheerfully and unanimously granted her £3,000 with which its provisions would be implemented. The purpose and the site of the house are described, and then its specifications are given, as follows:

And that the said house be built of brick, fifty-four foot in length, and forty-eight foot in breadth, from inside to inside, two story high, with convenient cellars underneath, and one vault, sash windows, of sash, glass and a covering of stone slate, and that in all other respects the said house be built and finished according to the discretion of the overseer, which shall be employed by virtue of this act to take care of the same, under the direction of the governor and council.

And be it further enacted, That a kitchen and stable, suitable for such an house be likewise built upon the land before mentioned, according to the discretion of the said overseer, and by the direction aforesaid.

The overseer is to "have full power to send to England for iron work, glass, lead, stone, slate, or any other necessarys," as well as to buy "slaves, horses, carts, and other materials as in his discretion he shall think fitt." The procedure for drawing on the treasury of the colony up to the sum of £3,000 is laid down, and the use of that sum exclusively for the building of the house is assured. And then the overseer is named:

And be it further enacted, That Henry Cary be appointed, and he is hereby appointed an overseer to inspect, oversee, and provide for the building aforesaid, with full power to begin, carry on, and finish the same . . .

Provision is made for the appointment, by the Governor, of a new overseer to succeed Cary should his death or disability call for it; Cary's salary is set at £100 per annum, and he is required to give a bond of £500 and lay his accounts before the

Assembly. Finally it is enacted that the cost of repairs to the finished building shall be met out of the export duty on tobacco of two shillings a hogshead; in effect this was a disclaimer of responsibility for maintenance on the part of the Burgesses, since the duty was directly at the disposal of the Governor and Council.

Evidently the Assembly felt that Cary had done a good job at the Capitol. It has been thought by more than one recent writer that the Palace (as, following later eighteenth-century usage, we shall here call it) would have been designed in England. However, the wording of the Act, in conjunction with the letter from Nott quoted above, makes it clear enough that Cary was virtually the architect. There is no mention of a draught and the specification leaves everything except internal dimensions, structural materials, number of storeys, type of windows and the provision of a vaulted cellar to his discretion.

THE BUILDING GOES UP

The digging for the foundations of the Palace can scarcely have begun when, in August 1706, Edward Nott died. When his successor, Robert Hunter, was captured at sea by the French, the duties of the chief executive devolved upon the President of the Council, Edmund Jenings. For thirty years Virginia had stood in need of an official residence for her governors; for nearly four years, until Alexander Spotswood arrived in June 1710, there was no governor in the colony to witness that need being supplied.

Jenings never called an Assembly, and information about the progress of the work is not so plentiful as it would be if the House of Burgesses had been sitting and counting the cost. The first indication of how things were going is given in the Journals of the Council under the date April 28, 1708, when Cary reported that he had "well nigh expended the whole Fund appropriated for building the said house" and asked for instructions. The Council accordingly asked the Treasurer of the colony for an extra £400 out of the proceeds of the duty on slaves and liquor (which had produced £1,000 more than the £3,000 voted for the Palace); in the event of there being no Assembly in the fall this was to be paid back out of the proceeds of the sale of "severall Negroes and other goods . . . wch if sold would raise a considerable sum of money for carrying on the work, but are now usefull therein." In June, Jenings told the Board of Trade that it was expected that all the outside work would be finished that summer;[5] but in September he had to report that the roof was not raised, "nor any inside work done."[6] Late in October Cary asked for further directions; the money advanced was all spent and the building "not near finished." The Council ordered

> that Mr. Henry Cary sell by Outcry or otherwise as may best advance the price so many of the s^d Negros and of the Utensils not usefull for finishing the building as will Satisfy the four hundred pounds advanced by Mr. Harrison and that he take care to cover the said house at least with planks to preserve it from injury of weather this winter, for payment whereof the Council conceive the remaining Negros and other things in his hands will be sufficient security till the Gen^ll Assembly hath provided for defraying the Charge and finishing the work.

Still there was a crisis to be surmounted: on November 2 Cary reported that the workmen refused to cover the house unless the arrears due to them, which amounted to nearly £200, were first paid—"but that done they are willing to cover the same and wait for their pay from the General Assembly." So another £200 was advanced by the Treasurer, the Council promising "that the said sum shall be refunded him out of the 2s per hogshead if the Assembly do not allow the same in his accounts."

Although the house was safely covered for the winter, Cary had more trouble to report when the building season of 1709 came round. His petition to the Council is worth quoting at length:

> That whareas your Petetinor was orderdd and Empowered by the late Generall Assembly to build a dwelling house & out houses for ye Quens Govornor have acordingly used the best of my Endevor to performe the same & have buielt & almost finished the Kitchen & Carryed up the wall & raysed the roffe of the Dwelling house and Covored itt with planks & layed on the lead upon the flat of the roffe & where as the s'd Assembly ordered the s'd house to be covored with stone slate which was sent for accordingly & are Com in butt are soe broke in Coming that not two thirds of them are fitt for use & those that are fitt Cannot mett with or here of any workeman that understands how to lay them soe that the house is still uncovered only with planks which is not suffishant to make itt tite & soe Consequently the timber worke will receave much Damadg by the rain that Come in doe therefore most humbley pray that your Honors will please to take the s'd buielding into your Considderation & Give such directions therein as you think fitt.[7]

Three matters of interest emerge from this: that the kitchen specified by the Act, but not the stable, was almost finished, that the roof platform was covered with lead, and that the slates for the roof had been obtained. With regard to the kitchen, this must have been the dependency flanking the forecourt on the west; later a new kitchen was built behind it. As for the lead and the slates, the use of these costly materials shows that only the best was thought good enough for the Governor's house. Sir

Balthazar Gerbier had written in *A Brief Discourse Concerning the Three Chief Principles of Magnificent Building* (1662): "I must not forget that the roof of a palace should be covered either with lead or blue slates." Lead was never used on the roofs of ordinary houses in colonial Virginia, and rarely on those of the grandest ones. Nor is it surprising that no workman could be found who knew how to lay slates. Even in London, where in the eighteenth century roofs were ordinarily covered with pantiles, slates were a scarce commodity. In the colonies they were so seldom seen that the house of the wealthy Philadelphia merchant Samuel Carpenter, which was roofed with them, came to be known simply as the Slate House.

Because of the condition in which the slates arrived, the Council told Cary to get the roof shingled.

THE DOUBLE PILE

The finishing of the Palace belongs to the story of Alexander Spotswood's architectural activities. However, since the main structure was built by Cary before Spotswood's arrival, this will be as suitable a place as any to consider its architectural character and its place in the history of Anglo-American architecture. The chief sources of our knowledge of its appearance and planning are three: the Bodleian plate

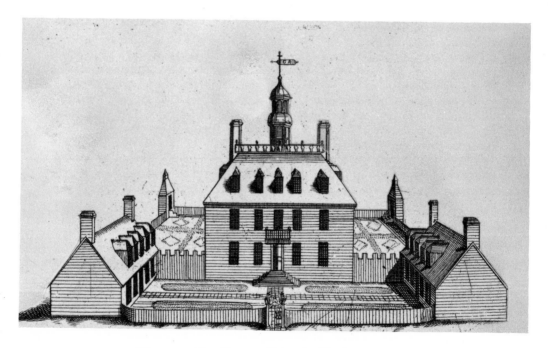

Figure 14. THE PALACE. From the "Bodleian plate."

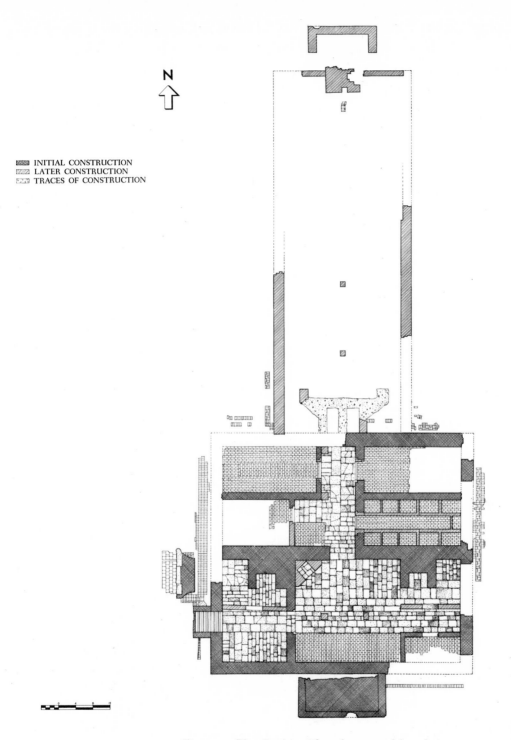

N

INITIAL CONSTRUCTION
LATER CONSTRUCTION
TRACES OF CONSTRUCTION

Figure 15. THE PALACE. Plan of excavated foundations.

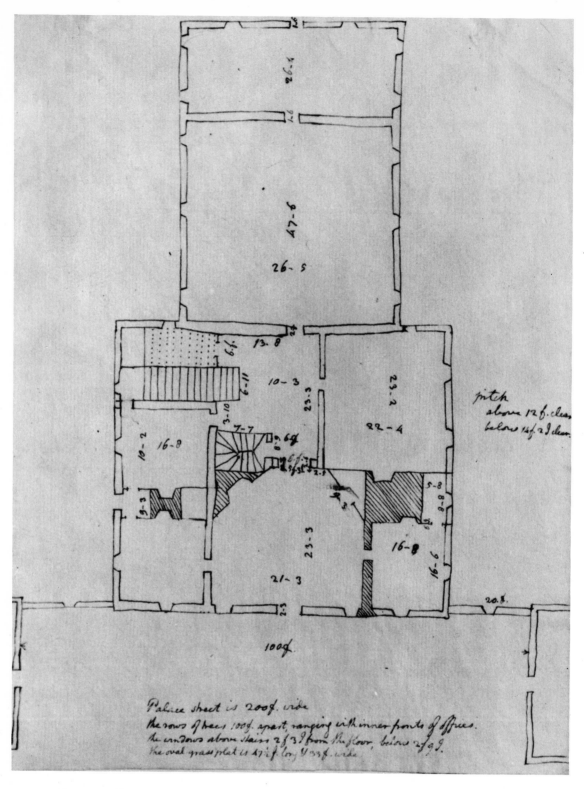

Figure 16. THE PALACE. Measured plan by Thomas Jefferson. Included in the annotations
are the heights of the two main storeys and of the window sills.

Figure 17. CHEVENING HOUSE, KENT.
From *Vitruvius Britannicus*.

Figure 18. DESIGN BY SERLIO.
From *Architettura*, Book VII.

(Fig. 14), the foundations as excavated in 1930–1932 (Fig. 15), and a plan drawn by Thomas Jefferson (Fig. 16).

The class of house to which it belonged was that which Sir Roger Pratt, fifty years before, had called the "double pile."[8] Two rooms deep, compact and block-like, the double pile was fundamentally different from the houses of the older Elizabethan-Jacobean tradition, which near Williamsburg was represented most notably by Green Spring. A very early—perhaps the first—English example was Chevening House, Kent, which a family tradition attributes to the 1620's and to Inigo Jones. (Fig. 17) Then come the houses designed by Pratt himself. The finest of them was Coleshill, Berkshire,[9] designed about 1650 and burnt in 1952. Here the main fronts were given life by the scheme of fenestration, with the three central windows more widely spaced than those at the ends. At Kingston Lacy, Dorset,[10] built in the mid-1660's, Pratt employed the opposite arrangement, spacing the central windows more closely than the rest. This is the arrangement at the Palace; but at Kingston Lacy the center section of the front breaks forward for additional emphasis. For grouped openings in an unbroken facade, as we see them at Williamsburg, we may go to Longnor Hall, Shropshire,[11] which dates from 1670. Or we may turn to an engraving in Serlio's seventh book,[12] which shows a front five windows wide, as is that of the Palace; this is a design which Pratt, if not Cary, certainly knew (Fig. 18).

Two other well-known English examples of the double pile are Thorpe Hall, Lincolnshire,[13] completed in 1656 to the design of Peter Mills, and the post-Resto-

Figure 19. EDIAL HALL, STAFFORDSHIRE. From a water-color by Paul Braddon.

ration Ashdown, Berkshire.[14] The architect of Ashdown is not known; Sir Balthazar Gerbier is a likely candidate. It is a very tall, almost towerlike house, with much to remind one that France had played a large part in the development of the type. French influence is still perceptible in Nether Lypiatt Manor, Gloucestershire (Fig. 20), which was built about 1705 and so is more nearly contemporaneous with the Palace than any of the other double-pile houses that have been mentioned. But the English house most like the Palace (at least externally) was the apparently rather earlier Edial Hall, Staffordshire (Fig. 19).[15] We may be certain that the resemblance was due to collateral descent from common ancestors rather than to any more direct relationship.

Some of the English double-pile houses have detached pavilions containing the

Figure 20. NETHER LYPIATT MANOR,
GLOUCESTERSHIRE. The garden front.

kitchen and stables, like the Palace; others do not. Some have pavilions attached to
the *corps de logis* by covered passages. Some have roof platforms and cupolas, some
have platforms without cupolas, some have cupolas without platforms, while some
have neither platforms nor cupolas. Few, if any, have cupolas as tall in relation to the
total height of the building as the cupola of the Palace, whose loftiness may be supposed to be due to a Williamsburg fashion set by the first College building, and
followed by the Capitol also. In general effect the Palace cupola is more than a little
Dutch.

A GREAT HALL?

As soon as we turn from the general form of the Palace to consider its planning
in detail, we are faced with a conflict in the evidence. When the foundations were
excavated, they were found to agree with Jefferson's plan of the building, which had
been published by Fiske Kimball in his monumental study of Jefferson's architectural drawings,[16] in every important respect save one: there was no foundation for
the partition wall between the entrance hall and the south-east room, although every
other partition was represented in the basement. That is to say, the foundations suggested that the house had had a *great hall* on the medieval model, entered near one
end, while Jefferson's plan showed it otherwise.

In 1946 Thomas T. Waterman proposed a solution of this difficulty.[17] Observing
that in Jefferson's plan certain parts of the building were distinguished by hatching,
and that those parts included the partition in question and the entrance hall fireplace, the foundations of which were not bonded into the adjoining walls, he
suggested "that Jefferson's plan, instead of being a measured drawing, as has been
thought, was a working drawing for an alteration actually carried out about 1773-

76." (The chimneys, also hatched in the plan, "perhaps were rebuilt of necessity, after sixty or more years of constant use.")

When one has discounted the description of the plan as a "working drawing"—with which its general character and the presence on it of notes giving such information as the width of Palace Green scarcely comport—and when one has allowed that 1773–1776 is too late a period for the alterations—because the room-by-room inventory of the building made after Lord Botetourt's death in 1770 shows that it was by then divided internally as in the plan—there remains much that is attractive in Waterman's theory. In England the great hall survived later than we are apt to think. Thorpe Hall, already mentioned, has one, and so—among later seventeenth-century houses—had Highmeadow, Gloucestershire,[18] and Cliveden, Buckinghamshire;[19] in 1702 no less a classicist than Nicholas Hawksmoor designed Easton Neston, Northamptonshire,[20] with a great hall that was medieval in plan, though nobly Roman in elevation and detail; in 1715 Newbold Hall, Warwickshire,[21] probably designed by Francis Smith of Warwick, was built with something much like a medieval great hall; Rainham Hall, Essex,[22] brings the theme down to 1729. It would be easy to multiply instances. Only with the country-wide diffusion of Palladian ideals in domestic planning in the 1730's did the medieval great hall as a room-type cease to be employed, while in at least one of the American colonies—South Carolina—it was the rule rather than the exception in the larger houses of the first third of the eighteenth century.[23]

There is therefore nothing inherently improbable in the supposition that the Palace had a great hall; indeed, it would fit into its historical context as neatly with one as without. But there is documentary evidence that proves conclusively that at least as early as 1727 it did not have one: namely, an Order of Council dated May 2 in that year "that the great Dining room and Parlour thereto adjoining be new painted, the one of pearl colour the other of cream colour." Since a parlour was always on the ground floor—Neve describes it as "a fair lower Room, design'd principally for the Reception, and Entertainment of Company"[24]—we are forced to conclude that "the great Dining room" was either the north-east room on that floor (which is called the dining room in the Botetourt inventory of 1770) or the (presumptive) great hall. The latter alternative cannot be seriously entertained. Hall and dining room were by no means interchangeable terms. Moreover, the documents mention "the hall" both before and after 1727, and it is hardly conceivable that an Order of Council should suddenly, and on one occasion only, call the same room by another name.[25]

Yet the absence of a foundation for the partition between the entrance hall and the south-east room, and the fact that the partition is hatched in Jefferson's plan, have still to be explained. The most likely explanation is that the house was indeed planned and begun with a great hall, and that the partition was the result of second thoughts on Cary's part or was one of the "many alterations" for which, according to Beverley, Spotswood was responsible.[26] The hatching in Jefferson's drawing could still represent recent work, for nothing could be more likely than that such a partition would have needed to be rebuilt after fifty or sixty years. Support is given to the structural evidence that the corner fireplace in the entrance hall was an afterthought by a "Proposal For rendering the new House Convenient as well as Ornamental,"[27] dating from *circa* 1710; this lists "*four* Chimney Glasses . . . for the furniture of the lower Apartments" and "*four* Chimney Glasses for the . . . second Floor." The same document refers to "the great Room in the second Story," which was to be "furnished with gilt Leather hangings 16 Chairs of the same, two large looking glasses with the Arms of the Colony on them according to the new Mode. two small Tables to stand under the Looking Glasses and two Marble Tables Eight Glass Sconces." It is a tempting guess that this "great Room" extended over the whole of the great hall below—not as yet divided into entrance hall and parlour by Spotswood; but it is no more than a guess and the "upper middle room" (as it is called in the Botetourt inventory) might be meant. In either case, the allotment to it of the richest "standing furniture"[28] in the whole house indicates that it was a state apartment and not, as was the upper middle room in Botetourt's day, a private living room for the Governor and his family.

THE PALACE'S INFLUENCE

Both as the first double pile in Virginia and as the official residence of the representative of the Crown, the Palace could scarcely fail to affect the subsequent development of architecture in the colony. Yet it did so by offering a new ideal of domestic amplitude rather than a model for close imitation. Among the larger plantation houses of the 1720's, Nomini Hall, Westmoreland County,[29] and Westover, Charles City County,[30] are double piles that might seem to have something in common with the Palace; but when their plans are analyzed it will be found that with their end chimneys and stairs in the central passage or entry they owed more to indigenous practice. Elsewhere book-learning played its part. The unknown architect of Stratford, Westmoreland County, turned to Serlio for inspiration;[31] the plan of Rosewell, Gloucester County,[32] combined themes from three English houses, Easton Neston, Buckingham House, and Roehampton House—all three to be found in the first volume of Colen Campbell's *Vitruvius Britannicus,* which was published in 1715. Knowledge of recent developments on the other side of the Atlantic was not so readily accessible to Cary in 1706. The Palace, as we have seen, was a late example of its type. That it was little imitated was not due to any intrinsic failing; rather it was due to the fact that those who could not be content with modes long established in the colony were soon offered more nearly up-to-date alternatives.

1710-1726
Church and State

ALEXANDER SPOTSWOOD landed at Jamestown on June 21, 1710 and assumed the duties of Lieutenant Governor of Virginia two days later. He was thirty-four. Born at Tangier, where his father was physician to the garrison, he came of a Scottish family which had played a conspicuous part in affairs of church and state since the middle of the sixteenth century: his great-great-grandfather had been a close associate of John Knox, his great-grandfather Archbishop of St. Andrews, his grandfather Secretary for Scotland. In 1693 he had joined the Earl of Bath's regiment of foot in Flanders as an ensign; in the War of the Spanish Succession he rose to the rank of lieutenant-colonel, was wounded at Blenheim, and captured at Oudenarde. During his twelve years as Governor he was to prove himself one of the most vigorous and able men to hold that office. The best known and most picturesque episode of his administration was the expedition that he led over the Blue Ridge, which gains in significance if one regards it as symbolic of the western movement of settlement that he did much to encourage. Always the soldier, he could exhibit what may seem to us an egregious lack of tact in dealing with the Councillors and Burgesses. In this he somewhat resembled Francis Nicholson. But whereas Nicholson, to the very end, saw his duties as Governor wholly in terms of loyalty to the Crown and the advancement of the Church, Spotswood at least progressed toward a broader view of the matter, that should give equal value to the internal welfare of the colony. Like Nicholson again, and like Andros too, he made a firm enemy in the person of James Blair; and it is highly probable that Blair was responsible for his eventual dismissal—as he certainly had been for the recall of Andros and Nicholson. Unlike Nicholson and Andros, however, Spotswood determined to make Virginia his permanent home. After a six year visit to England to straighten out some little difficulties about the tenure of his vast holdings of land in the new county of Spotsylvania, in the course of which he acquired a wife, four children, and the office of Deputy Postmaster-General for the American colonies, he returned to spend the last ten years of his life in the colony, supervising his plantations and the iron-works (the first in Virginia) that he had established.[1]

In his *History of the British Plantations in America*[2] Sir William Keith wrote of Spotswood (who was still alive, though the past tense suggests otherwise):

> He was well acquainted with Figures, and so good a Mathematician, that his skill in Architecture, and in the laying out of Ground to the best Advantage, is yet to be seen in Virginia, by the Building of an elegant safe Magazine, in the Centre of Williamsburgh, and in the considerable Improvements which he made to the Governor's House and Gardens.

That is true as far as it goes, but the half is not told. The very plan of Williamsburg, as we see it today, was due largely to Spotswood; and besides completing the Governor's House and laying out its gardens and designing the Public Magazine, he was architect of an addition to the Gaol, of a new church for Bruton Parish, and in some degree of the second building of the College. It was the day of the amateur architect, and another ex-soldier had already made good in the art in England with no more technical training (to all appearances) than Spotswood had. It would be a mistake to push the parallel between Alexander Spotswood and John Vanbrugh too far: the latter's achievements as an architect were incomparably greater. Yet in character and tastes they had something in common; both for instance married late in life after disparaging the matrimonial state, and were exemplary husbands.[3] And even if Spotswood did not write plays, as Vanbrugh did, at least he patronized the first theatre in the English colonies, opened at Williamsburg between 1716 and 1718.

In treating of the public buildings that went up during the administration of Spotswood (1710–1722) and that of his successor Hugh Drysdale (1722–1726), we shall abandon chronology, a strict attention to which would be impracticable because two or more buildings were often going up concurrently. And for convenience sake, rather than any logic in the arrangement, the College and the Playhouse will be deferred to the next chapter.

THE DEBTORS' PRISON

The first architectural work of Spotswood's to which we turn, though a minor one, has a special interest in that it possessed a feature which, whatever its precise nature may have been, was a novelty in the colony.

Figure 21. ALEXANDER SPOTSWOOD. Portrait by Charles Bridges, 1735/6.

The Public Gaol as we left it in 1704 was a brick building—house, one could say —measuring 30 ft. by 20 ft. on plan, with an exercise yard at its west end; it was designed to hold defendants until trial. In his speech to the Assembly in the fall of 1711 Spotswood referred to the need for accommodation for another class of prisoners, the debtors. The Committee of Propositions and Grievances considered the matter and in agreeing to its report the Burgesses resolved:

> That a Publick goal for Debtors which shall be committed by the General Court be built at Williamsburgh. That the Same be built with Brick and be well Secured with Plank That it be made thirty two foot in Length and Twenty foot in breadth from out side to out side . . . .

The act for building the Debtors' Prison, which became law in January 1711/12, appropriated funds not to exceed £200 out of the duty on slaves and liquor and gave the Governor himself power to "contract and agree with any person or persons, for the erecting, building and finishing the prison aforesaid." The new building stood. as Robert Beverley tells us, to the west of the exercise yard.

Beverley also tells us that all the public buildings at Williamsburg were roofed with shingles "except the Debtors Prison which is flat roofed anew; a very useful Invention of the present Governor [Spotswood] also."[4] From this it would appear that the Debtors' Prison was re-roofed between 1712 and the date of Beverley's revisions for the 1722 edition of his book. John Oldmixon, in his *British Empire in America*, misquotes Beverley as saying that the Debtors' Prison was "flat roofed, a new and very useful invention of Governor Spotswood," and adds scornfully: "Mr. R. B. Gent was very ignorant if he thought flat roofs a new invention." Although Oldmixon misread Beverley, it is true that the problem of the "flat roof" had exercised architects and others long before Spotswood's time.

In the sense of the term accepted in the seventeenth and eighteenth centuries, flat roofs need be only relatively flat. Godfrey Richards at the end of *The First Book of Architecture by Andrea Palladio*, published in 1663, gives two "flat roofs," both of king-post type, with rises of an eighth and a sixth of the span (Fig. 22); these were designed by William Pope, who in 1675 became Master of the Carpenters' Company.[5] But "flat roof" could also have a more special meaning. The antiquary-naturalist, Robert Plot, in his *Natural History of Oxfordshire* (1677) wrote: "It was an excellent Device, whoever first contrived it, of making Flat-Floors or Roofs *of short pieces of Timber continued to a great Breadth*, without either Arch or Pillar to support them." He goes on to mention the "flat floor" in the tower of the Schools at

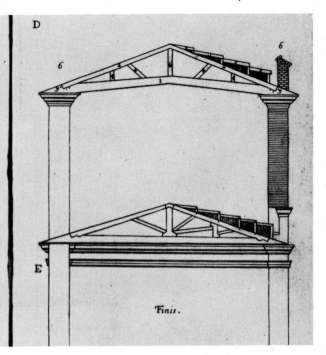

Of Flat Roofes D.

With a *Camber-Beam* and *Rafters* joggled in, whose weight lyeth not chiefly in the middle, and may be so made that without hanging up the Beam, the principals may discharge the weight; And how Drips may be made to walk on.

1. *Camber-Beam.*
2. *Principals joggled into the Camber-Beam.*
3. *The place where the principals are joggled in.*
4. *Punchons or Braces.*
5. *Drips to walk on, and may be made with the lesse current that the Roof may be made the more pitch for the strengthening thereof: And may be made higher or lower according to the Building and Discretion of the Architect.*
6. *Battlements.*

CHAP. LI.

Of a Flat Roof, with a Crown post, or King piece E.

If any of these Roofes be hipt, the former generall Rules may serve for a Rule to find out the back and the length of the Hip-Rafter or Sleeper for these also: Except the *Roof Bevells*, or be out of square, then the *Bevel Line* (instead of the *Horizontal*, or *Level line* of the Floore, with the back of the *Hip Rafter*) shall always become the *Angle lines*, by which the back of the *Hip Rafter* shall be made. And for *Dormers* if *Bevell*, must be the same thing Reversed.

Figure 22. FLAT ROOFS BY WILLIAM POPE. From Godfrey Richards' edition of Palladio.

Figure 23. SERLIO'S FLAT FLOOR OR FLAT ROOF. From *Architettura*, Book 1.

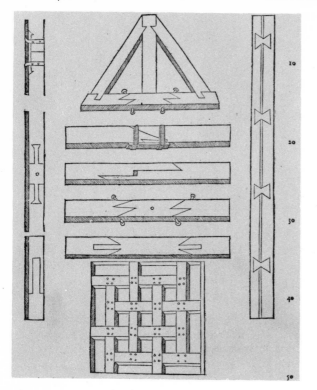

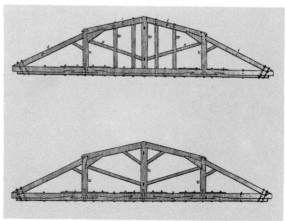

Figure 25. ROOF OF THE SHELDONIAN THEATRE, OXFORD. From Wren's *Parentalia*.

Figure 24. TRABES COMPACTILES.
From Barbaro's edition of Vitruvius.

Oxford (built in 1625) and the example of this kind of construction, which was truly flat, given by Serlio in his first book, published in 1545 (Fig. 23). Serlio's design reappeared under the head of *trabes compactiles* in Barbaro's edition of Vitruvius (1567), with examples of another kind of construction, to be touched upon in a moment (Fig. 24). The theoretical basis of the Serlian system was worked out by John Wallis, Savillian Professor of Geometry at Oxford, who in 1670 published diagrams demonstrating it in his *Mechanica*. Wallis also gave a model to the Royal Society, and this was illustrated by Nehemiah Crew, the vegetable physiologist, in his *Museum Regalis Societatis* (1681). Before this, in 1663, a young friend of Wallis, the Savillian Professor of Astronomy, had applied his extraordinary mind to the problem of roofing outsize areas and given to Oxford a practical demonstration of his own solution (Fig. 25). The building of which this forms a part is the Sheldonian Theatre, and the name of the Professor of Astronomy, whom in 1663 nobody would have regarded as primarily an architect, was Christopher Wren. In 1734 Wil-

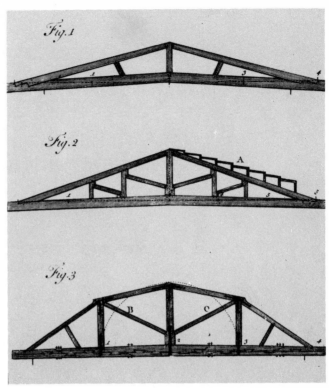

Figure 26. FLAT ROOFS AND "A ROOF PARTLY FLAT." From William Salmon's *Palladio Londinensis.*

liam Salmon published in his *Palladio Londinensis* variants of the Richards-Pope flat roofs and of the Sheldonian system (Fig. 22). The latter he describes as "a Roof partly flat" and says that "by scarfing, or piecing the Beams together in this Manner [i.e., the manner shown in the engraving], [it] will be capable of spanning any Breadth whatsoever."

Keith, it will be recollected, said that Spotswood was a good mathematician, and indeed there is plenty of other evidence of his interest in mathematics: he was responsible for Hugh Jones's appointment at the College, and while in England he put his Spotsylvania lands and iron-works in charge of a mathematical cousin, whose mismanagement of them he described to William Byrd with the reflection "that indeed he was rightly serv'd for committing his Affairs to the care of a Mathematician whose thoughts were always among the Stars." His "very useful Invention" may well have owed something (or everything) to Wallis or to Wren. Or he may have taken the idea from Serlio. On the other hand, the spanning of only twenty feet

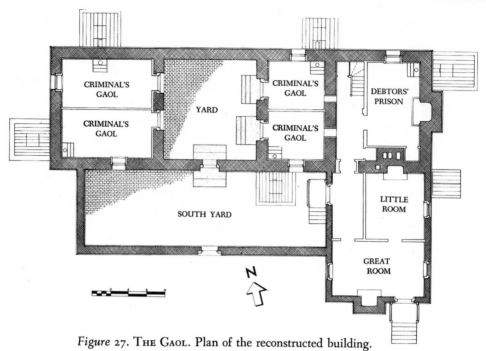

Figure 27. THE GAOL. Plan of the reconstructed building.

with a structure designed to utilize timber of insufficient length seems a somewhat gratuitous expenditure of ingenuity, and the possibility that the flat roof of the Debtors' Prison was nothing more than a king-post structure of exceptionally low pitch is not to be ruled out.

In 1722 *A Bill for Making the Public Prisons in Williamsburg more convenient, and for building a House for the Keeper thereof* was passed by the Assembly; it was one of the last bills to which Spotswood gave his assent. In accordance with its provisions a walled yard and a keeper's house were built adjoining the south side of the existing building and various alterations necessitated by a re-allocation of cells were carried out. The debtors, who never came in very fast, were moved from the possibly uncertain shelter of Spotswood's flat roof into the east end of the older portion. The sum of £359 was allowed for the work, and a committee consisting of John Holloway, the first Mayor of Williamsburg, John Clayton, the Attorney-General of the colony, and Archibald Blair, Burgess for James City County and brother of the Commissary, was put in charge. The Gaol retained the form thus given it for half a century, until in 1772 an Act of Assembly ordered an addition to the gaoler's house —"to consist of brick walls, and a shingled roof, not exceeding thirty one feet in length, and of the height and width of the old house." (Fig. 27)

BRUTON PARISH: THE FIRST BRICK CHURCH

The church that stood at Middle Plantation when the place became Williams-burg was a rectangular brick structure, 60 ft. by 24 ft. internally, which had been completed in 1683 (Fig. 28). It occupied a site north-west of the present church, near the center of the churchyard. The first vestry book of Bruton Parish, which was formed in 1674 by uniting two earlier parishes and named after Bruton in Somerset (the home of the Ludwell family and of the then Governor, Sir William Berkeley), disappeared in the last century, but fortunately not before extracts from it had been published.[6] From these we know that the original contractor, in 1679, was one George Marable, and that he was to be paid £350 sterling. However, something miscarried, for Marable went to law, arresting two of the vestrymen. In 1681 Francis Page undertook the building. The plan was altered in several respects and Page agreed to accept £150 "and sixty pounds of good sound, merchantable, sweet scented Tobacco and Caske, to be levied of each Tytheable in the parish for three years to-gether, the first payment to commence this next ensuing crop." In November 1683, the building having been finished, two 28-gallon barrels of tar were ordered for the roof; eleven months later Page gave bond and security to keep the church in good order and repair for four years. In 1685 there was talk of building a steeple, but it came to nothing.

As with the first College building, we have to thank Michel, the Swiss, for our only record of the appearance of this first brick church of Bruton Parish (Fig. 29). Michel's drawing shows a shaped gable in the Anglo-Flemish tradition at the west end; there are two windows above the west door, suggesting the presence of a western gallery inside; in the north wall of the churchyard is a lychgate with a ball-topped triangular pediment supported by baluster-like columns. Michel's drawing does not show the buttresses, five on each side, whose existence was revealed by excavation in 1939. These buttresses, like those of St. Luke's, Isle of Wight County, and of the church at Jamestown, were a medieval survival. So was the practice of specify-ing features by reference to another building, exemplified in an entry in the vestry book under a date in June 1679:

> The West door and Chancill door [to] be according to the demensions of James City Church doors, only to be one foot higher and ½ a foot wider than they are.

However, these survivals were not due to any "colonial time-lag." Church architec-

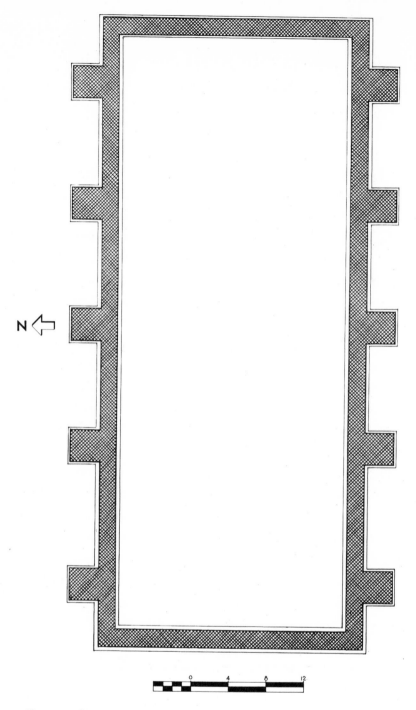

Figure 28. THE FIRST BRICK CHURCH OF BRUTON PARISH. Plan of foundations.

ture and the vestries that commissioned it were apt to be just as old-fashioned in country districts in England. The brick church in Minsterley in Shropshire, for example, was built with buttresses in 1692;[7] many seventeenth-century instances of features being directly imitated to order have been collected by Colvin.[8]

SPOTSWOOD'S CHURCH

Structurally, Francis Page's church was not an unqualified success. Repairs were ordered by the Vestry as early as 1693, and again in 1699, 1702, and 1703. In July 1705 one of the vestrymen was "desired to procure Carpenters to Visit the Church, and to report their opinion to the next Vestry whether it can be repaired or not"; fifteen months later the Vestry, "considering the great charge the parish hath been at for the repairing of the Church," ordered that 20,000 lbs. of tobacco be levied for building a new one. Another four years went by before enough money was raised, and all the time the demand for space by the extra-parochial worshippers who crowded into Williamsburg at the "public times" was increasing. Reasonably enough, the Vestry felt that the parish could not be expected to foot the whole bill for a church of the size necessary. So in November 1710 they petitioned the Assembly "for their Generous Contribution towards the same," promising that they would "consider of such a building as in their wisdoms shall be thought proper for the said Occasions, & to give directions that a Draught thereof be laid before your Honours dureing this Assembly: the Vestry on their part being willing to advance towards the same, what may be thought necessary for the building a Suitable Church for their Parish." The petition received the blessing of Spotswood and the Burgesses voted £200 from the duty on liquor and slaves, asking the Governor to "take the trouble of laying it out for Enlarging the said Church and building pews for the Governor Council and Burgesses." To this Spotswood replied "that he thanked the house for the confidence they had in him, that tho he had never been concerned in business of this nature, he would use his best endeavours to have the money laid out to answer their intentions." At a meeting of the Vestry on March 1, 1711 James Blair, who had been elected minister of Bruton Parish in December, reported that

> he had received from the Honble. Alexr. Spotswood, a platt or draught of a Church, (whose length is 75 foot, and bredth 28 foot in the clear, with two wings on each side, whose width is 22 foot) which he Laid before the Vestry for approbation—Adding further, that the Honble. the Governor proposed to the Vestry to build only 53 of the 75 foot, and that he would take care of the remaining part.

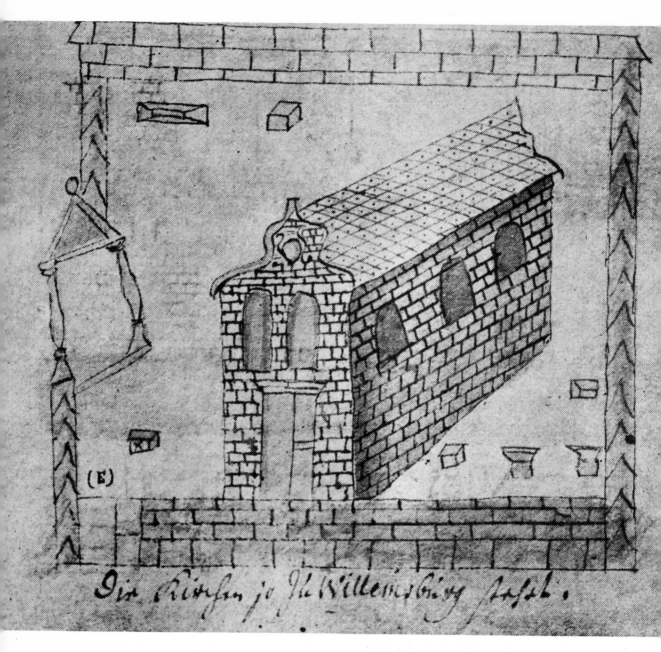

Figure 29. THE FIRST BRICK CHURCH OF BRUTON PARISH.
An early copy of a drawing made by Franz Ludwig Michel in 1702.

The Vestry approved Spotswood's design for "commodiousness and conveniency." It also, "not knowing what scantlings were suitable for such a building, nor number of bricks the said worke would take," empowered one of its members "to agree with some skillful workman to lay down the said scantlings" and calculate the number of bricks needed for that part of the building which the parish was to pay for; he was to report his findings to the next meeting. A fortnight later tenders for supplying the materials from John Tullitt and Henry Cary were considered, and thought exorbitant. "Whereupon the Honorable Alexr. Spottswood proposed together with the Hon. Edmund Jennings, to deliver in place as many bricks as shall be thought necessary in building the Church, at the rate of 15s. per thousand, in order to beat down the extravagant prices of workmen, provided some of the Vestry would undertake other parts." On November 17, 1712 the Vestry ordered that a building contract be entered into with James Morris, giving him twenty-three months to finish the work. Ten days later Spotswood told the House of Burgesses that he would "Diminish the Wings projected for the Publick use," since he perceived that they would be "Contented with less Room therein," and each arm of the transept was accordingly shortened from 19 ft. to 14 ft. 6 in.

James Morris was a carpenter by trade. His grandson, writing in 1762 in the vestry book of St. Peter's parish, New Kent County, tells us that he "came in Virginia with Coll. Ludwell Gen.ᵗ and was Cheif workman in the City of Williamsburg, and was an Englishman Born." [9] In 1704 he owned land to a total of 1,150 acres in York, James City and Gloucester Counties. He died in December 1717, leaving personal estate worth a little more than £100; the inventory is among the Jones family papers in the Library of Congress, the big landowner Thomas Jones having been his executor. Also among them is a bill from another carpenter,[10] Lewis Delony, whom we shall meet again during the building of the second Capitol. This shows that Delony worked for Morris at Bruton Church, and some items relating to his work there are worth quoting:

To 16 Square flooring done at the Church @ 3/6	£2 : 16 : —
To framing and putting in the ground floor	1 : — : —
To setting up the pews and making the Ends & some doors . . .	3 : — : —
To the Gallery forty shillings and the Stairs 15/	2 : 15 : —
To the pulpit and Canopy	1 : 10 : —
To the Communion Table with rail and banister	1 : 5 : —

For the transept, which was the responsibility not of the Vestry but of the Assembly, John Tyler (whom also we shall meet again) acted as "overseer." The specification,[11] which gives its dimensions as first planned, contains a list of rates for piece work:

> The Laying of the Bricks, including the Labourers work, shall be rated at 7s 6d
> per: Thousand—
> The framing, raising and covering the Roof at 18sh 6d p' Square—
> The framing & raising the Floor at 10 sh pr' Square—
> The Working & Setting the Eves at 20sh pr foot—
> The Rubbing, Cutting, & setting the Window Arches at 5sh pr: Arch—
> The Rubbing & Cutting the Foot lesses[12] at one penny pr: foot—
> The Rubbing the Returns at 2sh pr: hundred—
> The framing & Setting the Window & Door Cases at 10sh each—

The church was in use by the end of 1715, although the roof was not shingled until 1717.

BEAUTY FROM GEOMETRY

All the principal dimensions on plan of the Capitol and of the Palace were commensurable, those of the Capitol yielding integers when divided by 5 and those of the Governor's House being exactly divisible by 6; at the College we have seen the Golden Section ratio used to determine proportions. Remembering this, we should beware of assuming that the plan dimensions of Bruton Parish Church as designed by Spotswood—length, 75 ft; breadth of nave, 28 ft; breadth of transept, 22 ft; projection of transept 19 ft.—were as arbitrary in fact at first sight they may appear to be. Nothing indeed could be less likely than that the mathematical Governor, given the opportunity to design a church, should pick its dimensions out of a hat. Spotswood lived in an age which had inherited from the Renaissance the belief that the arts should reproduce the harmonies of nature, which could be expressed in mathematical terms; as Wren put it, "natural" beauty was "from Geometry." It would be wrong to say that in designing Bruton Church Spotswood called Geometry to his aid: he practically handed the job over to her.

There are several ways by which the dimensions on plan could have been arrived at; the system shown in the accompanying diagram (Fig. 31) has been chosen for the sake of simplicity of demonstration, rather than as that most probably used by Spotswood in the act of design. An equilateral triangle with sides of 75 ft., the internal length of the building, has an altitude of 66 ft., its internal breadth across the transept—and a measurement that would have been of great practical utility in staking out the plan because it is the length of a surveyor's chain. The projection of the transept is equal to the altitude of a triangle with sides of one-third of a chain, 22 ft.; the position of the eastern walls of the transept is determined by a triangle with sides of double that length, or two-thirds of the breadth of the building. The

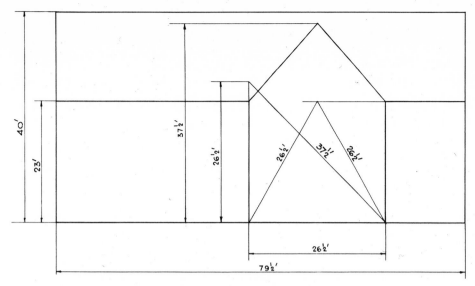

Figure 30. Bruton Parish Church. Diagrammatic elevation of the building as originally designed, showing system of proportion.

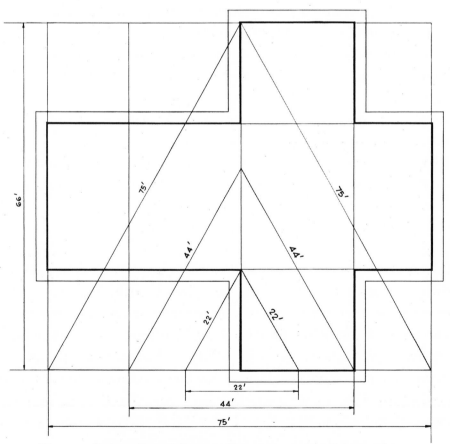

Figure 31. Bruton Parish Church. Diagrammatic plan of the building as originally designed, showing system of proportion.

projection of the transept in the revised design, 14 ft. 6 in., is half the diagonal of the transept arms as first designed.

Turning to the elevation (Fig. 30) we notice first that the height of the building to the roof-ridge is approximately half its length. The height of the walls, 23 ft., will be found to be the altitude of an equilateral triangle whose sides are 26 ft. 6 in., this being one third of the total external length of the building and also the external breadth of the transept at ground level. Finally (at least for the purposes of the present analysis) the height above ground of the apex of the transept gable is 37 ft. 6 in. This is not only half the internal length of the building: it is also the diagonal of a square on the external breadth of the transept. That is to say, the whole transept elevation may be inscribed in a Golden Section rectangle. Now the specification for the transept already quoted says: "The Rooff to raise in proportion to the breadth that it spans." Tempting though it may be to assume that "the proportion" refers to the Golden Section rectangle, there can be little doubt but that something else is meant. For the rake or pitch of the roof is in fact what William Salmon, in *Palladio Londinensis,*[13] tells us was "called true (or common) Pitch, it being most in Use"; it was "a proper Pitch for covering with Plain-Tiles" and he writes "To find the perpendicular Height, divide the Breadth of the Building . . . into 4 Parts, for the Length of the Rafter." Spotswood had made sure that his proportional system did not conflict with traditional carpenters' practice.

It would no doubt be possible to carry the analysis of the proportions of Bruton Church further. But enough has been said to show that its dimensions, far from being arbitrarily chosen or even a matter of taste, were related to each other according to a tight-knit scheme which is perhaps the more effective aesthetically for not being obvious to the eye.

THE CRUCIFORM PLAN

The cruciform church-plan is almost as old as Christian church architecture. Its longevity must be attributed to its symbolic appropriateness, for the practical use to which the arms of the cross or transept have been put has varied from age to age. In churches of the reformed faith it lent itself to the centralization that the concept of a church as an "auditory" (as Wren called it) demanded, and the transept facilitated the provision of galleries, which could very conveniently be supported by beams spanning each arm from east to west. Bruton Church as we see it today exemplifies this last advantage. However, the transept galleries, unlike the gallery at the west end of the nave, were not features of the building as completed in 1715, although a gallery was installed in the south arm as early as 1720.

An entry in the vestry book under a date in January 1716 gives the original seating arrangements:

> Ordered that the Men sitt on the North side of the Church, and the Women on the left.
> Ordered that Mr. Commissary Blair sitt in the head pew in the Church, and that he may Carry any Minister into the same.
> Ordered that the Parishioners be seated in the Church, and none others.
> Ordered that the Vacant room in the west end of the Church be made into three convenient pews, and that the Church Wardens agree with some workmen to do the same.

The order that only parishioners are to be seated in the church becomes intelligible when one understands that "church" here means the nave, built by and belonging to the parish, and does not include the Assembly's "wings"; the fact that there was room for an uneven number of pews at the west end suggests that the font stood near the west door, as it usually did in Anglican churches, on one side of the central passageway. The students of the College, as another entry in the vestry book shows, sat in the west gallery. Spotswood sat in a state pew, which was "raised from the floor, [and] covered with a canopy, around the interior of which his name was written in gilt letters." [14]

It would seem that the only cruciform churches in the American colonies before Bruton were the Roman Catholic "chapel" at St. Mary's, Maryland, built in the 1630's,[15] the first St. Anne's at Annapolis, designed in 1699, and the Swedish Lutheran church of Gloria Dei at Wicaco, Pennsylvania, built in 1698–1700 and added to in 1705; [16] it is improbable that Spotswood was thinking of any of these when he designed the Williamsburg church. As for the early writers who compared Bruton to the churches of London—meaning the City churches designed by Wren to take the place of those destroyed in the Great Fire—they were presumably referring to the general effect of the interior, with galleries and pews and lofty pulpit, rather than to the fabric itself. For none of Wren's churches, with the scarcely comparable exception of St. Paul's Cathedral, is cruciform externally, although in some of them an internal cross is produced through the use of columns. In the English provinces cruciform churches of seventeenth-century date are exceedingly rare. There is one at Buntingford, Hertfordshire, built in 1614–26 on a Greek-cross plan, one at Euston, Suffolk, built in 1676, with an aisled nave, and a third, of c. 1685, at Farley, Wiltshire.[17] And that would seem to be all. In post-Reformation Scotland, however, the cruciform plan was relatively common.[18] Can it be that the plan of Bruton was due to Scottish usage—seeing that both the architect, Spotswood, and the minister, Blair, were Scots? It is an attractive hypothesis; yet it must be confessed that it would be even more attractive if Spotswood had ever visited Scotland, which it seems he had not. Perhaps, after all, this is a case in which we need not look beyond practical considerations: part of the church was to be built by the Parish, part by the Assembly, and the cruciform plan made it possible to keep the parts distinct.

BRUTON'S PROGENY

Whatever led Spotswood to give Bruton Parish a cruciform church, there can be no questioning the effect of its example on subsequent church architecture in Virginia, which was demonstrably much greater than that of the Palace on domestic architecture. In Virginia, alone of the American colonies, the cruciform church became a normal eighteenth-century type. Christ Church, Lancaster County,[19] built in 1732, is the least altered example, and the finest; there are few country churches of the time in England that equal it in quality. Unlike Bruton, Christ Church has a hipped roof, as had also the cruciform Pongoteague Church of c. 1738 in Accomack County on the Eastern Shore.[20] St. John's, Hampton,[21] completed in 1728 by Henry Cary, Jr., son of the overseer of the Capitol and the Palace, and St. Paul's, Norfolk,[22] of 1739, resemble Spotswood's Bruton so very closely that one can only suppose that their vestries specified it as the model to be followed; except that at Hampton the transept was as wide as the nave, the dimensions on plan of the three churches (before additions) differed by inches only. Mattapony Church,[23] built probably about 1732, is another clear case of direct imitation; its builder, David Minitree, was a Williamsburg man. Abingdon Church,[24] of 1751–1755, shows its later date by the more academic treatment of the gable ends as pediments.

One respect in which Bruton differs from most of its progeny is the treatment of its doorways, which are plain arched openings. With the exception of Pongoteague, the other Virginian churches mentioned have or had pedimented doorcases of cut brick. This feature perhaps shows the influence of the builders' pattern books, which began to be published in England in the 1720's and which contained many such "frontispieces." When Bruton was built there were no English pattern books, and only a handful of translations of Italian and French architectural treatises, which were usually of a more theoretical nature even if some of them contained designs that could be lifted cold. Spotswood relied upon no such adventitious aids:

the virtues of his church were fundamental virtues of proportion. But its general simplicity was evidently relieved by features corresponding to the shaped gables of its predecessor, the first brick church of Bruton Parish, for in 1742 the Vestry ordered "the brick Ornaments of the Gavel ends to be taken down, and finished with wood, answering the rest."

THE MAGAZINE

There was a magazine at Middle Plantation at the time of Bacon's Rebellion. This we know from an Order of Assembly of 1676/7 "that for as much as the armes and ammunition sent by the kings majestie cannot be disposed of untill Mr. Secretary arrives, that therefore it remaine in the publique magazene at the *Middle plantation* untill the next assembly." And Michel mentions the existence of a magazine at Williamsburg in 1702. However, this building either was destroyed or came to be thought inadequate, and in December, 1714 the Assembly passed *An Act for erecting a Magazine,* which gave Williamsburg the building that stands in Market Square to this day.

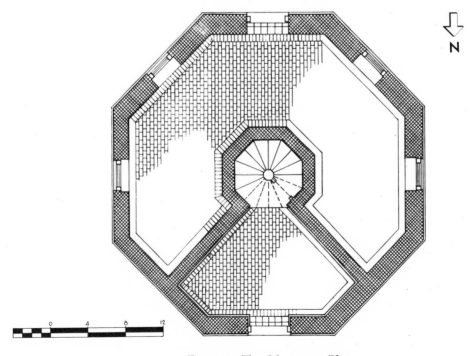

Figure 32. THE MAGAZINE. Plan.

The occasion for the introduction of the Bill was afforded by Queen Anne's gift to the colony of a quantity of arms and ammunition. In reporting the arrival of this to the Burgesses, the Governor suggested that measures to enable him to take better care of it than such military supplies had formerly received would not only be the best return they could make for so generous a gift, and a full recompense for any pains he had taken in soliciting and procuring it, but might "also Render it an Estate of Inheritance" to their posterity. To expedite the passage of the Act Spotswood offered to advance his own money, without interest, for the building; although it was not to cost more than £200, the public funds (he told the Board of Trade) were "so much anticipated that they could not possibly raise even that Sum in a considerable time." The Act laid the already hard-worked duty on liquor and slaves under contribution for both the cost of the building and the salaries of keeper and armourer, with the proviso that the Virginia Indian Company, which was authorized as monopolist of the trade with the Indians by another Act of the same Assembly, should contribute £100 as soon as it was incorporated. Spotswood was empowered to direct the work and issue warrants for payment for materials and labour.

Thanks no doubt to the nocturnal exploits of Lord Dunmore's men on April 20, 1775, a notion has got about—and even into print—that the Public Magazine was in some way a symbol of British tyranny. Of course nothing could be further from the truth. The erection of such a building was a rational measure of defense on the part of the colony.

John Tyler, who had been overseer of the transept of Bruton Parish Church, was employed in the same capacity at the Magazine, as we know from the petition of 1727 in which he prayed the Assembly to be allowed some recompense for both jobs. Even if we did not have Sir William Keith's word for it, we could guess that Spotswood gave the design. The program was one that appealed to the soldier and gave scope to the mathematician. Previous colonial magazines, such as the brick ones of 1660 at Jamestown [25] and of 1712 at Charleston,[26] and the modest frame structure of 1701 at Annapolis,[27] had been rectangular: very well, this one should be octagonal and should stand near the centre of the town like nothing so much as the *praetorium* in a Roman camp (Figs. 32, 33). Its beauty, like Bruton's, is "of Geometry." Walls and roof are of exactly the same height, and the total height from the ground to the apex of the roof is equal to the diagonal of a square constructed on the diameter; thus the whole design is regulated by the Golden Section. The result is satisfying, and aesthetically considered the Magazine is a most successful building.

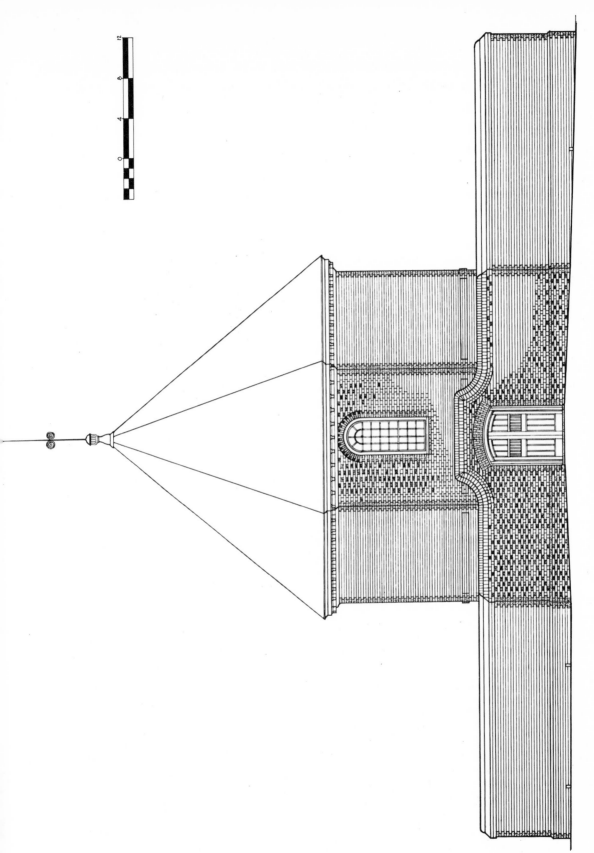

Figure 33. THE MAGAZINE. North elevation.

Judging it by functional criteria, one may have reservations. Although Keith called it safe, it broke the first rule for powder magazines in having an armourer's repair shop incorporated in it. Nor, with its wooden floors, stairs and roof, was it fireproof. A writer in the *Gentleman's Magazine* in 1760 says that powder magazines should always be vaulted [28]—though admittedly he was treating of fortress magazines, liable to bombardment. That Spotswood's design seemed functional enough to those who had no love for the form of government he had represented is shown by an advertisement in Purdie's *Virginia Gazette* for October 13, 1775:

> The Committee of Safety having appointed Edmund Pendleton and Carter Braxton, esquires, to let the building of a PUBLIC MAGAZINE at *Hanover* town, which is to be of *brick,* and in the *form* and *size* of that in *Williamsburg,* with such a *wall* around it, they hereby give notice that they will attend . . . to let the said building . . .

The wall referred to was not built until 1755. But the Magazine was enclosed with a fence or stockade by June 1722, when the younger Henry Cary was paid for the work.

THE FINISHING OF THE PALACE

We left the Palace, in the spring of 1709, structurally complete but still only a shell. In his first speech to the Burgesses, in October 1710, Spotswood informed them that he was commanded to remind them to appropriate funds for finishing it. "This is a Matter" he added, "in which Your Own Honour is now so far Engaged, That I no ways Doubt of your Ready complyance."

And indeed their compliance was ready enough. It expressed itself in *An Act for finishing a House for the Governor of this Colony and Dominion,* passed early in December. This Act not only appropriated £1,560 for the finishing of the house, kitchen and stable specified in the original Act, but went further in granting an additional £635, of which £250 was to be spent on standing furniture, and the remainder on works specified as follows:

> And be it enacted . . . That a Court-Yard, of dimentions proportionable to the said house, be laid out, levelled and encompassed with a brick wall four foot high, with ballustrades of wood thereupon, on the said land, and that a Garden of the length of two hundred fifty-four foot and of the breadth of one hundred forty-four foot from out to out, adjoining to the said house, to be laid out and levelled and enclosed with a brick wall, four foot high, with ballustrades of wood upon the said wall, and that handsome gates to be made to the said court-yard and garden, and that a convenient kitchen garden be laid out on the said land and be enclosed with pailes, and that an orchard and pasture

ground be made on the said land and be enclosed with a good ditch and fence, and also that a house of wood be built and finished for housing cattle, and that a house of wood for poultry be built and finished, with a yard thereto enclosed, on the said land.

Henry Cary, Sr., was again appointed overseer. The day before the bill was introduced he had, as it happened, petitioned the Assembly for arrears of salary. He stated that when work came to a stop he had asked the President of the Council, Jenings, to discharge him and appoint someone else to look after the building. Jenings had replied that he had no power to do this,

> whereupon your Peticon^r lookt upon himself to be under necessity of continuing to look after the said building and thinking himself lyable to answer any damages that might happen for want of his due care therein, and hath don severall things and services towards the same, dureing such intervall, as primeing and painting the Timber work in severall parts of it and burning a Large Kill of Bricks and Other small services and accordingly, the better to enable your Peticon^r to be the more carefull and diligent in looking after the said building, he did break up Housekeeping at his own Plantacon and remove his wife and other of his Domesticks to the said work or building all which was very prejudiciall to your Peticon^r . . . .

Unfortunately for Cary, not everyone thought that he was the party most prejudiced by this change of residence. At a meeting in April 1711 the Council decided that his methods were "extravagantly chargable and expensive both in the pay of the Workmen and charge of housekeeping." The Journal continues:

> This Board are therefore of Opinion that it is the duty of the said Cary to endeavour the lessening the said Expence by a more frugal management of the money wherewith he is entrusted by the General Assembly, and do request the Governor to give directions that Workmen may be imployed to undertake the finishing that Building by the peice or such other way as he shall find most usefull for carrying on the said Work to the best Advantage.

This is not as ambiguous as might at first appear, for the Act of 1710 stated that Cary was to carry on as overseer "under and with the direction of" the Governor. In fact Cary was on the way out. In December the Council held that "amongst divers other mismanagements and misapplications of . . . publick money" he had "under pretense of dieting the workmen imployed in the said building taken the liberty to maintain his whole family at the publick charge," and called for his accounts. He was succeeded as overseer by John Tyler.

Needless to say, the money voted in 1710 was not enough. In November 1712 Spotswood asked the Burgesses for more, so that the building should not remain "to all Strangers a Visable Testimony of an Imprudent undertaking." Twelve members were sent to ask how much would be needed, and reported back "that his Honor was pleased to say it was very Difficult to make Computations in this Country but that he would Manage it as thriftily as he could and believed according to the best Computation he could make That Six hundred pounds besides what is already expended would finish the work." The sum of £900 was accordingly appropriated.

But there were other more urgent claims on the yield from the duty on liquor and slaves, from which the £900 was to come. On December 8, 1713 the following message from Spotswood was read in the House of Burgesses:

> Mr. Speaker and Gentlemen of
> the House of Burgesses ·
> I have now ordered the overseer of the Governor's house to attend you with his Accompt, that you may thereby observe the Building has been carryed on, notwithstanding, no part of the nine hundred pounds you last appropriated is yet raised, for the allowing no interest for that sum might pass for frugal management—Yet I judge it would still be ill Husbandry to suffer Unfinished Works to stand long exposed, and an overseer's Sallary to run on, while nothing was doing, or at best to hire Workmen upon Credit; And therefore wherever any money has been wanting I have supplyed it—
> What now remains to be finished may, in my opinion, be either let out, or performed by so few workmen, as the Country needs no longer be at the Expense of an Overseer; for I will take care of the work, if these Gentlemen who are entrusted with the Repairs of the Capitol, or some others, have the charge of the Accompts.

The following day the House resolved "that the Governor be Desired that he would be pleased to take care of Finishing the Work and that the Overseer be Discharged." A bill to appoint two treasurers to the Trustees of the City of Williamsburg was before the House at the time, and a clause was added to it making them responsible for the building accounts and empowering the Governor to direct the works.

As before, the duty on liquor and slaves was to supply the money. This time, however, no limit was set on the amount to be spent. Spotswood congratulated himself on this in a letter to the Board of Trade, designed to ensure a continuance of the allowance for house rent; but the freedom conferred on him made it all the easier for his political enemies in the troubled middle years of his administration to bring charges of extravagance. In December 1714 we find the building referred to for the first time as "the Palace" in the Journal of the Council; it was an ill omen, for the term lent itself to sarcastic use. Matters came to a head in 1718. In May that year the House of Burgesses appointed a committee to wait on the Governor to see what still

needed to be done. Spotswood refused to discuss the subject with it. He said that if
the Burgesses sent deputations to him they should make sure that they were composed of men who were for treating him with decent good manners, adding: "Some
of those I See here present being Accustomed to Speak very irreverently of the Kings
Governours should I enter into Conversation with them may perhaps forget what
House they are in and be apt to speak to me in their usual rude Termes." Next,
a bill for repealing the Act of 1713 was introduced; it was rejected by the Council.
Then in November the House instructed William Byrd, in England as agent for the
colony, to make complaint to the King about Spotswood's conduct under four heads,
the second being "his Construction of the Law for finishing the Governors house,
whereby he lavishes away the Countrys money, contrary to the intent of the Law,
and even beyond what the words of the Law will bear and hath hitherto refused any
Redress therein."

Spotswood sent his reply to the Board of Trade on Lady Day, 1719.[29] It is a long
letter, of which a few excerpts will suffice. He had, he said, already pressed his
accusers to explain what precisely they meant by their general charge of lavishing
away the country's money about the Governor's House, but to no avail; "being then
put to guess at the sence and meaning of this Article . . . I can do no otherwise
than trouble your Lordship's with a Random Defence." If it was a question of the
discharge of his trust, he had directed no other work than what was projected before
the passing of the law that had given him full control, had ordered no extravagant
rates to be paid nor any extraordinary work to be performed, and had seen that the
men and materials had been duly employed and expended in finishing the Governor's House with its appurtenances and in no other way. Moreover, he could
demonstrate on the spot to anyone that the craftsmen and labourers had "wrought for
wages much under what are generally given in this country at Private Buildings."

> And should I descend to particular Remarks on the Management of this Build-
> ing since my time, I could point out such Generosity on my part towards
> carrying it on, as heartily grieves me now to have bestow'd, since I perceive
> the ungratefull Return that these people make for the same. But as I think it
> not fitting to trouble Yr Lordships with little particulars, so neither do I see
> there is any need thereof, since taking their clamour in gross, it appears upon
> the face of the Accompt, which they would presume to perplex his Majesty
> with, to be unreasonable & ungenerous, For deducting the Credit given, and
> sundry Sums which ought to have been brought into the Overseers Accompt
> before my time, it will be found that from Christmas 1713, to this day, I
> have expended about their Building and Gardens but little above Two Hundred
> pounds pr annum. A mighty sum indeed, to demonstrate that I have Lavished

away the TREASUR of a PROVINCE! and at such a time too, when their publick Treasury so abounds in Cash, that they have chosen to place Ten Thousand pounds out at Interest for Two pʳ cent yearly profitt.

As for his having refused any redress,

> I'm sure no one of their Articles surprised me more, than this, when I saw it exhibited against Me; I till then taking the Country in General, by the Conversation I held with the Gentlemen thereof, to be delighted with the Building, & having been used to hear nothing but Commendations of the Contrivances & Frugality of the Works . . . . And their Speaker & Many of their Members must own that . . . . [in May 1718] I often walked & freely talked with them concerning the Works then in hand, & offered, if the Assembly did not care to be at the Expence of the Fish-Pond & Falling Gardens, to take them to my Self; these improvements happening to be upon the Town Land & such as would not long want Purchasers. Besides from the first moment I discovered that any Burgesses were disposed to cavil at the Expense of the Building, I slackened my hand in carrying on the Works & thereupon frequently & Publickly said, Let them hire again an Overseer (which expence I have saved them for five Years past) to finish after their own fancys what remains to be done . . .

Having thus displayed his injured innocence, Spotswood brings in his counter-charges. Instead of the building accounts being submitted to the Committee of Claims in the normal manner, they had been turned over to a Select Committee "of four of the most prejudiced Members."

> Privately at their own lodgings having pull'd to pieces plain quarterly accounts that had their proper vouchers laid in order to justify each Article, They presented to the Consideration of the House a Scheme (as they call'd it) maliciously calculated to startle & puzle the weaker sort of Members, the same being drawn up after a confused unintelligible manner, with some wilfull Errors & spitefull Mistakes of their own, & formed upon the supposition of a Mansion-House Kitchin & Stable (as the first Act described) being all that was to be built. And to carry on the Deceit, the second Act passed in 1710, which allows an Orchard, Gardens and other Appurtenances, was conveyed away & not to be met with in the office: So that by this Concealment They found means to possess some members that what the first Act directed, was all that I was Impower'd to finish . . .

Though he could not know it, Spotswood might have saved his labour. For the Board of Trade had refused to recognize Byrd's credentials. "We take notice" the Board wrote back, "of the Complaints that you mention the Assembly have lately exhibited against You; All that we can say at present (no Body having yet apply'd on that Subject) is that You may depend upon all the Countenance & Support that We can give you which We think You have deserved."

The whole dispute was in reality but a symptom of a chronic disease in the body politic of the colony, the conflict between the old planter families and the royal authority. In 1720, after Byrd had returned from England disappointed in his hope of succeeding Spotswood, came reconciliation. That November the Burgesses appointed a committee to ask the Governor what he thought should be done for "the finishing the Governours House Gardens and other works which he is Impowered by Law to finish," and also to view and compute the cost of everything that had been done in the gardens since Christmas 1717. But Spotswood had had enough. In a letter, he recalled the former trouble over the accounts and concluded:

> Whereupon you'l Excuse me if I decline all future Concern in these works and whoever you are pleased to appoint to Oversee them may inform you what still remains to be done as he or they may likewise have in Charge if you think fit to get justly computed and valued the Works of the Gardens that are left unrated, Especially since it seems to be too Troublesome an Affair for your Committee to set about the computation thereof and that I am loath to offer any valuation of my own Gardeners and Servants performances.

So three of the Burgesses, accompanied by Henry Cary, Jr., were sent to inspect the Palace and its gardens, the Magazine, and the Gaol. It was found that £52 . 11s . 6d. would be needed to finish the house and that £469 . 2s . 9½d. was due to Spotswood. Before Christmas an Act had been passed to enable Cary to finish the building that his father had begun more than fourteen years before.

"MANY ALTERATIONS AND DECORATIONS"

The early history of the Palace is summed up by Beverley in a sentence: "It was granted by the Assembly in Governor Nott's time, begun in President Jennings' time but received its beauty and conveniency from the many alterations and decorations, of the present Governor, Colonel Spotswood."

Of the alterations, a probable one, affecting the internal planning of the building, has already been discussed. Then the Bodleian plate shows the forecourt and the parterre enclosed by six-foot brick walls instead of the four-foot walls "with ballustrades of wood thereupon" specified in the Act of 1710. Perhaps this was considered an extravagance; the higher walls of the forecourt certainly accorded better with the official character of the house. A minor alteration was carried out by the younger Cary when the balcony doors were made to open outwards instead of inwards as previously. The estimate for finishing the house, which supplies this information, shows that there was a billiard room—its plaster needed mending—but its location can only be guessed at. There was also a "bannio," or bath-house, the cost of finishing which was estimated at thirty shillings.[30]

Among the decorations may be included the array of arms, which in Hugh Jones' phrase were "nicely posited by an ingenuous [sic] contrivence of Governor Spotswood's," in the hall; in 1715 the collection, whose purpose was by no means purely decorative, included 160 muskets. Beverley no doubt intended the term decorations to be taken to include the garden. Here again we have the evidence of the Bodleian plate, supplemented by references in the records and corroborated by the archaeologist's spade.

For gardening in England, the decade 1710–1720 was a period of transition. Sentiments in favour of naturalism were expressed by Shaftesbury and Addison; practitioners of the art, notably Henry Wise, were beginning to introduce irregular elements into layouts that still retained the overall symmetry of the Franco-Dutch tradition, to which the majority of gardens continued to belong. There was nothing about the garden of the Palace as laid out by Spotswood that would have been novel in England at the time; nor would it have appeared particularly old-fashioned there. In the forecourt, entered through wrought-iron gates of English manufacture, were four flower-beds, with paved walks between. Beyond the house was the parterre with lozenge-shaped beds, no doubt edged with dwarf box, and a necessary house[31] in either of its far corners; the twelve lead flower-pots listed as standing furniture in Lord Botetourt's time may already have been there, though it is more likely that these were products of John Cheere's yard in the Haymarket, London, which flourished in mid-century. Over to the west were the fish-pond and the falling gardens that Spotswood had offered to "take to himself."

Spotswood bequeathed his books to the College of William and Mary. Only one of them has survived the fire of 1859 and the other mischances that beset books in college libraries—the first volume of the *Description des Châteaux et Parcs de Versailles, de Trianon, et de Marly* by Piganiol de la Force, published in Amsterdam in 1715. Here was inspiration perhaps; of more practical use would have been the architect John James' *Theory and Practice of Gardening* from the French of Le Blond, published in 1712. Stephen Switzer's *Ichnographia Rustica*, which to judge from library inventories and booksellers' advertisements in the *Virginia Gazette* was to become well known in the colony, did not appear until 1718—too late for Spotswood to have used it much. Where questions of horticulture rather than garden design were concerned, it would be surprising—so many copies of the book found their way to

Virginia—if he did not consult Jean de la Quintinie's work, of which John Evelyn's translation was published in folio under the the title of *The Compleat Gard'ner* in 1693 and in octavo, "compendiously abridg'd, and made of more Use, with very considerable Improvements" by George London and Henry Wise, in five editions between 1699 and 1710.

Ideally the garden of the Baroque age was not a self-contained entity: its axes pushed out to penetrate the surrounding countryside. Given the broad acres of a Beaufort or a Cavendish, such penetration could be peaceful enough. The acres at Spotswood's disposal were not so broad, and his attempt to achieve the Baroque ideal led to trouble. The story is told in a letter from John Custis III to Philip Ludwell II, dated April 18, 1717.[32] Custis had happened to be at the Governor's, when the Governor

> was pleased to ask my consent, to cut down some trees that grew on My land to make an opening, I think he called it a vista and told me he would cut nothing but what was only fitt for the fire, and for that he would pay me as much as any one gave for firewood, to please his honour, I told him he might if he pleased cutt such trees down, Sometime after I happened to dine with him, and he then told me there was a Swamp that did belong to me in which grew a great deale of wood, and alledged it would never be of much Service to me, by reason I could not come at it with a Cart without going through his pasture (but that was a mistake) . . .
>
> As to the Clearing his vista he cut down all before him such a wideness as he thought fitt, amongst which there was two very good oak Timber Trees, that my Tenant had reserved to cover my Tenement . . .

It really must have been most annoying for Mr. Custis, and the Governor's new-fangled talk of vistas can have done little to help matters. Yet to us today this attempt to impose Baroque order on the Virginian wilderness may seem not the least significant of Spotswood's ventures as a man of taste.[33]

VI

1710-1726
Learning and the Stage

ALTHOUGH a committee of the Council and Burgesses inquired into the cause of the burning of the College, when all the evidence had been heard there was "nothing but a large field for conjecture to loose it self in," as Mongo Ingles put it.[1] More than four years went by before arrangements for rebuilding were made; in view of the magnitude of the disaster, hardly to be grasped by an age which takes fire insurance for granted, this was no long delay. The income from which salaries would normally have been paid was saved for the new building. ("I have freely parted with my salary for that use," Blair took care to tell the Archbishop of Canterbury.[2]) It was a royal gift, however, that enabled a start to be made. In March 1708/9 Queen Anne, in response to a petition from the Visitors and Governors of the College, granted £500 out of the revenue of quit-rents. William Byrd, at Westover, heard the news on June 20;[3] the royal warrant for the payment of the sum to Visitors and Governors was communicated to the Council by President Jenings on the following day. On August 4 Byrd, accompanied by William Randolph, rode to Williamsburg "to the meeting of the College" and "went to the school house where we at last determined to build the college on the old walls and appointed workmen to view them and [compute] the charge."[4] There was another meeting on September 13 at which "after some debate the majority were for building on the old wall," though Byrd himself "was against this and was for a new one for several reasons."[5] On October 31 the building committee met to receive tenders and John Tullitt undertook the building for £2,000, "provided he might wood off the College land and all assistants from England to come at the College's risk."[6] The agreement with him was confirmed on December 8.[7]

96

Figure 34. THE COLLEGE OF WILLIAM AND MARY.
General view from the east, and the main building
from the south-west, from the "Bodleian Plate."

When Alexander Spotswood arrived, in June 1710, he brought with him a warrant for a further £500 to be paid out of quit-rents towards the new building; the warrant, issued in April, notes that the Crown had been informed that "Workmen have been employed to clear the Foundation and prepare Lyme and Timber for such Building, that more will be laid out than the Governours have at present in Cash before they can expect Our further Supply and that they depend very much thereupon." In November 1711 Byrd noted a payment to Tullitt of £500,[8] and in January 1711/12 he recorded that the Governors agreed to give Tullitt £400 "to build up the College hall."[9] After that there is nothing to show how things progressed until in June 1716 we find a Matthew Allen being paid for turning bannisters, and the Visitors and Governors concerning themselves with the furnishing of the building:

> Resolved, That the bedsteads of the scholars be made of Iron according to the model prepared by Daniel Jones.
> Ordered, That it be referred to the Committee to send to England for Standing furniture for the Colledge Kitchen, Brewhouse, and Laundry, & that they also send for a bell of 18 inches Diameter at the Brimms for the use of the Colledge.[10]

Other things to be sent from England included "1 Ingine for Quenching Fire."[11] It was not until October of this year, 1716, that it was ordered "that Sash Glass be provided from England for the Colledge Hall and that the same be fitted up in frames and that some spare Glass be also writ for to repair the windows of the Colledge."[12] That was seven years after Tullitt's tender had been accepted.

THE SECOND COLLEGE BUILDING

Whereas we have so little information about the erection of this second building

Figure 35. THE COLLEGE OF WILLIAM AND MARY. A daguerreotype,
showing the main building in its second form, taken before the fire of 1859.

of William and Mary, we have sufficient and trustworthy records of its appearance
(Figs. 34, 35) and we have Jefferson's plan (Fig. 36). And whatever may be
thought of Hugh Jones' attribution of the first building to Wren, there is no reason
to question his statement that the College was "rebuilt and nicely contrived, altered
and adorned by the ingenious Direction of Governor *Spotswood.*" [13] Although the
agreement with Tullitt was confirmed late in 1709, the work had not proceeded
far before Spotswood's arrival in June of the following year.

The dimensions of the building on plan (Fig. 37) were settled by the decision to
use the old walls. As we noted in discussing the first building, the west wall of the
main range was probably little damaged by the fire and retained *in toto.* The other
walls of the main range were pulled down or built up, as their condition demanded,
to approximately the level of the third floor. The third storey, which in the first
building was enclosed by walls on all four sides, could therefore be enclosed in the
roof and lighted by dormer windows on all sides but the west, where it was lighted

Figure 36. THE COLLEGE OF WILLIAM AND MARY. A plan by Thomas Jefferson,
showing the main building in its second form together with a proposed extension.

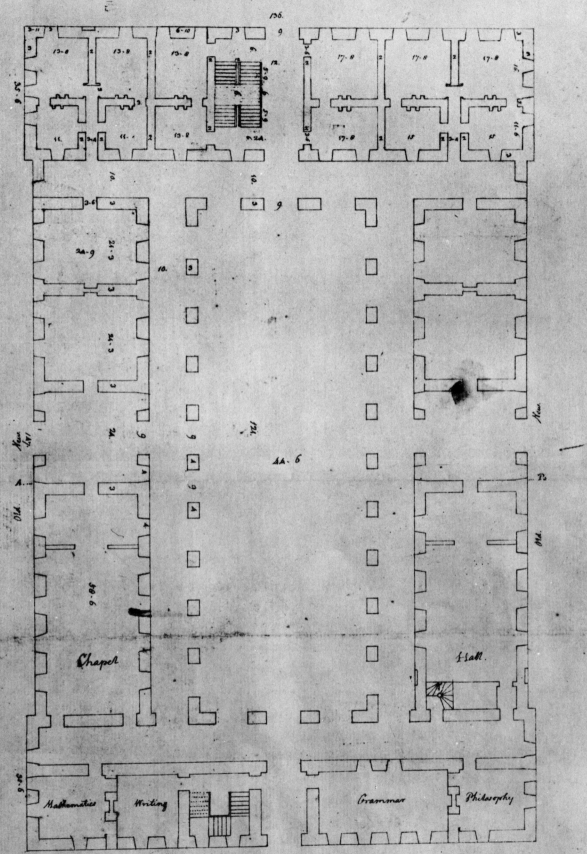

Western Front.

Chapel

Mathematics   Writing   Grammar   Philosophy

Eastern Front.

Plan for an addition to the College of William and Mary, drawn at the request of L.ᵈ Dunmore. this Eastern
end with the wings as far as the letters A. B. is the present building. the rest is the proposed addition.

by the windows in the original west wall. The difficulty presented by the difference of height between this wall and the others, which if the whole range was to be covered by a single hip roof would have necessitated a different angle of rake for its western slope, was solved by providing a series of transverse roofs over the western half of the range.

Although we have no positive evidence that the hall range in the first building was of the same height as in the second, it is most likely that it was, and that its roof ridge determined the height of the new roof of the main range; roofs being a highly standardized department of carpentry, it could have done so even if it had been completely burnt. In any case, the five transverse roofs of the main range are in effect repetitions of the hall roof cut short; in 1716 there must have been a sixth where later the chapel roof was to come. In the second building the height of the hall from ground to eaves is about 32 ft.; since its width also is 32 ft. and its length 64 ft., it has the form (below the roof) of a double cube. Since the main range of the first building (less its roof) was in form a triple cube of 46 ft., this may be regarded as circumstantial evidence that the hall was rebuilt to its original dimensions. Moreover, 32:46, as we saw, is the ratio of the side of a square to its diagonal—the Golden Section ratio. So Spotswood could adopt the eaves height of the hall for the main range and still be left with facades which obeyed the rules of geometrical proportion. The end walls of the main range, instead of being squares of 46 ft., as we have seen reason to believe they were in the first building, became rectangles of 32 by 46 ft.; the east front became three such rectangles instead of three squares. An essentially practical solution of the problem of rebuilding was amenable to a system of proportion because the original building had been regulated by a similar system.

With the regrading of the east yard the main entrance had to be moved up from the basement to the main floor. In the first building some emphasis had been given to the centre of the east front by the balustraded steps to the entrance and by balconies. Spotswood evidently felt that the lower front of the second building needed a more emphatic centre and added a pavilion of 1 ft. 6 in. projection and a width of 17 ft. 6 in. The latter dimension was determined by the outer faces of the lateral walls of the entrance lobby behind, and is equal to one eighth of the total length of the front. The pediment surmounting the pavilion is right-angled, and like most right-angled pediments has a rather harsh effect; here the rule of geometry has been a little too strict, and one would rather that Spotswood had left the question of rake to the builder's rule-of-thumb methods, as in the transept gables of Bruton Church.

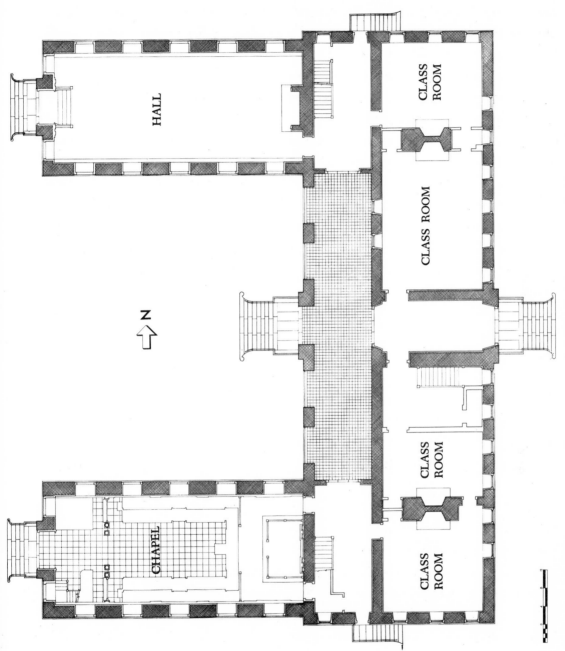

Figure 37. The College of William and Mary. Plan of the main building as restored.

A similar pavilion was added to the west side of the main range. The new cupola, though not as tall as that of the first building seems to have been, plays an important part in the total design. From the ground to its apex is 68 ft., so that the main range of the College, like Bruton Church as first built to Spotswood's design, is just half as high over all as it is long.

It would be a mistake to try to affix any stylistic label too firmly to the second College building—as indeed to much English building of its time. Nor would a search for specific prototypes be a profitable occupation. Hugh Jones, it is true, said that it was "not altogether unlike Chelsea Hospital," and later writers, hypnotized by the name of Wren, have sometimes seen fit to put the matter rather less negatively. As it happens, there *was* a colonial college, begun when the second building of William and Mary was going up, that in many respects was a direct imitation of Chelsea Hospital. Codrington College in Barbados (Fig. 39) was designed by the military engineer Christian Lilly [14] in 1713. Like William and Mary, it was to be a quadrangular building but was never completed; its building history is a tale of

Figure 38. THE COLLEGE OF WILLIAM AND MARY.
East elevation of the main building as restored.

difficulties and delays unparalleled in even the most protracted of building operations at Williamsburg.[15] Where building materials were concerned, in Barbados there was a complete reversal of the Virginian situation: stone was plentiful, while timber and brick had to be imported. To compare the elevations of Codrington College (as engraved for the Society for the Propagation of the Gospel) with William and Mary is to reflect how much more easily Spotswood could have achieved an impressive effect if an abundance of good stone had been at his disposal. At the same time one may feel that his regard for the fundamentals of design served him better than reliance on a thirty-year-old model served Lilly.

ROOMS AND CHAMBERS

The engraved plan of Codrington College (Fig. 40) shows us that the students were to be lodged in rooms arranged by staircases, as in the colleges of Oxford and Cambridge. Unfortunately we do not have such precise information about the students' lodgings at William and Mary. For here they were on the upper floors only, and the sole early plan known to us is of the principal floor. This was drawn by Thomas Jefferson in 1771 or 1772, when it was proposed to complete the quadrangle. The classroom names—from south to north: mathematics, writing, grammar, philosophy—are those of Jefferson's day; but at least the grammar school had occupied the same room from the beginning, and indeed the corresponding room in the first building also. In March 1716 the class room labelled mathematics by Jefferson was made available for livelier activities when William Levingston—of whom more later—was granted the use of it "for teaching the Scholars and others to dance untill his own dancing school in Williamsburg be finished."[16] We have already seen reason to believe that the position of the main stairs represents a departure from the plan of the first building, which the second in general followed. A smaller stair ascends from the hall; it will be remembered that a stair here had served as a fire escape in 1705. The kitchen, in both buildings, was underneath the hall. This is an unorthodox arrangement, the usual place for the kitchen in an English college being across the screen passage from the hall, on the same floor. The basement kitchen was an Italianism which reached England early in the seventeenth century; Virginian houses of that century incorporating it included Bacon's Castle, Surry County, and Criss Cross, New Kent County. In Williamsburg the Blue Bell and Blair's Brick House, both built early in the eighteenth century, had basement kitchens. Later, climatic considerations led to their general abandonment in the colony.

The precise arrangement of the upper floors can only be guessed at. Over the "piazza" was the gallery, or "long passage." To the north of the centre—if tradition is to be trusted—was a large room in which after the Revolution the faculty held disciplinary courts; it was then called the Blue Room. (Was this the convocation room of early years, for which two dozen "handsome leather chairs" were ordered in 1716?[17]) In 1747 there was a Common Room,[18] which might however have been the philosophy classroom of Jefferson's day, on the first floor. Among the other rooms was the library for which a "convenient chamber" had been set apart by 1729.[19] Then there were rooms for the Professors, and until the President's House was built in 1733 for the President too. We do know that the quarters for the students who lived in College—this, though encouraged, was not compulsory—were of two kinds. A statute of 1736 says: "Let the spare Chambers of the College over and above what are necessary for the President and Masters, and other Officers of the College, be let out at moderate Rents to the better Sort of big Boys."[20] (A resolution of the President and Masters of 1733 allots four rooms to fourteen boys, three and four to a

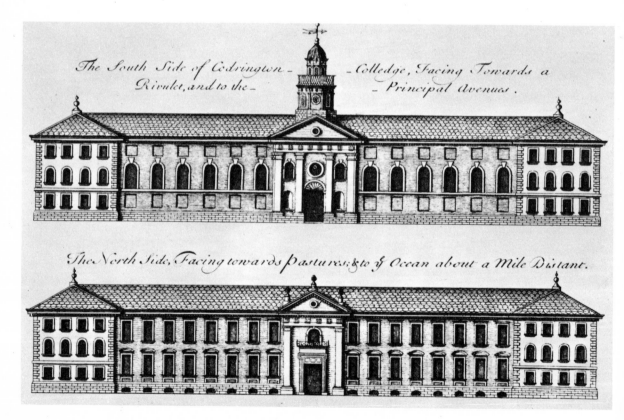

Figure 39. CODRINGTON COLLEGE, BARBADOS. The south and north fronts, from an engraving made for the Society for the Propagation of the Gospel in 1713.

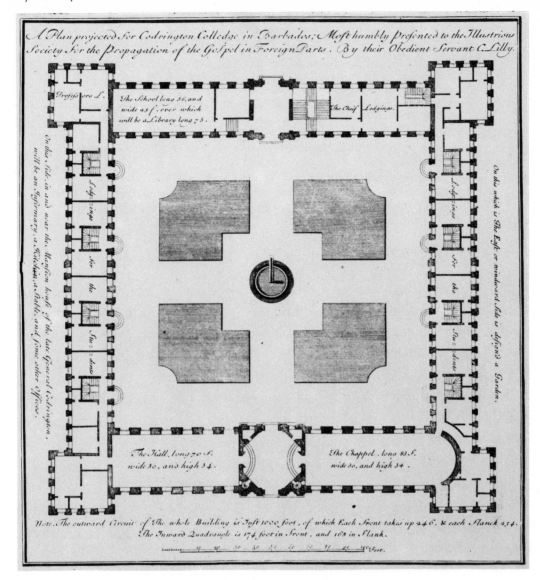

Figure 40. CODRINGTON COLLEGE, BARBADOS. The plan, as engraved
for the Society for the Propagation of the Gospel.

room.) [21] At least as early as 1751, [22] and no doubt from the first, there was also a
dormitory; by 1773 there were two, known as the Old Dormitory and the New Dormitory, each with its own staircase. [23] They were probably on the third floor, and one
of them may have been over the hall. [24]

Were sections of the students' chambers partitioned off as "studies," as at Harvard
and elsewhere? The word seems not to occur in the records; but that does not prove

that the thing did not exist. Unfortunately we do not have even a second-hand account of a student's accommodation at William and Mary in colonial times, such as we do have of the rooms of a professor:

> You have two rooms—by no means elegant tho' equal in goodness to any in the College—unfurnished—& will salute your Eyes on your Entrance with bare plaister Walls—however Mr Small assures me they are what the rest of the Professors have & are very well satisfied with the homeliness of their appearance tho' at first rather disgusting—he thinks you will not chuse to lay out any money on them.
>
> You may buy Furniture there, all except bedding & blankets, which you must carry over—Chairs & Tables rather Cheaper than in England—he says his Furniture consists of 6 Chairs, a Table, Grate bed & Bedstead & that is as much as you'll want.[25]

THE EDUCATION OF THE INDIANS

In 1723 the College received its first additional building, known today as Brafferton Hall or the Brafferton, but at first simply as Brafferton. It was built as an Indian school. So the education of the Indians produced architectural results almost exactly a century after the project of a Henrico College for "the Children of the Infidels" had been brought to nothing by the Great Massacre.

The Brafferton was named for the source of the funds with which Indian education at William and Mary was carried on. In 1691 Robert Boyle, the inventor of the air pump, directed in his will that the residue of his personal estate, after the payment of debts and legacies, should be applied by his executors to charitable and pious uses. The executors accordingly agreed "to lay out five thousand four hundred pounds . . . in the purchase of lands, and to apply the yearly rent thereof towards the propagating the Christian religion amongst infidels."[26] The lands so purchased were the manor of Brafferton, in the East Riding of Yorkshire, ninety pounds out of the rents of which were granted in perpetuity for propagating the gospel in New England while the remainder was to be "laid out for the advancement of the christian religion in Virginia, in such manner, and subject to such methods and rules as the . . . Earl of Burlington, and the Bishop of London . . . should appoint."[27] In December 1697 the Earl and the Bishop—James Blair, in England at the time, being at least within call—drew up and signed a settlement by which the money was to be paid over to the President and Masters of William and Mary. The latter were to

> keep att the said Colledge soe many Indian Children in Sicknesse and health in Meat drink Washing, Lodgeing Cloathes Medicines books and Educacon

from the first beginning of Letters till they are ready to receive Orders and be thought Sufficient to be sent abroad to preach and Convert the Indians at the rate of fourteen pounds per Annum for every such Child.[28]

In 1700 Francis Nicholson set about implementing the scheme with instructions to two westward-bound traders that they should tell the Indians "that a great & good man who lately died in England . . . having a great love for the Indians, hath left money enough to the College here in Virginia, to keep 9 or 10 Indian children at it, & to teach them to read, write & all other arts & sciences, that the best Englishmen's sons do learn," and that rooms would be ready for them the following summer; the children were to be young, about seven or eight, and if the Indians wished they could come and see the College for themselves.[29]

During the years between the fire and the rebuilding, the grammar school and the Indian school were held in the schoolhouse where William Byrd (as we have seen) attended meetings of the Visitors and Governors of the College in 1709. In 1711 Spotswood conceived the idea of getting the Queen of Pamunkey and the "great men" of the Chickahominy Indians to send children to the College as "Hostages for their fidelity"; the Queen of Pamunkey thought this such a fine scheme that she sent more boys than were asked for. In 1716 a Christopher Smith was made Master of the Indian children, of whom there were "but few of them now at the school," and at his request the Visitors and Governors ordered the erection of a partition in the grammar school to separate them from the English children.[30] It was presumably the fewness of the Indians, and the consequent smallness of the demands made upon the Boyle Charity, that made possible the provision, seven years later, of what Hugh Jones called "a good house and Apartments for the *Indian Master* and his Scholars."[31] This was not simply a measure of segregation, for according to the same authority the Indians were formerly boarded in the town, where "abundance of them" used to die from disease or unsuitable food or ("as some will have it") from sheer neglect.[32]

THE BRAFFERTON

The date of the Brafferton, 1723, is established by an inscribed brick to the right of the window on the west side of the south door. The available records do not tell us who built it, but Henry Cary, Jr., is a safe guess. He had taken over the completion of the Palace three years before; in the course of the next ten he was to build the President's House and the Chapel at the College. If he was the builder, he was

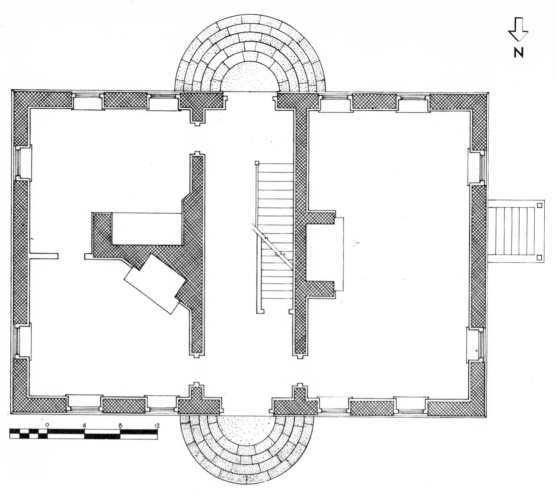

Figure 41. THE BRAFFERTON. Ground floor plan.

probably the designer too. As we have by now learned to expect, a simple system or proportion gives cohesion to the design. The length of the building is approximately one and a half times its breadth, the respective dimensions being 52 ft. and 34 ft. (Fig. 41) (The internal length, 48 ft., is equal to the internal breadth of the Governor's House.) From the ground to the chimney caps is 52 ft., so that the north and south elevations fit exactly into a square (Fig. 42), and the east and west very nearly into a square and a half. The height of the walls is 26 ft.—half the overall height of the building and also half its length.

On each of the main floors there are three rooms—a large room to the west and two smaller rooms to the east; the stairs ascend from the entry to a central passage

Figure 42. THE BRAFFERTON. North elevation.

above. We do not know just how the rooms were used when the building was still an Indian school. It would seem that the large room on the ground floor was most probably the schoolroom. In 1732 the Professor of Philosophy told the Bishop of London: "We have a very convenient room for a library over the Indian School," [33] and since £500 was to be spent on this library,[34] and Lord Burlington had promised Robert Boyle's portrait for it, it is reasonable to suppose that the large upper room was meant and that it was literally "over" the schoolroom. Of the smaller rooms, the Master presumably had two, since the Professors in College each had two rooms;

Figure 43. THE BRAFFERTON. Exterior from the south-west.

Figure 44. THE OLD RECTORY, SUTTON COLDFIELD, WARWICKSHIRE.
Built, and probably designed, by William Smith in 1701.

another of them may have served as an infirmary. The young Indians doubtless slept on the third floor, under the roof. The corner fireplaces in three of the smaller rooms are examples of a feature that became common in England in the reign of William III.[35] It was to become common in Virginia too, but the Brafferton was among the first houses, if not the first house, to have it; Scotchtown, Hanover County, and the Chiswell and Peyton Randolph houses, both in Williamsburg, are other candidates for priority.[36]

It is interesting to compare the Brafferton (Fig. 43) with the Old Rectory at Sutton Coldfield, Warwickshire (Fig. 44). An example of a well-defined late Stuart type, this house was built in 1701 by William Smith of Warwick, who as Colvin observes "during the early part of the eighteenth century appears to have been the leading master builder in the West Midland counties."[37] Its size (45 ft. long, 35 ft. deep, and 25 ft. to the eaves) is nearly that of the Brafferton, and the resemblance in other respects is striking enough. One difference is due to the fact that Smith had stone available for quoins and other dressings, whereas Cary (if it was Cary) did not. Another difference is in the form of the dormers, so squat in the English house; the tall dormers of the Brafferton, with roofs of the same rake as the main roof, are of a standard Virginian form whose origin has yet to be traced and whose ubiquity in the colony has yet to be explained.

Of course there is no need to postulate any knowledge of Sutton Coldfield Rectory on the part of the designer of the Brafferton. One could no doubt find other English examples of the class of house to which both belong that resemble the Brafferton just as closely.

THE THEATRE COMES TO AMERICA

William Levingston has figured in these pages once already, as prospective holder of a dancing class in one of the classrooms at the College. He now re-enters in the capacity that gives him his own place in the history of colonial culture—as promoter of the first theatre at Williamsburg, which was also, by a matter of eighteen or twenty years, the first theatre in the American colonies.[38]

In September 1715 (as appears from an indenture[39] to be discussed) Levingston bound a certain Charles Stagg and Mary his wife by articles of agreement "to Serve him in the colony of Virginia in the Arts, Professions"—or specifically to teach dancing classes for him. In March 1716, as we have seen, he obtained permission to hold a dancing class in the College until his own dancing school in Williamsburg should be finished; no doubt the Staggs were to teach this class. Three and a half months later, in July 1716, he entered into a new agreement with the Staggs. Under the terms of this, the Staggs were released from their obligations and allowed to keep such profits as had accrued from the dancing classes; in return they were to pay back what Levingston had spent on their travel between the places where the classes were held, and were also to "pay unto the said William Levingstone or his Assignes the Sum of Sixty pounds Current money Yearly during the Space of Three years next Ensueing the date hereof. . . Provided always"—and here we come to the first mention of the new venture in which Levingston and the Staggs were to be associated—

> Provided always & it is the true intent & meaning hereof that the said William Levingstone & his Assigns shall be & are hereby Obliged to Abate & deduct out of the said respective Yearly payments after the rate of five pounds Current money for Each Month which the said Stagg shall be diverted from teaching to dance in Consideration of his the said Charles Staggs being imployed in the preparation & Acting of Plays for the joint benefit of himself & the said William Levingstone.

Later we read:

> And it is further Covenanted & Agreed . . . that the said William Levingstone & Charles Stagg shall with all convenient Speed . . . use their best Endeavours to Obtain a Patent or Lycence from the Governour of Virginia for the Sole Privilege of Acting Comedies, Drolls or Other kind of Stage Plays within any part of the said Colony not only for the Three Years next Ensueing the date hereof but for as much longer time as the said Governour Shall be pleased to grant the Same.

The indenture goes on to fix the terms of the partnership. The Staggs were to be the producers of, and actors in, the plays. Levingston, who had already "at his own Proper Cost & Charge Sent to England for Actors & Musicians," was to provide the theatre:

> And the said William Levingstone doth further Covenant & Agree with all convenient Speed to cause to be Erected & built at his own proper Costs & Charge in the City of Williamsburgh One good Substantial house commodious for Acting Such Plays as shall be thought fitt to be Acted there.

In November that year, 1716, Levingston purchased three lots on the east side of Palace Street.[40] Since the holding of the lots was subject to the usual condition that houses should be built upon them within two years of purchase, the theatre had to be up by November 1718. A letter from Spotswood to the Board of Trade,[41] complaining that when he gave an entertainment in celebration of the King's birthday in May 1718 "eight Counsellors would neither come to my House nor go to the Play w'ch was Acted on that occasion," shows that it had been opened before then—that it had in fact been built "with all convenient Speed," as the indenture stipulated.

THE FIRST PLAYHOUSE

The remains of the foundations of this theatre, identifiable beyond all reasonable doubt by their location and their character, were excavated in 1947 (Fig. 45). They show that it was about 30 ft. wide by 86 ft. 6 in. long, and stood end-on to the street. The slightness of the foundation walls suggests a frame building, and a reference to weatherboards in a *Virginia Gazette* advertisement of 1745 (quoted below) confirms the structural evidence. It had no basement.

In the absence of more positive information about the form and character of the building, one may fairly ask if it was a proper theatre, with the internal arrangements of a typical English theatre of the period, or something nearer to a barn. However, there is nothing at all to suggest that it was not a proper theatre, or playhouse (as it is called in most of the contemporary references). And the determination of those who lived in Williamsburg or frequented the town during the public times to have everything after the London mode surely makes it unlikely that they would have put up with anything less.

Granted that it was a proper playhouse, it is possible to picture it, if not with accuracy, at least with some assurance of not being wildly wrong.[42] Externally it is plain to the point of bareness, with a gable roof, shingled, rising to a height of between thirty-five and forty feet; the weatherboards of the walls are painted red. Doors of domestic size, placed laterally, admit to the auditorium and (at the end farther from the street) to the stage; in deference to the climate of Virginia there are several small windows. Passing inside by the south-west entrance we find ourselves in a lobby; opposite the door is the pay-box, while to the right is one of the two "pit passages," which flank that part of the house and provide the only means of access to it. (The gallery pay-box and stairs are reached separately by the north-west entrance.) Traversing the pit passage, which is about twenty feet long, only three feet wide, quite unlit, and not altogether savory, we emerge into the pit itself. Our first impression, accustomed as we are to a later tradition of theatre architecture, is of extreme smallness; if a play was being given, an impression of extreme overcrowding would be added to this. On either side of the house, in two tiers, are the boxes; at the back

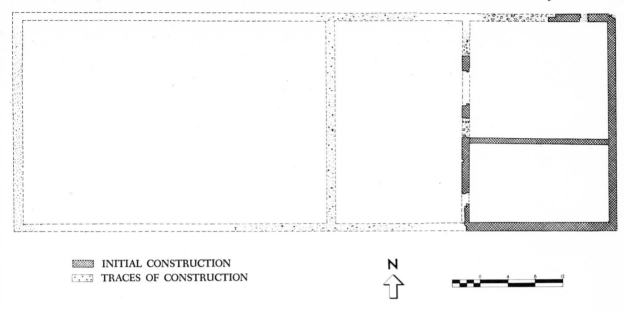

INITIAL CONSTRUCTION
TRACES OF CONSTRUCTION

N

0   4   8   12

Figure 45. THE PLAYHOUSE. Plan of excavated foundations.

is the gallery; the seats in both pit and gallery are plain wooden forms, without backs. The interior is painted generally a blue-green, but fine splashes of colour are supplied by drapes of red moreen in the boxes, hung there as much for acoustical as for decorative reasons. Turning towards the stage, we find the orchestra where we would expect it. But the proscenium doors, giving on to the forestage in front of the curtain on either side, with balconies above them, are "legacies from Elizabeth's day"[43] that were abandoned in the nineteenth century; it is through these doors, not through the scenery, that the actors make their exits and their entrances. The curtain is of green baize, though not precisely what is meant by baize today, and the scenery behind it slides in horizontal grooves; this method of scene changing, "almost unknown outside the British stage,"[44] is one of the factors that has enabled Mr. Levingston to build his theatre without a deep basement, such as the Continental European system demands. The character of the scenery, and the workings of such intriguing accessories as the cloud machine and the thunder run, are matters of theatrical rather than architectural history; the reader who has a curiosity about them must be referred to the luminous pages of Southern.[45]

PLAYHOUSE INTO COURTHOUSE

Levingston is described in the indenture of 1716 as a merchant, elsewhere as a gentleman and sometimes as a surgeon. His varied talents did not save him from financial difficulties, and about 1723, having mortgaged and lost possession of the Playhouse and his own dwelling (which stood next to it), and having acquired much experience of litigation, he moved to Spotsylvania County; he died at Fredericksburg in 1729.[46] His wife survived him; she was evidently a woman of parts, for in 1732 William Byrd, visiting Fredericksburg, noted that she was acting there "in the Double Capacity of a Doctress and Coffee Woman," and adds mysteriously: "And were this a populous City, she is qualify'd to exercise 2 other callings."[47] To inquire into his meaning might, one suspects, be indelicate.

Levingston's partner, Charles Stagg, lived on until January 1735/6[48]—the year, incidentally, which saw the opening of the second American theatre, at Charleston. Before 1736 there was no *Virginia Gazette,* and we do not know whether he continued to produce and act in plays at the Theatre; since he was in rather comfortable circumstances when he died, it is likely that he did. In 1735, before Stagg's death, John Blair, as executor of Archibald Blair to whom the property had been mortgaged in 1721,[49] sold the three lots by Palace Street to George Gilmer, surgeon and apothecary. Gilmer moved into the house that Levingston had built for himself, but conveyed the Theatre to a group of thirty-one subscribers, which included Governor Gooch and many other prominent people.[50] A period of amateur productions, with plays acted by "the young Gentlemen of the College" or "the Gentlemen and Ladies of this Country," followed.[51] But it did not last long: by December 1745 the Playhouse had "not been put to any Use for several Years," and was "now going to decay." The words are those of a petition to the subscribers from the City Corporation, representing "that they have no Publick Building within the City, wherein to hold their Common Halls & Courts of Hustings," and no money to build one with—

> Wherefore they shall esteem, and always acknowledge it as singular Mark of your Good Will and favour, if you will be pleased to bestow Your present Useless House on this Corporation, for the use aforesaid They intending to repair and alter it by their own Subscription, If this request be granted.[52]

The request was granted, and the *Virginia Gazette* for December 19 contained the following advertisement:

The Play-House in Williamsburg, being by Order of the Common-Hall of the said City, to be fitted up for a Court-House, with the necessary Alterations and Repairs; that is to say, to be new shingled, weatherboarded, painted, five large Sash Windows, Door, flooring, plaistering and proper Workmanship within; Notice is hereby given to all such as are willing to undertake the doing thereof, That they offer their Proposals to the Mayor who will inform them more particularly what is to be done.

In a sense the wheel had come full circle. For the second recorded theatrical performance in the American colonies had taken place ninety years before in Accomack Courthouse; the play was *The Bear and the Cub* and the king's attorney had brought an action against the three actors, who had given the first performance of it just previously and who were ordered by the justices to act it again (in full dress) in court.[53]

The Playhouse-turned-Courthouse was demolished in 1769 or 1770.[54] Long before that, in 1751, Williamsburg had received its second theatre, which stood east of the Capitol. Our knowledge of this building is not sufficient to justify more than a bare mention of it in the pages of an architectural history, in which the Palace Street Playhouse—though we know little enough about it, indeed—has been given as it were an honorary place on account of its historical priority in British America.

The Reign of George II

IN THE HISTORY of English architecture the reign of George II, which lasted just a third of a century, is the age of Palladianism. The first buildings of the Palladian movement, designed by William Benson, Colen Campbell, Lord Burlington and Giacomo Leoni, were already up by the time the reign opened; during the later 'twenties and the 'thirties a spate of publications, ranging from the grand folios of the leaders of the movement to the pocketable octavos put out by the more enterprising of the hangers-on, spread the gospel of Palladianism into every quarter of the kingdom. The result of this making of books was a degree of architectural standardization unprecedented in earlier times, even though there was much in English Palladianism that the sixteenth-century Italian architect from whom the movement took its name would scarcely have owned to—variations owing something to the Baroque of the age that was past, variations deriving from a still older tradition of domestic architecture, and variations tending towards an even stricter classicism.

The colonial builders were not slow to acquire and use the new books. As in England, one result was a more correct use of the classical elements, together with a greater refinement of detail—and a resultant loss of some of that hardly definable quality which we can only call "character." As in England, designs for chimneypieces and doorcases were lifted cold from the printed page. The "Venetian" window, a hall-mark of the style, appeared in Virginia at Nomini Hall around 1730—placed, in a very English and un-Italian way, at each end of the front. The desire for internal symmetry—no novelty in itself—was reinforced by the example of the pattern-book plans. Yet for all that there are few Virginian houses of the years 1727–1760 that one could call Palladian with much conviction, especially when they are compared with houses of later decades connected with the name of Thomas Jefferson; indeed, what is perhaps the *most* Palladian of them, Mount Airy in Richmond

County, was based on a design by James Gibbs, who was the most prominent British architect to preserve a certain independence of the Palladian movement. Above all, one looks in vain for that motif which was Palladio's prime contribution to European architecture: the temple portico with free-standing columns employed as the central feature of a facade. In houses, that is, one looks in vain; however, one of the public buildings that we have to discuss had a monumental portico which, if weak in detail, was at least remarkable as the earliest Virginian attempt to realize a noble idea. But before we come to that we must return for a time to the College, which during the first seven years of George II's reign was brought to the state to which we see it restored today.

THE COLLEGE CHAPEL

At William and Mary a chapel had long been, as might be said today, high on the list of priorities; the reader will remember the pother about Governor Andros' bricks back in 1697. In the first building the hall served as a chapel; this we know because a Quaker visitor in 1705 recorded that Blair, who evidently supported his other Scottish qualities with a pawky humour, told him that it was "the most useful Place in all the College; for, said he, 'Here we sometimes preach and pray, and sometimes we fiddle and dance, the one to edify, and the other to divert us.'"[1]

Later, Hugh Jones went so far as to suggest that the hall of the second building might actually be converted into a chapel. "There is as yet no great Occasion for the Hall," he wrote, "so that it might be made a Chapel and Divinity School, for which Purpose it would serve nobly with little or no Alterations."[2] Fortunately, the College was able to rise above so faint-hearted a policy of making do. On February 14, 1727/8 William Gooch, who had succeeded Drysdale as Governor the previous September, wrote to the Bishop of London: "We are going to build the Chappel as fast as we can."[3]

The first step, it having been decided to let the work "by the great," was to advertise for bids. This was done by posting up a notice at the Capitol, as the following letter shows:

> To the Honble the Governors of the Colledge of William and Mary—
> Hon^d Sirs
>   I understand by the advertisement of a noat set up at the Capitol by the reverend Mr Comisary Blair, that a Chappell is to be erected to the said Colledge in form of the Hall and well ffitted for the use of a Chappell workman like all which Building I will doe for Eight hundred Ninety Eight pounds

Curr^t money Except the Sashes and Glasses in the Body of the Building, I am Gen^t

Your most Obliged
Humble Servt to Com^d

Mar: 26. 1728   James Hughes[4]

Of James Hughes we know nothing. However, it does not much matter, for the contract was awarded to Henry Cary, Jr. The authority who gives us this information, writing in 1903, adds: "The original contract signed by him was preserved at the college till a few years ago, when it disappeared on a sudden."[5] (A loss that is much to be regretted, since colonial building contracts do not lie too thick on the ground.)

Although bids were invited early in 1728, construction did not begin until well on in the following year. There is no mention of a chapel in the article of Transfer of the College from the Trustees to the President and Masters, which is dated February 27, 1729, and the bricks were still being burnt on June 28 that year. However, Blair wrote to the Bishop of London on the latter date: "Our Undertaker puts us in hope that he will have it inclosed before winter."[6] Cary was evidently as good as his word. On September 8 Blair wrote to the Bishop again:

> I acquainted you Lop in my last that we had laid the foundation of the chappel. That work has since carried on with that expedition that the walls are now finished and we are going to set on the roof, so that I make no doubt it will be all inclosed before winter.[7]

But finishing and furnishing such a building, when "necessaries" like glass and paving stones had to be obtained from England, took time. The best part of three years were to pass before the formal opening took place, in the summer of 1732. William Dawson, the young Professor of Moral Philosophy who in due course was to succeed James Blair as President, described the occasion for the Bishop:

> My Lord:—I beg to acquaint your Lordship that on June 28th. 1732, our new chapel was opened with great solemnity. The Governor and his family were pleased to honour us with their Presence, and it being the assembly time, the members of both Houses came in great numbers. An holy Joy appeared in every countenance.[8]

THE CHAPEL INTERIOR

Any display of originality in the design of the College chapel would have been precluded by the requirement that it should be "in form of the Hall," even if originality had been a quality sought or valued by master-builders of Cary's type—which in fact it was not. Except for the absence of basement windows the elevations of the new wing exactly repeated those of the older one. In the matter of craftsmanship, it is true, there was a difference: the walls were laid up in Flemish bond, instead of the English bond that the second College building had inherited from its predecessor. The double-cube proportions, which as we saw may also have been an inheritance from the first building, were something of which the strictest of the Palladians could have approved, for the double cube was thought one of the most desirable shapes for a building or a room.

Evidence about the original internal arrangement and the furnishings of the chapel is scarce, and what there is of it is difficult to interpret. Jefferson's plan shows what would appear to be a screen near the west end, dividing off an ante-chapel as in an Oxford or Cambridge college. The central aisle was paved with stone (probably Purbeck or Shrewsbury, imported from England), as we learn from a letter of 1812:[9] in 1929 the area beneath it was found to be unexcavated and flanked by retaining walls of brick. One would suppose that the seating followed the usual plan of the English college chapel, with stalls facing inwards. However, the earliest mention of any kind of seating in the chapel is an item in a college account of 1740 recording the payment of 25s. to a certain Bowler "for new covering the Chappel Forms."[10] No doubt it could be argued that this referred to the seats of the stalls, on the grounds that the Medieval Latin *forma,* as the *Oxford English Dictionary* tells us, was sometimes "applied . . . to the stalls in a choir, with back, and book-rest," and that it is not impossible that this sense had survived. However, the usual meaning of a form is, and was, a backless bench, and it is worth remark that *O. E. D.* cites a passage from a book published in 1745 contrasting church seats with forms. So it would seem that in addition to the main seating there was an inferior kind, consisting of covered forms. The question remains: inferior to what? Both the other eighteenth-century references to seating in the chapel are to *pews.* On October 19, 1770, Lord Botetourt, the most popular of the royal Governors, was given a grand funeral and interred in a vault in the College chapel. On the following day the carpenter and joiner Joshua Kendall, who had made two of the three coffins for his lordship (the third being of lead), received a payment of £3 . 10s. for

> Taking up the Pew in Colledge & Floor and making good D° with a Cover of Planks & Centers for Arch to Vault for D° [in this case 'the Governor'] [11]

The second reference to pews—and to the same pew, as it happens—occurs in a

memorandum written some months later by Robert Carter Nicholas for the Duke
of Beaufort, who had expressed a desire to erect a monument to his uncle, Lord
Botetourt. This document tells us as much as anything we have about the chapel
interior and may be quoted in full:

> The Monument cannot be conveniently erected over the Grave, as it would
> spoil two principal Pews & incommode the Chapel considerably in other respects.
>
> If it is proposed to have it in the form of a Pyramid, it can be placed con-
> veniently in no part, except at the Bottom of the Isle fronting the Pulpit, where
> it would appear to advantage, if the Dimensions should not be thought too
> much confined; the Isle itself is about ten feet wide; there must be a Passage
> left on each side of the monument at least two feet & an half, so that the width
> of the monument, which will form the Front can be no more than five feet.
>
> A flat monument may be fixt still more commodiously in the side of the wall
> nearly opposite to the Grave. Between two large windows, there is a strong
> brick Pier six feet and an half wide; the length of this pier from the ceiling
> down to the wainscot is twelve feet and an half, & from the Top of the wainscot
> to the floor eleven feet and an half more; if the Height from the Wainscot to
> the ceiling should not be thought sufficient, we suppose there would be no
> Inconvenience in letting the monument down into the wainscot as low as the
> Floor, but then the bottom Part of it would be hid by the Front of the Pew.[12]

If we are to make full use of this, clearly the first thing to know is the position of
Botetourt's grave. For a century this has been a matter of dispute, a favoured view
being that Botetourt was buried in Sir John Randolph's vault in the north-east corner of the chapel. Since, as we have seen, Kendall made the centering for a new
vault for Botetourt, and since, as the same account reveals, Humphrey Harwood built
the vault,[13] this view can no longer be entertained, and the alternative view that he
was buried near the west end of the chapel must be correct. There is a substantial
amount of additional evidence bearing on the question;[14] a consideration that will
have occurred to the reader already is that a pew over Sir John Randolph's vault in
the north-east corner would have blocked the north-east entrance.

Whether or not there were stalls in part of the chapel, the latter part of Nicholas's memorandum suggests that the pew or pews over Botetourt's vault were box
pews; for there would surely have been a good deal of "Inconvenience in letting the
monument down into the wainscot as low as the Floor" if that wainscot had formed
the backing of banked tiers of stalls. The height of the wainscot, 11 ft. 6 in., is one of
the few positive pieces of information about the interior of the chapel that we have;
another is the width of the central aisle, about 10 ft. A third is that there was a pul-

pit. This is a piece of furniture that one would not expect to find in a college chapel; its presence might even be held to suggest that the whole interior was more like a Virginian parish church than an Oxford or Cambridge college chapel, though it would certainly be rash to insist on the inference. For what the comparison is worth, it may be noted that the chapel of Chelsea hospital contained box pews and a pulpit, and plain forms for the pensioners.[15] There, however, the pulpit stood against the middle of the south wall, whereas in the chapel at William and Mary it stood, to judge from Nicholas's remarks, on the east-west axis in front of the communion table. This was a common position for the pulpit in eighteenth-century Anglican churches, although in the former American colonies it survives today only in Trinity Church, Newport, Rhode Island. The sentiment that the altar should be visible to all worshippers at all times dates from a later age. For eighteenth-century churchmen the central pulpit helped to express the functional difference between the two parts of the church—the nave for prayer and preaching and the chancel for the celebration of Holy Communion.

No monument to Lord Botetourt was ever erected in the chapel, for the Assembly honoured his memory with a statue in the Capitol instead. The man whom some have thought to have been his posthumous host, Sir John Randolph, was commemorated by a monument "of curious Workmanship, in Marble" [16] set up in 1739. A hundred and twenty years later it was calcined; the present monument to Sir John, in the style of the London masons' yards of the 1730's, is his third in the chapel, having replaced a plain tablet which was set up in 1903.[17]

THE PRESIDENT'S HOUSE

The College Statutes of 1727 provided that the President's annual salary should be "One Hundred and Fifty Pounds Sterling, with an House and Garden suitable to the place, so soon as the College Revenues will bear all these Expenses." When the chapel had been completed and put into use it was felt that the time had come to implement the whole of this provision, and on July 31, 1732 there took place a ceremony recorded in the College Journal as follows:

> The foundation of the Presidents house at the College was laid, the President, [and the Masters] Mr Dawson, Mr Fry, Mr Stith, and Mr Fox, laying the first five bricks in order, one after another. The reason of the foundations being laid that day was, that Mr Henry Cary the Undertaker, had appointed his bricklayers to be ready that day, and that they could not proceed till the foundation was laid.[18]

Figure 46. THE PRESIDENT'S HOUSE. Exterior from the south-west.

Dawson, writing to the Bishop of London, gave the information that the new building, which he described as "a common brick House," was to be finished for £650
current money by October 1733.[19]

To all appearances the President's House (Fig. 46) and the Brafferton might be
twins, yet not identical twins. The President's House is 4 ft. larger than the Brafferton in each main dimension: 56 ft. long by 38 ft. deep by 56 ft. high to the top
of the chimneys. By itself this slight increase of size would scarcely be noticeable
or significant. However, Cary introduced variations in the design which give the
President's House its own individuality. First, he allotted three-quarters of the extra
height to the roof and chimneys, making the walls only 1 ft. higher than those of
the Brafferton. Then in the south elevation (Fig. 47) he varied the scheme of fenestration by giving all the extra 4 ft. of length to the intervals between the inner
windows and door, so that this front has a more open effect than that of the Brafferton opposite. On the north front, on the other hand, he produced an effect of
greater compression by giving the extra length to the walls between the quoins and
the outermost windows, and an even more nearly perfect regularity than that of the
Brafferton fronts by reducing the width of the doorway. The principal elevations of
the President's House, the Brafferton and the Palace exemplify the variety of effect
that the colonial builder could achieve through the manipulation of purely functional elements of design.

Inside, Cary gave the extra space to the rooms themselves, making the central passage the same width as that in the Brafferton (Fig. 48). There were four rooms on
each main floor, those to the south being slightly the larger. Despite the fact that
the house was extensively rebuilt in 1786, it is probably safe to say that there were
never any corner fireplaces such as the Brafferton had.

The group of three College buildings thus completed with the President's House
evinces the same disregard of mechanical symmetry that allowed Cary to vary the
theme of the Brafferton facade in the building that balances it. The town of Williamsburg was laid out by compass. The main building of the College, however,
had been set out in such a way that its east front, whether by accident or design, lay
along a line running nearly true north and south; it was therefore not quite at right
angles to Duke of Gloucester Street. Then came the Brafferton, whose long axis was
made parallel with Duke of Gloucester Street. When the President's House was to
be built to balance it, three possibilities presented themselves: it could be placed di-
agonally so as to repeat the angle between the Brafferton and the main building, it

Figure 47. THE PRESIDENT'S HOUSE. South elevation.

could be built parallel with the Brafferton, or it could be built at right angles to the main building. Both the first two courses would have made the divergence of the axis of the main building from that of Duke of Gloucester Street more noticeable, while the second of them would in addition have had an unhappy result in opposing to the acute angle between the Brafferton and the main building an obtuse one between the latter and the President's House. So the third was adopted, and the President's House was built at right angles to the main building. On the spot one is not conscious of the slight irregularity of the layout. But it may be that it gives the group of buildings a life that it would otherwise lack.

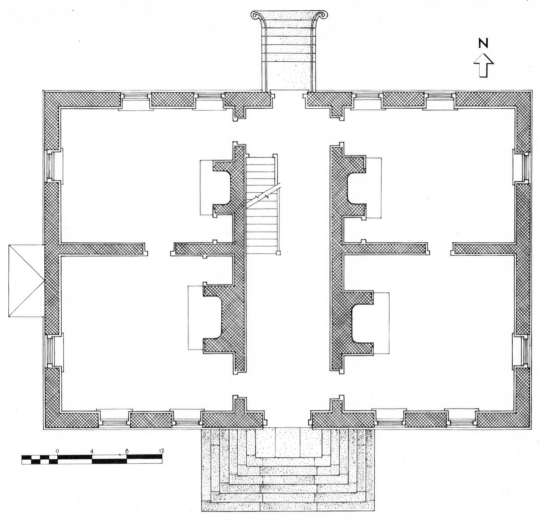

Figure 48. THE PRESIDENT'S HOUSE. Ground floor plan.

FIRE AND SMALLPOX

After the completion of the President's House, a dozen years and more went by, with nothing to record in these pages except the remodelling of the first theatre as a Courthouse, which has already been touched upon. Then, in 1747, came catastrophe at the Capitol. A detailed account was given by the *Pennsylvania Gazette:*

"Williamsburg
[Thursday] Feb. 5, 1747

Last Friday, [Jan. 30] the fatal and ever memorable Day of the Martyrdom of King Charles the First, a most extraordinary Misfortune befel this Place, by the Destruction of our fine Capitol. Between 7 and 8 o'clock in the Morning the Inhabitants of the City were surprised with the Sight of a Cloud of Smoke, issuing from the upper Part of the Capitol; but no Fire appeared on the Out-side. Soon after some of the Shingles began to kindle on Fire from within, and immediately a Blaze burst out, which presently reached the Cupola, and thence communicated the Fire to the Covering of the whole Fabrick. The Cupola was soon burnt, the two Bells that were in it were melted, and, together with the Clock, fell down, and were destroyed; and the whole Covering and Roof soon followed: Then the upper Floor of the several Rooms took Fire, soon burnt thro', and descended to the second Floor, and so to Bottom, till the whole Timber and Wood-work was destroyed, and the naked Brick Walls only left standing, which, however, seem good, except one or two small Cracks in the Semi-circles. During this Consternation and Hurry, all the Records deposited in the Capitol, except a few loose, useless papers, were, by great Care and Diligence, and in the Midst of Danger, happily preserved; as were also the Pictures of the Royal Family, and several other Things. The Wind, early in the Morning, was at Southwest, but just before, or at the Beginning of Fire, shifted to Northwest, and blew very fresh, so that the Fleaks of Fire, which flew about plentifully, were carried from the Town, and by that Means, thro' the kind Interposition of Divine Providence, the Houses escaped the Flames, and many Families were saved from Ruin.[20]

The Capitol fire, breaking out as it did in daylight, cannot have been as spectac-ular as the College fire of 1705. But people were just as unwilling to think it ac-cidental, and if the account of its origin given by Governor Gooch in a speech to the Assembly on March 30 is true they had rather better reason to put it down to "the Effect of Malice and Design." "I must indeed own it is difficult to comprehend how so flagitious a Crime could be committed, or even imagined, by any rational Creature," Gooch said—

> But when you have considered that the first Emission of the Smoke through the Shingles, was from an upper retired Room without Chimney, or Wainscot; that the Persons who on its first Appearance hasten'd thither to discover the cause, found all the Inside of the Roof in one blaze, impossible to be extinguished; and that a Fire kindled by Accident could not have made so rapid a Progress; you will be forced to ascribe it to the horrid Machinations of desperate Villains, instigated by infernal Madness.

Gooch was careful to add that he was sure that "such superlative Wickedness could never get Admittance into the Heart of a Virginian." But undoubtedly there were those in the colony who were not altogether displeased to see the building go up in smoke. The movement of settlement to the west had long deprived Williamsburg of any claim to be central that it may have had when it was founded: many of the Burgesses had to make long and tedious journeys to attend the Assemblies. More-over, the growth and the mercantile success of Norfolk pointed up other disadvan-tages of inland Williamsburg. In short, a new capital was needed as much as a new Capitol. And the Burgesses, in their address in reply to the Governor's speech, said so:

> On this Occasion, we hope to manifest the same Public Spirit as usual, by erecting a good and sufficient Edifice, for the Meeting of our General Court and the General Assemblies, a Work so necessary as to claim the Concurrence of this House; and we shall readily join in the proper Measures for effecting it: To lay the Foundations of a new City, to raise this Building in a Place commodiously situated for Navigation, will compleat the Glory of your administration, and transmit your Name with the highest Lustre to the Latest Ages: With what Pleasure then may we extend our Views thro' future Centuries, and anticipate the Happiness provided for Posterity!

Gooch was no Nicholson to fancy himself in the city-founding role of Marcus Hostilius. He could, however, appreciate the weight of the arguments in favour of removal, and went so far as to recommend this course in a letter to the Board of Trade.[21] It was not followed. In April 1747, although leave to bring in a bill for rebuilding the Capitol on the old site was refused by the Burgesses by forty-five votes to twenty-six, the *Act for Establishing a Town on Pamunkey River*, passed by forty-three votes to thirty-three, was thrown out by the Council; and the same fate overtook the compromise. *Act for appointing Persons to view the Places and Landings on Pamunkey River and on James River from the Falls to the Mouth of Appamattox.* On April 18 Gooch prorogued the Assembly, his speech containing some stern words tempered by "Hopes, that, after revolving in [their] retirement, the Motives and Objections on both Sides the Question, [they] would, another Session, cordially unite, either in repairing the old, or in building a new Capitol."

Their retirement, owing to an epidemic of smallpox, lasted longer than any could have foreseen. Eighteen months passed before, on October 27, 1748, Gooch addressed the Assembly again. "The very pressing Necessity for Erecting a Royal Edifice" was the subject of his speech. Williamsburg, he pointed out, "being intirely purged from the Virulency of the Small-Pox," was "a City of Refuge"; it was reasonable to suppose that it would be some years before the rest of the colony was free from the disease. Would the Assembly avail themselves of the dispensation and build in this place of safety, "where the most timid of our inhabitants may attend and prosecute their Business"? Or would they "remove to another Situation, where, the same Cause producing the same Effect, and High and Low terrified with the Dread of Infection, we are no less sure, all Authority and Power must be again suspended; the Government, in the Absence of its Guardians, exposed to insupportable Difficulties; and the Subject made liable to the additional Vexation of the like expensive

Delays they suffer'd during the late Visitation"? These considerations, said the Governor, had made him "an Advocate for building upon the old Foundations."

Those in favour of removal were not ready to admit defeat. On November 11 a Committee of the House resolved that it was its opinion that Williamsburg was "very remote from the far greatest Part of the Inhabitants of this Colony, and by Experience has been found altogether unfit for Trade and Navigation; . . . that a Town [should] be Established on some convenient Place on *York* River, or the Branches thereof; and that a Building for holding General Courts and General Assemblies [should] be erected in the said town," which was to be built "on the Lands of Thomas and William Meriwether, adjoining the Town of Newcastle," in Hanover County, five hundred acres being laid off for the purpose. A week later *A Bill for establishing a Town on Pamunkey River* was presented, and refused a second reading by forty-one votes to thirty-six. It was followed by *A Bill for Rebuilding the Capitol in the City of Williamsburg*, which achieved its second reading by the narrow margin of two votes (thirty-nine to thirty-seven), passed its third by the same margin (with one more Ay offset by one more No) on November 23, and received the Governor's assent on December 17. The status of Williamsburg was saved. But it had been a near thing.

THE SECRETARY'S OFFICE

The rescue of the bulk of the public records from the flames of the Capitol confronted the authorities with a need about which there could be no difference of principle: something had to be done to ensure their future preservation, and done at once. But when it came to details there proved to be room for disagreement, and *A Bill for erecting a Building for the Preservation of the Public Records and Papers of this Colony*, introduced in April 1747, foundered upon the Burgesses' refusal to adopt an amendment proposed by the Council. After the prorogation of the Assembly the Council took matters into its own hands; on April 29 it ordered

> That a Building be erected for the Preservation of the Records and that John Blair Esqr William Nelson Esqr John Robinson jun^r Esqr and Thomas Nelson Esqr be appointed Managers to treat with workmen about the same.

The building was evidently completed in the course of the year 1748. A petition of the Keeper of the Public Gaol presented to the House of Burgesses in November 1748 stated that the records had been put under his care after the fire and that "the Room they took up in his House obliged him, *for some Time,* to board out two of

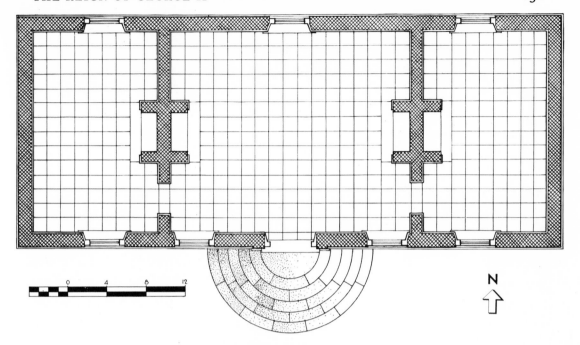

Figure 49. THE SECRETARY'S OFFICE. Plan.

his Children"; we may infer from the phrase here italicized that the records had already been removed to their new place of keeping. And at a meeting of the Council on December 2, 1748 a warrant was paid:

> For building a House to preser[v]e the Records . . £367 . 19 . 7.

This house was the handsome little building known today as the Public Records Office, and in the eighteenth century as the Secretary's Office.

The documents do not name the designer or the builder of the Secretary's Office. Its plan (Fig. 49) is an adaptation of an old type of Virginian house plan, that had two rooms on the ground floor and a central passage containing the staircase. In this case no staircase was needed, for there was to be neither upper floor nor basement, and the passage was expanded into what may here be properly called a hall. The chimneys were moved in from the end walls to the partitions, and each served a fireplace in the hall in addition to one in a terminal room. In view of the fate from which the papers and records had so recently been saved, this may seem a plethora of fireplaces. However, it should be remembered that if Gooch is to be believed the fireplaces installed in the Capitol in 1723 had nothing to do with its destruction; and those fireplaces were installed because the humidity of the Tidewater climate was

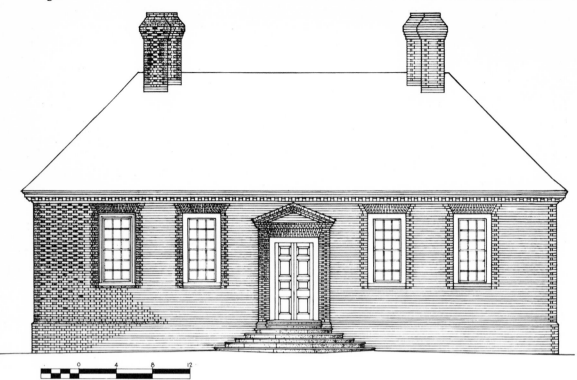

Figure 50. THE SECRETARY'S OFFICE. South elevation.

spoiling the very records that the new building was erected to accommodate. In fact the Secretary's Office represents about as good a solution of the double threat of fire and damp as the knowledge and the materials of the time could supply. It would of course have been possible, though expensive, to cover the building with a brick vault instead of a wooden roof. As it was, the use of brick for the walls was probably thought to increase the threat of damp. The principles of condensation were not generally understood in the eighteenth century, and as late as the 1780's Thomas Jefferson saw fit to explain them, and to refute the vulgar error that the water that appeared on brick walls in rainy weather was rain that had penetrated.[22] The floors of all three rooms were originally paved with stone, and one can imagine that their "sweating" in hot and humid weather must sometimes have led to the lighting of summer fires. The carpentry of the king-post roof, which was probably covered with round-butt shingles, is remarkable, the structural members being finished with a care that was uncommon in colonial Virginia.

Figure 51. THE SECRETARY'S OFFICE. The south front.

The precise functions of the three rooms in the Secretary's Office cannot now be determined. The absence of openings in the end walls suggests that book-cases or presses for records were ranged against them. Examination of the walls has shown that there was no wainscot to increase the hazard of fire; there were, however, chair-rails.

Externally the glazed bricks establish a definite pattern over the surfaces of the walls, laid up as usual in Flemish bond (Figs. 50, 51). The doorway of rubbed brick is of a kind that we have noted as a feature of many Virginian churches. There are doorways of practically identical design at Ware Church (c. 1720) and Abingdon Church, Gloucester County (1751–1755, Fig. 52), Vauter's Church, Essex County (in the addition of 1731), St. John's, King William County (in the post-1734 addition), Mattapony Church, King and Queen County (c. 1732), and—a domestic example—Carter's Grove, James City County (1751, Fig. 53); the last two mentioned were the work of the Williamsburg bricklayer David Minitree. Under the eaves there is an admirably detailed modillion cornice of wood. The chimneys are of the T-plan type, which had been used in Virginia since the seventeenth century. It may be held that since the four fireplaces were all of the same size chimneys of this type were not strictly functional. However, their use is justified aesthetically by the contribution which their sculptural interest makes to the building as a whole. And the designer of the Secretary's Office, whoever he may have been, was a man with whom aesthetic considerations counted.

THE REBUILDING OF THE CAPITOL

The Act for rebuilding the Capitol appointed a committee of eight and empowered them, or any five of them, "to covenant, agree with, hire and employ such and so many undertakers, workmen, and labourers, and to provide, furnish and buy such materials as they . . . shall think convenient and proper . . . for re-building, repairing, and altering the said Capitol, on the old Foundations." The cost was not to exceed £3,000.

Much of the work on the Capitol was done in the interval between the return of Gooch to England in 1749 and the arrival of Robert Dinwiddie as Governor late in 1751. Three Presidents of Council carried on the administration during this period, but no Assembly was called. The Palace, it will be remembered, had been built at a similar time, with a consequent scarcity of records. In the case of the Capitol there would be no records of the progress of the work but for the fortunate survival of two private diaries, that of Robert Rose, who in 1748–1751 was minister of St. Anne's Parish in Albemarle County, and that kept in the year 1751 by John Blair (nephew of the Commissary), who was chairman of the building committee.[23]

From Robert Rose's diary we learn the name of the first contractor or undertaker. On March 1, 1748/9 he noted:

> Stopt at Mr W Fitzhughs dined, returned to Mr Walkers, who had got Home from Wmsburg where he had undertaken the Capitol for £2600.

This Mr. Walker was William Walker, who when he had contracted to build the steeple of St. Peter's church, New Kent County, to his own design in 1740 had been described as "of the Parish of St: Paul in the County of Stafford Builder"—a rare instance of the use of this generic term instead of the specific "carpenter" or "bricklayer."[24] Other works of his were a glebe house for St. Paul's Parish, Hanover County, built in 1739–1740, for which also he drew the plan,[25] and a toll bridge over the Pamunkey at Newcastle.[26] When he made his will, in February 1748/9,

Figure 52.
ABINGDON CHURCH, GLOUCESTER COUNTY, VIRGINIA.
The south doorway.

Figure 53.
CARTER'S GROVE, JAMES CITY COUNTY, VIRGINIA.
The north doorway (before restoration).

he had "many buildings now on hand, many workmen, many tools & many Materials for carrying on the same"; "& many more I daily Expect from London & other parts of great Britain." [27] Evidently he was well equipped for the public work that he had undertaken. But he was fated not to carry it out, for a year later he was dead. On February 11, 1749/50 Rose wrote in his diary:

> Went to Overwharton Church where heard of Mr. Wm Walkers death which will I hope delay the Building of the Capitol.

Rose (who, as the last remark shows, was of the party for removal from Williamsburg) attended Walker's funeral on February 15.

There is an interval of nearly twelve months before John Blair's diary takes up the tale. The first entry relating directly to work at the Capitol is under the date January 25, 1751:

> Wheatly shew[e]d me that he had finish[e]d Mr. Skelton's work, but Skelton took no care of it.

This introduces us to the contractor who succeeded Walker, James Skelton, and to one of the carpenters to whom he had sublet part of the work, John Wheatly. James Skelton (whose youngest son's widow[28] became Thomas Jefferson's wife) was a builder of some prominence in the colony. In 1719–1720 he had built the churchyard wall at St. Peter's, New Kent County ("the s[d]: Wall to be in all Respects as well Done as the Capitol wall in Williams-Burgh") and repaired the church, by contract.[29] In 1721–1723 he built a church at Poplar Spring, Gloucester County, which followed the cruciform plan of Bruton and was evidently a building of some pretensions; he received the considerable sum of £1,190 for this work, and while it was going on he lived on the site in a small house—the equivalent of the medieval mason's lodge—which the vestry subsequently got him to fix up for permanent use and bought from him for £12.[30] In 1733 he was a resident of Goochland and also owned land in Hanover County;[31] in 1737 the Governor's Council ordered him a payment of £10 for viewing and valuing a house at Point Comfort fort; he was appointed Sheriff of Hanover County for 1739–1740, a Justice of the Peace in 1741, and Sheriff again for 1742–1743.[32] If he was *distrait* at the end of January, 1751, taking no care of his work, the reason may perhaps be found in an earlier entry in Blair's diary, dated January 5: "Skelton sett off to go up to bury his wife, having got a black coat for it." Skelton himself was to die in 1754.[33]

Of John Wheatly less can be told. At the time of the building of the second Capitol he was living in Williamsburg on the lot now occupied by the Custis-Maupin house, on Duke of Gloucester Street opposite Bruton Church; he had rented this in 1746.[34] He performed the carpentry at Carter's Grove, under contract, in 1751–1753,[35] and, as we shall see, he also worked at the Palace.

To return to Blair's diary, the next entry that tells us anything about the progress of work at the Capitol is under the date March 1, 1751: "Balconies taken down." A month later construction succeeded demolition, for on April 1 Blair noted: "I laid a found[atio]n Brick at Capitol." On May 18 a kiln of bricks was fired; on June 11 Blair "endeav[oure]d a meeting ab[ou]t the Capitol"—a phrase that suggests something less than enthusiasm on the part of the other building committee members; on June 24 "they raised the first Window on Cap[ito]l." On August 29 Blair "settled a new modell of the seats for the Burgesses"; on September 14 he found the building as he had "left it the 3d, and as it had been for some time before, not at all advanced." However, on September 16 and 18 the great door cases were put up, and on September 20 he noted:

> The gr[ea]t gate the Burgesses went in at stopt, and begun to be brick'd up. The foundation frame of the cupulo fitted into its place in framing.

This is an important entry for us, because it shows that not only the foundations but parts of the walls of the first Capitol were re-used in the second; for "the great gate the Burgesses went in at" must have been one of the doorways in the east wing of the first building. The ambiguity as to which way the first building might be supposed to face was resolved in the second in no uncertain way by the erection of a portico on the west front, to which the first reference appears in Blair's diary under the date September 24: "Lay[in]g bricks for the grand steps; but fear." What did he fear? Apparently the security of blocks of stone as unwontedly large as those which formed the steps of the portico, for two days later he noted: "Steps bro[ugh]t in place, but no fasten[in]g prepar[e]d." On September 28 he wrote: "The first stone of the grand stairs of the portico was set today, on w[hi]ch I stood when but 2 more were laid, w[i]thout cramps." But it was not until November 26 that he "saw the gr[ea]t steps at the capitol all up in their places."

Before that, on September 27, there had been a visit from Richard Taliaferro, whom we shall meet again at the Governor's House, and he had viewed Wheatly's sash work. On October 1 "Delony beg[a]n to raise the 2d Floor." This was Lewis Delony, whom we met working for James Morris at Bruton Church; in the meanwhile he had gone up in the world, becoming one of the first Justices of Lunenburg County in 1746, and designing that county's first courthouse and building its gaol.[36] There follow some entries, dated October 2, 3 and 5, about the raising of timbers— on the last date over the General Court. On November 1 Blair obtained a warrant on the colony's Treasurer to pay Skelton £500 and also transacted a piece of business in which William Walker's estate was involved:

> This even[in]g I assigned to Skelton at Mr. Waller's the bond of Walker's ex[ecuto]rs to repay the £500 advanced to him towards his rebuild[in]g the capitol.

Mr. Waller was Benjamin Waller, Burgess for James City County and a member of the building committee.

Blair tells us that Skelton fired the last kiln for the Capitol on November 15, 1751. Just under a month later, on December 12, he wrote:

> This afternoon I laid the last top brick on the capitol wall, and so it is now ready to receive the roof, and some of the wall plates were rais[e]d and laid on this day. I had laid a foundation brick at the first build[in]g of the capitol above 50 year ago, and another foundation brick in April last, the first in mortar towards the rebuilding, and now the last as above.

Nearly two years more were to pass, however, before the Assembly, which in February 1752 sat in the College, was summoned to the rebuilt Capitol, on November 1, 1753. Soon afterwards Skelton petitioned for "a further Allowance for rebuilding the Capitol" and was granted £500, of which £200 was not to be paid "until the said Rebuilding be compleated." In 1755 Governor Dinwiddie presented the royal arms for the pediment of the western portico. But the building was not yet altogether finished, for an issue of the *Virginia Gazette* contained an advertisement for "about 280 feet of purbeck and 80 feet of blue Shrosberry Stone for completing the Piazzas of the Capitol" in August 1756.[37]

THE SECOND CAPITOL

The external appearance of the first Capitol can be reconstructed with some confidence from the evidence supplied by the specification in the Act of 1699, by the foundations as they existed in 1929, and by the Bodleian plate. The second Capitol is not nearly so well documented; we have no detailed specification, and no eighteenth-century view of the building. Moreover, all the nineteenth-century views were based either on "a drawing preserved by a lady of the place" or on other views based on that same lost drawing; and the drawing in question was made after the cupola had been removed and the portico altered. Originally the latter had four columns in each storey, as Ebenezer Hazard tells us in an account to be quoted shortly, and they were Doric below and Ionic above, as we know from Jefferson's description:

> The Capitol is a light and airy structure, with a portico in front of two orders, the lower of which, being Doric, is tolerably just in its proportions and ornaments, save only that the intercolonnations are too large. The upper is Ionic, much too small for that on which it is mounted, its ornaments not proper to the order, nor proportioned within themselves. It is crowned with a pediment, which is too high for its span.[38]

In 1796 Benjamin Henry Latrobe wrote that the wooden pillars [sic] had been "stripped of their Mouldings & twisted and forced out of their planes in all directions."[39]

As has been hinted already, the portico of the second Capitol was the first monumental portico in Virginia. Away to the south, Drayton Hall near Charleston had been built with a two-storey portico a dozen years earlier. It was a Palladian motif, but Palladio himself in employing it either recessed the porch within the body of the building, so as to keep the columns nearly in the same plane as the front wall, or—in one instance [40]—built flanking walls to the portico itself. Drayton Hall, where part of the porch is recessed within the house, approaches Palladio's own practice more closely that did the Capitol, where the portico was simply applied to an unbroken front. Yet incorrect or not the Capitol portico was to find its imitators. At least it would seem reasonable to regard the two-story porticoes of Shirley and perhaps that of the destroyed Tedington,[41] both in Charles City County, as its progeny. And one might claim that a far more distinguished example of the type stood in some degree of relationship to it. For is it not possible that Jefferson, in his early designs for Monticello, was induced to substitute columns for the arches originally planned as the lower part of the frontispiece by the thought that he could thus give Virginia a corrected version of the portico of the Williamsburg building he knew so well?

A major difference between the first and second Capitols was produced by the squaring off of the south ends of the wings in the latter. A complete rebuilding of this end of the wings was no doubt necessitated by the development of the "small Cracks in the Semi-circles" that the *Pennsylvania Gazette* had described among the results of the fire, and new tribunes or "semi-circles" would have conflicted with the portico. A few other features of the building are described in, or can be inferred from, a passage in the journal of Ebenezer Hazard, who was in Williamsburg in 1777:

> The Capitol is a large two Story Brick Building in the Form of an H: it is surrounded with a Brick Wall; you enter the Court Yard by an elegant Iron Gate. In the Front of the Building is a Portico & Balcony, each supported by four Pillars; above these the King's Arms (elegantly carved & gilt) were formerly placed, but upon Independence being declared they were taken down & burned. Upon entering the Capitol you get into a Room in which the Courts of Justice are held; it is large & convenient; here is a fine whole Length Picture of Queen Anne by Van Dyck [!]. Opposite to the Door by which you enter this Room (in another Apartment, which is a Kind of Hall) is an elegant white marble pedestrian Statue of Lord Botetourt in his Robes, made by Richard Hayward, London, 1773. . . . From the Hall where this Statue is placed you go into the Lobby of the House of Burgesses, & thence into the Room where they sit; the latter is large, convenient, & plain: the Speaker's Chair & a large Iron Stove are at the Upper End, on Each Side the Seats for the Members, & at the lower End a Gallery for the Use of Spectators. . . . On one Side of this Room hangs

a whole Length of King George the 2d & on the other another of Queen Caroline. The other Rooms in the Capitol are large but contain nothing worthy of Observation. On the Top of the Capitol is a Cupola, & a Clock with four Dials.[42]

Hayward's statue of Lord Botetourt must await treatment in the next chapter. For the rest, it may be noted that Hazard's statement that one went from the piazza into the *lobby* of the House of Burgesses ties in neatly enough with Blair's notes about the new plan of the seating and about the bricking up of "the great gate the Burgesses went in at." In the first Capitol the House of Burgesses was of the same length as the General Court—50 ft.—and was entered directly from the piazza or through the east doorway; in the second it had a lobby which diminished the floor area within the House, though if the public gallery was over the lobby the accommodation would have been the same. Finally, the cupola, which we know from another source to have been covered with lead,[43] must have been either square or—as is more likely—octagonal; for no one would put a clock with *four* dials in a hexagonal cupola, such as the first Capitol had.

REPAIRS AT THE PALACE

When in 1747 Gooch urged upon the Board of Trade the advisability of moving the capital of the colony, one of the considerations that he put forward was that the Palace was "so old and decayed it would require an annual repair of at least £100."[44] It is a surprising statement, made as it was of a brick house that had been begun no more than forty-one years previously—and finished less than twenty-five. However, records of payments for repairs during the period 1723–1747 show that Gooch's estimate of future needs was if anything on the modest side. The total spent was £3,294 . 8s. 4d., which give an average of over £131 per year.[45] Even if payments for new outbuildings, such as smoke-houses and kitchens, were included under the head of repairs (as seems most probable), one can hardly escape the conclusion that the Palace was a flagrant example of jerry-building.

In 1749, Williamsburg's continuance as capital of the colony having been assured and Gooch having returned to England, action was taken towards remedying what in the Council Journal for September 4 was called "the ruinous Condition" of the Palace. On that date the Council "thought proper that it should be surveyed by some skilful Persons and an estimate made by them of the Charge of putting it in good Repair, and were pleased to appoint Mr. James Wray and Mr. Richard Taliaferro for

that Purpose, and ordered the Clerk to . . . desire that they would forthwith carefully view & inspect the said House and make a Report as soon as possibly they could
of the Expense which they should judge the Reparation might amount to." On
November 2 the Council themselves inspected the building and thought "that it
should be generally and thoroughly repaired." On November 7 Thomas Lee, President of the Council, told the Board of Trade: "The Governor's House, gardens, etc.,
has been Viewed and Examined by our most Skillful Architect, and he reports that
the necessary repairs will cost £1259 - 6, Curt Money." [46]

It has been assumed that by "our most Skillful Architect" Richard Taliaferro,
who certainly (though not immediately, as we shall see) carried out the repairs, was
meant. Even if the assumption is correct and we disallow the apparently equal claim
of James Wray, a carpenter who did some repairs at the College in 1739,[47] from
1745 lived in the Timson House on the corner of Prince George Street and Nassau
Street,[48] and died in 1750,[49] it is surely a mistake to make too much of the phrase,
"our most Skillful Architect." The President of the Council would naturally, in
writing to the Board of Trade, wish to convey the impression that the best possible
advice had been sought; what he said should not be taken to indicate that Richard
Taliaferro was a towering figure, or even a prominent one, in the Virginian architectural scene. In 1737 Taliaferro had been appointed a Justice of the Peace for
James City County,[50] and in 1741 Sheriff.[51] At the time of the Palace repairs he was
living in a house called Powhatan,[52] about three miles west of Williamsburg, which
he had built (and perhaps designed) for himself at an undetermined date; he may
also have designed the Wythe House, on the west side of Palace Green, which he
bequeathed to his son-in-law George Wythe.[53] In 1756 his tender for paling in the
College yard and repairing the President's House was accepted.[54] He died in 1779,
aged 73, of what was grimly described as "the gout in the head." [55] Until some tan-
gible proof of his skill as a designer turns up, it is fair to picture him as a substantial planter whose capital and credit were important qualifications for such an
undertaking as the repair of the Palace.

Another year, 1750, went by without anything much being done. Payments for
repairs that year totalled only £38. 2s. 11d. and in 1751 £71 . 1s. 8d. However, it
was in 1751 that the final arrangements for the work were made. Again, as in the
case of the Capitol, we owe what little we know of the matter to John Blair's diary.
Entries in January and May show that at first there was some thought of entering
into an agreement with a Mr. Richards. But he proved rather unbusinesslike—he

"gave in proposals in a very loose manner," Blair complains—and the last we hear of him is in an entry for May 27:

> Mr. Richards now with me ab[ou]t the Gov[erno]rs house, and said if he did it he must have four years to finish it. Qr. what to be done.

It seems safe to identify him with the strangely christened Mourning Richards, who a month after his last interview with Blair contracted to build a glebe house for Christ Church, Middlesex County,[56] and in September the same year was awarded the contract for building, to his own design, Aquia Church in Stafford County—a job which, owing to a fire in 1755 when the building was almost ready to hand over to the vestry, he did not finally complete until 1757.[57]

On June 12, 1751 Blair was able to record that the Council approved of his proposal for repairing the Palace. In the absence of evidence to the contrary, it is to be supposed that this proposal involved bringing Richard Taliaferro back on the scene. In any case, on August 30 Blair "finish[e]d the Contract with Taliaferro for the Gov[erno]rs house." Under the date September 28 there is an entry which explains Taliaferro's inspection of John Wheatly's sash work at the Capitol on the previous day:

> Went w[i]th Taliaf[err]o, Wheatly & Taylor to Gov[erno]r [i.e., the acting Governor, Lewis Burwell, President of the Council]. Taliaf[err]o agr[ee]d w[i]th Wheatly & made out an invoice.

So Wheatly executed some at least of the new carpentry at the Palace.

The new Governor, Robert Dinwiddie, the imminence of whose arrival had added urgency to the need for the repairs, reached Williamsburg on November 21 and was escorted to what is called today the Carter-Saunders house, which had been purchased for his accommodation until such time as the Palace would be fit for occupation again. There is no record of the actual date of his moving into the Palace. However, in November 1752 the King's birthday was celebrated with "a Ball, and a very elegant Entertainment, at the Palace, where were present the Emperor and Empress of the Cherokee Nation, with their Son the Young Prince, and a brilliant appearance of Ladies and Gentlemen."[58] Moreover, the sum paid for repairs in 1752 was £818 . 8s. 10d.[59]—a figure which suggests that the building must have been nearly habitable by November (when the second payment was normally made). In the following year, 1753, the total drops to a mere £195 . 4s. 3d. By December 19, 1753 Dinwiddie had certainly moved in; for on that day the Carter-Saunders house was sold.[60]

THE PALACE BALL-ROOM AND SUPPER-ROOM

The work at the Palace at this stage in its history included more than mere repairs, even though the treasury warrants specify nothing else. Thomas Jefferson's plan of the building shows a large extension to the north, about 75 ft. long by about 31 ft. wide, and the excavations of 1929 confirmed its accuracy in this respect. The inventory of Lord Botetourt's estate and of the standing furniture at the time of his death shows that the two rooms in this extension were the ball-room and supper-room.[61] In only two periods do the records of payments for repairs name sums which could cover this addition—1752–1754 and 1768–1770. The payments in the latter period, which total little more than half those of 1752–1754, can be accounted for under another head. In November 1749, as we have seen already, the cost of necessary repairs was estimated at £1,259 . 6s. 0d. Between that date and the end of 1753 we have noted annual totals which should now be put down sum-wise:

1750:	£ 38	.	2s.	11d.
1751:	£ 71	.	1s.	8d.
1752:	£818	.	8s.	10d.
1753:	£195	.	4s.	3d.
	£1,122	.	17s.	8d.

The total payments in these four years thus amount to rather less than the cost of repairs as first estimated. The first payment in 1754, £112 . 10s. 6d.,[62] brings the total to £1,235 . 8s. 2d., which is not far short of the estimate. However, with the second payment in 1754, no less a sum than £853 . 4s. 10d., the total soars far beyond it—to £2,088 . 13s. 0d. In 1755 the relatively small sum of £159 . 17s. 5d. was spent. It seems safe to assume that the large payment in 1754 was for the building, or at least the finishing, of the addition containing the ball-room and the supper-room.

Many houses in England were receiving similar additions at this time. Isaac Ware, in *A Complete Body of Architecture* (1756), complains that "the custom of routs"—that is, large assemblies or evening parties—"brings in the necessity of a *great room*, which is opened only on such occasions, and which loads and generally discredits the rest of the edifice." He adds:

> In houses which have been some time built, and which have not an out of proportion room, the common practice is to build one to them: this always hangs from one end, or sticks to one side, of the house, and shews to the most careless eye, that, though fastened to the walls, it does not belong to the building.

The Palace addition, as Ware would doubtless have allowed, had a better justification than mere fashion, for it provided space that must have been much needed for the balls given by the Governor in celebration of royal birthdays and other anniversaries of public significance. Moreover, the fact that its external width was made equal to the height to the eaves of the main body of the house—probably in order that its end elevation might fit into a perfect square—indicates an attempt to preserve unity. But although its furnishings are listed in the inventory of the contents of the Palace taken upon Lord Botetourt's death in 1770,[63] and although the same inventory reveals that it had a porch and store-rooms in the roof, we have no record of its architectural character or even of its general appearance, inside or out.

Figure 54. THE NOTT TOMB, BRUTON PARISH CHURCHYARD. Governor Edward Nott died in 1706; this table tomb, voted by the Assembly in 1718, was set up in 1720.

Figure 55. The Bray Monument,
Bruton Parish Churchyard.
David Bray and his wife died in 1734.

THE 1750's AT BRUTON

Some lesser works of the 1750's remain to be noticed. The first of them to be initiated was the building of a new churchyard wall. In December 1749 a certain Emery Hughes agreed with the Vestry to build the wall for £290.[64] However, he failed to carry out his contract, and in July 1752 Samuel Spurr, whom we shall meet again in the next chapter, took on the job for £320, promising to finish it by October 1754.[65] By this decade the churchyard already contained most of the finer tombs, which were imported from England. These include the table tomb of Governor Nott, voted by the Assembly in 1718 and set up in 1720 (Fig. 54)—excellent London work, with trophies at either end of the gadrooned tomb-chest and curtains held back by cherubs' heads and a skull on either side;[66] the tall marble monument to David Bray and his wife, both of whom died in 1734, with an obelisk supported by four eagles' feet in allusion to the bearings on the Bray escutcheon, which is carved on the base of the tomb (Fig. 55): and the boldly Baroque table tomb of Edward Barradall (d. 1743), with splayed scrolls at the corners (Fig. 56). (A post-Revolution monument which in its Neo-Classical delicacy provides an interesting contrast with the last is the elliptical table tomb of the merchant John Greenhow [d. 1787] with its four fluted pilasters.)

Inside the church, the south gallery had been enlarged, but this was not enough to solve the space problem. So in February 1751 the Vestry decided to build an addition to the church and an advertisement in the *Virginia Gazette*[67] announced that a meeting would be held "to agree with Workmen" on March 15. What came of this is not clear; rather more than a year later the House of Burgesses resolved to make the enlargement of the church, together with the purchase of an organ, a "country charge." The result was *An Act for enlarging the Church in the City of Williamsburg, and purchasing an Organ to be placed therein.* This appointed a building committee, with John Blair again at its head, and allocated £300 for the extension of the building and £200 for the organ. The question of an organ for the church had been raised back in 1729, when Governor Gooch had written to England asking that the King or the Queen be approached about presenting one. "One of £200 value would be large enough," he added.[68] But by this time £200 was not nearly enough: an additional £100 . 7s. 6d was subscribed by private individuals and in 1755 the Assembly voted £120 . 7s. 8d. more, bringing the total amount spent to £420 . 15s. 2d. It was a celebrated organ in its day, and a traveler of 1783 describes Bruton as "fam'd for its noble Organ of one hundred tones."

In the summer of 1752 Blair used the pages of the *Virginia Gazette*[69] to announce two meetings at which the building committee would be prepared to award the contract for enlarging the church. (The first meeting was prevented by the intervention of other business.) We do not know whose tender was accepted. The addition took the form of a 22 ft. extension at the chancel end, making that part of the church east of the crossing precisely equal in size to the nave to the west of it. Late in 1755 an organ loft was ordered. This was erected at the west end of the nave,[70] as was normal in churches of the time.

PROTECTING THE MAGAZINE

While the organ loft was being installed in Bruton, there was building activity in a sterner cause over on Market Square. In 1754 Virginia had become involved in the French and Indian War and it was apparent that the Public Magazine, protected by

Figure 56. THE BARRADALL MONUMENT, BRUTON PARISH CHURCHYARD.
Edward Barradall died in 1743.

nothing more than the wooden fence or stockade for which Henry Cary, Jr., had been paid in 1722 (if indeed that still existed), stood "exposed to the designs of evil minded persons." To remedy this, in August 1755 a clause was inserted in *An Act for raising the Sum of Forty Thousand Pounds, for the protection of His Majesty's Subjects on the Frontiers of this Colony:*

> That Peyton Randolph, esquire, Carter Burwell, John Chiswell, Benjamin Waller, and James Power, gentlemen, or any three of them, be, and are hereby appointed directors, to treat and agree with workmen, to erect a high and strong brick wall, to inclose the said magazine, and to build a guard house convenient thereto.

This committee advertised twice in the *Virginia Gazette*, in September 1755, that it would meet intending workmen.[71] Once more we do not know who did the job, and the remaining pictorial evidence of the form of the Guard House, consisting of a half-view in one of L. J. Cranston's drawings of about 1858 (Fig. 81) is both too slight and too late to be of much value. However, military architecture was highly standardized in the eighteenth century, the normal constituents of a guard house being a room for the officers, another for the men, and a piazza or porch for the sentry. Thanks to this circumstance, the reconstructed Guard House of 1949 (Fig. 91), built on foundations which corresponded to what could only be the Guard House on the so-called "Frenchman's Map" [72] and adapting general formulae to local building practice, probably resembles the original structure closely enough.

VIII

1760-1780
Steeple, Courthouse,
and Hospital

E HAVE NOW reached the last twenty years of Williamsburg's life as capital of Virginia—a life which exceeded the three score years and ten
named by the psalmist as the human span by a mere decade, and one
from which the labor and sorrow noted by the same authority as the result of such
longevity was by no means absent. To the historian of England and her American
colonies, as indeed to the English-speaking world at large, 1760 is first of all the year
of the accession of George III, whose reign was to see the separation of those colonies
from the mother country. To the historian of Williamsburg, where so much that
preluded that separation was worked out, the year has an added significance: it was
on March 25, 1760, that young Thomas Jefferson went into residence at the College
of William and Mary. Thus began an association between the great statesman-
humanist and Williamsburg which was to last through the remainder of the town's
years as capital, reaching its apogee when in June 1779 Jefferson moved into the
Palace (as by then it was called even in the official records) as Governor of Virginia
—the last Governor to occupy the old house.

Jefferson's architectural activities at Williamsburg were not what they might
have been if the times had been more settled, or if the town had lived out the century as capital of the state. His most original projects remained on paper; his most
considerable work to be actually begun got no further than the foundations. For all
that, Jefferson's Williamsburg designs, executed or unexecuted, are so important in

relation both to the history of American architecture and to his personal development as an architect (not to mention the architectural history of Williamsburg) that they must have a chapter to themselves. In the present chapter, therefore, we have to treat of three structures with which Jefferson was not, as an architect, concerned—the steeple of Bruton Parish Church, the Courthouse, and the Public Hospital; in addition, the statue of Lord Botetourt claims our attention as a major embellishment of the Capitol. These works all fall within a period of five years, beginning in October 1768, when a building committee for the steeple was appointed, and ending in September 1773, when the Directors of the Public Hospital took possession of their completed building.

BRUTON STEEPLE

It was in December 1768 that the first step towards implementing the decision of October to build a steeple for Bruton was taken, with the insertion of an advertisement in Purdie and Dixon's *Virginia Gazette*:

> To be Let, on Wednesday the 4th of January next, if fair, otherwise next fair day,
>   The Building of a Steeple to Williamsburg Church. All Gentlemen that incline to undertake the same are desired to attend that day at the said church with proper plans, and just estimate to each plan.
>
>   John Pierce   } Church-Wardens [1]
>   William Eaton }

The contract was awarded to Benjamin Powell. According to McCabe[2] this was in September 1769. But he must have misread the vestry book; for in the previous month of August John Blair's daughter Anne sent a gay letter to her sister Martha in which she wrote:

> They are Building a steeple to our Church, the Door's for that reason, is open every day; and scarce an Evening as Dickey can tell you but we are entertained with the performance of Felton's Handel's Vi Vally's, &c, &c, &c, &c.[3]

Benjamin Powell was one of the more prominent tradesmen of Williamsburg. He is first met with in 1753, when he bought a lot southeast of the Capitol; in the deed he is described as a wheelwright.[4] In 1764–1765 he carried out extensive repairs at the Public Gaol, receiving over £388 for them, and he received nearly £80 for repairs to the Capitol late in 1769. In 1771 he undertook his largest building, the Public Hospital. In 1774 he was made a member of the Williamsburg Committee for the enforcement of the Continental Association, his fellow members including men of such high standing as Robert Carter Nicholas, Peyton Randolph and George

Figure 57. BRUTON PARISH CHURCH. The steeple from the churchyard.

Wythe.[5] In 1776 he was paid £590 . 2s . 10d. for work "on the Barracks & for the Troops in Williamsburg,"[6] and in the following year he again carried out repairs at the Capitol. In 1777–1778 he was City Marshal.

Under the terms of his agreement with the Vestry, Powell was to receive £410 for building the steeple and repairing the church; we are not told what the repairs comprised. As usual, the payments were to be made in installments—£150 in 1769, £130 in 1770, and £130 in 1771. He was also to have "the Old Bell, and the Materials of the old Steeple." In this context, "steeple" must mean bell-cote; for before 1769 Bruton certainly had nothing more. The old bell was presumably that salvaged from H. M. S. *Garland,* wrecked on the North Carolina coast, which Spotswood had given to the parish in 1711.[7] A new bell had recently been presented.

It is interesting to compare the plum-coloured brick of Powell's tower (Fig. 57) with the lighter brick of the body of the church. The design of the steeple as a whole belongs to the Wren-Gibbs tradition; with its repeated octagons it could have been inspired by the vastly more elaborate steeple of St. Michael's, Charleston, completed ten years before. It was the first steeple of its kind in Virginia, and not everyone approved. A correspondent asked in the *Virginia Gazette:*

> Would it not be more eligible, ye Brutonians, and would ye not with more cheerfulness pay the assessment, to have money raised upon you to mend the streets of Williamsburg, and the roads to the College and Capitol landing (which are very much in want of repair) than to be taxed to pay for a STEEPLE, which is much about as like one as the Emperour of Morocco's pigeon house, or the thing upon the Turkish mosques which they call a minaret, where a fellow knocks upon a piece of wood with a mallet to call the Mussulmen to prayers?[8]

In justice to this critic it must be granted that the upper part of the steeple seen from a distance can, owing to the curve of the roofs, remind one of the ventures into exoticism in the pattern-books of William Halfpenny and his like.

THE COURTHOUSE OF 1770

While Bruton steeple was being built, a much more sophisticated structure began to rise some 250 yards to the east. The Courthouse of 1770 (Fig. 61) is a building whose designer one would like to be able to name; but owing to the destruction of the James City County records in the Revolution one cannot. The first courthouse at Williamsburg had been built in 1715, near the junction of Francis and England Streets —approximately where the present James City County Courthouse stands. After the incorporation of the City of Williamsburg in 1722, the Mayor and Corporation

Figure 58. BRUTON PARISH CHURCH. General view from Duke of Gloucester Street.

shared this courthouse with the County, until in 1745, as we have seen, the Playhouse was altered to serve as a city courthouse and the Court of Hustings moved there. In 1764 the Corporation was empowered by Act of Assembly to levy taxes for building a new courthouse. Then on March 23, 1769 an advertisement appeared in the two rival *Virginia Gazettes:* [9]

WILLIAMSBURG, *March* 16, 1769.

THE COMMON HALL having this day determined to build a commodious BRICK COURT-HOUSE, in this city, and having appointed us to agree with an undertaker to build the same; we do hereby give notice that we shall meet at Mr. *Hay's* [the Raleigh Tavern], on *Tuesday* the 4th day of *April*, to let the building thereof. We are also appointed to dispose of the present Court-House, and the ground on which the same stands.

JAMES COCKE,
JAMES CARTER,
JOHN CARTER,
JOHN TAZEWELL.

N. B. The Plan of the above Court-House, may be seen at Mr. *Hay's* at any time.

There is nothing in this to show that the new Courthouse was to serve the county as well as the city. However, fourteen months later, in May 1770, both city and county petitioned the Assembly to alter the boundary so that the site on Market

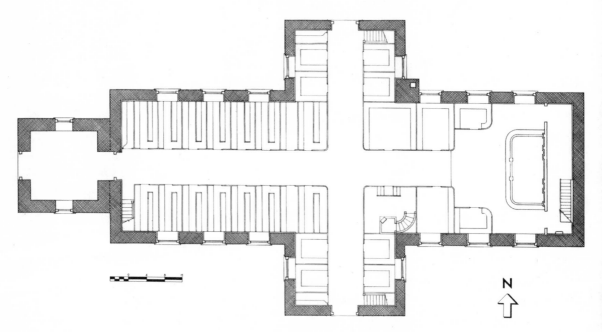

Figure 59. BRUTON PARISH CHURCH. Plan.

Figure 60. BRUTON PARISH CHURCH. South elevation.

Square might be taken into James City County, with the consequence that *An Act to annex Part of the County of York to the County of James City* became law at the end of June. By September the new building must have been ready for use, for the city sold the former Playhouse in that month; [10] the county clerk had given notice that the old James City County Courthouse would be sold "at the next court" in a July issue of the *Virginia Gazette*.[11]

It would be wrong, however, to say that the Courthouse was *finished* in 1770: in one important respect it never was finished. There can be no question at all but that its designer intended the portico on its south side to have four columns; it is almost

Figure 61. THE COURTHOUSE. Exterior from south.

certain that the columns were never erected. The type of entablature, with its pulvi-
nated frieze, indicates that they were to have been of the Ionic order, and it is reasonable to suppose that they were to have been of stone and imported from England.
The original steps came from England, as we know from what William Nelson,
President of the Council, wrote to a London merchant in 1772:

> I am particularly to thank you for procuring the Stone-steps for the Court-house
> in Williamsburg, which came in good Order, and are to the entire Satisfaction
> of those concerned in the Building.[12]

The T-plan, with the courtroom forming the upright of the T and rooms for justices and jury on either side, was a common form for courthouses in Virginia. Unfortunately we know nothing of the character of the James City Courthouse of 1715;
in 1706 the bricks of the Jamestown Statehouse were appropriated for a courthouse,
when one should be built, but there is no proof that they were used for it. In view of
the spread of the cruciform church through the colony from Williamsburg, it is
tempting to think that it may have been the prototype of the T-plan courthouse, and
perhaps at the same time the first courthouse to adopt the piazza of the Capitol.
However that may have been, in the 1730's Charles City, York, King William and
Hanover Counties all built T-plan courthouses, and Isle of Wight County followed
at mid-century with a two-story building of the same plan. In 1767 the T-plan was
employed for the Chowan County Courthouse at Edenton, North Carolina.

Thanks to the prostyle (though in execution astylar) portico, a feature possessed
by no previous courthouse in Virginia, the plan of the Courthouse of 1770 (Fig. 62)
may also be read as a Latin cross. The cross is formed from a rectangle, measuring 61
ft. from west to east and 52 ft. from north to south, by taking away squares of 16 ft.
from the north-west and north-east corners, and by taking away rectangles measuring
16 ft. by 8 ft. from the south-west and south-east corners. The internal planning follows Palladio's system of proportion, as demonstrated—or rather, perhaps, implied—
in his Book II.[13] The main divisions are formed of three 3 : 2 rectangles and a square
on the longer side of one of them. To appreciate this, one should continue the line of
the north walls of the wings containing the jury rooms across the courtroom. It will
be found that the part of the courtroom to the south of this line is a square, while
the part to the north is a rectangle of the same size and shape as the interior of the
wings. (It seems highly probable that the division was actually expressed in the
building as originally furnished, by a barrier separating the court proper from the
public space). The ceiling height is equal to the length of the shorter side of this rec-

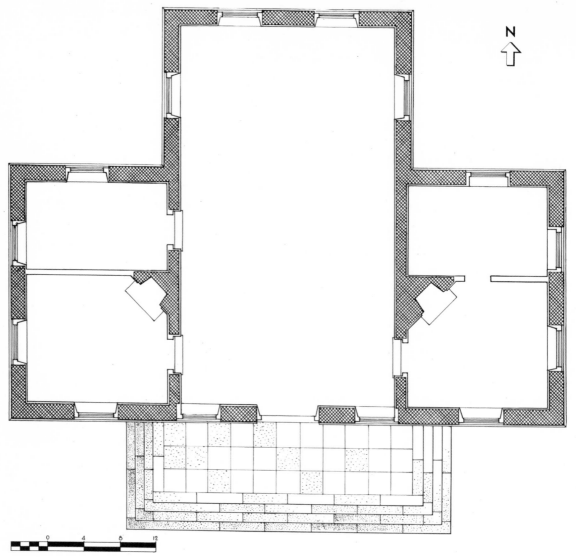

Figure 62. THE COURTHOUSE. Plan.

tangle, so that the same ratios are repeated in the internal elevations of the court-room—which some may consider the most nobly proportioned room in Williams-burg.

Turning to the external elevations, we find that these are regulated by the over-all dimensions of the plan. For instance, if we take the south elevation (Fig. 63) we find that the height to the weathervane from the 1770 grade of Market Square (about 6 in. lower than the present grade) is equal to the total length of the build-

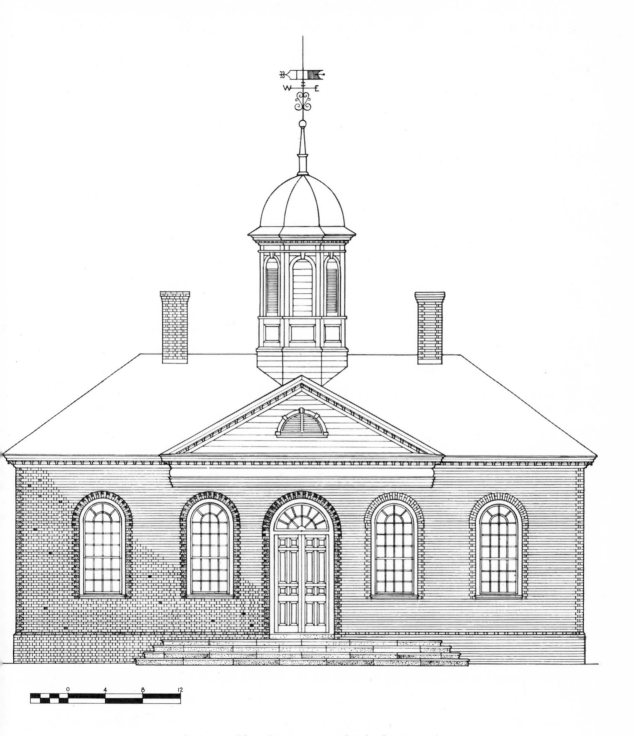

Figure 63. THE COURTHOUSE. South elevation.

ing, and that the diagonals of a square constructed on the length of the building as base intersect at the apex of the pediment of the portico. We may then proceed to construct a series of three more squares upon the original grade level, letting the median line of the elevation bisect each square perpendicularly; the base of the first square to be half the length of the diagonal of the outermost square, the base of the second to be half the diagonal of the first, and the base of the third to be half the diagonal of the second—that is to say, a series of squares each of which is of half the area of the previous one. We find that these three squares determine, respectively, the height from the ground of the architrave of the cupola, the width as well as the height of the pediment, and the height of the soffit of the main cornice. Continuing the series, we find that the fourth square determines the height from the ground of the springing of the window arches or, if we raise the base to the level of the water table, the distance between that feature and the architrave of the portico; the fifth gives the height of the doorway to the top of the lintel and the height of the windows from the sill to the crown of the arch. We may then lay over the elevation the rectangle of 61 ft. by 52 ft., still using the original grade as base. This gives us the height to the crown of the cupola, while if we draw the diagonals of the rectangle we find that they bisect the sills of the outer windows and the intradoses of the arches of the inner windows and also cut the chimney caps at their outermost angles. The designer of the Courthouse had evidently acted upon the principle enunciated by Robert Morris in his *Lectures on Architecture, Consisting of Rules Founded upon Harmonick and Arithmetical Proportions in Building*:

> In delineating the Plan or Elevation of a Building, the Out-line is to be first form'd . . . it is from thence the internal Parts, as well as the *ornamenting* and *disposing* the proper Voids, and Decoration of the Front, are to be regulated.

And it may be noted that Morris's book, published in London in 1734–1736 reached Williamsburg at least as early as 1751, when it was advertised for sale in the *Virginia Gazette* under the title of *Harmonic Architecture*.[14]

Stylistically, the Courthouse may be described as Early Georgian. Its octagonal cupola is of a form employed throughout Britain in the reigns of the first two Georges; since there is evidence that some of the engravings subsequently collected into the volume called *Vitruvius Scoticus* were known in Virginia by the time the Courthouse was built, it is worth remark that several rather similar cupolas are to be seen in designs of William Adam illustrated in that collection.[15] A contemporary public building in England would probably have embodied some awareness of the

new architectural ideals of William Adam's more famous sons, Robert and James;
but these were not to affect any American building to a noticeable degree until the
1780's. As for the Courthouse's influence on architecture in Virginia, this was not
great. At least it is safe to say that it was the fore-runner rather than the fore-father
of the many porticoed courthouses erected in the state in the first half of the nineteenth century; for the line doubtless sprang from Jefferson's Capitol at Richmond.
Jefferson himself, in his *Notes on the State of Virginia*, dismisses it without individual mention among the "churches and courthouses in which no attempts are made at
elegance."

We do not know precisely how the interior of the Courthouse was furnished; nor
has the interior of any other colonial courthouse in Virginia survived. We do, however, have a specification dating from 1740 for Lancaster County Courthouse, and
this lists what may be presumed to have been standard courthouse furnishings in
the colony and indicates their arrangement:

> The floor to be flaged to the outer barr & planked within, the Justices' bench
> to be neatly railed & ballastered and raised from the floor three foot and to be
> divided Wainscot fashion above & below into twelve seats besides the Chair
> A seat for the Jury under the Justices on the lower floor A Clark's Table & Chair
> also a Chair for the King's attorney A seat for the sherif and another for his
> deputy and two barrs at least benches to each of them and one Gate neatly
> railed . . . [In the jury room] a Table for the use of the Jurymen.[16]

In addition, there are records of repairs done at the York County Courthouse after
the Revolution. These mention "a Circuling Seat for the Jury to Set on," a "Bal-
luster Rail in a Circule," a "Righting Desk at the Bar 15 feet & half Long," "Two
boxes for the Sherifs to Sett in wainscoted with three Steps to Each," a lawyers'
bench, and "the Chair wainscotted 7 feet High 4 feet wide two pilasters Dentle
Cornish." [17]

"A HOSPITAL . . . FOR PERSONS OF DISORDERED MINDS"

The first public mention of the need for "a hospital at Williamsburg for persons
of disordered minds" was made in an address to the Burgesses by Governor Fauquier,
himself the son of a physician, in November 1766:

> It is expedient I should also recommend to your Consideration and Humanity
> a poor unhappy set of People who are deprived of their Senses and wander
> about the Country, terrifying the Rest of their Fellow Creatures. A legal Con-
> finement, and proper Provision, ought to be appointed for these miserable Ob-

jects, who cannot help themselves. Every civilized Country has an Hospital for these People, where they are confined, maintained and attended by able Physicians, to endeavour to restore to them their lost Reason.

The recommendation did not go unheeded: a couple of weeks later the Burgesses passed a resolution "that an Hospital be erected for the Reception of Persons who are so unhappy as to be deprived of their reason," and ordered the appropriate committee to prepare a Bill. But the Bill was not forthcoming, and Fauquier raised the matter again the following April. Still nothing happened, and it was not until November 1769 that a bill "to make Provision for the Support and Maintenance of Ideots, Lunatics, and other Persons of unsound Minds" was actually drawn up.

In the meantime the new Governor, Lord Botetourt, had four lunatics committed to the Pennsylvania Hospital at Philadelphia, to be kept there until Virginia could provide accommodation more suitable for them and their like than the Public Gaol. The Pennsylvania Hospital, which had been begun to the design of Samuel Rhoads in 1755, was not exclusively for the insane, as the Williamsburg hospital was to be. But it did have one floor—the basement—with cells specially designed for them, and that was something unique in British America. So when the Directors of the Hospital for the Reception of Idiots, Lunatics, and Persons of Insane Mind (which from now on we shall call the Public Hospital) came to choosing an architect for the new building, it was natural that they should look to Philadelphia for him. And it was natural that having done so they should choose Robert Smith, the most successful master-builder of that great city.

Smith was a man (some say a Scotsman) of forty-seven or forty-eight when he was asked for a design for the Public Hospital.[18] He was a carpenter by trade, and his first recorded work would seem to be the construction in 1752–1754—perhaps to his own design—of the exceedingly Gibbsian steeple of Christ Church, Philadelphia. In 1753 he designed Nassau Hall at Princeton; in 1758 he built St. Peter's Church, Philadelphia; in 1761 he designed Pennsylvania "New College," and in 1766 the Third Presbyterian Church, both in Philadelphia; in 1766–1767 he served (it is said) as master carpenter for the Philadelphia "Bettering House," which was a kind of almshouse-cum-workhouse, and in the latter year he was architect of the Zion Lutheran Church in Philadelphia, which Ebenezer Hazard, whose description of the Capitol we have considered, called the "largest and finest in North America." In 1768 he supplied the plans for the building for which he is generally remembered, Carpenters' Hall in Philadelphia.

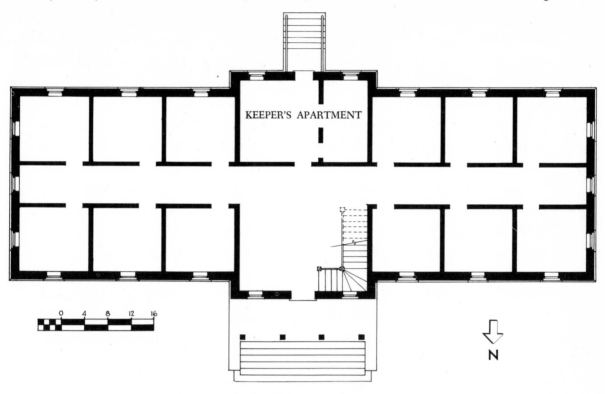

KEEPER'S APARTMENT

Figure 64. THE PUBLIC HOSPITAL. Restoration of the plan,
based on Robert Smith's description and Benjamin Powell's agreement,
by A. Lawrence Kocher and Howard Dearstyne.

Owing to the loss of the first eight pages of the minutes of the Public Hospital
Directors' meetings, we have no details of the circumstances of Smith's appointment. We do, however, have the "description" that he sent to Williamsburg with
his drawings; and this valuable document, when read in conjunction with the builder's agreement, tells us as much about the plan (Fig. 64) and the construction of this
long destroyed building as anyone could fairly ask to know.

For a complete transcript of this description, which bears the date April 9, 1770,
the reader is referred to Appendix III. It will be noticed that Smith specifies brick
or stone as alternatives for the cellar and basement walls, going so far as to suggest
hewn stone for the latter. Clearly he did not know Tidewater Virginia; and indeed
it is more than likely that he never visited Williamsburg at all. The safety measures
to which a large part of the report is given up were no doubt the fruits of study of
the Pennsylvania Hospital.

The Act establishing the Hospital was passed in June, 1770—a couple of months after Smith's design had been sent. The sum of £1,200 was voted for the site and the building. In August the building committee appointed by the Directors advertised in the *Virginia Gazette* that it had agreed on a plan for the building and was "ready to treat with all Undertakers, who may incline to engage in the Work." [19]

Benjamin Powell was awarded the contract. For £1,070 he was to "furnish all the materials . . . except the Grates and such other things as are usually imported from England and . . . finish and compleat the whole in a neat strong and workmanlike manner agreable to the plan and explanation thereof . . . within two years." The articles of agreement between him and the building committee are printed in full in Appendix IV. As a carpenter, he had to sublet the brickwork to another tradesmen. His choice was Samuel Spurr, whom we saw building the churchyard wall and who at this time was living next door to Benjamin Powell's nephew Seymour, who had inherited the house built by Benjamin on the Yorktown road lot that he had purchased in 1753 and sold to Seymour's father in 1760.[20] On October 3, 1771 the following advertisement appeared over Samuel Spurr's name in the *Virginia Gazette*:

> The Subscriber will give good Wages, and Accommodations, to two or three Journey-men BRICKLAYERS, for the remaining Part of the Season, to work upon the Hospital building in this City. Plenty of Bricks and Lime is ready, so there will be no Delay.[21]

In the matter of brickwork the ideas of Philadelphia and Williamsburg differed, for in the fall of this same year, 1771, the Directors ordered that the walls should be increased in thickness by half a brick.[22]

As usual, the funds first voted for the building proved to be insufficient. In February 1772 the Directors presented a memorial to the House of Burgesses in which they stated that they had thought of making up the difference by subscription but conceived that such a course might be deemed improper; the cost of the ground and building would amount to about £1,600, while it would be necessary to enclose a garden and yards for patients to walk and take the air in, to employ a Keeper and Matron and to meet other incidental charges not yet provided for. (The original Act had allowed £25 per annum for each patient.) At this the Burgesses voted a further £800. The minutes of the Court of Directors show that £188 odd had been spent on imported materials by mid-1772; [23] this did not include the stone steps from England, the importation of which was ordered in May 1773.[24] On September 14, 1773

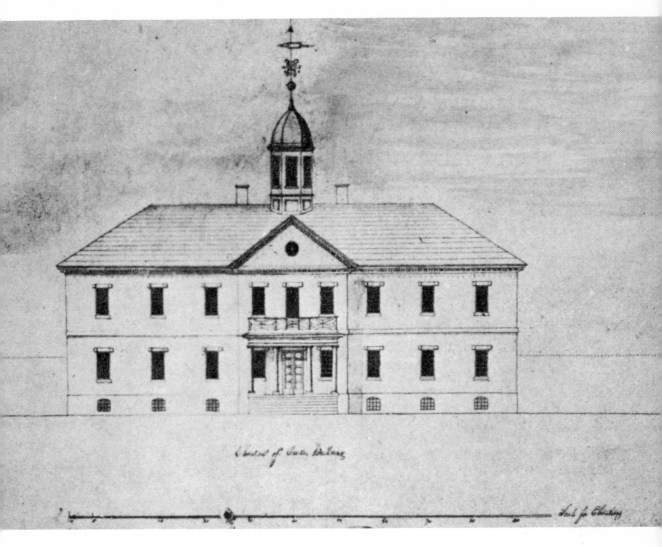

Figure 65. THE PUBLIC HOSPITAL. A drawing of *circa* 1825.

the President of the Court of Directors called a meeting and announced that he was informed that the Hospital was completed. "Whereupon the Court proceeded to examine the said Hospital, and finding it finished according to Agreement, the same was received of Benjamin Powell the Undertaker."

THE PUBLIC HOSPITAL IN HISTORY

The most famous hospital for the insane in the eighteenth century was Bethlem Hospital, or Bedlam, in Moorfields, London, which had been built to the designs of Robert Hooke in 1674–1676. The Pennsylvania Hospital, both as designed in 1751 and as completed in an Adamesque style in the first decade of the nineteenth century, was with its terminal pavilions surmounted by cupolas and its raised centre distinctly reminiscent of Hooke's building.[25] The Public Hospital at Williamsburg, besides being smaller, was much simpler, with the "neat Pediment" and "neat Mundelian Cornice" supplying the only touches of architectural ceremony. There is no evidence that it originally had a cupola, while there being no mention of such a feature either in Smith's description or in Powell's agreement is presumptive evidence that it did not. The earliest known drawing of the Hospital, in which it has a cupola and is supported by two ancillary structures, shows a state to which it was brought between 1821 and 1830.[26] (Fig. 65)

Smith's experience in designing the Public Hospital must have been useful to him when, in 1773, he came to design his next (and apparently his last) considerable public building. This was the Walnut Street Prison in Philadelphia, a building much admired in its day both for its plan and for its fire-proof construction. That a prison and a lunatic asylum should resemble each other so closely is not surprising in view of the acceptance in the eighteenth century of what has been called "the moral treatment of insanity." As Granville L. Jones, from whose account of the founding of the Hospital I take the phrase, has put it: "There was considerable feeling, as a matter of fact, that there was little difference between the punitive confinement of the criminal and the preventive confinement of the insane." [27] Dr. Jones continues— and his words may be borrowed for their assessment of the significance of the Public Hospital at Williamsburg in medical history—as follows:

> The 'able physicians' referred to by Governor Fauquier were few and far between and his proposal for a 'hospital' was largely an expression of his idealism and hope. . . . The attending physicians in Williamsburg were well trained and highly skilled for their times and were no doubt thoughtful, sincere and sympathetic, but from the sources available we cannot assume anything but the customary practice of the day. The important thing is the philosophy of its founding. The name given it and the character of the governing board, the administrator, and the attending physicians all point to a vision and a hope for the future.

THE BOTETOURT STATUE

Norborne Berkeley, Baron de Botetourt, died on October 15, 1770, aged 58. He had been Governor for just under two years, but that had been long enough for his administrative ability, which was happily supported by a talent for show and "a becoming and proper Degree of Affability," to gain him a special place in the affections of the Virginian gentry. "The best of Governours and the best of men," wrote his obituarist in Purdie and Dixon's *Virginia Gazette,* and many agreed. Although more than eight months were to pass before the official tributes were paid in the Assembly, one detects in them an uncommon note of sincerity. And on July 11, 1771, the Burgesses took an unprecedented step, when they resolved, *nemine contradicente,*

> That an elegant Statue of his late excellency the Right Honourable Norborne, Baron de Botetourt be erected in Marble at the Public Expence, with proper Inscriptions, expressing the grateful Sense this House entertains of his Lordship's prudent and Wise Administration, and their great Solicitude to perpetuate, as far as they are able, the Remembrance of those many public and social Virtues which adorn his illustrious Character . . .

A committee of six, headed by the President of the Council, William Nelson, was appointed to direct the obtaining of the statue from England, and it was resolved that the Treasurer was to pay for it out of public funds, without any limit being set upon the price.

The committee forthwith informed Botetourt's nephew and executor, the fifth Duke of Beaufort, of the Assembly's intention. In thanking them, the Duke promised to "give their Agent in England all the Assistance in [his] power to render their wishes effectual that the Statue may be like," but added that he feared

> it must be in some measure imperfect as there is no Portrait of Lord Botetourt that has been taken within the last five and Twenty or Thirty Years, but there is a Medal in Wax that is reckon'd tolerably like that shall be communicated to the person imploy'd by the Assembly.[28]

The person employed was John Norton, a London merchant who had set up a branch under his son at Yorktown; the medallion, as later correspondence reveals, was the work of Isaac Gosset (1713–1799), an artist of Huguenot descent who modelled portraits, in a wax composition invented by himself, of pretty well everyone of importance in England between 1750 and 1780.[29] Early in March 1722 Norton showed the Duke a drawing for the statue, and on March 10 he wrote to his son:

> I have fixed on an Artist to execute the Statue for L. Bottetourt since the Duke of Beaufort came to Town, his name is Havard and lives in Picadilly, he's to be finished in 12 months completely with Iron Rails packages &ca & to be put on ship for £700 I shall send the Design to Mr. Nicholas framed pr Capt. Robertson, also 4 Medallions done by Gossette an exceed'g good likeness of L. Bottetourt wch I have bought and send as presents, one for Mr. President Nelson, 1 for the Treasurer, 1 for the Speaker, and 1 for yourSelf.[30]

"Havard" was Richard Hayward, whose signature is to be read on the base of the statue. Born in Warwickshire in 1728, he had gone to Rome in 1753, remaining there about a year. Church monuments were doubtless the mainstay of his practice, as they were of the practices of most English sculptors of the time; Gunnis lists thirteen by him, including six in Westminster Abbey. He also supplied chimney-pieces, including one for Kedleston, six for Woburn Abbey, and a number for Somerset House.[31]

When the drawing reached Williamsburg there was some discussion of the inscription, and it was decided that the word Peace should be omitted as exceptionable. (Why anyone should have objected to it does not appear.) Alternative designs for the pedestal were offered; Robert Carter Nicholas told Norton: "We highly approve either of the Designs for the back Front but, of the two, should prefer that which has the Vine or Branch running up the inner Edge as we think it fills up better & makes the figure more compleat."[32] In August 1772 Norton was able to tell his son:

> The Statue of Lord Bottentourt is in forwardness, I carried Mrs. Horrocks to see it, she thinks with me, there will be a great resemblance of His Person, the famous Gossett, who did the small pieces I sent over, has been kind enough to give me his Assistance in that respect, the artist has luckily hit on a Block of fine Marble and 'tis the general Opinion of those who have seen the Figure, that it will be well perform'd.[33]

Seven months, later, in March 1773, he reported:

> Ld. Botetourts Statue is on board the *Virginia* 'tis much admir'd here by all the Curious and Artists, hope it will please in Virga by many Friends advice, I have been induc'd to send a person over to set it up, lest any accident shou'd happen to it, of which the Statuary seem'd very apprehensive, and he spar'd me one of his Masons to go over, tho' it was very inconvenient to him.[34]

Norton's hopes for the favourable reception of the statue in the colony, where it arrived safe after a two months voyage, were not disappointed. "It is a Masterly piece of Work," wrote Nicholas, "tho' the likeness is not so striking as of the Medallion,"[35] and again: "The Statue is universally admired."[36] John Hirst, the mason who accompanied it and set it up in the piazza of the Capitol by early June, was if possible admired even more. "Every Gentleman, whom I have conversed with, highly approves of your sending him over; indeed I don't know what we should have done without such a Man. He has given entire Satisfaction." Understandably enough, "being very fearful of the Effects of our hot Weather, & withall anxious to re-

Figure 66. THE BOTETOURT STATUE. Richard Hayward, sculptor. Set up in the Capitol in 1773, now at the College.

Figure 67. THE BOTETOURT STATUE.
Relief of Britannia and Virginia on pedestal.

turn to his Family," he stayed little more than a month. His fee was increased from the £35 originally agreed upon to £50.[37]

Botetourt's was the third public statue to be set up by order of Assembly in the American colonies, and the first and last to commemorate a royal governor (Fig. 66). The two earlier statues were both of the elder Pitt, and were voted in 1766 by the Assemblies of South Carolina and New York out of gratitude for Pitt's part in the repeal of the Stamp Act; both were the work of Joseph Wilton and were set up in Charleston and New York City in 1770. (The Charlestonians greeted theirs with a degree of enthusiasm that can hardly be mustered up for effigies of the dead, however beloved: "it was landed amidst a vast concourse of inhabitants . . . who received it with cheers and, preceded by music, drew it by hand to the place where it was to rest until the pedestal for it was raised.") [38] Like Hayward's Botetourt, Wilton's Pitt was a standing figure. But he was clothed in classical toga, as was thought most suitable for an orator, whereas Botetourt wears court dress of the time. Botetourt's pose is strikingly similar to that of Michael Rysbrack's Sir Hans Sloane, set up in the Physic Garden at Chelsea *circa* 1737.[39] Vandalism and long exposure to the weather has made it impossible to evaluate "the likeness" today. However, we can still—especially if we make a mental restoration of the right hand holding a rolled parchment—admire the balance of the figure as a whole, and the way in which Hayward, with Gosset's help, has managed to convey an impression of dignity, both official and personal, tempered by that "becoming and proper Degree of Affability": it might be a portrait by Sir Joshua Reynolds translated into marble. The pedestal, which bears inscriptions on three sides, together with the arms of Virginia on the front, and on the back a relief showing Britannia and Virginia meeting over an altar inscribed CONCORDIA (Fig. 67), has in its mouldings the kind of rich delicacy that we associate with the brothers Adam. Yet it would probably be wrong to ascribe its character to their influence. Hayward was in Rome just before Robert Adam, and there he would have discovered the archaeological etchings of Piranesi, in which enrichments of this kind were first given prominence, for himself.

IX

Jefferson at Williamsburg

THE PALACE had been left by the works of the early 'fifties in pretty good shape. At least that is a deduction that may be made from the warrants for repairs in the twelve or thirteen years following their completion.[1] In 1755, as we saw, the total amount paid under this head was £159 . 17s. 5d. In 1756 it dropped to £86 . 13s. 6d., in 1757 to a mere £20 . 10s, and during the accounting period October 25, 1757—April 25, 1758 only £10 worth of work was done. For the next six months of 1758 the figure was £162 . 15s. 2d. Francis Fauquier had taken over the administration of the colony on June 7; the increase is what one would expect about the time of the arrival of a new Governor, while the small amounts spent during the later years of Robert Dinwiddie's administration may be partly accounted for by his preoccupation with the French and Indian War. In 1759–1762 the annual average was just over £144; for 1763 the record is incomplete; in 1764 the relatively large sum of £274 . 3s. 5d. was spent; for 1765 and 1766 the records are missing. For the period April—October 1767 the figure was £57 . 10s. Then there is a re-markable rise, treasury warrants "for repairs to the Governor's House" being issued at meetings of the Council during the next two and a half years as follows:

May 1768	£382 . 11s. 0d.
November 1768	£ 91 . 12s. 0d.
November 1769	£505 . 2s. 7d.
May 1770	£312 . 17s. 9d.
	£1292 . 3s. 4d.

And that, unfortunately, is as far as the available records take us.

Surely it was no coincidence that this costly program of "repairs" was embarked upon less than ten months after William Tryon, Governor of North Carolina, and his architect-builder John Hawks signed the contract for the other colonial Palace, at New Bern.[2] It was intended that Tryon's Palace should "exceed for Magnifi-

172

cence & architecture any edifice on the continent." [3] Virginia could hardly ignore such a challenge from her upstart neighbor to the south, and we may suspect that the works carried out at the Williamsburg Palace between October 1767 and May 1770 included rather more than strictly necessary structural repairs, especially when we take Botetourt's tastes into account.[4] Nevertheless, such repairs were doubtless carried out, and it is reasonable to suppose that if the hatching on Thomas Jefferson's measured plan of the Palace (discussed in Chapter IV) means anything at all it must show what was rebuilt at this time. This is not to say that Jefferson was directly concerned with the work; we shall see shortly that the drawing was not even contemporary with it. But he would have been an observant spectator. In 1767 he was already planning his own house, his enthusiasm for architecture having been aroused by contact with the connoisseur Dr. John Morgan in Philadelphia the previous year,[5] if not even earlier by conversation at the Palace dinners to which Fauquier (who in London had been a tenant of no less an architect than James Gibbs [6]) so often invited him.

THE PALACE INTERIOR AS JEFFERSON KNEW IT

The inventory of the contents of the Palace taken after Botetourt's death makes it possible to name the various rooms for what they were in 1770, though it should be remembered that their functions had undoubtedly changed from time to time as the requirements of different Governors varied. To the right of the entrance hall as one came in was the *front parlour*, and to the left the *pantry*; the large north-east room on the ground floor was the *dining room*, under the stairs was a *powder room*, and between that and the pantry the *little middle room*, through which the food passed on the way from the outside kitchen to the dining room (Fig. 69). On the second floor the north-east and south-east rooms are called in the inventory the *chamber over the dining room* and the *chamber over the front parlour*; over the hall was the *middle room*, the south-west room was *his Lordship's bed chamber*, the north-west the *library*. The inventory then lists the contents of four *store rooms*. These were clearly in the roof of the ball-room wing, because the inventory goes on to mention in the roof of the main block two *closets*, a *garret room over his Lordship's bed chamber*, a *room over the study* (or library), and a *garret room over the front parlour*. Then we descend to the *rum cellar, stone cellar, cook's cellar, bin cellar, vault, cider cellar, strong beer cellar*, and *Maderia and cheese store*—an impressive particularization.

While the inventory lists the standing furniture in addition to Botetourt's per-

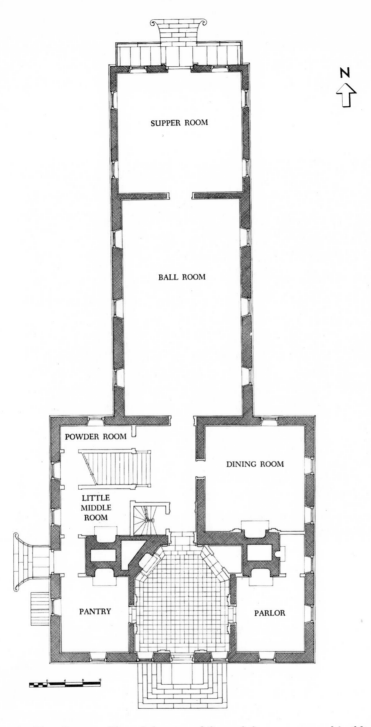

SUPPER ROOM

BALL ROOM

POWDER ROOM

DINING ROOM

LITTLE
MIDDLE
ROOM

PANTRY

PARLOR

Figure 69. THE PALACE. Plan of the ground floor of the reconstructed building.

Figure 70. THE PALACE. Mantelpiece, restored from original fragments, in the front parlour.

sonal belongings, it naturally does not tell us anything about what is more the concern of the architectural historian, the character of the interior trim and fixtures. It does contain an item that shows that the still fairly new fashion of wall paper was followed in the supper room,[7] and an upholsterer's account shows that the ball room was papered too;[8] a letter written in 1771 adds the information that Botetourt "had hung a room with plain blue paper & border'd it with a narrow stripe of gilt Leather."[9] When the foundations were excavated many Dutch tiles were found, together with fragments of mantelpieces of veined and coloured marbles and two nearly complete tablets of statuary such as commonly formed the central feature of mantel friezes. One of these last is carved with a swag of fruit and flowers in high relief, the other with deer in a landscape. After the mantelpiece ornamented with the latter had been reconstructed on the evidence of the surviving fragments (Fig. 70), it was noticed that it bore a close resemblance to a mantelpiece installed in the course of the third quarter of the eighteenth century at Eltham Lodge, Kent.[10]

JEFFERSON'S DESIGNS FOR REMODELLING THE PALACE

In his *Notes on the State of Virginia* Jefferson wrote: "The Palace is not handsome without: but it is spacious and commodious within, is prettily situated, and, with the grounds annexed to it, is capable of being made an elegant seat." And his interest in its architectural potentialities is further attested by several studies for remodelling it, to which we must now turn.[11]

The first two, Figs. 71 and 72, are in the form of rough sketch plans, back to back on tracing paper and consequently not easy to read in reproduction. They adumbrate a scheme for greatly increasing the size of the building by building a second *corps de logis* of the same dimensions as the original building; the ballroom (or, in the revised version in Fig. 72, about half of it) becomes a central hall linking the two blocks, with a columned loggia on either side. This scheme may owe something to the Capitol or Tuckahoe, but surely more to the plan of the Villa Thieni at Cicogna, as given by Palladio in his second Book. In both schemes the stairs are brought forward into the southern portion of the old block, but neither of the two different arrangements proposed for them is very intelligible.

The ballroom wing does not appear in any of the other three plans, while the execution of one of them would inevitably have involved its demolition. Two of these plans, Figs. 73 and 74, are carefully drawn and to scale. In each the hall becomes a complete octagon with two fireplaces. In Fig. 73 the octagon is obtained by building a three-sided bay out from the entrance front, and therefore is deeper than it is wide; passages provide circulation around its farther sides, and additional staircases are cut through the great chimney-stacks. In Fig. 74 the opposite method is employed for forming the octagon, which is a regular one with equal sides: the central portion of the front is left standing and the front walls of the smaller rooms

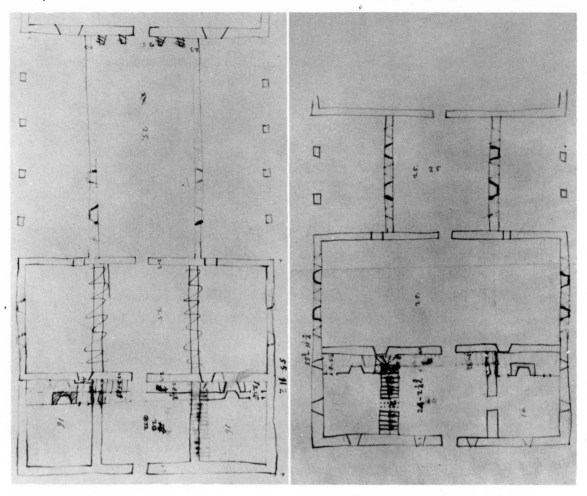

Figure 71. THE PALACE.
Design for remodelling, by Thomas Jefferson.

Figure 72. THE PALACE.
Design by Thomas Jefferson on the back of that in *Figure 71.*

flanking the hall are moved back about six feet. Inside, in order to preserve the square
proportions of these two rooms, the chimneys are reduced in size and the partitions
moved back the same distance; the stairs are moved into the passage between the hall
and the garden front. While reducing the total area of the ground plan, this scheme
increases the actual living space by providing a third 16 ft.-square room in the north-
west corner of the house in place of the "little middle room" (as the Botetourt inventory calls it) south of the stairs in the house as it stood.

The remaining plan, Fig. 75, was probably drawn before those in Figs. 73 and 74. There is an octagon of the same dimensions as that in Fig. 73, but internal change is kept to a minimum. Outside the walls, on the other hand, a remarkable and indeed epoch-making novelty is proposed. Along the north front are eight columns, with the notation "Pediment front whole width of roof." And the south front is treated in the same way, except that there is an extra column between each angle column and the walls of the house—an arrangement necessitated by the projection of the octagon.

Had this design been executed, Williamsburg would have gained the first temple-form house of the Neo-Classical movement, whose leaders sought to avoid what they regarded as the impurities of Palladianism and the Baroque by returning for inspiration direct to the fountainhead of classical antiquity. In England the garden building in the form of a temple had been a commonplace for half a century and more, but that is by no means the same thing; churches too, following the examples of St. Paul's, Covent Garden, and St. Martin-in-the-Fields, had sometimes been given the form, which in their case had an obvious propriety. In America the Redwood Library at Newport, Rhode Island, built to the design of Peter Harrison in 1748–1750, is an adaptation of the form; but it is an adaptation derived from Palladio, who used the theme of interpenetrating temple fronts in his Venetian churches, and therefore not Neo-Classical in the strict sense. For a dwelling house the pure temple form had been used neither in America nor anywhere in eighteenth-century Europe. And the amphiprostyle building—that is, the building with a portico at either end—was to remain rare even when in the nineteenth century the temple-form house, first realized in actual bricks and mortar by Jefferson at the University of Virginia, became a widespread American type.

The historical importance of this design makes its correct dating highly desirable. Kimball first assigned all Jefferson's Palace drawings to 1779; subsequently he thought that with the possible exception of the measured plan they had been made for Lord Dunmore in 1771 or 1772.[12] Strangely enough, in view of his use of the evidence of paper and watermarks in dating other drawings by Jefferson, he overlooked the presence of a watermark of the type called *cardinal* in the paper of the amphiprostyle design. The measured plan is on the same paper;[13] and so is a letter from Jefferson to Richard Henry Lee dated January 2, 1780.[14] This last is a valuable piece of evidence. Cardinal was a paper of French origin,[15] by no means in general use in the colonies; Jefferson may well have obtained a supply direct from·a French

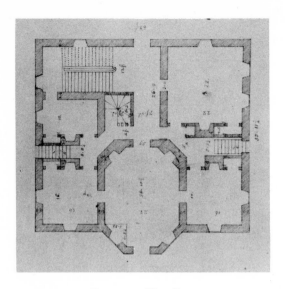

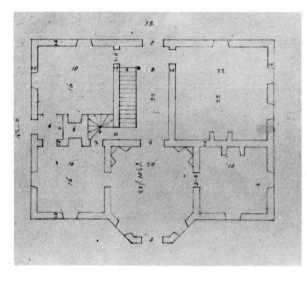

Figure 73. THE PALACE.
Design for remodelling, by Thomas Jefferson,
in which a projecting bay is added to the south front.

Figure 74. THE PALACE.
Design for remodelling, by Thomas Jefferson,
in which the south wall is moved back.

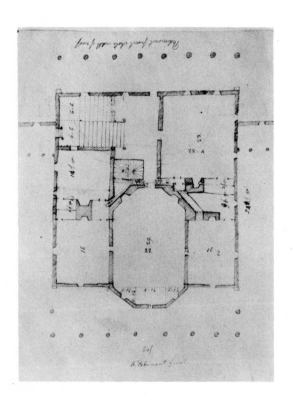

Figure 75. THE PALACE.
Design for remodelling, by Thomas Jefferson,
with two porticos.

source.[16] That he used it for a letter in 1780 strongly suggests that Kimball's first dating of the drawings was the nearer the mark. The argument that Jefferson would not plan a remodelling of the Palace after the introduction, in June 1779, of the bill for removing the capital to Richmond is not a cogent one. His *Notes on the State of Virginia,* containing the statement that the Palace was "capable of being made an elegant seat," was written in 1780–1781, after the actual removal. The character of the more fully thought out designs, with the removal of the ballroom wing, accords well enough with the supposition that they were essays in the conversion of the building into a private house. In that case they must have been made between June 1779 and December 1781 (when the Palace burned). Corroborative evidence for assigning them to this period is supplied by two other designs—an early plan for the Governor's House at Richmond and an amphiprostyle scheme for the new Capitol there. When Jefferson made these, in 1780–1783,[17] the Palace projects were surely still fresh in his mind.

AN EXTENSION AT THE COLLEGE

At the College, nearly forty years had followed the building of the President's House without any major work being undertaken. Then on September 3, 1772 the following advertisement appeared in Purdie and Dixon's *Virginia Gazette:*

> The Visitors and Governors of the College intending to make an additional Building to the College, have directed us, who are appointed a Committee for that Purpose, to procure an exact Estimate of the Expense thereof, to be laid before them at their next Meeting. Notice is therefore given, to all Persons willing to undertake this Work, that a Plan thereof is lodged with Mr. *Matthew Davenport,* who will be ready at all Times to show the same, and to whom they are desired to send their Estimates and Proposals, sealed up, on or before the first Day of *October* next.
>
> > DUNMORE
> > PEYTON RANDOLPH
> > RO. C. NICHOLAS
> > LEWIS BURWELL
> > JOHN BLAIR

This plan, or at least a copy of it (Fig. 36), survives.[18] Jefferson was its author, and it is inscribed in his hand: "Plan for an addition to the College of William and Mary drawn at the request of Ld. Dunmore." John Murray, Earl of Dunmore, the last of the Royal Governors, had arrived in Virginia in August 1771; Jefferson had been at Williamsburg for the Assembly from October until mid-December that year, and again in April and May 1772.

Jefferson's proposals would have completed the main building of the College as a closed quadrangle. This, as we know, it was to have been from the beginning, had the funds allowed. But whereas the building as originally designed would have been square on plan, Jefferson proposed to complete it as a rectangle with the east-west axis much the longer. The arcaded loggia or "piazza" was to have been continued around all four sides of the court. (How this was to have been done without interfering with the windows of the chapel and the hall is not clear.) Next to the chapel and hall were to have been spacious vestibules, with doors both on the outside and towards the court; beyond these the plan shows two classrooms aside, and at the western end a range of building of the same dimensions as the old range to the east. On the ground floor—and it may perhaps be assumed on the upper floors too—this west range was to contain rooms for the masters or students, arranged in pairs or "sets," with a large room to the west and a smaller one towards the piazza or corridor, every room being provided with an outside door in addition to that communicating with its neighbour to the east or west. (The four rooms at either end could have been used as a unit, an *appartement* on the French model.) The scheme differs fundamentally from that employed in the Colleges of Oxford and Cambridge, and proposed for Codrington College in Barbados, in its adoption of corridor access instead of separate staircases.

This west range, as archaeological excavation has shown, was the only part of Jefferson's design upon which a beginning was made. John Saunders, a carpenter who had built stables for the President of the College in 1761,[19] was awarded the contract, as we know from a reference to him as "the Undertaker" in the faculty minutes of June 1776. By that time building work had come to a stop; the subject of the minute in which Saunders is named was a distribution among the faculty of nails that had been imported for the new building, and which no doubt were included in John Norton's bill for £205 odd, appearing in the bursar's book under the heading "New Building" and paid in November 1774. In 1777 Ebenezer Hazard noted "the Foundation of a new Building which was intended for an Addition to the College, but has been discontinued on Account of the present Troubles."[20] By September 1780 any idea of continuing the building had been abandoned and two issues of Dixon and Nicholson's *Virginia Gazette* announced:

> The college has for sale, a considerable quantity of scantling, originally intended for an additional building. Any person taking the whole which cost about 500 l. in the year 1775, may have it upon the most reasonable terms.[21]

Figure 76. DESIGN FOR A CHAPEL. Plan by Thomas Jefferson.

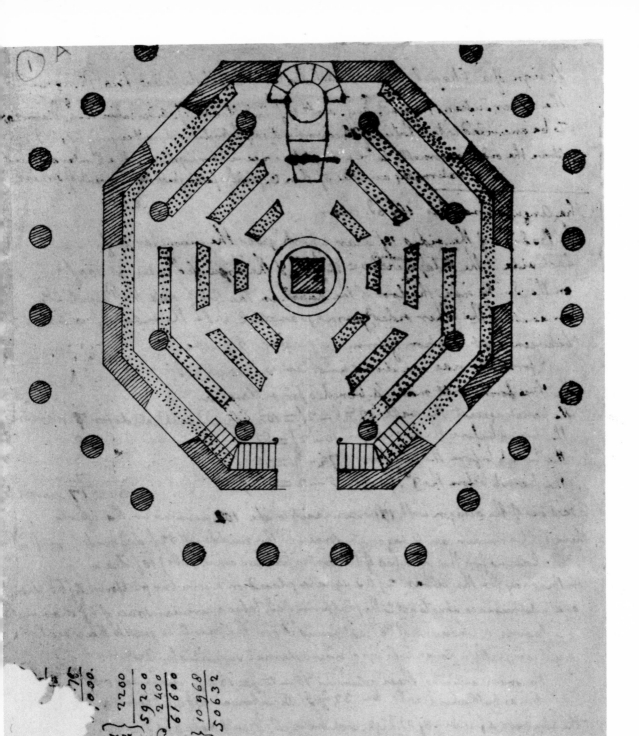

2 walls 1 br thick
30 f long. 3/9 9 high
to upper windle } 7200

of filler -- 59200
1 f deep in ground 2400
61600

deduct for front } 10968
windows --
50632

Design of a Chapel. the Model the temple of Vesta. Pallad. B. 4. Pl. 38. 39.

the Order Tuscan: Basement 3. 9. shaft 12 f. Entablature 3 f. order entire 18. 9. diam. 2. 0.9.

to be encircled with a Portico of 20 columns. it's depth (including column & capping) 6 f 1 2/3 9

Above the order, internally to be a ~~cupola~~ concave hemisphere with a circular aperture at top

externally an Attic 5 f. then a plinth falling back. then segment of sphere.

___

the Angular radius 16 f 3 9. clear.

the Radius of the sides 13 f. clear, which gives the diameter 30 f.

each side of the Octagon (internally) will be 12 f 6 9. & the circumference internal 100 f.

in the South side the door of the chapel. in the North side the Pulpit &c.

in each of the other sides forms parallel with the sides 3 f. asunder.

between each section of forms. a passage 2 f. wide.

each forms to rise one above another. viz each 6. 9.

the three forms will make 4. benches for sitters. viz.

the bench against the wall 12½ f — 2 f. = 10½ f (@ 18 9. each) will do for 7 person

the bench before the first form 10 — 2 f = 8 f — — — — — — 5

the bench before the 2d form 7½ — 2 = 5½ f — — — — — — 3

the bench before the 3d. form 5 — 2 = 3 f — — — — — — 2

17 persons

6. sections of the octagon with 17 persons each make 102 persons in the whole.

there will remain an Octagonal space in the middle of 12 f. diameter. or (al-

-lowing for the benches of the center form on each side) 10 f diam.

in this may be the Altar 2 f 6 9. square placed on a circular platform 4 f 6 9. diam.

one intermediate steps to get to the platform of 9 9. takes a circular space of 6 f. diameter &

leaves a vacancy of 2 f. all round it for the people to pass to their seats.

a gallery, within, level with top of order external, supported by 8 columns

the order entire of these columns 15 — 1½ f = 13½ f. diameter will be 1. 0 ¾

the entablature will be 32 2/5 9. which leaves 10 f 9. 6 9 external to

the windows 4 f. wide: of 8 9. high. architrave abt 8 9. will make 9 f 4 9. in all.

this leaves 17 9. for height of window sill, i.e. even with the bench.

the gallery 3 f. deep with 2 rows of benches. the back bench will hold 8. the for

6 pair of the benches will hold 90 persons.

so whole contents of church will be 193 persons.

Figure 78. DESIGN FOR AN
OCTAGONAL CHAPEL. Plan
from Robert Morris,
Select Architecture (1755).

The unused timber and the nails were not the only materials put to other uses. Excavation in 1950 revealed most of the foundations in the form of backfilled trenches, indicating that even used brick was salvaged. It also revealed that the two halves of the building as shown in Jefferson's existing plan were to have been exchanged in execution, so that the larger rooms would lie to the south of the central axis and the stairs and smaller rooms to the north.

"DESIGN OF A CHAPEL"

One more design by Jefferson remains to be considered. It is a plan for an octagonal building with a peristyle (Fig. 76), inscribed "Design of a chapel the model the temple of Vesta. Pallad. B. 4. Pl. 38. 39." [22] The temple by the Tiber in Rome that used to be known as the Temple of Vesta, to Palladio's illustrations of which Jeffer-

Figure 77. DESIGN FOR A CHAPEL. Notes by Thomas Jefferson
on the back of the plan in *Figure 76* (transcribed in Appendix V).

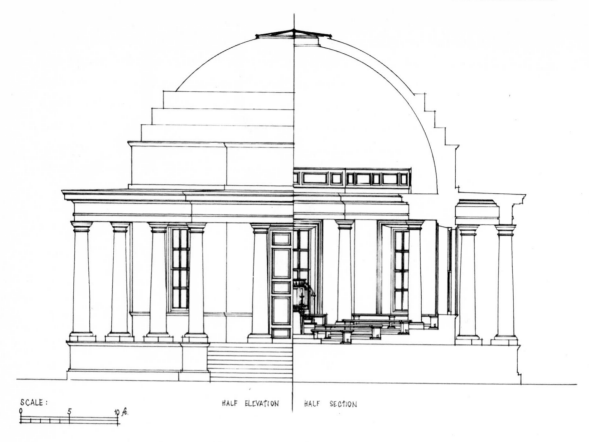

SCALE :
0   5   10 ft.

HALF ELEVATION | HALF SECTION

Figure 79. DESIGN FOR A CHAPEL. Elevation and section,
based on Jefferson's plan and notes, drawn by Anthony D. C. Hyland.

son refers, is a circular building; and it is of the Corinthian order, whereas this chapel, as the annotations on the back of the drawing (Fig. 77, printed in full in Appendix V) show, was to be Tuscan. Perhaps it suggested the peristylar scheme to Jefferson; certainly Palladio's reconstruction of the upper part of the temple was the model for the upper part of the chapel, with "externally an Attic 5f. then 3 plinths falling back. then segment of sphere." But the internal planning owes more to plate 31 of Robert Morris' *Select Architecture* (1755), which was one of Jefferson's chief sources of architectural inspiration. (Fig. 78)

Kimball dated this drawing, on the evidence of the paper used, *circa* 1770. Its connection with Williamsburg may be assumed, he pointed out, because at the time Jefferson could have had no other place in mind, Charlottesville as yet being nothing more than a hamlet. It would be tempting to see the design as a proposed remodelling of the Magazine, which as it happens has exactly the same dimensions on plan, were it not for the presence on the front of the drawing of calculations of the number of bricks needed: these indicate that it was to be built from the ground up. Whether or not there was ever any serious thought of executing the design, restored in Fig. 79, it is of great interest. A number of octagonal churches were built in England in the second half of the eighteenth century; [23] preachers—John Wesley among them—were with the architects in liking the form. None of them had a peristyle, and in giving his chapel such a feature Jefferson was working in the same Neo-Classical spirit as in his project for adding porticoes to the Palace.

Since 1780

O N CHRISTMAS EVE, 1779, the House of Delegates, sitting in what had been the Chamber of the House of Burgesses, adjourned until the following spring. Before the adjournment, the order was given

> That the clerk of this House do remove, at the public expense, the books, papers and records of this House, together with such of the books, papers and records of the General Assembly, as are in his possession, to the town of Richmond, in the county of Henrico, previous to the next session of the General Assembly.

A bill "for the removal of the seat of Government" had been introduced the previous May and passed early in June. The last meeting of the Council in Williamsburg was held on April 7, 1780; the Governor, Thomas Jefferson, took his final departure from the Palace a few days later.[1] The first Assembly to be held at Richmond convened on May 1, 1780.

The days of Williamsburg as capital of Virginia were ended; the buildings that were the outward and visible sign of its former pre-eminence remained. One part of my business in this last chapter will be to sketch the history of those buildings during the century and a half that intervened between Williamsburg's loss of capital status and its assumption of a new role in the life and culture of America—and here the word "sketch" is used advisedly, for nothing more than an outline would be in place in these pages. The other part will be to relate, very briefly, how the same buildings were restored to, or reconstructed in, the form that the visitor to Williamsburg sees today; here "how" needs some qualification, because neither a detailed history of the restoration, nor a description of the techniques employed, can be attempted: each would require—and should be given—a volume to itself.

WAR AND PEACE

Reasons of war had reinforced the older arguments for the need for a new capital, and it was not long before the public buildings became subject to the effects of war. By December 1780 the lead had been stripped from the cupola of the Capitol by militia quartered in the building; Jefferson wrote to the commanding officer that orders should be given "to secure the clock & cupola by stopping up the open part of the Cupola, or raising a roof over it, or such other measure as an intelligent workman shall think best," and added: "It must be made absolutely secure in some way or other."[2] (After all, was not the Capitol "on the whole . . . the most pleasing piece of architecture we have"?) In the fall of 1781 Capitol, College and Palace all became hospitals, the first two being occupied by the French and the last by the American army. Neither the Capitol nor the main building of the College suffered materially from the change of use. But on November 23 the President's House at the College was gutted by fire,[3] and a month later—to the day—the Palace burned.[4]

The French were prompt in recompensing the College for the burning of the President's House and its contents, to the tune of over £1,500, and it was soon restored to use; the structural work cost £752. 14s. 8d.[5] No one had the slightest desire to rebuild the Palace. Contemporary accounts agree that it was in a poor state of repair, and an even poorer state of decoration, before the fire. In May 1782 orders were given for the sale of the bricks of its tumbling walls. There was some thought of disposing of the Palace lands by lottery;[6] eventually, in 1784, they were conveyed to the College, with power to sell, and in 1785 the College sold them. The buildings flanking the forecourt survived the fire and became private houses.

Meanwhile, new uses were being found for the public buildings in Capitol Square. The Gaol was still a gaol, but from 1784 was shared by the City of Williamsburg and James City County. The Capitol itself, which had continued to be the official seat of the Court of Admiralty after 1780, was in December 1782 vested in the City Corporation for ten years, together with the Secretary's Office, to serve as a grammar school. The school was opened in January 1784, "under the direction of Mr. Walker Maury, a gentleman, who for several years has conducted an institution of a similar nature, in the County of Orange."[7] In 1785–1786 Maury employed the bricklayer and plasterer Humphrey Harwood to carry out various alterations and repairs in both the buildings; in the Secretary's Office the work included the formation of a habitable basement. In 1787 the Rev. John Bracken became master.[8] Two

Figure 80. THE MAGAZINE IN 1848.
From Lossing's *Pictorial Field-Book of the Revolution.*

years later a squatter, Philip Bidgood by name, had somehow installed himself in the former Secretary's Office.[9] In 1793 the Assembly passed an Act for pulling down the east wing of the Capitol, applying the proceeds of the sale of the materials to the repair of the western wing, and renting out the Secretary's Office and using the rent for the same purpose. Apparently the Act was not implemented at once, for Henry Latrobe records, as we have already seen, that the building was in a sad state in 1796. The sad state of the Botetourt statue is recorded in a drawing from the same hand.[10] In this case the damage was quite recent; during the early years of the Revolution the statue was still cleaned at the opening of each General Assembly, and it was in good condition at least as late as 1783.[11] In 1801 it was purchased by the President and Masters of the College for $100, and the head was "very dextrously stuck on with an iron plug by the bishop [James Madison] and Mr. Moody in conjunction";[12] it was then re-erected in the position in the College yard that, except for a brief Civil War sojourn at the State Asylum, it has occupied ever since. After the closing of the grammar school the district Court of Chancery sat in the remaining wing of the Capitol,

Figure 81. THE MAGAZINE IN 1858. From a water-color by L. J. Cranston.

and in 1824 the Secretary's Office was allotted to the clerk of the court and became known as the Clerk's Office. On April 10, 1832 the remaining wing of the Capitol was destroyed by fire.[13] Some of the walls survived for a year or two at least, but whether any part of them was incorporated in the Female Academy, which occupied the site from 1839, we do not know. The Secretary's Office, which had also been conveyed to the Female Academy in 1839, was in private ownership by 1855.

CHANGE AND DECAY, AND FIRE

Returning to the years immediately following the Revolution, we find that the Magazine had ceased to perform its original function by 1783; by 1795 it had become a market house.[14] However, there were still cannon balls lying about in the Magazine yard in 1805, when they had been, as the Corporation informed the authorities at Richmond, "for a long time Instruments in the hands of the mischievous to break down the walls thereof."[15] In the 1830's the upper floor of the Magazine became a Baptist meeting house, and in 1853 the Baptists completed the work that the mischievous with the cannon balls had begun, bearing off the remaining bricks of the yard wall for use in their new church. When the Baptists left, the building was "devoted to the fascinations of Terpsichore"[16]—which presumably means that it became a dance hall. (Figs. 80, 81)

Bruton Parish Church came through the Revolution unharmed, and under the ministry of John Bracken continued to serve the Anglican forms of worship. In 1787

a traveller noted: "They have regular service once a day, every sunday, not common in Virginia."[17] The organ was an attraction too. "A week rarely passes in which a number of the inhabitants do not assemble for the purpose of passing an hour or two at church while the ancient organist, or some of his pupils perform upon this instrument," we are told by a writer in 1795.[18] But not even the proximity of the first Bishop of Virginia, James Madison, at the College could do much to relieve the financial distress that had followed upon disestablishment, and before the end of the century the building was "much out of repair."[19] We do not hear of any repairs until 1827.[20] The interior began to lose its eighteenth-century character in 1829, when the pews were cut down.[21] In 1838–1840 it was altered radically, with the aid of funds raised by the Ladies' Working Society of Bruton Parish. A partition was built across the nave west of the transept and the altar placed against its east side (so that the orientation was reversed); three stoves were installed, and the tower entry was fitted up as a coal-shed. Much of the old woodwork was sold. (But the Governor's pew, set up by Spotswood, had gone some years before this[22].)

Figure 83. THE PUBLIC HOSPITAL ABOUT 1850. From a contemporary engraving.

The one public institution in Williamsburg that prospered and made large additions to its buildings between the Revolution and the Civil War was the Public Hospital. A "New Addition," standing north-east of the original building, had been built by 1821; by 1830 it was balanced by the "Western Addition."[23] In 1842–1846, by which time the official title had been changed to the Eastern Lunatic Asylum, a very extensive building campaign was carried out. The original building was increased a storey in height and linked to the "Additions" by two-storey wings, while three tetrastyle Doric porticoes were built fronting the courtyard.[24] (Fig. 83) The effect must have been handsome, but things were not to rest there: by 1853 there was the three-storey "Doric Building" joined to the north end of the western range by a covered way, while to the south of the main complex stood the "Gothic Building."[25] The latter, with twin towers at one end, could have been even more ecclesiastical-looking than it was if its designer had not been under the necessity of making the windows rather smaller than is customary in churches.[26]

As an institution, the College of William and Mary had its ups and downs during these years. Architecturally, its record was one of dilapidations and repairs and minor alterations—until in the small hours of February 8, 1859 the main building became, for the second time in history, a fiery spectacle for the awakened townspeople. The

Figure 82. DUKE OF GLOUCESTER STREET. A water-color by Thomas Charles Millington, showing Bruton Church and the College.

Figure 84. THE COLLEGE OF WILLIAM AND MARY.
The main building in its third form. Henry Exall and Eben Faxon, architects.

Figure 85. THE PALACE.
The east fore-building *circa* 1858, from a water-color by L. J. Cranston.

accounts of the blaze are oddly like those of the first fire in 1705. Again some of the students were in danger for a time but happily escaped, and again—there being "no fire engine in Williamsburg worthy of the name" [27]—nothing could be done to stay the progress of the flames. The whole building was gutted. The walls, most of which had come through the 1705 fire too, still stood, and were discovered to be sound enough for retention in the rebuilding. Henry Exall of Richmond was the architect first chosen for this; he lost the job through dilatoriness and was succeeded by Eben Faxon of Baltimore.[28] The work was carried out with dispatch and the building was in use again by November 1859. The western arcade was bricked up to supply more space for classrooms and a new stair; a low-pitched slate roof was substituted for the former hipped roof and half-storey; the east front was "relieved" (as the phrase went) "by two Towers of the Italian style of Architecture." [29] (Fig. 84) In view of the preservation of the old walls and the undoubted convenience of the "renewed building," it was possible to feel that things had all worked out for the best: "the effect of the fire will be only to make the appliances of the College equal to the demands of the day." [30] No one could know that the flames would so soon leap again.

THE CIVIL WAR

And so we come to the Civil War. In May 1861 the College suspended all lectures; shortly afterwards the buildings were taken over by the Confederate Army, to serve first as quarters and then—as for the French Army eighty years before—as a hospital. On May 5, 1862 the Battle of Williamsburg was fought. For the rest of the war the town was occupied by Union troops.

It was during this period that the fore-buildings of the Palace went, pulled down for the sake of the bricks. In 1835 they had been visited by a grandson of Lord Dunmore, who found that their possessor had fitted them up "in a neat cottage style," [31] and we have views of them as they appeared in the 1850's in drawings by T. C. Millington and L. J. Cranston. (Fig. 85) The last contemporary mention of the fore-buildings occurs in the Philadelphia *Inquirer* for May 16, 1862, where we read: "One of them is about undergoing repairs, and when completed will be a fine residence. One of the buildings is now the hospital of the above [i.e., the Third Pennsylvania] cavalry."

The greater part of the Gaol was also pulled down for its bricks. But these losses must have seemed trifling to the witnesses of the wanton burning of the College in September 1862. The story of this is best told in the words of a deposition made by a Williamsburg lady who was one of them, which despite the brevity proper to the form conveys something of the atmosphere of the times. She deposed:

> That she resided at the time on the College grounds in the President's house, and that she was alarmed, on the evening of the 8th of September, by the cry of fire. She went out and found that the College Building was on fire; that soon a crowd gathered and extinguished the flames; and that while carrying a bucket of water, she met three United States soldiers; one of them told her if the College was not burned that day, it would be the next, or words to that effect; that early the next day, a detachment of the Southern cavalry entered and, after a short contest, retired, the last of them leaving by ten minutes after ten o'clock, A. M.; that shortly afterwards, the College yard was crowded with United States soldiers, many of them drunk and boisterous; that she and her sisters were advised, so unruly were they, to leave the premises, which they did; that about five o'clock, P. M., she was told of the College being on fire, and advised to return, as the house in which she lived was in great danger. This she did, and soon after the College was a smoking ruin; and that there is no doubt of the destruction having been designedly effected by drunken United States soldiers.[32]

There was no doubt; everyone admitted that. But the admission did not prevent the woodwork of the Brafferton being torn out later on, and much damage being done to the President's House as well.[33]

1865–1900

The rebuilding of the College could not be undertaken until 1867; after a delayed start it was completed in 1869. The old walls had survived another ordeal by fire; for the oldest of them it was the third. At first it was thought that their condition was better than it had been after the 1859 fire.[34] In fact this was not so, and more than 400,000 bricks had to be laid.[35] The architect was Alfred L. Rives of Richmond.[36] At his bidding the Italianate towers disappeared and a pedimented pavilion with a triple-arched loggia became the central feature of the east front of the building in its fourth form, the form that it retained until the restoration of 1928–1931. (Fig. 86)

The 'seventies were a quiet time for the buildings with which we have been concerned. In 1881 the last traces of the Female Academy were removed from the Capitol site.[37] In 1885, on June 7, occurred another of the fires with which this history has been so liberally punctuated when the original Public Hospital building burned.[38] The following year, 1886, saw the beginning of a bout of repairs and alterations at Bruton, during which the church-furnisher's catalogue made its ominous appearance at vestry meetings and the Furnace Committee was much in evidence.[39]

But Virginians were beginning to feel a new sense of responsibility for their his-

Figure 86. THE COLLEGE OF WILLIAM AND MARY. The main building in its fourth form.
Alfred L. Rives, architect. From a photograph of the 1870's.

toric buildings. In Williamsburg there had long been a sentiment of reverence for
the town's colonial past, and much of this crystallized around the Magazine—which
people had taken to calling, strangely, the Powder Horn. So it is fitting that the Magazine should have been the first purchase of the Association for the Preservation of
Virginia Antiquities (founded at Williamsburg in January 1888.) [40] In 1861 the
Magazine had reverted to its original function for a time. [41] Then after the War the
town sold it and it became part of a livery stable. In February 1888 one of its sides
fell, soon to be followed to the ground by another; [42] in September 1889, shortly before its purchase by the Association was completed, the roof was burned. During the

Figure 87. THE COLLEGE OF WILLIAM AND MARY. The east front of the main building as restored to its second form.

last weeks of 1889 a restoration was carried out under the direction of Walter R. Higham, a Richmond architect, old bricks from the Palace and other destroyed buildings being employed. Subsequently it was used as a museum.

In 1897 the A. P. V. A. also acquired, by gift, the site and foundations of the Capitol.[43]

THE TWENTIETH CENTURY

One more fire has to be listed—that which early in April 1911 gutted the Courthouse.[44] Since the walls stood firm and the colonial furnishings had made way for

Figure 88. THE COLLEGE OF WILLIAM AND MARY.
The main building from the west.

others in the latter part of the nineteenth century—the interior of the building is said to have received rough treatment in the Civil War—the architectural loss was not great. The City Council and Board of Supervisors voted unanimously for the repair of the building,[45] and the work was completed within a few months.[46] The portico was equipped with Doric columns, whose attenuated proportions gave the building a distinctly Federal look.

But the prevailing theme of the twentieth century was to be not destruction but restoration. Already, nine years before, there had appeared on the Williamsburg scene the man in whose mind the dream (his own favorite word for it) of restoring

Figure 89. THE CAPITOL. The building as reconstructed in its first form, from the south.

the town to its colonial appearance took shape. In 1902 the Rev. William A. R.
Goodwin, then Rector of St. John's, Petersburg, was invited to be Rector of Bruton
Parish. He made it his condition of acceptance that the Vestry should allow him to
restore the church, and the result was the restoration of 1903–1907 for which J.
Stewart Barney of New York gave his services as architect.[47] By present standards it
was not, perhaps, a very accurate restoration. Nevertheless, it corrected the anom-
alies that had been introduced into the interior arrangement of the building in 1838–
1840, and it was a milestone both in the development of an appreciation of colonial
architecture and in the career of its remarkable initiator.

That career now becomes the thread to lead us on to those events of the later

Figure 90. THE PALACE. As reconstructed, from the south-east.

1920's which were to result in the restored colonial capital that we know today.[48] In 1908 it takes us to Rochester, New York, where Dr. Goodwin became Rector of St. Paul's Church. Then in 1922 Dr. Goodwin was asked to write the history of the Theological Seminary of Virginia, an institution which had its origin at William and Mary. Thus the connection with Williamsburg was renewed; in the following year, 1923, it was drawn tight when he returned to William and Mary as head of the Department of Biblical Literature and Religious Education and director of the college endowment campaign. In February 1924 Dr. Goodwin spoke at a dinner in New York about the projected Phi Beta Kappa Memorial Hall at William and Mary. Among those present was John D. Rockefeller, Jr., whom Dr. Goodwin invited to visit Williamsburg. As things turned out, Mr. Rockefeller was not able to accept the invitation until March 1926; he was at Williamsburg again, for the dedication of the Phi Beta Kappa Memorial Hall, the following November. On May 21, 1927 was held, in the Wythe House, the conference that led to his authorizing Dr. Goodwin to buy properties in the town, and on November 21–22, 1927, in New York, the conference at which he assumed responsibility for the execution of the entire restoration project. Throughout this period (during which nearly two hundred purchases of property were made), and for another six months and more, the fact that Dr. Goodwin's backer was Mr. Rockefeller was a well kept secret. It was not until June 12, 1928, that the news was allowed to break, at a mass meeting of the citizens of

Figure 91. THE MAGAZINE AND GUARDHOUSE. The Magazine as restored, with the reconstructed Guardhouse beyond.

Figure 92. THE GAOL. From the south-east.

Williamsburg called to consider the conveyance of Courthouse Green and the Court-house "to Dr. William A. R. Goodwin and his associates." Before that, in February, The Williamsburg Holding Corporation had been formed and granted a Certificate of Incorporation; and Perry, Shaw and Hepburn, of Boston, had been retained as architects.

The partner to whom the architects owed the commission was Perry. Born in Boston in 1883, William Graves Perry received his architectural training at Massachusetts Institute of Technology and the Ecole des Beaux Arts. For two periods, before and after his sojourn in Paris, he was draughtsman in the office of Shepley, Rutan and Coolidge, heirs to the practice of the great H. H. Richardson; after some

Figure 93. THE GAOL. From the south-west.

years of independent practice, in 1923 he joined his fellow New Englander Thomas Mott Shaw and the Pennsylvanian Andrew Hepburn in partnership. Shaw, who was born in 1878, is another *diplomé* of the Ecole; Hepburn, born in 1880, was also trained at M. I. T.; the bond between these two, who became partners in 1919, was former membership—at different times—of Guy Lowell's office in Boston.

Perry first visited Williamsburg in 1926. The Wythe House was then being restored, with funds raised by Dr. Goodwin, and he was able to offer some useful suggestions. So when, in December 1926, Dr. Goodwin failed to secure the services of Thomas E. Tallmadge in making preliminary studies for the restoration, it was of Perry that he thought next. And Perry, with the energy and enthusiasm that are still his, was in Williamsburg ten days after Dr. Goodwin's letter was mailed to him, in January 1927. In May several large boxes of drawings, which included preliminary plans and perspectives of the College, a perspective of the Capitol, and plans and aerial perspectives in color of Capitol Square and Palace Green restored, came down from Boston, to be employed with effect at the important Wythe House conference of May 21.

The Williamsburg office of Perry, Shaw and Hepburn was opened in 1928 with Walter Macomber in charge as Field Representative. Harold R. Shurtleff, to whom scholarship owes so much for *The Log Cabin Myth*, became Director of the Department of Research and Record. Thomas T. Waterman was an early member of the draughting force—he left the office in 1933—while Singleton P. Moorehead and A. Edwin Kendrew were early arrivals (coming in October 1929 and January 1930 respectively) whose association with the restoration has lasted unbroken up to the time of writing; Orin M. Bullock, Jr., was an original member who left in 1933 and returned to Colonial Williamsburg twenty years later as Supervisor of Architectural Research.

WILLIAMSBURG RESTORED

The restoration of the public buildings began with the College.[49] Work on the main building started in the summer of 1928 and was completed in 1931; the President's House was restored in April–September 1931 and the Brafferton in December 1931–June 1932. In the case of the main building, the second form was chosen in preference to the first because so much more was known about it, while the chapel had never been a part of the first. Yet although the pictorial documentation of the east front of the building (Fig. 87) was almost plentiful, when the work of restoration began relatively little was known about its west side (Fig. 88). In particular, the design of the roof was giving the architects trouble—when in December 1929 Mary F. Goodwin made her dramatic identification of the subject of the copper plate numbered C. 30 in the Rawlinson Collection of the Bodleian Library at Oxford. This, the "Bodleian Plate" of Williamsburg parlance, was described by Andrews and Davenport in their *Guide to Manuscript Material for the History of the United States* simply as showing "buildings, probably in some town in Virginia or Carolina, with figures of plants and animals." Its importance for the information it gives about the Capitol and the Palace, as well as the College, needs no stressing for readers of the earlier chapters of this book.

Figure 94. Bruton Parish Church. The interior, looking east.

Figure 95. BRUTON PARISH CHURCH. The nave, looking west.

In restoring the main building of the College it was found necessary to take down all the partition walls. A steel frame, on concrete footings, was then constructed within the outer walls, its outermost columns being hidden in slots in those walls. This frame carries all floor and roof loads—with the paradoxical result that the oldest walls in Williamsburg are also the town's earliest example of the modern device of curtain walls. The engineers were Cleverdon, Varney and Pike of Boston, whose skill was also employed in the reconstruction of the Capitol. In this case preservation of the old foundations was desired as a matter of principle; yet it would not have been practicable to use them as part of the new structure. The solution was to support the new walls on steel beams that rested on concrete piers passing through the old foundations to new footings below them, where the old foundations remained; where the latter had gone, normal concrete foundation walls were used.

The Capitol, whose site had been transferred to Colonial Williamsburg by the Association for the Preservation of Virginia Antiquities in 1928, was reconstructed in the period October 1931–January 1934 (Fig. 89), the Palace in December 1931–April 1934 (Fig. 90); the Courthouse was restored in April–October 1932 (Fig. 61), and the Magazine (leased from the A. P. V. A.) in May 1934–October 1935 (Fig. 91). In October 1934, when the original program of restoration was virtually complete, Colonial Williamsburg set up its own architects' office, with Kendrew as Director and Moorehead as Head Designer, to succeed Perry, Shaw and Hepburn, who were appointed consultants. The Gaol [50] was the first public building to be reconstructed under the new regime (Figs. 92, 93); work on it began in June 1935 and was finished in April 1936. In January 1939 Colonial Williamsburg and its architects took over the second restoration of Bruton Parish Church (Figs. 94, 95), which had been begun by the parish under Dr. Goodwin the previous year with Perry, Shaw and Hepburn as architects; the main work was pushed to completion by August, though some modifications were made in 1940–1942. Among the post-war works was the Guard House, reconstructed in June–August 1949 (Fig. 91). And so it has come about that every building whose history has been our concern in these pages, except the Playhouse and the Public Hospital, has either been restored or has been reconstructed in one of its early forms.

Notes

CHAPTER I

[1] It is told in full by R. H. Land, "Henrico and its College," *W. & M. Q.*, 2nd series, XVIII (October, 1938), 453–498.

[2] A. B. Cutts, "The Educational Influence of Aberdeen in Seventeenth Century Virginia," *W. & M. Q.*, 2nd series, XV (July, 1935), 231–235.

[3] The letter is printed in *W. & M. Q.*, 2nd series, IX (October, 1929), 301.

[4] P. R. O., C. O. 5/1305.

[5] W. S. Perry, ed., *Historical Collections relating to the American Colonial Church* (Hartford, 1870–1878), I, 3. (Hereafter cited as Perry, *Historical Collections*.)

[6] *Ibid.*, 8.

[7] *Ibid.*, 7.

[8] Hugh Jones, *The Present State of Virginia* (London, 1724), p. 28. (Hereafter cited as Jones, *Present State*).

[9] Nicholson Papers, Colonial Williamsburg Archives.

[10] W. Labaree in *D. A. B.*

[11] A 1743 copy of a plan of Annapolis made in 1718 by James Stoddert is reproduced by M. R. Radoff, *Buildings of the State of Maryland at Annapolis* (Annapolis, 1954), plate 1. This plan shows a "Bloomsbury Square," which is a further indication that the planner's mind was dominated by London: the original Bloomsbury Square, laid out by the Earl of Southampton, was the first London *square* to be so called.

[12] *Archives of Maryland* (Baltimore, 1883–19–), XIX, 501–2.

[13] *Ibid.*, XXII, 70.

[14] Robert Beverley, *The History and Present State of Virginia* (London, 1705), edited by L. B. Wright (Chapel Hill, 1947), p. 105. (Hereafter cited as Beverley, *History and Present State*).

[15] Jones, *Present State*, p. 25

[16] According to Beverley, *History and Present State*, 2nd edition (London, 1722), p. 250. Beverley's statement is borne out by entries in the Journals of the House of Burgesses in 1712, showing that Christopher Jackson was allowed £37. 14s. for "laying out the City of *Williamsburgh* and the Roads to the Ports belonging to the Said City" together with £34. 13s. for expenses.

[17] A. N. B. Garvan, *Architecture and Town Planning in Colonial Connecticut* (New Haven, 1951), pp. 29–30. (Hereafter cited as Garvan, *Colonial Connecticut*).

[18] Jones, *Present State*, p. 25, also emphasizes the health aspect, saying that Middle Plantation was "a healthier and more convenient Place, and freer from the Annoyance of *Muskettoes*."

[19] Garvan, *Colonial Connecticut*, p. 46.

[20] M. Vitruvius, *The Ten Books of Architecture*, translated and edited by M. H. Morgan (Cambridge, 1926), p. 17. (Hereafter cited as Vitruvius).

[21] *Ibid.*, 21.

[22] *Ibid.*

[23] Beverley, *History and Present State*, 2nd edition, p. 250.

[24] See letter from A. Matthews, *Nation* (New York), LX (May 9, 1895), 361; six examples of the use of the term between 1699 and 1776 are quoted, all referring to Williamsburg.

[25] First published 1696.

[26] The use of the bay system in colonial Virginia is discussed by T. T. Waterman in *W. & M. Q.*, 2nd series, XV (April, 1935), 117–122.

[27] See Joseph Moxon, *Mechanick Exercises: or the Doctrine of Handiworks*, 3rd edition (London, 1703), p. 126. Bricklayers used a ten foot and a five foot rod. (*Ibid*, p. 247.)

[28] Beverley, *History and Present State*, p. 289.

[29] Jones, *Present State*, p. 31.

[30] *Ibid.*, p. 30.

[31] "Observations in Several Voyages and Travels in *America* in the Year 1736," *The London Magazine*, July, 1746, reprinted in *W. & M. Q.*, 1st series, XV (April, 1907), 223.

[32] "Journal of an Officer in the West Indies, 1764–5," King's Ms. 213, ff. 54-b–60, British Museum, London.

[33] L. B. Alberti, *Ten Books on Architecture*, translated by James Leoni, edited by J. Rykwert (London, 1955), p. 130.

[34] Thomas Jefferson, *Notes on the State of Virginia,* edited by W. Peden (Chapel Hill, 1955), pp. 152–153. (Hereafter cited as Jefferson, *Notes.*)

[35] Letter to Bishop of Oxford, printed in *Wren Society [Publications]* (Oxford, 1924–1943), V, 20. (Hereafter cited as *Wren Society.*)

[36] For the best short accounts of the eighteenth-century architect in England, as also for the master-builder's business methods there, see H. M. Colvin, *A Biographical Dictionary of English Architects 1660–1840,* (London, 1954), pp. 2–15 (hereafter cited as Colvin, *English Architects*), and J. Summerson, *Georgian London* (London, 1945), pp. 53–63.

[37] For examples see L. Hall, "First Architectural School? No! But . . . ," *Journal of the American Institute of Architects,* XIV (August, 1950), 79–82, and Theophilus Hardenbrook's advertisement in the *New York Mercury* in 1758, reprinted in R. S. Gottesman, *The Arts and Crafts in New York, 1726–1776* (New York, 1938), pp. 180–181.

[38] See B. Little, *The Life and Works of James Gibbs, 1682–1754* (London, 1955), p. 61. (Hereafter cited as Little, *Gibbs.*)

CHAPTER II

[1] Ralph Wormeley to William Blathwayt, August 16, 1695, Blathwayt Papers, Colonial Williamsburg Archives.

[2] The evidence of Bland's survey is supported by the statement of Beverley, *History and Present State,* p. 266.

[3] Blair to Nicholson, January 2, 1693/4, Ms., Virginia Historical Society, printed in *V.M.H.B.,* VII (October 1899), 165.

[4] *Ibid.,* 275–276.

[5] Lambeth Mss., William and Mary College Papers, Folder 8, Bodleian Library, Oxford.

[6] P.R.O., C.O. 5/1307.

[7] *Archives of Maryland,* XX, 235–237.

[8] Fulham Mss., Maryland, no. 152, Lambeth Palace Library, London.

[9] Perry, *Historical Collections,* I, 36–65.

[10] *Ibid.*

[11] Blair to Bishop of London, January 21 [1697/8], Fulham Mss., Virginia Box II, no. 65, printed in *W. & M. Q.,* 2nd series, XIX (July, 1939), 347.

[12] P. R. O., C. O. 5/1309.

[13] Board of Trade: Virginia, VI, printed in "Accounts of the College," *W. & M. Q.,* 1st series, VIII (January, 1900), 167–171.

[14] The kiln in which the bricks were burnt was found by excavation in 1929. For the price of bricks for the Capitol, see p. 40.

[15] For oyster-shell lime and methods of burning see W. Bailey, "Lime Preparation at Jamestown in the Seventeenth Century," *W. & M. Q.,* 2nd series, XVIII (January, 1938), 1–12. Shells were used in Virginia because of the lack of limestone. But the special properties of shell-lime were appreciated in England. Moxon notes that "the shells of Fish, as of Cockles, Oysters, &c. are good to burn for *Lime*" (*Mechanick Exercises* (London, 1703), p. 241), and cock-shell lime was used in the vaults of St. Paul's (E. J. Enthoven and C. R. Ashbee, eds., *Life and Works of Sir Christopher Wren. From the Parentalia or Memoirs by his Son Christopher* [Campden, Gloucestershire, 1903], p. 195).

[16] E. M. Riley, "The Colonial Courthouses of York County, Virginia," *W. & M. Q.,* 2nd series, XXII (October, 1942), 407.

[17] *Papers Relating to an Affidavit made by his Reverence James Blair . . . against Francis Nicholson, Esq.* (London, 1727), p. 36. (Hereafter cited as *Papers Relating to an Affidavit.*)

[18] *W. & M. Q.,* 1st series, XVIII (January, 1910), 214.

[19] See note 11, above.

[20] *V. M. H. B.,* XXXI (April, 1923), 156.

[21] York County Records, Book XII (Deeds, Orders, Wills), 332, County Clerk's Office, Yorktown.

[22] The inventory of her personal estate is *ibid.,* Book XIV (Orders, Wills), 368.

[23] Perry, *Historical Collections,* I, 112–113.

[24] Issue of March 19–March 21.

[25] Its foundations (excavated in 1929–1930) are not bonded into those of the hall. Therefore it must have been begun after the completion of the latter. A flight of steps led from a doorway in the north end of the west wall to the basement. The lobby, if it was ever completed, was probably demolished when the chapel was added to the second building (in 1728–1732) and the present west wall—laid in Flemish bond, instead of the English bond of the first building—built then. Humphrey Harwood rebuilt the west doorway of the hall in 1786. (Humphrey Harwood Ledger, Colonial Williamsburg Archives).

[26] Perry, *Historical Collections,* I, 120–121.

[27] John Oldmixon, *The British Empire in America* (London, 1741), I, 437.

[28] *Papers Relating to an Affidavit,* p. 50. The date rather suggests that the College was at first provided with casements, as was the almost contemporary Stoughton Hall at Harvard, and that these were then replaced by the more modern type of window. The sash window may or may not have been an English invention: it was evidently perfected in England. The earliest use of it in quantity at present known was at Whitehall Palace in 1685 (*Wren Society,* VII, 14, 75 and *passim*); in 1686 glass for sash windows was advertised for sale in the *London Gazette* (*O.E.D.*).

[29] P. R. O., C. O. 5/1312.

[30] The information under this head given here comes from a report prepared in 1932 by the archaeologist in charge, P. Duell, "The Wren Building: Archaeological Report, including a Brief History of the Four Forms of the Building," typescript,

Colonial Williamsburg. I have adopted some of Duell's conclusions also.

[31] Nicholson Papers.

[32] A manuscript copy (see the next note) is in the Stadtbibliothek at Berne, Ms. X, 152. It is translated by W. J. Hinke in *V. M. H. B.*, XXIV (January, 1916), 1–43, (April, 1916), 113–141, (June, 1916), 275–288; the excerpts quoted are from this translation.

[33] Duell, in a letter to W. A. R. Goodwin dated August 10, 1937, states: "The volume measures about 7 in. by 9 in. and about ¾ in. thick; there are two tie strings at the front. The volume is written in German longhand and is entitled, 'Meines Bruder's Franze Ludwig Michel's kurze Americanische Reisebesschreibung'; it is marked '3rd Copy.' . . . The drawings themselves are unquestionably copies by the brother since they are on the pages of the book itself and were not inserted. . . . It appears that the drawings in the book were first laid out lightly in pencil and then ruled over in brown ink. The ink appears to be the same as that of the manuscript, and both have turned brown with time. . . ." (Department of Research, Colonial Williamsburg.)

[34] For illustrations and a summary account of these buildings see H. S. Morrison, *Early American Architecture from the First Colonial Settlements to the National Period* (New York, 1952), pp. 82–88 (hereafter cited as Morrison, *Early American Architecture*); for more details see S. E. Morison, *The Founding of Harvard College* (Cambridge, 1935), and *Harvard in the Seventeenth Century* (Cambridge, 1936).

[35] In both these possible prototypes the loggia goes right round the court, as in Jefferson's proposal for extending the College.

[36] Letter to Ralph Bathurst, President of Trinity, printed in *Wren Society*, V, 14.

[37] This alternative reading was suggested to me by Mr. A. Lawrence Kocher. Mr. Kocher has also suggested that what I take to be the basement wall is paving in front of the building; this I cannot accept because with the grade 3 ft. lower than it is today (as archaeological evidence tells us that it was) there must have been 3 ft. of wall showing below the basement window sills.

[38] For illustrations and discussion of this, see J. Piper, "A Cubist Folk Art," *The Architectural Review*, XCIV (July, 1943), 21–23; O. Lancaster, "Celtic Highlights," *ibid.*, CIII (January, 1948), 23–26; [M. Whiffen], "Painted Rustics," *ibid.*, CX (December, 1951), 263–265.

[39] See *Wren Society*, XI, plates 53–56.

[40] Nicholson Papers.

[41] The paragraph that follows is based upon testimony about the fire in the Virginia Archives, printed in *V. M. H. B.*, VI (January, 1899), 272–277, and in *W. & M. Q.*, 2nd series, VIII (October, 1928), 231–234.

[42] Letter from Fulham Mss., *W. & M. Q.*, 2nd series, X (January, 1930), 73.

CHAPTER III

[1] T. J. Wertenbaker, *The Old South: the Founding of American Civilization* (New York, 1942), p. 95, suggests Vanbrugh, whom he calls "one of King William's Dutch architects."

[2] Each wing of the Capitol measured 75 ft. by 25 ft. internally; the fourth Statehouse at Jamestown, 74 ft. 6 in. by 23 ft. For the Statehouse see H. C. Forman, *Jamestown and St. Mary's, Buried Cities of Romance* (Baltimore, 1938), pp. 172–174. (Hereafter cited as Forman, *Jamestown and St. Mary's*.)

[3] For the history and meaning of the term statehouse in America, see A. Matthews in *Dialect Notes* (New Haven), II (1902), 199–224.

[4] Doctor's Commons was demolished in 1867. For the interior of the hall, see T. Rowlandson and A. C. Pugin, *The Microcosm of London* (London, 1808), I, plate facing p. 224.

In Italy a *piazza* is of course an open space in a town—a square. When Covent Garden, London, was laid out in 1630, Inigo Jones—Englishman Italianate that he was—called it a piazza. He was thinking of the open space, but Londoners were most struck by the novelty of the arcaded loggias of the houses along its north and east sides and transferred the outlandish term to them. There were many spelllings current in England and the colonies: below we meet "Pe'ach," and the "Builders Dictionary" appended to Edward Hoppus's edition of William Salmon's *Palladio Londinensis* (London, 1748) says that it was "commonly called *Piache*." In the nineteenth century the term was used in America for any porch occupying all or a large part of the length of a house front.

[6] Acts of Virginia Assembly 1662–1702, Jefferson Collection, Library of Congress, printed in Appendix II. Hening took the easy way out when he printed it as H.

[7] The proportions of the building as shown by Bland do not correspond with those given in the Act —for instance, he makes the length of the wings four times their width—because he was primarily concerned to show its position in relation to the land laid out for the new town. He also squares off both ends of the wings, and it is just possible that they were so in the original plan and were altered before the passing of the Act.

[8] The account of the development of the plan given here is supported by archaeological evidence uncovered when the foundations of the Capitol were excavated in 1929. As the plan here reproduced shows, the brick foundation of a semi-circular porch was found against the west wall of the west wing on the central axis of the cross-bar of the H.

[9] For Virginian houses with cross- and T-plans see H. C. Forman, *The Architecture of the Old South* (Cambridge, 1948), pp. 54–73; for the Annapolis Statehouse, see Radoff, *Buildings of the State of Maryland at Annapolis*, pp. 1–11.

[10] P. R. O., C. O. 5/1312, being the report of "the Committee Appointed to Inspect the Act directing the building the Capitol &c. and to examine the proceedings of the Committee appointed by the said Act to oversee the building of it."

[11] *Ibid.*

[12] For the genealogy of the Carys see R. K. Brock, *Archibald Cary of Ampthill, Wheelhorse of the Revolution* (Richmond, 1937), pp. 1-4.

[13] Quit-rent rolls printed in *V. M. H. B.*, XXX (October, 1922), 345.

[14] Riley, "The Colonial Courthouses of York County, Virginia," *W. & M. Q.*, 2nd series, XXII (October, 1942), 401.

[15] "Council Papers 1698-1702," Ms., Virginia State Archives, printed in *V. M. H. B.*, XXIV (October, 1916), 401.

[16] Mr. Howard Colvin tells me that John Lumley of Northampton was described as "overseer to the Earl of Westmorland at Apethorpe" when he designed the Westmorland Building at Emmanuel College, Cambridge, about 1720. I know of no other instance of the use of the term in this sense in England in the seventeenth or the eighteenth century.

[17] In *A ryght frutefull Mater: and hath to Name the Boke of Surveyeng,* quoted by O. E. D.

[18] P. R. O., C. O. 5/1312, which is also the source of information in the paragraph following.

[19] *Ibid.*

[20] See R. T. Whitelaw, *Virginia's Eastern Shore: a History of Northampton and Accomack Counties* (Richmond, 1951), pp. 704-705 and *passim.*

[21] See Morrison, *Early American Architecture,* p. 551, fig. 470.

[22] P. R. O., C. O. 5/1313.

[23] There are numerous records in Virginia vestry books of the tarring of roofs of churches, and weatherboards were sometimes tarred also—as in England they often are to this day. Hugh Jones states that houses in Williamsburg were "covered with Shingles of *Cedar,* &c. tarr'd over at first." The building lease for a house at Hampton, Elizabeth City County, in 1765, required that it be "covered with good heart-pine or cypress shingles to be tarred once in every two or three years." (H. J. Campbell, "The Syms and Eaton Schools and their Successor," *W. & M. Q.*, 2nd series, XX [January 1940], 10-11). Tar to the value of £10 . 10s. 10d was bought for the College in 1697; its purpose is not stated in the accounts but it was undoubtedly for the roof. Edmund Jennings wrote to the Board of Trade in 1704: "Tarr is generally sold from ten to twelve Shillings . . . The barrll by the Law to containe att least 30 gallons . . . Some is made use of by the Inhabitants for their houses Boats &c" (*W. & M. Q.*, 2nd series, III [July, 1923], 209). In the eighteenth century tar became one of the chief exports of the colony, a number of Acts being passed to encourage its production for the use of the Navy,

which had been dependent on Scandinavia for its supply of the commodity.

[24] In York County Records, Book XIV (Orders, Wills), 108, 112, 139, 144, 151, 163-4.

[25] P. R. O., C. O. 5/1314.

[26] In Catholic allegory the sun was the symbol of papacy. Therefore Nicholson's motto should doubtless be read as an affirmation of Protestantism and loyalty to the Church of England. His arms, granted 1693/4, were: Azure on a cross argent between four suns in splendour or, a cathedral church gules (J. B. Burke, *The General Armory of England, Scotland, Ireland and Wales* [London, 1884], p. 734).

[27] On the symbolism that grew up around Queen Elizabeth see Frances A. Yates, "Queen Elizabeth as Astraea," *Journal of the Warburg and Courtauld Institutes,* X (1947), 27-82.

[28] This plate was formerly C.30 in the Rawlinson collection, Bodleian Library, Oxford; it was presented by the Curators of the Bodleian to Mr. John D. Rockefeller, Jr., and is now in the Courthouse museum, Williamsburg. The *terminus post quem* for dating it is set by its showing the President's House at William and Mary, which was built 1732-1733. It is probable that it was engraved to illustrate William Byrd's *History of the Dividing Line.* The pair to it in the Bodleian, C.29, is a map of the Virginia-Carolina line, and the date March 6, 1727/8 is inscribed on it by Currituck Inlet; this was when and where the survey that ran the line began. In July 1737 Byrd wrote to the naturalist Peter Collinson, in England, asking him to arrange for plates to be made to illustrate the *History,* which he was still writing. Previously he had sent Collinson a copy of his journal of the survey, and this had been seen by the naturalist and engraver Mark Catesby. It is quite possible that Catesby engraved the two plates in question, especially since (as Mr. Thomas E. Thorne has pointed out to me) the animals and plants are drawn with more skill and spirit than the buildings. The *History of the Dividing Line* was not published until 1841. (See J. S. Bassett, ed., *The Writings of "Colonel William Byrd of Westover in Virginia Esq."* [New York, 1901], p. lxxix, and W. K. Boyd, ed., *William Byrd's Histories of the Dividing Line betwixt Virginia and North Carolina* [Raleigh, 1929], pp. xv, xvi.)

[29] T. T. Waterman, *The Mansions of Virginia, 1706-1776* (Chapel Hill, 1946), p. 86. (Hereafter cited as Waterman, *Mansions.*)

[30] See below, p. 65 and p. 214, n. 31.

[31] E. C. Peirce, "Courthouses of Lancaster County, 1656-1950," *Northern Neck Historical Magazine,* I (December, 1951), 29. The building has been destroyed.

[32] T. T. Waterman, *The Early Architecture of North Carolina* (Chapel Hill, 1941), p. 249. I have not been able to find confirmation of the tradition that Leigh came from Williamsburg.

[33] G. L. Chumbley, *Colonial Justice in Virginia* (Richmond, 1938), p. 127.

CHAPTER IV

[1] See Forman, *Jamestown and St. Mary's*, pp. 52, 116–119.

[2] P. R. O., C. O. 5/1359.

[3] C. Headlam, ed., *Calendar of State Papers, Colonial Series, America and West Indies, 1700* (London, 1910), p. 490.

[4] Transcripts of Virginia Mss. From P. R. O., II, Part 1, 316–317, Virginia State Archives.

[5] C. Headlam, ed., *Calendar of State Papers, Colonial Series, America and West Indies, 1706–1708, June* (London, 1916), p. 766.

[6] *Ibid., 1708–1709* (London, 1922), p. 97.

[7] Ms. in Virginia State Archives, printed in *V. M. H. B.,* XVI (July, 1908), 83–84.

[8] See R. T. Gunther, *The Architecture of Sir Roger Pratt . . . from his Note-books* (Oxford, 1928).

[9] For photographs and plans see H. A. Tipping, *English Homes* (London, 1921–1928), Period 4, I, 1–22.

[10] For an elevation of the house drawn by Pratt himself see J. Lees-Milne, *The Age of Inigo Jones* (London, 1953), fig. 86. Kingston Lacy was altered by Sir Charles Barry *circa* 1854.

[11] For photographs see Tipping, *English Homes,* Period 4, I, 145–154.

[12] S. Serlio, *Architettura,* VII, 155.

[13] For photographs and plans see Tipping, *English Homes,* Period 4, I, 23–52.

[14] Photographs *ibid.,* xvi, xvii.

[15] The resemblance was first noticed by A. Pierce Middleton, who saw the small engraving of Edial Hall, which had served as the home of Dr. Samuel Johnson's short-lived school, in the National Illustrated Library edition of Boswell's *Life* (London, 1851), I, 75. (Information, S. P. Moorehead). This engraving was based on a larger engraving in Thomas Harwood, *The History and Antiquities of the Church and City of Lichfield* (Gloucester, 1806), facing p. 564, which in turn was doubtless made from the watercolor drawing, now at Johnson's Birthplace, Lichfield, that is here reproduced. According to P. Laithwaite, "Dr. Johnson's Lichfield Forebears and Dr. Johnson's Academy," *North Staffordshire Field Club Transactions,* LXVI (1932), 87, "it would seem that the hall was built, as were so many other substantial houses in and around Lichfield, shortly after the Restoration." The greater part of the house was demolished *circa* 1810.

[16] S. F. Kimball, *Thomas Jefferson, Architect: Original Designs in the Possession of Thomas Jefferson Coolidge, Jr.* (Cambridge, 1916). (Hereafter cited as Kimball, *Thomas Jefferson, Architect.*)

[17] Waterman, *Mansions* pp. 32–33.

[18] For plans and elevation see Campbell, *Vitruvius Britannicus,* II, 39, 40.

[19] Plan and elevations *ibid.,* 70–74.

[20] For plan and photographs see Tipping, *English Homes,* Period 4, II, 119–140.

[21] For plans and elevation see Campbell, *Vitruvius Britannicus,* II, 94.

[22] For plans and photographs see Tipping, *English Homes,* Period 5, I, 237–246.

[23] Examples are Mulberry (1714), Brick House, Edisto (*circa* 1725), Crowfield (1730), and Fenwick Hall (1730). (See S. G. Stoney, *Plantations of the Carolina Low Country* [Charleston, South Carolina, 1938], for plans and photographs.)

[24] [T.] N [eve], *The City and Countrey Purchaser, and Builder's Dictionary* (London, 1703).

[25] Waterman (*Mansions,* p. 33) uses a letter of Lady Gooch, wife of Governor Sir William Gooch, to support his great hall theory. Lady Gooch, writing on February 4, 1749/50, is describing her London house to a correspondent in Virginia and she says: "the great parlor is almost as broad as our dressing room at Wmsbg and within 2 foot as long, the other about the size of my closet, we have four chambers on the first floor and two light closets and as many garrots, and I believe they'd all stand in the hall." (L. H. Jones, *Captain Roger Jones, of London and Virginia* [Albany, 1911], p. 223.) The trouble about this, for Waterman's purpose, is that Lady Gooch was stressing the smallness of her London house; and if the great parlor was really slightly smaller than the dressing room in the Palace, the chambers and garrets almost might have fitted into the Palace entrance hall. Waterman could have found better support for his theory in a letter from Governor Dinwiddie to Lord Loudoun, dated July 1, 1756: "I am to acqu't You that the Gov't Ho. is a very good one, but there are only three Rooms besides the Garrets and Offices, seperate from the Ho." At least it could be argued that the count of three for the ground floor rooms—the second floor rooms or "chambers" are not mentioned at all—was due to the omission of the great hall as not being a living room. However, the true explanation surely is that the "little middle room" of the Botetourt inventory was omitted as a mere servery—just as the recently built ball-room and supper-room were omitted as unsuited for everyday purposes. Dinwiddie was expecting a visit from Loudoun, and he went on to say that he realized that the Palace would be sufficient only for Loudoun and his attendants; he himself would move with his family into a rented house. (R. A. Brock, ed., *The Official Records of Robert Dinwiddie* [Richmond, 1883–1884], II, 456.)

[26] Beverley, *History and Present State,* 2nd edition p. 250.

[27] Ms., Virginia State Archives.

[28] That is, the furniture provided by the colony, which remained permanently in the house—as distinct from the personal furniture brought over by each successive Governor.

[29] For a restoration of the plan of Nomini Hall see Waterman, *Mansions,* p. 142.

[30] Plan *ibid.,* p. 164.

[31] Plan of Stratford, *ibid.,* p. 97; the Serlian plan is in Book VII, cap. IX. On this, and on the prototypes of Rosewell, see M. Whiffen, "Some Virginian House Plans Reconsidered," *Journal of the Society of Architectural Historians,* XVI, no. 2 (May 1957), 17–19.

[32] For plan see Waterman, *Mansions,* p. 109.

CHAPTER V

[1] For Spotswood see L. Dodson, *Alexander Spotswood, Governor of Colonial Virginia, 1710–1722* (London, 1932).

[2] London, 1738.

[3] For William Byrd on this side of Spotswood's character see Bassett, ed., *The Writings of "Colonel William Byrd, of Westover in Virginia, esq."* p. 357. Byrd's account of his visit to Spotswood in "A Progress to the Mines in the Year 1732" is altogether delightful.

[4] Beverley, *History and Present State,* p. 250.

[5] Colvin, *English Architects,* p. 466.

[6] By J. C. McCabe, in *Church Review,* VIII (March, 1856).

[7] See M. Whiffen, *Stuart and Georgian Churches outside London* (London, 1948), fig. 16.

[8] Colvin, *English Architects,* p. 6.

[9] C. G. Chamberlayne, ed., *The Vestry Book and Register of St. Peter's Parish, New Kent and James City Counties, Virginia, 1684–1786* (Richmond, 1937), p. 414.

[10] Papers of the Jones Family, I, f. 41, Library of Congress.

[11] W. P. Palmer *et al.,* eds., *Calendar of Virginia State Papers* (Richmond, 1875–1893), I, 174–175. (Hereafter cited as *Calendar V. S. P.*)

[12] A foot less, or footlace or foot laceing, was a chamfered set-off—here the set-off of the water-table. (See Architectural Publication Society, *The Dictionary of Architecture* [London, 1852–1892], III, 71.)

[13] 1748 edition, p. 119.

[14] [Charles Campbell], "Notes on Jamestown, Williamsburg and Yorktown," *Southern Literary Messenger* (Richmond), III (1837), 237–238, reprinted in *W. & M. Q.,* 1st series, XXI (October, 1912), 137.

[15] For plan see Forman, *Jamestown and St. Mary's,* p. 202.

[16] In St. Anne's and Gloria Dei the cross was due to the projection of a porch on one side and a sacristy on the other; in the case of Gloria Dei the porch and sacristy were added to buttress the walls of the nave. For St. Anne's see Radoff, *Buildings of the State of Maryland at Annapolis,* pp. 17–20; for Gloria Dei (which is now within the City of Philadelphia), S. P. Dorsey, *Early English Churches in America* (New York, 1952), pp. 120–121.

[17] For Buntingford see N. Pevsner, *The Buildings of England: Hertfordshire* (London, 1953), fig. 14a; for Euston, Whiffen, *Stuart and Georgian Churches outside London,* fig. 13; for Farley, *Wren Society,* XIX, plates 48–51. The attribution of Farley to Wren cannot be maintained: it was most probably designed, and built, by Alexander Fort, the King's Master Joiner. (See Colvin, *English Architects,* p. 210.)

[18] See G. Hay, *The Architecture of Scottish Post-Reformation Churches 1560–1843* (Oxford, 1957), pp. 63–68.

[19] See Dorsey, *Early English Churches in America,* figs. 33–37.

[20] See above, p. 42.

[21] See G. C. Mason, *Colonial Churches of Tidewater Virginia* (Richmond, 1945), plate 22.

[22] *Ibid.,* plate 33.

[23] *Ibid.,* plate 69.

[24] *Ibid.,* plate 52.

[25] See Forman, *Jamestown and St. Mary's,* p. 24.

[26] N. M. Davis, "Public Powder Magazines at Charleston," *The Year Book of the City of Charleston* (Charleston, 1942).

[27] See Radoff, *Buildings of the State of Maryland at Annapolis,* p. 41. It was 15 ft. long, 10 ft. wide, and of 8 ft. pitch. However, in 1716–18 a much grander Magazine House was built. (*Ibid.,* 48–50.)

[28] [B. F. de] Belidor, "Of Powder Magazines," *Gentleman's Magazine,* XXX (June, 1760), 269–270, with diagram facing 265.

[29] P. R. O., C. O. 5/1318.

[30] An interesting item in the estimate, which was entered in the Journal of the House of Burgesses, is:

"450 yards painting on the roof of the House at 12d . £22 . 10 . 0".

Evidently the shingles in this case were painted instead of being tarred.

Another item is:

"Covering the flatt roof with Pitch, Sand, and Lime and laying a floor of Plank over the same £12 . 0 . 0"

This is puzzling. It will be remembered that the flat roof had been covered with lead by Henry Cary, Sr., twelve years before. Perhaps the climate had been too much for it, as it was to be for the lead on the public buildings at Washington in the early nineteenth century. (See T. Hamlin, *Benjamin Henry Latrobe* [New York, 1955], p. 422.) Another, and on the whole more likely, explanation is that the lead remained and that the purpose of the pitch, sand and lime was to protect it from the new floor of planks, the vegetable acids in wood having a deleterious effect on lead—though against this it must be admitted that lime tends to oxidize it. (For the use of sand and earth between lead and wood see L. F. Salzman, *Building in England down to 1540* [Oxford, 1952], pp. 265–266.)

[31] Identified as such by the foundations.

[32] Ludwell Papers, II, Virginia Historical Society.

[33] In April 1716 Spotswood, with the help of John

Fontaine, laid out an avenue "about half a mile long" at Fort Christanna, Brunswick County. (A. Maury, ed., *Memoirs of a Huguenot Family* [New York, 1853], p. 280.) The Palace Green avenue, however, would seem not to have been due to Spotswood; at least we find no mention of it before December 15, 1737, when the Council ordered "that there be paid to Mr. Philip Finch the Sum of Ten pounds for laying and planting the Avenue to the Governors House."

CHAPTER VI

[1] Letter to Francis Nicholson dated February 7, 1705 [/6], Nicholson Papers.

[2] Perry, *Historical Collections* I, 184.

[3] L. B. Wright and M. Tinling, eds., *The Secret Diary of William Byrd of Westover 1709–1712* (Richmond, 1941), p. 51.

[4] *Ibid.*, p. 67.

[5] *Ibid.*, p. 82.

[6] *Ibid.*, p. 99.

[7] *Ibid.*, p. 116.

[8] *Ibid.*, p. 434.

[9] *Ibid.*, p. 476.

[10] "Proceedings of the Visitors of William and Mary College, 1716," *V.M.H.B.*, IV (October, 1896), 170–171.

[11] *Ibid.*, 173.

[12] *Ibid.*, 175.

[13] Jones, *Present State*, p. 28.

[14] For Lilly, see article in *D. N. B.* There, and elsewhere, it is said that he laid out Kingston, Jamaica; this, however, has now been disproved. (See J. G. Young, "Who Planned Kingston?", *Jamaican Historical Review*, I [December, 1946], 144–153).

[15] For the history of Codrington College see Frank J. Klingberg, ed., *Codrington Chronicle: an Experiment in Anglican Altruism on a Barbados Plantation, 1710–1834* (Berkeley, 1949).

[16] *V. M. H. B.*, IV (October, 1896), 169.

[17] *Ibid.*, 173.

[18] Mentioned in letter of William Dawson, dated August 18, 1747, in *W. & M. Q.*, 2nd series, XX (April, 1940), 215–216.

[19] The Transfer of the College of William and Mary in Virginia, printed in *The History of the College of William and Mary in Virginia* (Baltimore, 1870) pp. 16–31.

[20] *The Charter and Statutes of the College of William and Mary in Virginia* (Williamsburg, 1736), reprinted in *W. & M. Q.*, 1st series, XXII (April, 1914), 293.

[21] Journal of the Meetings of the President & Masters of William & Mary College [1729–1784], p. 218, College Archives.

[22] Under the date November 16, 1751 John Blair, nephew of the Commissary, noted in his diary: "This evening Mr. Preston to prevent the young gentlemen at the college from playing at a rehearsal in the dormitory, how they could act Cato privately among themselves, did himself, they say, act the Drunken Peasant; but his tearing down the curtains is to me very surprising." (L. G. Tyler, ed., "Diary of John Blair," *W. & M. Q.*, 1st series, VIII [July, 1899], 15). The Mr. Preston who got so carried away was the Rev. William Preston, Professor of Moral Philosophy.

[23] The resolution of 1773, allotting rooms, names them in terms of their relationship to the old and new dormitory staircases.

[24] The ledger of Humphrey Harwood, in Colonial Williamsburg Archives, records work done at the College in 1777–1790. Entries for May 1788 include the items:

"To 12 days work Repairing Plastering
                in Garrott @ 6/ - £3:12
To white washing 12 Rooms, &
            4 Passages for   do   @ 4/6   3:12
To do   do   9 do   &
          4 Clossets @ 4/6 (Second Story) 2:14
To Repairing Plastering & larthing
    in Old Dormontory 12/ - &
             3 days lab^r 7/6 :19: 6"

But it cannot be said that the ledger helps us much in trying to settle the position of the rooms.

[25] Letter from Stephen Hawtrey to his brother Edward, dated March 26, 1765, *V. M. H. B.*, XVI (October, 1908), 210.

[26] The Transfer of the College. (See note 19 above.)

[27] *Ibid.*

[28] "Present Rules and Methods . . . for the disposition of the Rents and proffits of the Manor of Brafferton . . .," printed in *W. & M. Q.*, 2nd series, X (January, 1930), p. 68.

[29] Perry, *Historical Collections*, I, 123–124.

[30] "Proceedings of the Visitors . . .," *V. M. H. B.*, IV (October, 1896), 165, 172.

[31] Jones, *Present State*, p. 26.

[32] *Ibid.*, p. 94.

[33] Rev. William Dawson to the Bishop of London, August 11, 1732, *W. & M. Q.*, 1st series, IX (April, 1901), 220.

[34] Journal of the Meetings of the President & Masters of William & Mary College [1729–1784], p. 8.

[35] It is sometimes said, on the authority of a remark in John Evelyn's *Diary*, that it was introduced then. However, there are corner fireplaces in the Queen's House at Greenwich, which was built to the design of Inigo Jones in 1616–1635 and altered by John Webb in 1664.

[36] See Waterman, *Mansions*, pp. 66 and 70, for plans of these houses.

[37] Colvin, *English Architects*, p. 555.

[38] For the history of the theatre and the personalities connected with it see R. H. Land: "The First Williamsburg Theater," *W. & M. Q.*, 3rd series, V (July, 1948), 359–374. This goes into the non-architectural aspects of the subject more fully than is possible or desirable here.

[39] York County Records, Book XV (Orders, Wills), 52–54.

[40] The lease and release are recorded in York County Records, Book III (Deeds, Bonds), 204–206.

[41] R. A. Brock, ed., *The Official Letters of Alexander Spotswood* (Richmond, 1882–1885), II, 284.

[42] The account that follows is based upon S. P. Moorehead's reconstruction of the Playhouse made, with R. Southern as consultant, for Colonial Williamsburg. Mr. Moorehead has pointed out to me that the exterior may have looked very like that of the theatre of 1788 at Richmond, Yorkshire, translated from stone into wood. (For photograph of the Richmond theatre see R. Southern, *The Georgian Playhouse* [London, 1948], plate 34.)

[43] *Ibid.*, p. 23.

[44] *Ibid.*, p. 21.

[45] *Ibid.*, and, more particularly, *Changeable Scenery: its Origin and Development in the British Theatre* (London, 1952).

[46] See Land's article cited in note 38 above for this and more about Levingston.

[47] Bassett, *The Writings of "Colonel William Byrd of Westover in Virginia Esqr.,"* p. 373.

[48] William Byrd mentioned his death in a letter dated January 21, printed in *V. M. H. B.*, IX (January, 1902), 240.

[49] As evidenced by York County Records, Book XVI (Orders, Wills), 692.

[50] *Ibid.*, Book V (Deeds, Bonds), 153–154.

[51] Such performances were announced in the *Virginia Gazette*, September 10 and September 17, 1736; see also letter of Thomas Jones printed in *V. M. H. B.*, XXVI (April, 1918), 180. *The American Weekly Mercury*, no. 869 (August 26, 1736), contains the following item, dated May 3 at Williamsburg:

"This being the Time of our General Court, the Town was last Week filled with an extraordinary Concourse of Gentlemen and Ladies; who came hither to see our Governors Sister and Son, in company with one Dr. *Potter*, Apothecary *Gilmore*, *Abraham Nicholas*, a Painter, and several others, put Plays on the Public Theatre: And in Acting the *Recruiting Officer*, and *Busy-Body*, they performed their Parts with so much applause, that they have already got about One hundred and fifty Pounds Subscriptions to encourage their Entertaining the Country with the like Diversions at future Public Meetings of our General Court and Assembly.

N. B. *The terms of Subscriptions are, that a Ticket will be delivered for every Twenty Shillings Subscribed.*"

[52] York County Records, Book V (Deeds), 154–155.

[53] For an account of these curious doings see J. C. Wise, *Ye Kingdome of Accawmacke* (Richmond, 1911), pp. 324–326.

[54] On September 27, 1770, the city conveyed the land on which the playhouse *had* stood to John Tazewell. (York County Records, Book VIII [Deeds], 107.)

CHAPTER VII

[1] *A Journal of the Life of Thomas Story . . . and also, of his Travels,* (Newcastle-upon-Tyne, 1747) pp. 387–388.

[2] Jones, *Present State*, p. 88.

[3] Fulham Ms., printed in *W. & M. Q.*, 2nd series, XIX (October, 1939), 456.

[4] William and Mary College Papers, folder 241, printed in *W. & M. Q.*, 1st series, XI (January, 1903), 175 n.

[5] *Ibid.*

[6] Fulham Ms., printed in *W. & M. Q.*, 2nd series, XIX (October, 1939) 460–462.

[7] Fulham Ms., *ibid.*, 467.

[8] *W. & M. Q.*, 1st series, IX (April, 1901), 220.

[9] Elizabeth B. Kennon to Samuel Mordecai, printed in *V. M. H. B.*, XXXIV (April, 1926), 123.

[10] William and Mary College Papers, folder 282, College Archives.

[11] Papers concerning "His Excellency Lord Botetourt's Estate," R. A. Brock collection, Henry E. Huntington Library.

[12] Botetourt Papers, Virginia State Archives, printed in *Tyler's Magazine*, III (October, 1921), 115.

[13] "To Humphrey Harwood

1770

Oct. 19.

To 1450 Bricks at 2/9 & 25 Bushels
      lime at 9d . . . .   3 . 3 . 1-½
,, building a Vault 30/ and 7 days
      labor at 2/ . . . .   2 . 4 . 0"

[14] John Tyler, tenth President of the United States and fifteenth Chancellor of the College, always insisted that Botetourt was buried near the west end of the chapel. The protagonist of the east-end party was Hugh Blair Grigsby the historian, who succeeded Tyler as Chancellor. In 1858 Grigsby examined Sir John Randolph's vault, finding a second body in it but neither Botetourt's coffin plate nor a lead coffin. (He did not know that Botetourt was buried in lead.) In 1862, after the third College fire, a Union soldier found and stole Botetourt's silver coffin plate. (It was subsequently returned to the College.) Clearly he must have rifled another vault. And this vault must have been towards the west end, because the other two vaults at the east end are Randolph vaults of 1776 and 1784. When the floor was taken up in 1929 two vaults were revealed under the second window from the west on the north side; but they were not opened. One of them must be that of Bishop Madison, whose remains were "committed to a vault in the Northwest corner of the Chapel" in 1812. The east-enders would contend that the other belongs to Robert Nelson, who was buried in the chapel the following year, or to Madison's wife. However, in November 1859 Robert J. Morrison, himself a convinced east-ender, read a paper before the College faculty in which he stated:

"Near the North-west corner of the Chapel is the vault in which repose the ashes of James Madison the first Bishop of Virginia and on the same side, a few feet farther east is the grave of Chancellor Nelson." If this is correct and Nelson was really buried *east* of Madison, the vault by the side of Madison's cannot be his. Moreover, L. G. Tyler in a footnote to this passage, as printed in *W. & M. Q.*, states: "There is still another vault in the west end of the Chapel, which appears to have been overlooked by Mr. Morrison. It contains a copper [sic] coffin with a large skeleton, and was doubtless the vault of Lord Botetourt, who is known to have been buried in a coffin of that character." From all this it seems safe to conclude that Botetourt lies in one of the two vaults near the second window from the west on the north side of the chapel. (See editorial from *The Southern Argus* [Norfolk], July 31, 1856, reprinted in *W. & M. Q.*, 2nd series, X [January, 1930], 84–86; *V. M. H. B.*, XXXIV [April, 1926], 123; R. J. Morrison, "The Vaults in the East End of the Chapel of the College of William and Mary," Ms. dated February 8, 1859, Virginia State Library, printed in *W. & M. Q.*, 2nd series, VIII [October, 1928], 269–270; R. J. Morrison, paper read before Faculty of William and Mary, November 22, 1859, printed in *W. & M. Q.*, 1st series, XVI [October, 1907], 133–136.)

[15] See C. G. T. Dean, *The Royal Hospital, Chelsea* (London, 1950), p. 54.

[16] *Virginia Gazette*, April 20, 1739.

[17] The inscription repeats the original, which was copied by H. B. Grigsby and also is given in the *Virginia Gazette*, April 13–20, 1739.

[18] Journal of the Meetings of the President and Masters of William and Mary College [1729–1784], p. 8.

[19] Letter of Rev. William Dawson to the Bishop of London, dated August 11, 1732, *W. & M. Q.*, 1st series, IX (April, 1901), 220.

[20] *Pennsylvania Gazette* (Philadelphia), April 2, 1747.

[21] P. R. O., C. O. 5/1326.

[22] Jefferson, *Notes*, pp. 153–154.

[23] The Ms. diary of the Rev. Robert Rose, 1747–1751, is in the Colonial Williamsburg Archives. I am indebted to Mr. John Hemphill for drawing my attention to the entries referring to Walker and the Capitol. Blair's diary, edited by L. G. Tyler, is printed in *W. & M. Q.*, 1st series, VII (January, 1899), 133–153, VIII (July, 1899), 1–17.

[24] C. G. Chamberlayne, ed., *The Vestry Book and Register of St. Peter's Parish, New Kent and James City Counties, Virginia, 1684–1786* (Richmond, 1937) pp. 262–263. (Hereafter cited as Chamberlayne, *St. Peter's Parish*.); he is called builder again when the vestry order a payment to him (*ibid.*, p. 266). Mr. H. M. Colvin (in letter to author) writes: "It would certainly be unusual to find a man called a 'builder' in an English vestry-book as early as 1740 . . . . However, in January 1711/12 the contract for the rebuilding of Whitchurch Church, Salop., was drawn up between 'William Smith of the Wergs in the County of Stafford Builder of the one part and the Rector Churchwardens and Inhabitants of Whitchurch of the other part' (original in County Record Office). Now in this contract Smith was acting as the 'undertaker'—i.e., he was making himself responsible for the carpentry, glazing, and other trades besides his own—and I think that the word 'builder' was simply being used as a synonym for 'undertaker.' In other words, Smith did not habitually call himself a builder any more than he would habitually call himself an undertaker: it was just an expression of the function he was performing in relation to a particular contract." However, John Richardson of Yorktown was described in an apprenticeship indenture in 1750 as "Carpenter & builder"; the apprentice was to be taught "in the Arts and Misteries of a Carpenter & Builder." (York County Records, Book V [Deeds], 409–410.)

[25] C. G. Chamberlayne, ed., *The Vestry Book of St. Paul's Parish, Hanover County, Virginia, 1706–1786* (Richmond, 1940), pp. 157–158.

[26] As is shown by a petition laid before the House of Burgesses on December 2, 1748.

[27] Stafford County Deeds, Liber O (Wills, Inventories 1748–1763), 83, Virginia State Archives. The will, dated February 7, was proved on March 13. Walker's executors were Thomas Lee (who was to become President of the Council before the year was out), Charles Carter, John Tayloe, Nathaniel Harrison and Philip Lee—an impressive list of gentlemen. He left them his business and gave them "full power to Contract with other Workmen, to buy whatever they think proper towards finishing & compleating the same [i.e., the buildings on hand] in as full & ample manner as I could do were I living & the profits to be divided among all my Children."

[28] Martha (Wayles), widow of Bathurst Skelton.

[29] Chamberlayne, *St. Peter's Parish*, pp. 174, 177.

[30] C. G. Chamberlayne, ed., *The Vestry Book of Petsworth Parish, Gloucester County, Virginia, 1677–1793* (Richmond, 1933), pp. 156, 157, 166–168. Poplar Spring church was abandoned in the 1790's and in 1820 the bricks were removed to build the first Hygeia Hotel at Old Point Comfort. (See G. C. Mason, *Colonial Churches of Tidewater Virginia* [Richmond, 1945], pp. 249–253.)

[31] *W. & M. Q.*, 1st series, XXI (July, 1912), 56. In 1734 he conveyed the 393 acres in Hanover County, patented in 1733, to Benjamin Waller (*W. & M. Q.*, 2nd series, IX (July, 1929), 211).

[32] *V. M. H. B.*, XIV (April, 1907), 341; *W. & M. Q.*, 2nd series, IX (July, 1929), 212; *V. M. H. B.*, XV (April, 1908), 382.

[33] Francis Jerdone to Hugh Crawford, September 12, 1754, *W. & M. Q.*, 1st series, XI (April, 1903), 242.

[34] He leased it from John Custis II. (Ms. lease in possession of Mrs. Hunter Debutts.)

35 Carter's Grove Plantation account book, in possession of Mr. George H. Burwell.

36 L. C. Bell, ed., *Cumberland Parish, Lunenburg County, Virginia, Vestry Book 1746–1816* (Richmond, 1930), p. 201. In 1734 he worked on the glebe house of Blisland parish (Chamberlayne, *St. Peter's Parish*, p. 675.)

37 *Virginia Gazette* (W. Hunter), August 27, 1756.

38 Jefferson, *Notes*, p. 152.

39 Ms. Journal, quoted by T. Hamlin, *Benjamin Henry Latrobe* (New York, 1955), p. 70.

40 Villa Cornara, Piombino in Castelfranco.

41 For an old photograph of Tedington see A. L. Kocher and H. Dearstyne, *Shadows in Silver: a Record of Virginia 1850–1900* (New York, 1954), p. 88.

42 F. Shelley, ed., "The Journal of Ebenezer Hazard in Virginia, 1777," *V. M. H. B.,* LXII (October, 1954), 407–409.

43 From correspondence between George Muter and Thomas Jefferson following the stripping of the lead by militia quartered in the Capitol in 1780. (*Calendar V. S. P.,* I, 397.)

44 P.R.O., C.O. 5/1326.

45 The figures for 1723–1743 (first payment) are given in the Executive Journals of the Council; those for 1743 (second payment)–1747 in P. R. O., C. O. 5/1326, 1327.

46 Gooch Papers, Transcripts, III, 1015, Virginia Historical Society.

47 William and Mary College Papers, folder 282.

48 The purchase is recorded in York County Records, Book V (Deeds), 134. In 1736 Wray had bought two other lots on Prince George Street from David Menetree, bricklayer. (*Ibid.,* Book IV, 431.)

49 *Ibid.,* Book XX (Wills, Inventories), 206–208. It shows that he had glaziers' as well as carpenters' tools.

50 *V. M. H. B.,* XIV (July, 1906), 20–21.

51 *W. & M. Q.,* 1st series, IX (October, 1900), 128.

52 *Ibid.* Powhatan was burnt out in the Civil War and rebuilt within the original walls, which remain as an exceptionally fine example of colonial brickwork.

53 Elizabeth Taliaferro became George Wythe's second wife. Richard Taliaferro's will is printed in *W. & M. Q.,* 1st series, XII (October, 1903), 124–125.

54 The entry in the minutes of the meeting of the President and Masters is printed in *W. & M. Q.,* 1st series, II (January, 1894), 209.

55 *Virginia Gazette* (A. Purdie), July 3, 1779.

56 C. G. Chamberlayne, ed., *Vestry Book of Christ Church Parish, Middlesex County, Virginia, 1663–1767* (Richmond, 1927), p. 279. He also made a door for the middle church in the same period. (*Ibid.,* p. 290.)

57 The churchwardens of Overwharton Parish advertised for "all Persons inclinable to undertake it . . . to come [on September 5] . . . and give

in their Plans and Proposals" in the *Virginia Gazette,* June 6, 1751. On May 16, 1755 the *Virginia Gazette* contained an appeal by Richards, "To all charitable and well-disposed Christians." This relates the circumstances of the building of Aquia Church and continues: "He [Richards] had got the Church in such Forwardness, that he should have been able to have delivered the same to the Vestry in a short Time, and then was to receive the Ballance of his Tobacco, having received only 75,000 Pounds [out of 130,900 lbs.]; but, on the 17th Day of *February* last, while he was absent on his necessary Business, the whole Building was accidentally consumed by Fire, which has reduced him and his Family to very great Distress, he being utterly unable to re-build the said Church. And, therefore, he most humbly prays your Aid and Assistance." Whatever the success of this appeal may have been, Richards managed to rebuild the Church; and in 1757 the Assembly passed *An Act to impower the Vestry of the Parish of Overwharton . . . to levy for Mourning Richards a reasonable satisfaction for rebuilding a Church at Aquia.*

58 *Virginia Gazette,* November 17, 1752.

59 This and the 1753 amount from P. R. O., C. O. 5/1327.

60 York County Records, Book V (Deeds), 572.

61 Botetourt Papers, Virginia State Archives.

62 This and the next two amounts from P. R. O., C. O. 5/1328.

63 The standing furniture in the ball-room comprised: "19 Leather Bottom Mahogony chairs, 8 long stools, 8 stocker Brackets, 6 brass Branches"; in the supper-room: "2 long walnut dining Tables, 16 Walnut Leather bottom chairs, 2 Glass Lustre w[i]th 12 Branches." There were "2 large deal Benches" in the porch. Botetourt's own furniture in the ball-room comprised: "3 large mahog[an]y dining tables, 1 large round walnut do., 12 mahog[an]y chairs hair bottoms, 1 large dutch stove, 3 glass lustres with 6 branches each & gauze covers, 2 large paintings of the King & Queen gauze covers, 2 Venetian blinds"; in the supper-room: "1 large dutch Stove." (Inventory among Botetourt Papers.)

64 Vestry minutes, as abstracted by McCabe in *Church Review,* VIII (March, 1856), 614.

65 *Ibid.*

66 As Mr. Lawrence Kocher has pointed out to me, there is a tomb of identical design, dated 1717, at Braintree, Essex. (For photographs and measured drawings of it see *The Practical Exemplar of Architecture* [London, n.d.], plates 110, 111.)

67 Issue of February 28, 1751.

68 Gooch Papers, Transcripts, I, 135.

69 Issues of May 15 and June 25, 1752.

70 Mrs. Lelia Tucker, writing to Mrs. Frances Bland Coalter, June 8, 1812, says that young Gregory Page, drowned at Capitol Landing, was buried in the church aisle under the organ gallery. (Tucker Letters, transcript, Colonial Williamsburg Archives;

original of this letter in possession of Mrs. Frances Bland Coalter Saunders.)

[71] Issues of September 5 and September 12, 1755.

[72] A plan of Williamsburg, dated 1782, which was probably made by a French army cartographer for purposes of billeting. Showing the position of every building in the town, the Frenchman's Map (see endpapers), in the possession of the College of William and Mary, has been a document of prime importance in the restoration.

CHAPTER VIII

[1] *Virginia Gazette* (A. Purdie and J. Dixon), December 15, 1768.

[2] *Church Review and Ecclesiastical Register,* VIII (March, 1856), 615.

[3] Letter from Anne Blair to Martha Braxton, dated August 21, 1769, *W. & M. Q.,* 1st series, XVI (January, 1908), 179.

[4] York County Records, Book V (Deeds), 565.

[5] *Virginia Gazette* (Purdie and Dixon), December 22, 1774.

[6] *V. M. H. B.,* XXXI (October, 1923), 329.

[7] Brock, *The Official Letters of Alexander Spotswood,* I, 67.

[8] *Virginia Gazette* (Purdie and Dixon), February 15, 1770.

[9] Purdie and Dixon's, and William Rind's.

[10] See above, Chapter V, note 54.

[11] *Virginia Gazette* (Purdie and Dixon), July 19, 1770.

[12] William Nelson Letterbook, 1766–1775, p. 245, Virginia State Archives.

[13] On Palladio's system, see R. Wittkower, *Architectural Principles in the Age of Humanism* (London, 1949), pp. 111–115.

[14] In issue of May 24, 1751, as "Just Imported, and to be Sold reasonably, at the Printing-Office in Williamsburg," in a long list of titles which also includes "Ware's Palladio" (1738) and "Salmon's Palladio [Londinensis]" (first published 1734, second edition 1743).

[15] Gordon's Hospital, Aberdeen (p. 108), The Orphans' Hospital, Edinburgh (p. 140), Harden House (p. 142), Royal Infirmary, Edinburgh (p. 150), Watson's Hospital, Edinburgh (p. 151). For the influence of other *Vitruvius Scoticus* designs in Virginia, see Waterman, *Mansions,* p. 308 and *passim.* One may suggest that the subject of Scottish influence on American colonial architecture in general is one that would richly repay further investigation.

[16] E. C. Peirce, "Courthouses of Lancaster County, 1656–1950," *Northern Neck Historical Magazine,* I (December, 1951), 29–30. The specification as given here has been corrected with the aid of a photostat of the original, Lancaster County Records, Order Book VIII, 287, Virginia State Archives.

[17] Riley, "The Colonial Courthouses of York County, Virginia," p. 405. A plan of the foundations of this courthouse, built in 1733 and destroyed in 1814, faces p. 402, *ibid.*

[18] For an account of Robert Smith, on which what follows is based, see C. E. Peterson, "Notes on Robert Smith," being Appendix I to the same author's "Carpenters' Hall," *Transactions of the American Philosophical Society,* XLIII, part 1 (1953), 96–123.

[19] *Virginia Gazette* (W. Rind), August 2, 1770.

[20] York County Records, Book VII (Deeds), 274.

[21] *Virginia Gazette* (Purdie and Dixon), October 3, 1771.

[22] Minutes of the Court of Directors, p. 17, Eastern State Hospital, Williamsburg.

[23] *Ibid.,* p. 18.

[24] *Ibid.,* p. 20.

[25] See illustrations to E. B. Krumbhaar, "The Pennsylvania Hospital," *Transactions of the American Philosophical Society,* XLIII, part 1 (1953), 237–246. For Bethlehem Hospital see J. Summerson, *Architecture in Britain 1530–1830* (London, 1954), pl. 96.

[26] A plan accompanying insurance policy no. 1640 of the Mutual Assurance Society, dated May 25, 1821, Virginia State Archives, shows the eastern fore-building only, and calls it "the New Addition." The plan accompanying policy no. 6023 of the same Society, dated January 5, 1830, shows them both, calling them "the East Addition" and "the West Addition."

[27] G. L. Jones, "The History of the Founding of the Eastern State Hospital of Virginia," *American Journal of Psychiatry,* CX (March, 1954), 650.

[28] Letter dated Badminton, October 13, 1771, Botetourt Papers, Virginia State Archives.

[29] See R. Gunnis, *Dictionary of British Sculptors 1660–1851* (London, 1954), *sub nomine.* (Hereafter cited as Gunnis, *British Sculptors.*)

[30] F. N. Mason, ed., *John Norton & Sons, Merchants of London and Virginia* (Richmond, 1937), pp. 225–226. (Hereafter cited as Mason, *John Norton & Sons.*)

[31] See Gunnis, *British Sculptors;* also C. Hussey, "Woburn Abbey, Bedfordshire–II, Some Georgian Craftsmen," *Country Life,* CXVIII (September 8, 1955), 488–491.

[32] Mason, *John Norton & Sons,* p. 245.

[33] *Ibid.,* pp. 265–266.

[34] *Ibid.,* p. 313.

[35] Letter to John Norton, dated June 4, 1773, Norton Papers.

[36] Mason, *John Norton & Sons,* p. 332.

[37] *Ibid,* pp. 331–332.

[38] E. McCrady, *The History of South Carolina under the Royal Government 1719–1776* (New York, 1899), p. 677.

[39] See M. I. Webb, *Michael Rysbrack, Sculptor* (London, 1954), fig. 78.

CHAPTER IX

[1] The sources of the following figures are the Executive Journals of the Council 1753–74, Virginia State Archives, and P. R. O., C. O. 5/1328,1329.

[2] The precise date was January 9, 1767. For the history of the New Bern building see A. T. Dill, *Governor Tryon and his Palace* (Chapel Hill, 1955).

[3] John Whiting of Rhode Island, quoted *ibid.* p. 114.

[4] On his taste in architecture and landscape design see B. Little, "Norborne Berkeley: Gloucestershire Magnate," *V. M. H. B.*, LXII (October, 1955), 386, 394–395.

[5] See S. F. Kimball, "Jefferson and the Arts," *Proceedings of the American Philosophical Society* LXXXVII (July, 1943), 238–239.

[6] Little, *Gibbs*, p. 186, and the same author, "Francis Fauquier and an English Architect," *W. & M. Q.*, 3rd series, XII (July, 1955), 475–476.

[7] "In a Closet . . . Ozanabrigs intended to past the paper on in the Supper Room."

[8] Ms. notebook of accounts with the estate of Lord Botetourt, R. A. Brock Collection, Huntington Library. The upholsterer was J. Kidd; he was paid 2s. 4d. for mending paper in the ballroom in 1769 and 2s. 6d for taking down the supper room curtains and mending the paper in the ballroom in 1770.

[9] Robert Beverley to Samuel Athawes, April 15, 1771, Letter-book 1761–1793, Ms. Division, Library of Congress.

[10] See Tipping, *English Homes*, Period 4, I, fig. 140.

[11] These drawings were first published by Kimball, *Thomas Jefferson, Architect*. More recently Kimball published a *rotonda*-type plan which he suggested was a project for remodelling the Palace because it was attached to, and on the same kind of paper as, the College design that Jefferson made for Dunmore (see below). (S. F. Kimball, "Jefferson and the Public Buildings of Virginia: I—Williamsburg, 1770–1776," *Huntington Library Quarterly*, XII [February, 1949], 118–119, fig. 7.) (Hereafter cited as Kimball, "Public Buildings: I.") But unlike the schemes here reproduced it would have entailed an almost complete reconstruction of the building, and there would not seem to be any compelling reason for believing that it had in fact anything to do with the Palace.

[12] *Ibid.*, 119–120.

[13] No part of a watermark appears in the paper of the measured plan, but identity of weight, colour, texture and bridge-marks establishes that it is the same kind of paper.

[14] Among the Lee Papers, University of Virginia. Catalogued by C. E. Thurlow and F. L. Berkeley, Jr., *The Jefferson Papers of the University of Virginia* (Charlottesville, 1950), p. 6, item no. 36.

[15] See A. Nicolaï, *Histoire des Moulins à Papier du Sud-Ouest de la France 1300–1800* (Bordeaux, 1935), p. 19. Nicolaï quotes Panchouque's encyclopedia to the effect that the particular function of cardinal was to serve as a letter paper for merchants. The watermark in the paper used by Jefferson resembles that reproduced by Nicolaï on plate 24, and

also that reproduced by E. Heawood, *Watermarks* (London, 1940), plate 490, no. 3695.

[16] I have examined hundreds of Virginia letters and other papers of the period without finding another example. But paper with a cardinal watermark so similar to that of Jefferson's as to be attributable to the same manufacturer was used for an "itineraire de la marche de l'armée partout de Phillipsburg pour se rendre à Prince-town" in 1781. (Lafayette [Leclerq] Papers, Folder II, no. 38, Colonial Williamsburg Archives.)

[17] See S. F. Kimball, "Jefferson and the Public Buildings of Virginia: II—Richmond, 1779–1780," *Huntington Library Quarterly*, XII (May, 1949), 303–310. (Hereafter cited as Kimball, "Public Buildings: II.") The Governor's House plan is in the Coolidge Collection of the Massachusetts Historical Society, and was first reproduced by Kimball, *Thomas Jefferson, Architect*, plate 104. The Richmond Capitol plan is in the Huntington Library. In the article referred to Kimball reproduces another version of the Governor's House scheme, HM 9375.

[18] HM 9367, Huntington Library. Kimball reproduced and discussed it in "Public Buildings: I," but was not aware that the building was ever begun. The full story was first told by A. L. Kocher and H. Dearstyne, "Discovery of Foundations for Jefferson's Addition to the Wren Building," *Journal of the Society of Architectural Historians*, X, no. 3 (October, 1951), 28–31.

[19] Journal of the Meetings of the President & Masters of William & Mary College [1729–1784], p. 101. Saunders, who was a carpenter of some substance, also did repairs for the College from time to time. The land tax records indicate that he died in 1792 or 1793.

[20] F. Shelley, ed., "The Journal of Ebenezer Hazard in Virginia, 1777," *V. M. H. B.*, LXII (October, 1954), 405.

[21] *Virginia Gazette* (J. Dixon and T. Nicolson), September 13 and 20, 1780.

[22] HM 9387, Huntington Library. First discussed by Kimball, "Public Buildings: II," p. 116.

[23] E.g., Hartwell, Buckinghamshire (1753, Henry Keene, architect), Stony Middleton, Derbyshire (1759, attributed to James Paine), St. Mary's Chapel, Birmingham (1773, Joseph Pickford, architect).

CHAPTER X

[1] See Jefferson to Philip Mazzei, April 4, 1780, in J. P. Boyd, ed., *The Papers of Thomas Jefferson* (Princeton, 1950–) III, 342.

[2] See Chapter VII, note 43.

[3] Journal of Baron Louis von Closen, 1780–1782, II, 12, transcript, Library of Congress.

[4] *Ibid.* Also letter of Rochambeau to Washington, December 24, 1781, Rochambeau Papers, photostat, Library of Congress.

[5] Account for rebuilding of President's House, William and Mary College Papers, folder 13-A.

[6] Benjamin Harrison to Speaker of House of Dele-

gates, May 30, 1782, in H. R. McIlwaine, ed., *Official Letters of the Governors of the State of Virginia* (Richmond, 1926–1929), III, 238.

[7] *Virginia Gazette or the American Advertiser,* (Richmond: J. Hayes), January 10, 1784.

[8] *Virginia Gazette or the American Advertiser* (Richmond: T. Nicholson), January 4, 1787.

[9] *Calendar V. S. P.,* IV, 602.

[10] Reproduced by J. H. B. Latrobe, ed., *The Journal of Latrobe,* (New York, 1905), facing p. 250.

[11] When it was mentioned as "a beautiful white marble statute" by the anonymous author of "A Journey on Horseback from Philadelphia to Charleston, S. C. in the year 1783," Ms., Virginia State Archives.

[12] St. George Tucker to Henry St. G. Tucker, August 8, 1801, printed in *W. & M. Q.,* 2nd series, X (April, 1930), 164.

[13] *Calendar V. S. P.,* X, 574.

[14] [St. George Tucker], *A Letter, To the Rev. Jedediah Morse . . . ,* reprinted in *W. & M. Q.,* 1st series, II (January, 1894), 195, n.

[15] *Calendar V. S. P.* IX, 439.

[16] Appeal for contributions by Mrs. Robert Harrison, 1888, Letter-book of Mrs. Cynthia B. T. Coleman, in the possession of Mrs. George P. Coleman.

[17] Samuel Vaughan, Diary, 1787, p. 48, photostat, Library of Congress.

[18] [St. George Tucker], *A Letter, To the Rev. Jedediah Morse, A. M. . . . ,* p. 192.

[19] Isaac Weld, *Travels through the States of North America and the Provinces of Upper and Lower Canada during the Years 1795, 1796, and 1797* (London, 1799), p. 96.

[20] F. L. Hawks, *Contributions to the Ecclesiastical History of the United States of America* (New York, 1836–1839), I, 203.

[21] Vestry Book, Bruton Parish, 1827–1889, Bruton Parish House, Williamsburg.

[22] [Charles Campbell], "Notes on Jamestown, Williamsburg and Yorktown."

[23] See Chapter VIII, note 24.

[24] Tenders "for erecting three large Porticoes and one Smaller one, to the building of the Asylum" were advertised for in the *Richmond Enquirer,* May 31, 1844. A plan attached to policy no. 14389 of the Mutual Assurance Society, dated October 27, 1846, shows that the old building had by then been heightened and the connecting wings built.

[25] Policy no. 17639 of the Mutual Assurance Society, dated September 24, 1853.

[26] There is a drawing of it by L. J. Cranston in the possession of Colonial Williamsburg.

[27] Contemporary newspaper clipping pasted in an extra-illustrated copy of *The History of the College of William and Mary,* College Archives.

[28] Record Book of William and Mary College [1846–1879], College Archives, under date March 1, 1859 and *passim.*

[29] *Weekly Gazette and Eastern Virginia Advertiser* (Williamsburg: E. H. Lively), April 6, 1859.

[30] *Ibid.*

[31] C. A. Murray, *Travels in North America during the Years 1834–1836* (New York, 1839), I, 128.

[32] *The History of the College of William and Mary,* p. 52.

[33] Report from the President to the Board of Visitors and Governors, dated July 5, 1865 in Faculty Minutes under same date.

[34] *Ibid.*

[35] Report of the Building Committee to the Visitors and Governors, dated June 28, 1869, College Papers, folder 52–A.

[36] "Whose taste, skill and judgment the Committee gratefully acknowledge[d]" *ibid.*

[37] [T. R. Goodwin], *The Capitol in which the General Assembly of the Colony and Commonwealth of Virginia Met from 1704 to 1779* (Williamsburg, 1934), p. 18.

[38] *The One Hundred and Thirty First Annual Report of the Eastern State Hospital* (Richmond, 1904), p. 18.

[39] Vestry Book, Bruton Parish, 1827–1889.

[40] *Year Book of the Association for the Preservation of Virginia Antiquities for 1896 and 1897* (Richmond, 1896), introduction.

[41] M. L. Foster, *Colonial Capitals of the Dominion of Virginia* (Lynchburg, 1906), p. 70.

[42] The chief source for the events of 1888–1889 is the Letter-book of Mrs. Cynthia B. T. Coleman, in the possession of Mrs. George P. Coleman.

[43] [Goodwin], *The Capitol,* p. 18.

[44] It is described in *The Virginia Gazette,* April 6, 1911.

[45] *Ibid.,* April 27, 1911.

[46] According to the terms of the contract, which was let in June, the work was to be completed by October 1. (*Ibid.,* June 29, 1911.)

[47] For the history and details of this restoration see W. A. R. Goodwin, *Bruton Parish Church Restored* (Petersburg, 1907), and the Vestry Book of Bruton Parish, 1889–1912.

[48] Much of this and the two following paragraphs is based on Elizabeth Hayes, "The Background and Beginnings of the Restoration of Colonial Williamsburg, Virginia," 1933, typescript, Colonial Williamsburg Archives. Miss Hayes was Dr. Goodwin's secretary, and her valuable account was compiled from his files and her own diaries.

[49] Most of the information in this final section is derived from the Architectural Reports on the several buildings, typescript, Colonial Williamsburg Architectural Records Office.

[50] The Gaol was conveyed to Colonial Williamsburg in 1933 by the City, to which it had reverted after a brief period of ownership (1929–1931) by the A. P. V. A. Part of the Gaol lot belonged to the A. P. V. A. in 1933 and was conveyed by that body to Colonial Williamsburg about the same time.

APPENDIXES

I. Governors of Virginia
1690-1781

Note: The first dates given are those of the actual administration of the respective Governors.

June 1690–August 1692:

Francis Nicholson (1655–1728), Lieutenant Governor under Lord Howard of Effingham. (Commissioned, November 1689.)

September 1692–October 1698:

Sir Edmund Andros (1637–1714), Governor General. (Commissioned, March 1692.)

December 1698–August 1705:

Francis Nicholson, Governor General. (Commissioned, July 1698.)

August 1705–August 1706:

Edward Nott (1634–1706), Governor General. (Commissioned before April 12, 1705.)

Robert Hunter was appointed to succeed Nott, but was captured on the voyage out by a French privateer and held prisoner until 1709. In 1710 he became Governor of New York.

June 1710–June 1722:

Alexander Spotswood (1676–1740), Lieutenant Governor under Earl of Orkney. (Commissioned, February 1709/10.)

September 1722–July 1726:

Hugh Drysdale (d. 1726), Lieutenant Governor under Earl of Orkney. (Commissioned, April 1722.)

September 1727–August 1749:

> SIR WILLIAM GOOCH (1681–1751), Lieutenant Governor under Earl of Orkney (until January 1737) and Earl of Albemarle. (Commissioned, January 1726/7.)

November 1751–January 1758:

> ROBERT DINWIDDIE (1693–1770), Lieutenant Governor under Earl of Albemarle (until December 1754) and Earl of Loudoun. (Commissioned, July 1751.)

June 1758–March 1768:

> FRANCIS FAUQUIER (1703–1768), Lieutenant Governor under Earl of Loudoun (until April 1762) and Sir Jeffrey Amherst. (Commissioned, January 1758.)

October 1768–October 1770:

> NORBORNE BERKELEY, BARON DE BOTETOURT (1718–1770), Governor General. (Commissioned, July 1768.)

September 1771–June 1775:

> JOHN MURRAY, EARL OF DUNMORE (1732–1789), Governor General. (Commissioned, July 1771.)

June 1776–June 1779:

> PATRICK HENRY (1736–1799), Governor. (Elected by Convention of Delegates, June 1776, for term of one year; re-elected by House of Delegates and Senate, 1777 and 1778.)

June 1779–June 1781:

> THOMAS JEFFERSON (1743–1826), Governor. (Elected by General Assembly, June 1779; re-elected, June 1780.)

II. Specifications for the Capitol
in Acts of the Assembly

THE PROJECTED CAPITOL was described in *An Act directing the building the Capitoll and the City of Williamsburgh*, 1699, and certain modifications of the original design were authorized by an Act of 1701. A manuscript volume of Acts of Assembly of 1662–1702, among the Jefferson Manuscripts in the Library of Congress, gives the relevant part of the 1699 Act as follows:

> . . . the sd Capitoll shall be erected and built in manner and forme according to the rules and dimentions following (viz) that the sd building shall be made in the forme and figure **H** that the foundation of the sd building shall be four Bricks thick up to or near the surface of the ground and that the walls of the sd building from thence shall be three bricks and a halfe brick thick to the water table and from the water table to the top of the first story three bricks thick and from thence to the top of the second story two bricks and a halfe brick thick the length of each side or parte of wch building shall be seventy five foot from inside to inside the breadth thereof twenty five foot from inside to inside and the first story of each part or side shall be fifteen foot pitch one end of each pt or side of wch Shall be semicircular and the lower rooms at the sd end fifty foot long and shall be parted by a wall from the rest of the building on each side or part wch other part shall be divided into four divisions whereof one to be for a large and handsome staire Case that the midle of the front on each side of the sd building shall have a Circular Porch with an Iron Balcony upon the first floor over it & great folding gates to each Porch of Six foot breadth both and that four Galleryes shall be in the room below that shall be caled the generall Court house the upper Story of each Side to be tenn foot pitch and be divided as shall be directed by the Comitees appointed to revise the laws that the two parts of the building shall be joyned by a Cross Gallery of thirty foot long and fifteen foot wide each way according to the figure herein before speecified raised upon Piazzas and built as high as the other parts of the building and in the Middle thereof a Cupulo to surmount the rest of the building Wch shall have a Clock placed in it and on the top of the sd Cupulo shall be put a flag upon occasion that the windows to each story of the sd building shall be sash windows and that the roofe shall be a hip roof with Dormand windows and shall be well shingled with Cypress shingles and that the great roomes below of each building shall be laid

with flag stone one part or side of which building shall be and is hereby appropriated to the use of the Generall Court & Councill for the holding and keeping of
the sd generall Court and Councill therein and the severall offices thereto belonging the other part or side of the sd building shall be and is hereby appropriated to
the use of the house of Burgesses and the offices thereof and to no other use or
uses wtsoever . . .

The following is Hening's version of *An act giveing further directions in building the Capitoll and for building a Public Prison,* 1701:

WHEREAS it is concluded to be more suitable and comodius for the Uniforme
carrying on and finishing the Capitoll now erecting in the City of Williamsburgh
that some alterations be made in the modell of the said Capitoll laid downe and
expressed in an act of assembly made at James City the 27th day of Aprill Anno
Domini 1699,

Be it therefore enacted by the governour, councell and burgesses of this
present generall assembly and the authority thereof, and it is hereby enacted,
That the following directions be observed, vizt.

That the porches of the said Capitoll be built circular fifteen foot in breadth
from outside to outside, and that they stand upon Cedar columns (if to be had)
if not the same to be sett upon other good, lasting and substanciall wood; that
the cross building betwixt the two main buildings be of the same breadth with
the maine buildings that all the great doors be arched, and that it be left to the
comitee which now is or hereafter shall be appointed to oversee the building of
the capitoll to direct what other doors shall be made therein, that the placeing the
four galleryes be left to the committee which now is or hereafter shall be appointed
to oversee the building of the Capitoll, and that they have liberty to take so much
room out of the adjacent rooms as in their discretion they shall think fit for the
carrying up a suitable pair of staires.

That the windows in the lower story be arched, and that the lower floors be
raised two foot from the ground. . .

III. Robert Smith's "Description" of the Public Hospital

"A Description of the Plans and Elevation of a Hospital for Virginia," from the Minutes of the Court of Directors.

The Plan consists of a Hall for a Staircase, behind There is the Keepers apartment, and 12 other Rooms chiefly for the Reception of mad People, The Stairs begin near the front Door and lands on passages in the second Story. The second Story has 12 Rooms the same Dimensions as those in the first Story, and a Room over the Keepers Apartment which may serve the Managers of the Hospital to meet or may be divided which will make two other Rooms for Patients The Hall is designed to be open as far as the landing of the Stairs the whole hight of both Storys, The Cellers should be about eight feet high between the under sides of the Joices and the Surface of the Celler floor, And the foundation must go 12 Inches lower which will make the whole height of the Celler wall on which you lay the first floor 9 feet, This wall shou'd be 19 Inches thick either of Stone or very hard Brick and the Partition Walls shoud be 14 Inches thick, The first floor is designed 3 feet above the Surface of the Ground which will require the Wall about 2 feet or a little more raised above the said Surface, This part from the ground up to the top of the first floor shou'd be cased with hard Brick if the Celler Wall be of Stone, unless you go to the Expence of hewn Stone for this part which will be better; After the Wall is worked up as high as the first floor to the full Demensions of the plan set off about 4 Inches for the finishing of the plinth or Water table which may be of Moulding Bricks.

[Sketch of section of wall showing water table].

The first Story is ten feet high from floor to Cieling. The outside Walls all round 14 Inches Thick and the partitions nine Inches thick of Bricks. The second Story is designed the same thickness and to be Nine feet six Inches high. The Windows are 6 lights of Glass 10 by 8 Inches for the hight and 3 for the Width, There must be a grate of Iron to the inside of each Window which may be fixed in the follow Manner Suppose this to be the Jaums of a Window and Irons fixed ready to receive the grates when the Building is finished

[Sketch]

I would have 2 eyes of Iron made like the rough Scratch above, which shou'd be made of Common flat bar Iron with a hole of an Inch diameter to receive a hook which will be fixed to the Grate, the other End split and turned up or down one Inch and built in the Brick work. There two eyes shou'd be fixed about eight Inches above the bottom of the Window and two more fixed about the same distance from the top of the window, the Grate having four hooks to fit into those eyes may be set in and a hasp fixed to the Grate at top that will fall on a Staple drove into the lintel over the Window head fix on a padlock the whole will be safe.

See this rough Scratch. [*Sketch of "grate" in elevation*]

Dimensions of the Plan........................feet
The Keepers Apartment........................ 22.

                                                    feet In:
6 Rooms on one side............... 11.9...... 70.6
2 End Walls..................... 14...... 2.4
6   Ditto..................... 9...... 4.6
2 Water Tables.................. 4...... 8
Whole length of Building.................. 100.–

2 Rooms .... 10.9 each 21.6
1 Passage 6.2   6.2
2 Walls .... 14 thick 2 . 4
2 Ditto .... 9 Do 1 . 6
2 Water Tables.................. 4 Do   8
                                          32 . 2
Whole Width of Building.................. 32 . 2
NB The middle part projects 3 feet........... 6 . –
                                          38 . 2

If there shoud be occasion for Fire to warm the common Rooms, there may be Stoves fixed on the partition between two Rooms with the Mouth open to the Passage, by which means they make fires and the mad People cannot come at them. They shou'd be fixed about two foot above the floor for fear of the Patients falling against the Stoves. See to the left hand on the Plan the place of two Stoves.

This Building will require about Two hundred thousand Bricks each Brick about 8¾ Long 2⅜ Thick and 4¼ Broad about 13 of such Bricks with Mortar will make one foot Superficial of a Nine Inch Wall or 19½ of such to a fourteen Inch Wall The Bricklayer must order it so that the Chimneys come out in the Roof at Equal distance from the middle otherwise they will have a very ill Effect, This may be easily done.

About 40 Thousand feet of Scantling will be wanted Superficial, which we reckon at one Inch thick 12 such feet makes one foot Cubical Measure.

16 Thousand feet of plank for Doors and floors about 1½ thick 2 Thousand feet of plank very good for Sashes &c.

5 Thousand of Inch Boards for Cornice to the Eves and other finishing besides Boarding the Roof.

The above hints and a carefull inspection of the plan may be sufficient to perform any part of the Building

Philadelphia April 9th 1770   Robt Smith

IV. Agreement Between Benjamin Powell and the Directors of the Public Hospital

(From the Minutes of the Court of Directors.)

Articles of Agreement indented made and concluded this the eighteenth day of January in the year of our Lord one thousand seven hundred and seventy one *Between* Benjamin Powell of the City of Williamsburg carpenter of the one part and the Court of Directors of the Hospital for the Reception of Ideots Lunatics and persons of insane and disordered Minds of the other part *Witnesseth* that the said Benjamin Powell for and in consideration of the sum of Money herein after mentioned doth covenant and agree with the said Court of Directors that he will erect a large brick Building for an Hospital for the Reception of Ideots Lunatics and persons of insane and disordered Minds on the Lots lately purchased by the said Court of Directors of Thomas Walker agreable to the plan and explanation thereof hereto annexed The whole Walls to be of hard well burnt Bricks and laid with good Mortar the North front of the middle Building to have a neat Pediment the South East and West ends to be hipped to have a neat Mundelian Cornice round the whole the Roof to be covered with plank and good Cypress Shingles the Frame and Scantling to be of good Oak or poplar and of proper sizes for such a Building the Floors to be laid with good pine Plank well seasoned one and a half Inch thick and free from Sap the outward Doors and those to the Middle Rooms to be pannelled and the others strong batten Doors. and the said Benjamin Powell doth agree to furnish all the materials for the said Building except the Grates and such other things as are usually imported from England and that he will finish and compleat the whole in a neat strong and workmanlike manner agreable to the plan and explanation thereof aforesaid within two years from the date hereof *In Consideration* whereof the said Court of Directors do agree to pay the said Benjamin Powell one thousand and seventy pounds in the following manner that is to say two hundred and fifty pounds part thereof in hand and the Residue at such Times and in such proportions as the said Court of Directors shall think fit to direct having regard to the progress of the Work. *In Witness* whereof the parties . . . . [*etc*].

V. Jefferson's Octagonal Chapel

THE FOLLOWING is a transcript of the annotations on the reverse of Thomas Jefferson's plan of an octagonal chapel, HM 9387, Henry E. Huntington Library, San Marino, California.

Design of a Chapel. the Model the temple of Vesta. Palad. B. 4. Pl. 38. 39.

the Order Tuscan. Basemt 3–9. shaft 12f.Entablature 3f. Order entire 18–9. Diam. 20I.
the Order Tuscan. Basemt $\overset{f\ I}{3-9}$. shaft 12f.Entablature 3f. Order entire $\overset{f\ I}{18-9}$. Diam. 20I.
to be encircled with a Portico of 24 columns. it's depth (including column & capping)6f1⅔ I.
Above the order internally to be a concave hemisphere with a circular aperture at top
    externally an Attic 5f. then 3 plinths falling back. then segment of sphere.

---

the Angular radius 16f 3I. clear.
the Radius of the sides 13f. clear, which gives the diameter 30f.
each side of the Octagon (internal) will be 12f 6I. & the circumfer^ce internal 100f.
in the South side the door of the chapel. in the North side the Pulpit &c.
in each of the other sides 3 forms parallel with the sides 3f. asunder.
between each section of forms a passage 2f. wide.
each forms to rise one above another. viz each 6.I.
the three forms will make 4 benches for sitters; viz.
the bench against the wall 12½f — 2f. = 10½f(@ 18I. each) will do for 7 persons
the bench before the first form 10 — 2f = 8f 5
the bench before the 2^d form 7½ — 2f = 5½f 3
the bench before the 3^d form 5 — 2 = 3f 2
                                                         $\overline{}$
                                                         17 persons
6. sections of the octagon with 17 persons each make 102 persons in the whole.
there will remain an Octagonal space in the middle of 12 f. diameter. or (al-
    -lowing for the benches of the center form on each side) 10f diam.
in this may be the Altar 2f 6I. square placed on a circular platform 4f 6I. diam.
one intermediate step to get to the platform of 9I. takes a circular space of 6f. diameter &
    leaves a vacancy of 2f. all round it for the people to pass to their seats.
a gallery within, level with top of order external, supported by 8 columns
    the order entire of these columns 15 — 1½f = 13½f. diameter will be [*Ms. torn*]
    the entablature will be 32⅖I. which leaves 10f9.6I external be [*Ms. torn*]
the windows 4f. wide: 8f 8I. high. architrave ab^t 8I. will make 9f 4I. in all.
    this leaves 17I. for height of window sill, i.e. even with the bench.
the gallery 3f. deep with 2 rows of benches. the back bench will hold 8. the fo [*Ms. torn*]
    6 pair of the benches will hold 90 persons.
    so whole contents of church will be 193 persons.

BIBLIOGRAPHY

Bibliography

This bibliography lists:

1. Primary manuscript sources cited in the body of the work.

2. Secondary manuscript sources that proved especially valuable.

3. Printed books cited, with exceptions that fall into two categories:
   (a) standard works of general reference, such as *D. A. B.* and *O. E. D.*,
   and (b) works on architecture first published before 1660.

4. Certain printed books, not cited in the body of the work, of value for background information or for their illustrations.

5. Most of the articles and other matter in periodicals cited in the body of the work. Exceptions have been made in the case of a few items, such as genealogical notes and excerpts from quit-rent rolls, whose bearing on the main subject is quite indirect. When a collection of papers is printed in parts in several issues of a periodical, only those parts which contain pertinent matter are listed.

MANUSCRIPTS

Primary sources

BEVERLEY, ROBERT, Letter-book, 1761–1793. Manuscript Division, Library of Congress.

BLATHWAYT PAPERS. Colonial Williamsburg Archives.

BOTETOURT, LORD: papers concerning "His Excellency Lord Botetourt's Estate." R. A. Brock Collection, Henry E. Huntington Library, San Marino, California.

——— Botetourt Papers. Virginia State Archives.

BRUTON PARISH VESTRY BOOK, 1827–1889. Bruton Parish House, Williamsburg.

CARTER'S GROVE PLANTATION ACCOUNT BOOK, 1749–1756. Mr. George H. Burwell.

CLOSEN, BARON LOUIS VON, JOURNAL, 1780–1782, transcript. Manuscript Division, Library of Congress.

COLEMAN, CYNTHIA B. T., Letter-book. Mrs. George P. Coleman.

COLONIAL OFFICE PAPERS: C.O. 5/1305–5/1359. Public Record Office, London.

COUNCIL: Executive Journals of the Council, 1751–1774. Virginia State Archives.

FULHAM MANUSCRIPTS. Lambeth Palace Library.

GOOCH PAPERS, TRANSCRIPTS. Virginia Historical Society.

HARWOOD, HUMPHREY: Ledger. Colonial Williamsburg Archives.

JONES FAMILY: Papers of the Jones Family. Manuscript Division, Library of Congress.

"Journal of an Officer in the West Indies, 1764–5."
King's Manuscript 213. British Museum, London.

"A Journey on Horseback from Philadelphia to Charleston, S. C. in the year 1783." Virginia State Archives.

LUDWELL PAPERS. Virginia Historical Society.

MUTUAL ASSURANCE SOCIETY: Insurance Policies for "Lunatic Hospital" and "Eastern Asylum," nos. 1640 (May, 1821), 6023 (January, 1830), 14389 (October, 1846), 17639 (September, 1853). Virginia State Archives.

NICHOLSON PAPERS. Colonial Williamsburg Archives.

"Proposal for rendering the new House Convenient as well as Ornamental." Colonial Papers, Virginia State Archives.

PUBLIC HOSPITAL: Minutes of the Court of Directors. Eastern State Hospital, Williamsburg.

ROCHAMBEAU PAPERS, PHOTOSTATS. Manuscript Division, Library of Congress.

ROSE, ROBERT: Diary 1747–1751. Colonial Williamsburg Archives.

STAFFORD COUNTY DEEDS: Liber O (Wills, Inventories, 1748–1763). Virginia State Archives.

TUCKER-COLEMAN PAPERS. Colonial Williamsburg Archives.

VAUGHAN, SAMUEL: Diary, 1787, photostat. Manuscript Division, Library of Congress.

VIRGINIA ASSEMBLY: Acts of Virginia Assembly 1662–1702. Jefferson Collection, Manuscript Division, Library of Congress.

VIRGINIA MANUSCRIPTS: Transcripts of Virginia Manuscripts in the Public Record Office, London. Virginia State Archives.

WILLIAM AND MARY, COLLEGE OF: Journal of the Meetings of the President and Masters of William and Mary College [1729–1784]. College Archives.

——— Record Book of William and Mary College [1846–1879]. College Archives.

——— William and Mary College Papers. College Archives.

——— William and Mary College Papers. Lambeth Manuscripts, Bodleian Library, Oxford.

YORK COUNTY RECORDS. County Clerk's Office, Yorktown.

Secondary sources

ARCHITECTURAL REPORTS: Thomas Tileston Waterman, "The Wren Building of the College of William and Mary"; Milton L. Grigg, "Brafferton Hall"; Milton L. Grigg, "The President's House"; George S. Campbell, "The Public Magazine"; Singleton Peabody Moorehead, "The Public Gaol"; Alfred Lawrence Kocher, "The Public Records Office"; Ernest Maurice Frank, "The Guardhouse"; Alfred Lawrence Kocher and Howard Best Dearstyne, "The Courthouse of 1770"; Alfred Lawrence Kocher, "The Governor's Palace"; Howard Best Dearstyne, "The Capitol." Typescript, 1932–1956. Architectural Records Office, Colonial Williamsburg.

BULLOCK, HELEN CLAIRE, "The Botetourt Statue." Research Report, typescript, 1936. Department of Research, Colonial Williamsburg.

DUELL, PRENTICE, "The Wren Building: Archaeological Report, including a Brief History of the Four Forms of the Building." Typescript, 1932. Colonial Williamsburg Archives.

——— Letter to W. A. R. Goodwin, dated August 10, 1937. Department of Research, Colonial Williamsburg.

GOODWIN, MARY RANDOLPH MORDECAI, "The Courthouse of 1770." Research Report, typescript, 1954. Department of Research, Colonial Williamsburg.

HAYES, ELIZABETH, "The Background and Beginnings of the Restoration of Colonial Williamsburg, Virginia." Typescript, 1933. Colonial Williamsburg Archives.

STEPHENSON, MARY A., "The Eastern State Hospital at Williamsburg, Virginia." Research Report, typescript, 1950. Department of Research, Colonial Williamsburg.

——— "The First Theatre." Research Report, typescript, 1946. Department of Research, Colonial Williamsburg.

PRINTED WORKS

ADAM, WILLIAM, Vitruvius Scoticus; being a Collection of Plans, Elevations, and Sections . . . principally from the Designs of the late William Adam, Esq. Architect. Edinburgh: Adam Black and J. & J. Robertson; London: T. Underwood and J. Taylor, [1810].

ARCHITECTURAL PUBLICATION SOCIETY, The Dictionary of Architecture, 8 Volumes. London: the Society, 1852–1892.

ASSOCIATION FOR THE PRESERVATION OF VIRGINIA ANTIQUITIES: Year Book of the Association for the Preservation of Virginia Antiquities for 1896 and 1897. Richmond: the Association, 1896.

BAILEY, WORTH, "Lime Preparation at Jamestown in the Seventeenth Century," W. & M. Q., 2nd series, XVIII (January, 1938), 1–12.

BASSETT, JOHN SPENCER, ed., The Writings of "Colonel William Byrd, of Westover in Virginia, Esq." New York: Doubleday, Page and Co., 1901.

BELIDOR, BERNARD FOREST DE, "Of Powder Magazines," Gentleman's Magazine, XXX (June, 1760), 269–270.

BELL, LANDON COVINGTON, ed., Cumberland Parish, Lunenburg County, Virginia, Vestry Book 1746–1816. Richmond: The William Byrd Press, 1930.

BEVERLEY, ROBERT, The History and Present State of Virginia. London: R. Parker, 1705.
2nd edition. London: B. and S. Took, 1722.
New edition, edited by Louis Booker Wright. Chapel Hill: University of North Carolina Press, 1947.

BLANTON, WYNDHAM BOLLING, Medicine in Virginia in the Eighteenth Century. Richmond: Garrett and Massie, 1931.

BOLTON, ARTHUR THOMAS, AND HENDRY, H. D., eds., *The Wren Society* [*Publications*], 20 volumes. Oxford: Oxford University Press, 1924–1943.

BOYD, JULIAN PARKS, ed., *The Papers of Thomas Jefferson*, 12 volumes to date. Princeton: Princeton University Press, 1950–.

BOYD, WILLIAM KENNETH, ed., *William Byrd's Histories of the Dividing Line betwixt Virginia and North Carolina*. Raleigh: North Carolina Historical Commission, 1929.

BROCK, ROBERT ALONZO, ed., *The Official Letters of Alexander Spotswood*, 2 volumes. Richmond: Virginia Historical Society, 1882–1885.

—— ed., *The Official Records of Robert Dinwiddie*, 2 volumes. Richmond: Virginia Historical Society, 1883–1884.

BROCK, ROBERT KINCAID, *Archibald Cary of Ampthill, Wheelhorse of the Revolution*. Richmond: Garrett and Massie, 1937.

BROWNE, WILLIAM HAND, ed., *Proceedings and Acts of the General Assembly of Maryland, September, 1693–June, 1697* (being *Archives of Maryland*, XIX). Baltimore: Maryland Historical Society, 1899.

—— ed., *Proceedings of the Council of Maryland, 1693–1697* (being *Archives of Maryland*, XX). Baltimore: Maryland Historical Society, 1900.

[CAMPBELL, CHARLES], "Jamestown, Williamsburg and Yorktown," *Southern Literary Messenger* (Richmond), III (1837), 237–238, reprinted in *W. & M. Q.*, 1st series XXI (October, 1912), 136–138.

CAMPBELL, COLEN, *Vitruvius Britannicus*, 3 volumes. London: the author, 1715–1725.

CAMPBELL, HELEN JONES, "The Syms and Eaton Schools and their Successor," *W. & M. Q.*, 2nd series, XX (January, 1940), 1–61.

CAPPON, LESTER JESSE, and DUFF, STELLA F., *Virginia Gazette Index 1736–1780*, 2 volumes. Williamsburg: Institute of Early American History and Culture, 1950.

CHAMBERLAYNE, CHURCHILL GIBSON, ed., *Vestry Book of Christ Church Parish, Middlesex County, Virginia, 1663–1767*. Richmond: Old Dominion Press, 1927.

—— ed., *The Vestry Book of Petsworth Parish, Gloucester County, Virginia, 1677–1793*. Richmond: Virginia State Library Board, 1933.

—— ed., *The Vestry Book of St. Paul's Parish, Hanover County, Virginia, 1706–1786*. Richmond: Virginia State Library Board, 1940.

—— ed., *The Vestry Book and Register of St. Peter's Parish, New Kent and James City Counties, Virginia, 1684–1786*. Richmond: Virginia State Library Board, 1937.

CHANDLER, JULIAN ALVIN CARROLL, and SWEM, EARL GREGG, eds., "Pitch and Tar in Virginia, 1704, *W. & M. Q.*, 2nd series, III (July, 1923), 209–210.

CHUMBLEY, GEORGE LEWIS, *Colonial Justice in Virginia*. Richmond: The Dietz Press, 1938.

COLVIN, HOWARD MONTAGU, *A Biographical Dictionary of English Architects 1660–1840*. London: John Murray, 1954.

COUNCIL OF COLONIAL VIRGINIA: "Council Papers 1698–1700. From the Originals in the Virginia State Library," *V. M. H. B.*, XXI (April, 1913), 163–183; (July, 1913), 254–268; XXII (January, 1914), 29–43.

—— "Journals of the Council of Virginia in Executive Sessions, 1737–1763," *V. M. H. B.*, XIV (July, 1906), 1–35.

CUTTS, A. BAILEY, "The Educational Influence of Aberdeen in Seventeenth Century Virginia," *W. & M. Q.*, 2nd series, XV (July, 1935), 229–249.

DAVIS, N. M., "Public Powder Magazines at Charleston," *The Year Book of the City of Charleston*, 1942.

DEAN, C. G. T., *The Royal Hospital, Chelsea*. London: Hutchinson and Co., 1950.

DILL, ALONZO THOMAS, *Governor Tryon and his Palace*. Chapel Hill: University of North Carolina Press, 1955.

DODSON, LEONIDAS, *Alexander Spotswood, Governor of Colonial Virginia, 1710–1722*. London: Oxford University Press, 1932.

DORSEY, STEPHEN PALMER, *Early English Churches in America*. New York: Oxford University Press, 1952.

EASTERN STATE HOSPITAL: *The One Hundred and Thirty First Annual Report of the Eastern State Hospital*. Richmond: Superintendent of Public Printing, 1904.

ENTHOVEN, ERNEST JAMES, and ASHBEE, CHARLES ROBERT, eds., *Life and Works of Sir Christopher Wren. From the Parentalia or Memoirs by his Son Christopher*. Campden, Gloucestershire: Essex House Press, 1903.

FORMAN, HENRY CHANDLEE, *Jamestown and St. Mary's, Buried Cities of Romance*. Baltimore: The Johns Hopkins Press, 1938.

—— *The Architecture of the Old South*. Cambridge: Harvard University Press, 1948.

FORTESCUE, JOHN WILLIAM, HEADLAM, CECIL, and NEWTON, ARTHUR PERCIVAL, eds., *Calendar of State Papers, Colonial Series, America and West Indies*, 30 volumes covering period 1693–1739. London: H. M. Stationery Office, 1903–1953.

FOSTER, MARY L., *Colonial Capitals of the Dominion of Virginia*. [Lynchburg: J. P. Bell Company, printers, 1906.]

GANTER, HERBERT LAWRENCE, ed., "Documents Relating to the Early History of the College of William and Mary and to the History of the Church in Virginia," *W. & M. Q.*, 2nd series, XIX (July, 1939), 347–375; (October, 1939), 446–470; XX (January, 1940), 114–137; (April, 1940), 212–236.

GARVAN, ANTHONY N. B., *Architecture and Town Planning in Colonial Connecticut*. New Haven: Yale University Press, 1951.

GILLIAM, RICHARD D., "Skelton and Shelton Two Distinct Virginia Families," *W. & M. Q.*, 2nd series, IX (July, 1929), 209–216.

GOODWIN, THOMAS RUTHERFORD, *A Brief and True Report Concerning Williamsburg in Virginia*. Williamsburg: Colonial Williamsburg, 1941.

[GOODWIN, THOMAS RUTHERFORD], *The Capitol in which the General Assembly of the Colony and Commonwealth of Virginia Met from 1704 to 1779*. Williamsburg: Colonial Williamsburg, 1934.

GOODWIN, WILLIAM ARCHER RUTHERFORD, *Bruton Church, Williamsburg, Virginia; Brief Historical Notes*. [Williamsburg], 1903.

——— *Bruton Parish Church Restored and its Historic Environments*. Petersburg: Franklin Press, 1907.

——— *The Record of Bruton Parish Church*. Edited by Mary Frances Goodwin. Richmond: The Dietz Press, 1941.

GUNNIS, RUPERT, *Dictionary of British Sculptors 1660–1851*. London: Odhams Press, 1954.

GUNTHER, ROBERT WILLIAM THEODORE, *The Architecture of Sir Roger Pratt . . . from his Notebooks*. Oxford: printed for the author at the University Press, 1928.

HAMLIN, TALBOT, *Benjamin Henry Latrobe*. New York: Oxford University Press, 1955.

HARWOOD, THOMAS, *The History and Antiquities of the Church and City of Lichfield*. Gloucester, 1806.

HAWKS, FRANCIS LISTER, *Contributions to the Ecclesiastical History of the United States of America*, 2 volumes. New York: Harper and Brothers, 1836–1839.

HAY, GEORGE, *The Architecture of Scottish Post-Reformation Churches 1560–1843*. Oxford: Clarendon Press, 1957.

HEAWOOD, EDWARD, *Watermarks, mainly of the 17th and 18th Centuries*. Hilversum: Paper Publications Society, 1950.

HENING, WILLIAM WALLER, ed., *The Statutes at Large; being a Collection of All the Laws of Virginia*, 13 volumes. Richmond: the editor, 1810–1823.

HINKE, WILLIAM JOHN, trans. and ed., "Report of the Journey of Francis Louis Michel from Berne, Switzerland, to Virginia, October 2, 1701–December 1, 1702," *V. M. H. B.*, XXIV (January, 1916), 1–43, (April, 1916), 113–141, (June, 1916), 275–288.

JEFFERSON, THOMAS, *Notes on the State of Virginia*. London: J. Stockdale, 1787.

New edition, edited by William Harwood Peden. Chapel Hill: University of North Carolina Press, 1955.

JONES, GRANVILLE L., "The History of the Founding of the Eastern State Hospital of Virginia," *American Journal of Psychiatry*, CX (March, 1954), 644–650.

JONES, HUGH, *The Present State of Virginia. Giving a Particular and Short Account of the Indian, English, and Negroes Inhabitants of that Colony*. London: J. Clarke, 1724.

New edition, edited by Richard Lee Morton. Chapel Hill: University of North Carolina Press, 1956.

JONES, LEWIS HAMPTON, *Captain Roger Jones, of London and Virginia*. Albany, New York: Munsell's Sons, 1911.

KEITH, WILLIAM, *History of the British Plantations in America*. London: Society for the Encouragement of Learning, 1738.

KIMBALL, SIDNEY FISKE, "Jefferson and the Arts," *Proceedings of the American Philosophical Society*, LXXXVII (July, 1943), 238–245.

——— "Jefferson and the Public Buildings of Virginia: I–Williamsburg, 1770–1776," *Huntington Library Quarterly*, XII (February, 1949), 115–120.

——— "Jefferson and the Public Buildings of Virginia: II–Richmond, 1779–1780," *Huntington Library Quarterly*, XII (May, 1949), 303–310.

——— *Thomas Jefferson, Architect: Original Designs in the Collection of Thomas Jefferson Coolidge, Jr.* Cambridge, Massachusetts: Riverside Press, 1916.

KLINGBERG, FRANK JOSEPH, ed., *Codrington Chronicle: an Experiment in Anglican Altruism on a Barbados Plantation, 1710–1834*. Berkeley: University of California Press, 1949.

KOCHER, ALFRED LAWRENCE, and DEARSTYNE, HOWARD BEST, *Colonial Williamsburg: its Buildings and Gardens*. Williamsburg: Colonial Williamsburg, 1949.

——— "Discovery of the Foundations for Jefferson's Addition to the Wren Building," *Journal of the Society of Architectural Historians*, X, no. 3 (October, 1951), 28–31.

——— *Shadows in Silver: a Record of Virginia 1850–1900*. New York: Charles Scribner's Sons, 1954.

KRUMBHAAR, EDWARD BELL, "The Pennsylvania Hospital," *Transactions of the American Philosophical Society*, XLIII, part 1 (1953), 237–246.

LAND, ROBERT HUNT, "Henrico and its College," *W. & M. Q.*, 2nd series, XVIII (October, 1938), 453–498.

LATROBE, BENJAMIN HENRY BONEVAL, *The Journal of Latrobe*, edited by J. H. B. Latrobe. New York: D. Appleton and Co., 1905.

LEES-MILNE, JAMES, *The Age of Inigo Jones*. London: B. T. Batsford, 1953.

LITTLE, BRYAN, "Francis Fauquier and an English Architect," *W. & M. Q.*, 3rd series, XII (July, 1955), 475–476.

——— "Norborne Berkeley: Gloucestershire Magnate," *V. M. H. B.*, LXII (October, 1955), 379–409.

——— *The Life and Works of James Gibbs, 1682–1754*. London: B. T. Batsford, 1955.

LOSSING, BENSON J., *The Pictorial Field-Book of the Revolution*, 2 volumes. New York: Harper and Brothers, 1859.

McCABE, JOHN COLLINS, "The Old Vestry Books of Bruton Parish," *Church Review*, VIII (March, 1856).

McIlwaine, Henry Read, and Hall, Wilmer Lee, eds., *Executive Journals of the Council of Colonial Virginia*, 5 volumes to date. Richmond: Virginia State Library, 1925–.

McIlwaine, Henry Read, ed., *Journals of the House of Burgesses of Virginia*, 8 volumes. Richmond: Virginia State Library, 1909–1915.

—— *Legislative Journals of the Council of Colonial Virginia*, 3 volumes. Richmond: Virginia State Library, 1918–1919.

—— *Official Letters of the Governors of the State of Virginia*, 3 volumes. Richmond: Virginia State Library, 1926–1929.

McCrady, Edward, *The History of South Carolina under the Royal Government 1719–1776*. New York: The Macmillan Company, 1899.

Mason, Frances Norton, *John Norton & Sons, Merchants of London and Virginia*. Richmond: The Dietz Press, 1937.

Mason, George Carrington, *Colonial Churches of Tidewater Virginia*. Richmond: Whittet and Shepperson, 1945.

Matthews, Albert, letter to editor on the term Capitol, *Nation* (New York), LX (May 9, 1895), 361.

—— "The Term State-House," *Dialect Notes* (New Haven), II (1902), 199–224.

Maury, Ann, ed., *Memoirs of a Huguenot Family*. New York: George P. Putnam and Co., 1853.

Morison, Samuel Eliot, *The Founding of Harvard College*. Cambridge: Harvard University Press, 1935.

—— *Harvard in the Seventeenth Century*. Cambridge: Harvard University Press, 1936.

Morris, Robert, *Lectures on Architecture Consisting of Rules Founded upon Harmonick and Arithmetical Proportions in Building*, 2 volumes. London, 1734–1736.

—— *Select Architecture. Being . . . Designs of Plans . . . Well Suited to Both Town and Country*. London, 1755.

Morrison, Hugh Sinclair, *Early American Architecture from the First Colonial Settlements to the National Period*. New York: Oxford University Press, 1952.

Morrison, Robert J. "The College after the Fire of 1859," *W. & M. Q.*, 1st series, XVI (October, 1907), 132–136.

—— "The Vaults in the East End of the Chapel of the College of William and Mary," *W. & M. Q.*, 2nd series, VIII (October, 1928), 269–270.

Moxon, Joseph, *Mechanick Exercises: or the Doctrine of Handy-Works*. 3rd edition. London, 1703.

Murray, Charles Augustus, *Travels in North America during the Years 1834–1836*, 2 volumes. London: R. Bentley, 1839.

N[eve, T.] *The City and Countrey Purchaser, and Builder's Dictionary*. London, 1703.

Nicholson, Francis: *Papers Relating to an Affidavit Made by His Reverence James Blair . . . against Francis Nicholson, Esq*. London, 1727.

Nicolai, Alexandre, *Histoire des Moulins à Papier du Sud-Ouest de la France 1300–1800*. Bordeaux: G. Delmas, 1935.

Oldmixon, John, *The British Empire in America*, 2 volumes. London: J. Brotherton, J. Clarke, 1741.

Palmer, William Pitt, et al., eds., *Calendar of Virginia State Papers and Other Manuscripts, Preserved in the Capitol at Richmond*, 11 volumes. Richmond: varying imprint, 1875–1893.

Peirce, Elizabeth Combs, "Courthouses of Lancaster County, 1656–1950," *Northern Neck Historical Magazine*, I (December, 1951), 23–35.

Perry, William Stevens, ed., *Historical Collections Relating to the American Colonial Church*, 5 volumes. Hartford: Church Press Company, 1870–1878.

Peterson, Charles E., "Carpenters' Hall," *Transactions of the American Philosophical Society*, XLIII, part I (1953), 96–128.

Pevsner, Nikolaus, *The Buildings of England: Hertfordshire*. London: Penguin Books, 1953.

Radoff, Morris Leon, *Buildings of the State of Maryland at Annapolis*. Annapolis: The Hall of Records Commission, State of Maryland, 1954.

R[ichards, Godfrey], ed., *The First Book of Architecture by Andrea Palladio*. London, 1663.

Riley, Edward Miles, "The Colonial Courthouses of York County, Virginia," *W. & M. Q.*, 2nd series, XXII (October, 1942), 399–414.

Rowlandson, Thomas, and Pugin, Augustus Charles, *The Microcosm of London*, 3 volumes. London: R. Ackerman, 1808.

Salmon, William, *Palladio Londinensis, or the London Art of Building*. London, 1734.

3rd edition, edited by Edward Hoppus, with "Builder's Dictionary" appended. London, 1748.

Shelley, Fred, ed., "The Journal of Ebenezer Hazard in Virginia, 1777," *V. M. H. B.*, LXII (October, 1954), 400–423.

Southern, Richard, *Changeable Scenery: its Origin and Development in the British Theatre*. London: Faber and Faber, 1952.

—— *The Georgian Playhouse*. London: Pleiades Books, 1948.

Stoney, Samuel Gaillard, *Plantations of the Carolina Low Country*. Charleston, South Carolina: The Carolina Art Association, 1938.

Story, Thomas, *A Journal of the Life of Thomas Story . . . and also, of his Travels*. Newcastle-upon-Tyne: I. Thompson and Company, 1747.

Summerson, John Newenham, *Architecture in Britain 1530 to 1830*. London: Penguin Books, 1954.

—— *Georgian London*. London: Cresset Press, 1945.

Swem, Earl Gregg, "Some Notes on the Four Forms of the Oldest Building of William and Mary College," *W. & M. Q.*, 2nd series, VIII (October, 1928), 217–307.

[Swem, Earl Gregg, ed.,] "Supplementary Documents Giving Additional Information concerning the Four Forms of the Oldest Building of William and Mary College," *W. & M. Q.*, 2nd series, X (January, 1930), 68–86.

SWEM, EARL GREGG, ed., *Virginia Historical Index*, 2 volumes. Roanoke: Stone Printing and Manufacturing Company, 1934–1936.

TECHNICAL PRESS, publ., *The Practical Exemplar of Architecture*. London: Technical Press, n.d.

THURLOW, CONSTANCE E., and BERKELEY, FRANCIS L., JR., *The Jefferson Papers of the University of Virginia*. Charlottesville: University of Virginia Press, 1950.

TIPPING, HENRY AVRAY, *English Homes*, 9 volumes. London: Country Life, 1921–1928.

[TUCKER, ST. GEORGE], *A Letter, to the Rev. Jedediah Morse, A. M., Author of the "American Universal Geography."* Richmond: T. Nicholson, 1795. Reprinted in *W. & M. Q.*, 1st series, II (January, 1894), 184–197.

TURNOR, REGINALD, *The Smaller English House*. London: B. T. Batsford. 1952.

TYLER, LYON GARDINER, ed., "Correspondence Relating to Lord Botetourt," *Tyler's Quarterly Historical and Genealogical Magazine*, III (October, 1921), 106–126.

––– ed., "Diary of John Blair," *W. & M. Q.*, 1st series, VII (January, 1899), 133–153, VIII (July, 1899), 1–17.

––– ed., "Observations in Several Voyages and Travels in *America* in the Year 1736; from *The London Magazine*, July, 1746," *W. & M. Q.*, 1st series, XVI (January, 1907), 1–17; (April, 1907), 215–224.

––– ed., "Unpublished Letters at Fullham [*sic*], in the Library of the Bishop of London." *W. & M. Q.*, 1st series, IX (April, 1901), 218–227.

––– "The Walls of the College," *W. & M. Q.*, 1st series, XI (January, 1903), 174–179.

––– *Williamsburg, the Old Colonial Capital*. Richmond: Whittet and Shepperson, 1907.

VIRGINIA: "Miscellaneous Colonial Documents. From the Originals in the Virginia State Archives," *V. M. H. B.*, XVI (July, 1908), 72–84; XVII (January, 1909), 34–46.

VIRGINIA GAZETTE. Williamsburg, 1736–1780. From 1736 until 1766 there was one newspaper of this title; from 1766 until 1780 there were always two and for a period three. The printers were as follows:–*Virginia Gazette [I]*, William Parks, 1736–1750; William Hunter, 1751–1761; Joseph Royle, 1761–1765; Alexander Purdie and Co., 1765–1766; Alexander Purdie and John Dixon, 1766–1775; Dixon and William Hunter (Jr.), 1775–1778; Dixon and Thomas Nicolson, 1779–April, 1780. *Virginia Gazette [II]*, William Rind, 1766–1773; Clementina Rind, 1773–1774; John Pinkney, 1774–1776. *Virginia Gazette [III]*, Alexander Purdie, 1775–1779; John Clarkson and Augustine Davis, 1779–December, 1780.

WARE, ISAAC, *A Complete Body of Architecture. Adorned with Plans and Elevations, from Original Designs*. London, 1756.

WATERMAN, THOMAS TILESTON, "The Bay System

in Colonial Virginia Building, *W. & M. Q.*, 2nd series, XV (April, 1935), 117–122.

––– *The Mansions of Virginia 1706–1766*. Chapel Hill: University of North Carolina Press, 1946.

––– and JOHNSTON, FRANCES BENJAMIN, *The Early Architecture of North Carolina*. Chapel Hill: University of North Carolina Press, 1941.

WEBB, MARGARET I., *Michael Rysbrack, Sculptor*. London: Country Life, 1954.

WELD, ISAAC, *Travels through the States of North America and the Provinces of Upper and Lower Canada during the Years 1795, 1796, and 1797*. London: J. Stockdale, 1799.

WERTENBAKER, THOMAS JEFFERSON, *The Old South: the Founding of American Civilization*. New York: Charles Scribner's Sons, 1942.

WHIFFEN, MARCUS, *Stuart and Georgian Churches: the Architecture of the Church of England outside London 1603–1837*. London: B. T. Batsford, 1948.

––– "Some Virginian House Plans Reconsidered," *Journal of the Society of Architectural Historians*, XVI, no. 2 (May, 1957), 17–19.

WHITELAW, RALPH T., *Virginia's Eastern Shore: a History of Northampton and Accomack Counties*. Richmond: Virginia Historical Society, 1951.

WILLIAM AND MARY, COLLEGE OF: "Accounts of the College," *W. & M. Q.*, 1st series, VIII (January, 1900), 166–171.

––– *The Charter, and Statutes, of the College of William and Mary in Virginia*. Williamsburg: William Parks, 1736. Reprinted in *W. & M. Q.*, 1st series, XXII (April, 1914), 282–296.

––– "Depositions as to the Burning of William and Mary College, 1705," *V. M. H. B.*, VI (January, 1899), 271–277.

––– "Description of William and Mary College, 1765," *V. M. H. B.*, XVI (October, 1908), 209–210.

––– *The History of the College of William and Mary in Virginia, from its Foundation, 1693, to 1870*. Baltimore: J. Murphy and Co., 1870.

––– "Papers Relating to the Administration of Governor Nicholson and to the Founding of William and Mary College," *V. M. H. B.*, VII (October, 1899), 153–168.

––– "Proceedings of the Visitors of William and Mary College, 1716. (Ludwell Papers, Virginia Historical Society Collections)," *V. M. H. B.*, IV (October, 1896), 161–175.

WISE, JENNINGS CROPPER, *Ye Kingdome of Accawmacke; or, The Eastern Shore of Virginia in the Seventeenth Century*. Richmond: The Bell Book and Stationery Co., 1911.

WITTKOWER, RUDOLF, *Architectural Principles in the Age of Humanism*. London: The Warburg Institute, University of London, 1949.

WRIGHT, LOUIS BOOKER, and TINLING, MARION, eds., *The Secret Diary of William Byrd of Westover 1709–1712*. Richmond. The Dietz Press, 1941.

YATES, FRANCES A., "Queen Elizabeth as Astraea," *Journal of the Warburg and Courtauld Institutes*, X (1947), 27–82.

INDEX

Index

A

Aberdeen (Scotland), 2, 4, 219.
Abingdon Church (Gloucester
  County, Va.), 84, 133, 135.
  doorway of (*illus.*), 135.
Accomac County (Virginia), 42,
  84, 117.
  play presented in, 117.
Accomac Courthouse, 117.
Acquia Church *see* Aquia Church.
Actors, 113, 115, 116, 117, 216.
  in Accomac, 117.
  in Williamsburg, 113, 116, 216.
Adam, James, 161.
  Robert, 161, 171.
  William, 160, 161.
Addison, Joseph, 94.
Admiralty, High Court of, 36.
The Age of Inigo Jones, 213.
Albemarle, Earl of, 226.
Albemarle County (Virginia), 134.
Alberti, L. B., 14, 209.
*Alexander Spotswood, Governor of
  Colonial Virginia*, 214.
Allen, Matthew, 97.
American Colonial Architecture
  see Architecture.
American Journal of Psychiatry,
  219.
American Revolution, 11, 189, 191,
  193.
The American Weekly Mercury,
  216.
Amherst, Sir Jeffrey, 226.
Amsterdam, 94.
Andrews, C. M., 205.
Andros, Sir Edmund, 18, 19, 20,
  21, 22, 23, 67, 119, 225.
  bricks for chapel promised by,
  20–21, 22, 119.
  charges against, 18–19, 20–21,
  gift of sashing for College, 23.
  governor of Virginia (1692–
  1698), 225.
  recalled as governor, 21, 67.
Annapolis (Maryland), 8, 9, 10,
  20, 39, 83, 86, 214.
  church at, 83, 214.
  magazine at, 86, 214.
  planned by F. Nicholson, 8–9.
  plans of (1696), 9; (1718), 209.

statehouse at, 39.
town plan of, 8–9.
Anne, Queen, 25, 43, 48, 55, 86,
  96, 139.
  accession of proclaimed in
  Williamsburg, 25, 48.
  arms of, 43.
  gift of arms and ammunition to
  Virginia, 86.
  gift of funds to William & Mary
  College, 96.
  name of on Capitol, 48.
  portrait of, 139.
Anne Arundel County (Mary-
  land), 9.
Apethorpe (Northamptonshire),
  212.
Apothecaries, 116, 216.
Appleby (Leicestershire), 32.
Appomattox River, 129.
Apprentices, 46, 217.
Apses, 36, 42, 50.
  See also Capitol, semicircular
  ends of.
Apulia (Italy), 11.
Aquia Church (Stafford County,
  Va.), 142, 218.
Arcaded loggias, 211.
Archaeological investigation in
  Williamsburg, 23, 24, 25,
  26, 63, 182, 210, 211.
  plans of foundations (*illus.*), 47,
  59, 76, 115.
  See also under names of build-
  ings.
Archbishop of Canterbury *see*
  Canterbury.
Archibald Cary of Ampthill, 212.
Architects:
  American, 15–17, 41, 50, 65,
  141, 162, 172, 179, 194,
  195, 196, 198, 200, 203,
  204, 212.
  training of, 16–17.
  See also under names.
  English, 15, 16, 17, 61, 62, 64,
  118, 119, 210, 214, 220.
  methods of, 15–17, 210.
  remuneration of, 17.
  training of, 16.
  See also under names.
  Scottish, 29.

Architectural Department, Colonial
  Williamsburg, 208, 221.
*Architectural Principles in the Age
  of Humanism*, 219.
Architectural Publication Society,
  214.
Architectural Records Office,
  Colonial Williamsburg,
  221.
Architectural Review, 211.
Architectural schools, 16–17.
Architecture:
  American colonial, 14–15, 49,
  118–119, 179.
  baroque in, 9, 14, 49, 95, 146,
  179.
  Dutch influence on, 63.
  Neo-classicism in, 15, 146,
  179, 187.
  Palladianism in, 64, 118–119,
  121, 179.
  Scottish influence on, 29, 219.
  English, 14, 28–29, 31, 32, 36,
  49, 50, 58, 61, 62, 63, 64,
  65–66, 68, 83, 84, 102, 103,
  118–119, 121, 143, 160–
  161, 179, 210, 211.
  baroque in, 14, 31, 118, 179.
  Elizabethan, 28, 36, 50, 61.
  French influence on, 62.
  Georgian, 160–161.
  Italian influence on, 31, 103,
  118.
  Jacobean, 28, 61.
  Neo-classicism in, 179.
  Palladianism in, 64, 118–119,
  121, 179.
*Architecture and Town Planning
  in Colonial Connecticut*,
  209.
Architecture in Britain, 219.
*The Architecture of Scottish Post-
  Reformation Churches*, 214.
*The Architecture of Sir Roger
  Pratt . . . from his Note-
  books*, 213.
The Architecture of the Old South,
  211.
Architettura, 29, 30, 61, 71, 72,
  213.
  plans from (*illus.*), 29, 61, 71.
Archives of Maryland, 209, 210.
Armourers, 86, 88.

Arms and ammunition, 86.
The Arts and Crafts in New York,
    210.
Ashbee, C. R., 210.
Ashdown (Berkshire), 62.
Association for the Preservation of
    Virginia Antiquities, 197,
    198, 208, 221.
Astraea, 212.
Asylums *see* Public Hospital.
Athawes, Samuel, 220.
Atlantic Ocean, 31, 32, 66.
Attorney-General of Virginia, 74.
Avenues, 214–215.

B

"The Background and Beginnings
    of the Restoration of Colo-
    nial Williamsburg, Vir-
    ginia," 221.
Bacon's Castle (Surry County,
    Va.), 39, 103.
Bacon's Rebellion, 53, 85.
Badminton (Gloucestershire), 219.
Bailey, W., 210.
Baker, Samuel, 22.
Balconies *see* under Capitol; Pal-
    ace; Playhouse; William &
    Mary College–Main Build-
    ing.
Ballrooms, 143–144. *See also* under
    Palace.
Baltimore (Maryland), 195.
Baptist church (Williamsburg),
    191.
Barbados, college in, 102, 104, 105,
    182.
Barbaro, Daniele, 72.
Barney, J. Stewart, 200.
Baroque architecture, 14, 31, 49,
    95, 118, 146, 179.
    town planning, 9, 14.
Barracks, 152.
Barradall, Edward, 146, 147.
Barret, Robert, 9.
Barry, Sir Charles, 213.
Bassett, J. S., 212, 214, 216.
Bath, Earl of, 67.
Bath-houses, 94.
Bathurst, Ralph, 211.
Bay System, 12, 209.
"The Bear and the Cub" (play),
    117.
Beard, Richard, 9.
Beaufort, Duke of, 95, 167.
Bedlam, 165.
    See also Bethlem Hospital.
Beds, 106.
Belidor, B. F. de, 214.
Bell, L. C., 217.
Bells, 97, 152.

Benches, 218, 233.
Benjamin Henry Latrobe, 214,
    218.
Benson, William, 118.
Berkeley, F. L., 220.
    Norborne, Baron de Botetourt
    see Botetourt.
    Sir William, 53, 75.
Berkshire (England), 61, 62.
Bermuda, 2.
Berne (Switzerland), 25, 211.
Bethlem (Bethlehem) Hospital
    (London), 165, 219.
Beverley, Robert, 9, 11, 14, 54,
    65, 70, 93, 94, 209, 213,
    214.
    history by quoted, 9, 11, 14, 70,
    93.
    letterbook of, 220.
Bidgood, Philip, 190.
*A Biographical Dictionary of Eng-
    lish Architects,* 210, 214,
    215.
Birmingham (England), 220.
Birthdays, royal *see* King's birthday
    celebrations.
Bishops, Anglican, 5.
    See also Canterbury, London,
    St. Asaph, Salisbury.
Bishops of Virginia, 216.
Blackwater Swamp (Virginia), 6.
Blair, Anne, 150, 219.
    Archibald, 74, 116.
    Rev. James, 2, 3, 4, 5, 6, 18, 19,
    20, 21, 22, 25, 29, 32, 33,
    46, 47–48, 67, 74, 83, 84,
    96, 106, 119, 120, 210,
    215.
    at University of Edinburgh,
    4, 29.
    at Varina (Henrico Co., Va.),
    4.
    commissary of Bishop of Lon-
    don, 4, 25, 74, 83, 119,
    215.
    councillor, 19, 20.
    criticism of, by Gov. Andros,
    19–20.
    founder of William & Mary
    College, 2, 4–6.
    in England, 4, 5–6, 18, 20,
    21, 22, 32, 106.
    letters of, 5, 18, 21, 22, 120,
    210.
    opposition of to Gov. Andros,
    18–19, 20, 67.
    to Gov. Nicholson, 47–48,
    67.
    to Gov. Spotswood, 67.
    overseer of, 33.
    pew of, 83.

    portrait of (*illus.*), 3.
    president of William & Mary
    College, 2, 6, 18, 96,
    120.
    quoted by Quaker, 119.
    salary of as college president,
    96.
    Scottish background of, 2, 4,
    29, 84, 119.
    sermon by (1702), 25.
    servants of, 21, 46.
    John, 116, 130, 146, 150, 181.
    diary of, 135–136, 137, 138,
    140, 141, 142, 215, 217.
    Martha, 150, 219.
    Rev. Robert, 2.
Blair's Brick House (Williams-
    burg), 103.
Bland, Theodoric, 12, 19, 25, 37,
    39, 211.
Bland Survey of Williamsburg
    (1699), 12, 19, 25, 37, 39,
    211.
    Capitol on (*illus.*), 39.
Blathwayt, William, 210.
Blathwayt Papers, Colonial Wil-
    liamsburg Archives, 210.
Blenheim, Battle of, 67.
Blisland Parish (Virginia), 218.
Bloomsbury Square (Annapolis),
    209.
Bloomsbury Square (London),
    209.
Blue Bell (Williamsburg), 103.
Blue Ridge Mountains (Virginia),
    67.
Boadicea, statue in London of, 1.
Board of Trade, 21, 54, 56, 86, 90,
    91, 92, 113, 129, 140, 141,
    210, 212.
Bodleian Library (Oxford), 19,
    205, 210, 212.
Bodleian Plate (copperplate), 48,
    49, 58, 61, 93, 94, 138,
    205, 212.
    date of, 212.
    discovery of, 205, 212.
    illustrations of buildings from,
    49, 58, 97.
    presentation of, 212.
Bologna (Italy), 31
Bona Nova (ship), 2.
Books, 11, 84, 94–95, 118, 160,
    186, 219.
    in Virginia, 11, 94–95, 160, 186,
    219.
    on architecture, 11, 84, 118,
    160, 186, 219.
    on gardening, 94–95.
Boston (Massachusetts), 203, 204,
    205, 207.

Botetourt, Norborne, Berkeley, Baron de, 64, 65, 94, 121, 122, 123, 143, 144, 162, 166–167, 168, 171, 174, 176, 178, 213, 216, 217, 218, 219, 220, 226.
  buried in William & Mary Chapel, 121–122, 123, 216–217.
  coffin-plate of, 216.
  furniture of, 143, 144, 218.
  See also inventory of.
  governor of Virginia (1768–1770), 226.
  inventory of estate at Palace, 64, 65, 94, 143, 144, 174, 176, 178, 213, 218.
  medallions of, 167, 168.
  monument proposed for, 122–123.
  papers concerning estate (Brock Mss.), 216, 220.
  popularity of, 121, 166–167.
  portrait of mentioned, 167.
  statue of see Botetourt Statue.
Botetourt Papers (Virginia State Archives), 216, 218, 219.
Botetourt Statue, 123, 139, 140, 150, 166–171, 190.
  at Capitol, 139, 140, 150, 168.
  at Public Hospital, 190.
  at William & Mary College, 168, 190.
  photographs of (illus.), 169, 170.
  sculptor of, 139, 140, 167, 168, 171.
  See also Richard Hayward.
  sketch of by Latrobe, 190.
Bow windows, 36.
Bowler, Mr., 121.
Bowling Green (Virginia), 50.
Boxwood, 94.
Boyd, J. P., 220.
  W. K., 212.
Boyle, Richard see Burlington, Richard Boyle, Earl of.
  Robert, 106–107, 109.
  portrait of, 109.
Bracken, Rev. John, 190, 191.
Braddon, Paul, 62.
The Brafferton (William & Mary College), 106, 107–112, 125–126, 196, 205.
  compared to President's House, 125–126.
  compared to Sutton Coldfield Rectory, 111, 112.
  damage to (1862), 196.
  date of building, 107.
  designer of, 107, 108, 112.

  dimensions of, 108, 125.
  elevations of, 109, 125.
    north (illus.), 109.
  fireplaces in 112, 125.
  floor plan of (illus.), 108.
  funds for building, 106.
  Indian school in, 106, 109, 112.
  library in, 109.
  photograph of (illus.), 110.
  restoration of (1931–32), 205.
  rooms in, 108–109, 112, 125.
  stairway in, 108.
  woodwork of removed (1862), 196.
Brafferton Hall see The Brafferton.
Brafferton Manor (Yorkshire), 106, 215.
Braintree (Essex, England), 218.
Brandy, 25.
Braxton, Carter, 88.
  Martha, 219.
Bray, David, 145.
Brick House (Edisto, S. C.), 213.
Brick-kilns, 89, 136, 138, 210.
Bricklayers, 15, 21, 22, 41, 44, 123, 134, 164, 189, 209, 218, 230.
  for Capitol, 41.
  for President's House, 123.
  for Public Hospital, 164, 230.
  for William & Mary College, 21, 22.
  from England, 21–22, 41, 44.
  measures of, 209.
  See also Workmen.
Brick-makers, 2, 21, 41.
Bricks, 19, 20, 21, 22, 40, 41, 48, 79, 80, 84, 89, 103, 119, 133, 157, 163, 164, 185, 187, 189, 191, 195, 198, 210, 216, 217, 227, 229, 230, 231.
  Andros' promise of for chapel, 20–21, 22, 119.
  cost of, 21, 40, 41, 79, 80, 210, 216.
  cut, 48, 84.
  for Bruton Parish Church, 79, 80.
  for Capitol, 40, 41, 48, 136, 137, 138, 210, 227.
    sold, 190.
  for Gaol, re-use of, 195.
  for Palace, 89.
    sold from ruins of, 189, 195, 198.
  for Public Hospital, 163, 164, 229, 230, 231.
  for William & Mary College, 19, 20, 21, 22.
    for chapel of, 119, 216.

  from Jamestown, 157.
  glazed, 133.
  moulding, 229.
  re-use of, 157, 185, 189, 190, 191, 195, 198, 217.
  rubbed, 133.
Brickwork, 35, 80, 121, 133, 164, 210, 218, 227, 229–230, 231.
  bond of, 121, 133, 210.
  See also under buildings by name.
Bridges, Charles, 69.
A Brief Discourse Concerning the Three Chief Principles of Magnificent Building, 58.
Bristol (England), 40.
The British Empire in America, 70, 210.
British Museum (London), 209.
Brock, R. A., 213, 216, 219, 220.
  R. K., 212.
Brown, Mather, 172.
Bruce, Sir William, 29.
Brunswick County (Virginia), 215.
Bruton (Somerset, England), 75.
Bruton Parish (Virginia), 75.
  name of, 75.
Bruton Parish Church (built 1683), 75–77, 78, 85.
  plan of foundations (illus.), 76.
  sketch of by Michel (illus.), 78.
Bruton Parish Church (built 1711–15), 14, 15, 77–85, 86, 145–146, 150–155, 191–192, 196, 200, 218.
  addition to (1751–55), 146.
  alterations to, 146, 150, 152, 192, 196, 200.
  bells of, 152.
  building materials for, 79, 80.
  communion table for, 79.
  compared with London churches, 14, 83.
  contract for building, 79.
    for building steeple, 150, 152.
  cruciform plan of, 15, 82, 83, 84, 136.
  diagrammatic plan of (illus.), 81.
  dimensions of, 77, 79, 80, 82.
  doors of, 79, 80.
  doorways of, 84.
  draught or platt of, 77.
  elevation, south, (illus.), 155.
  floors of, 79, 80.
  font in, 83.
  galleries in, 79, 82, 83, 146.
  governor's pew in, 77, 83, 192.

Bruton Parish Church (continued)
  organ in, 146, 150, 192.
  organ-gallery in, 146, 218.
  overseer for building, 79, 86.
  pews in, 77, 79, 83, 192.
  photographs of (illus.), 151,
    153, 192.
  photographs of interior (illus.),
    206, 207.
  plan of (illus.), 154.
  pulpit in, 79, 83.
  rectors of, 77, 83, 191, 192, 200.
  repairs to, 152, 192, 196.
  restoration of (1903–07), 200.
  restoration of (1939), 208.
  roof of, 80, 82, 84.
  seating arrangements in, 83. See
    also pews in.
  Spotswood's design of, 68, 77,
    79, 80, 82, 83, 84, 100,
    102.
  Spotswood's pew in, 77, 83, 192.
  steeple added, 150–152.
  transept of, 79, 80, 82, 86, 100,
    192.
  windows of, 80.
  woodwork of, 192
  workmen for, 79, 80, 83, 137.
    for addition to, 146.
    for steeple of, 150, 152.
Bruton Parish Church Restored,
  221.
Bruton Parish Churchyard, 144,
  145, 146, 147, 164.
  tombs in, 144, 145, 146, 147.
  wall around, 145, 164.
Bruton Parish House, 221.
Bruton Parish Vestry Books, 75,
  77, 79, 83, 196, 221.
Buckinghamshire (Eng.), 64, 220.
Buglers, 25.
Builders, 15–17, 134, 217.
  use of word, 134, 217.
  See also Carpenters; Bricklayers
    etc.
Building contracts, 15, 16, 17, 21,
  42, 46, 79, 120, 217, 221,
  231.
  for Bruton Parish Church, 79.
  for Capitol, 42, 46.
  for Public Hospital, 231.
  for William & Mary College, 21,
    120.
  in England, 15–16, 217.
  in Virginia, 16, 217.
Building in England down to 1540,
  214.
Building materials see Bricks;
  Glass; Ironwork; Lime;
  Nails; Scantling; Shingles;
  Slate; Stone; Timber, etc.

Building methods, 15–17.
Building trades, 16.
  See also Bricklayers; Carpenters;
    Joiners; Masons, etc.
The Buildings of England: Hert-
  fordshire, 214.
Buildings of the State of Maryland
  at Annapolis, 209, 211,
  214.
Bullock, Orin M., Jr., 205.
Buntingford (Hertfordshire), 83,
  214.
Burgesses, Virginia House of, 40,
  67.
  activities of concerning the
    Botetourt Statue, 167.
    concerning Bruton Parish
      Church, 77, 79.
    concerning the Capitol, 34,
      35, 37, 38, 40, 42, 43, 45,
      46, 47, 48, 51, 134.
    concerning the Gaol, 42, 51,
      70, 74.
    concerning the Magazine, 85,
      86, 147.
    concerning the Palace, 53, 54,
      55, 56, 57, 88, 89, 90, 91,
      92, 93.
    concerning the Public Hos-
      pital, 161, 162, 164.
    concerning the removal of the
      capital (1699), 7, 34, 35;
      (1747), 128–130.
    concerning the Secretary's
      Office, 130.
    concerning William & Mary
      College, 5, 6, 7, 18, 20,
      23, 96.
  clerks of, 37.
  journals of, 209, 214.
  meets at Capitol for first time,
    45.
  meets at Jamestown, 43.
  meets at William & Mary Col-
    lege (1700–04), 23.
  pews for in Bruton Parish
    Church, 77.
  room for in Capitol, 35, 43, 188,
    228.
    See also Capitol, Burgesses
      Room in.
  speakers of, 46, 47, 167.
  See also General Assembly of
    Virginia.
Burke, J. B., 212.
Burlington, Richard Boyle, Earl of,
  106, 109, 118.
Burton, George, 33.
Burwell, Carter, 147.
  George H., 217.
  Lewis, 142, 181.

"Busy-Body" (play), 216.
Buttresses, 75, 77, 214.
Byrd, William I, 21.
  William II, 24, 73, 91, 92, 93,
    96, 107, 116, 212, 214,
    216.

C

Calendar of State Papers, Colonial
  Series, 213.
Calendar of Virginia State Papers,
  214, 218, 221.
Cambridge University, 29, 103,
  121, 123, 182, 212.
  chapels at, 121, 123.
  quadrangular colleges at, 29.
  students' rooms at, 103, 182.
Campbell, Charles, 214, 221.
  Colen, 66, 118, 213.
  H. J., 212.
Cannon balls, 191.
Canterbury, Archbishop of, 5, 20,
  21, 22, 23, 96.
Capital of Virginia, removal of
  (1699), 7, 34, 35.
  removal of (1779–80), 188.
  removal of considered (1747–
    48), 128–130, 140.
  See also Jamestown; Richmond;
    Williamsburg.
Capitol (Richmond, Virginia),
  220.
Capitol (Williamsburg):
  first building (1701–1747), 7,
    8, 11, 12, 14, 15, 16, 34–
    50, 51, 54, 80, 84, 127–
    128, 130, 138, 140, 210,
    211, 212, 227–228.
  acts of General Assembly con-
    cerning, 7, 8, 11, 12, 34–
    35, 37, 38, 39, 40, 42, 43–
    44, 45, 46, 51, 211, 212,
    227–228.
  archaeological investigation of,
    47, 211.
  plan of foundations
    (illus.), 47.
  architectural character of, 48-
    50.
    See also design of.
  balconies of, 35, 43–44, 227.
  bar in Burgesses room, 43.
  bells in cupola, 128.
  building accounts for, 44, 45.
  building materials for, 40, 41,
    42, 44, 45.
    from England, 41, 44–45.
    See also Bricks; Lime;
      Scantling; Shingles; Tim-
      ber.
  bricks for, 40, 41, 138, 210.

brickwork of, 35, 227.
burgesses first use, 45.
Burgesses Room in, 35, 36, 43, 44, 45, 140, 228.
burning of (1747), 127–128.
chimneys added (1723), 48–49, 128.
clock in cupola of, 128, 227.
committees to superintend building of, 40, 41, 42, 46, 51, 212, 227, 228.
compared to Jamestown State-house, 36, 39, 50.
completion of, 43, 44, 45–47.
Conference Room in, 39.
contract for building, 16, 42, 46.
costs of building, 40, 41, 42, 44–45, 54.
Council Chamber in, 35, 228.
cross gallery of, 35, 37–39, 42, 227, 228.
cupola of, 35, 44, 48, 49, 128, 227.
descriptions of (1705–1736), 14.
design of, 34, 35, 36, 37, 38, 39, 40, 42, 49, 50, 51, 211, 227–228.
  changes in, 36–39, 51, 228.
designer of, 34, 36.
dimensions of, 12, 35, 36, 37, 38, 80, 140, 211, 227, 228.
directions for building, 34–35, 37, 38, 40–48, 227–228.
doors of, 41, 42, 43, 137, 140, 228.
dormer windows of, 44. See also windows of.
draught of mentioned, 34, 37.
fireplaces in, 48, 49, 131. See also chimneys added.
flag on, 227.
flagstone for, 35, 228.
floor plans of (illus.), 44, 45.
flooring for, 35, 41, 44, 228.
"form of" see design of; H-plan of.
foundations of, 35, 41, 42, 47, 48, 134, 138, 211, 227.
  excavated, 47, 211.
  laid (1701), 41, 42, 138.
  plan of (illus.), 47.
  re-used in second Capitol, 134.
  See also Capitol—Second Building.
furnishings in, 43, 128.
galleries in, 227, 228.
  See also cross gallery of.
gates of, 227.

General Court Room in, 35, 37, 43, 44, 45, 140, 227, 228.
  court first sits in, 43, 44.
glazing of, 44. See also windows of.
H-form of, 37, 38, 39, 50, 211, 227.
inscriptions on, 48.
iron balconies of see balconies of.
named "Capitol," 11, 37.
Nicholson's arms on, 48.
overseer for building, 40, 41, 42, 48, 84.
  See also Henry Cary.
painting of woodwork in, 44, 45.
paving stone for, 43, 44, 45, 228.
piazza of, 35, 37, 50, 140, 227.
pictures in, 128.
pictures of, 48, 49, 138.
  on Bodleian plate, 48, (illus.) 49, 138, 205.
  reconstructed building, 200.
plans of, floor-plans (illus.), 44–45.
  foundations (illus.), 47.
platted on survey (1699), 37, 39, 211.
  (illus.), 39.
"plot or draught" of mentioned, 34, 37.
porches of, 211, 227, 228.
privy for, 46.
Queen's arms at, 43, 48.
reconstruction of (1931–34), 205, 207–208.
  photograph of reconstructed building (illus.), 200.
records in, 128, 130.
roof of, 35, 44, 45, 49, 128, 227.
rooms in, 35, 39, 43, 44, 45, 128, 227, 228.
  See also Burgesses Room in; Council Chamber in; General Court Room in.
sash windows of, 42, 227. See also windows of.
scantling for, 41.
seats in, 43.
semi-circular ends of, 36, 37, 128, 139, 211, 227.
semi-circular porches of, 211, 227, 228.
shingles of, 44, 128, 227.
specifications for, 138, 227–228.

staircases in, 227, 228.
steps of, 44.
stone for see paving stone for.
sundials on, 46, 48.
undertaker for building mentioned, 35, 40, 41, 42.
wainscoting in, 43, 45, 128.
wall around, 136.
walls of, 35, 128, 137, 211, 227.
window frames of, 41.
windows of, 35, 41, 42, 44, 45, 227, 228.
  arched, 42, 228.
  dormer, 44, 227.
  glass for, 45.
  sash, 42, 227.
woodwork in, 43, 45, 128.
workmen for, 40, 41, 42, 44, 46, 49.
  from England, 41, 44.
second building (built 1751–53), 14, 15, 79, 117, 123, 134–140, 142, 150, 157, 162, 168, 177, 189, 190, 191, 196, 198, 205, 207, 208.
act of General Assembly concerning, 134.
alterations to (1785–86), 189, 190.
balconies of, 136, 139.
Botetourt statue in, 123, 139, 140, 150, 168.
  See also Botetourt Statue.
brick kiln for, 136, 138.
bricks for, 136, 137, 138.
brickwork of, 136, 137, 140.
building committee for, 134, 136, 137.
building materials for, 134, 135, 136, 138.
built on foundations of first Capitol, 134, 137.
  See also foundations of.
Burgesses Room in, 137, 139, 140.
burned (1832), 191.
clock in cupola of, 140, 189.
columns of, 138, 139.
compared with first Capitol, 139.
completion of building, 138.
contractors for, 134, 136.
costs of building, 134, 137, 138.
Court of Admiralty in (1780), 189.
Court of Chancery in, 190.

Capitol, second building (continued)
cupola of, 137, 140, 189.
damage to (1780–1832), 189, 190, 191.
descriptions of, by Gordon, 14.
by Hazard, 138, 139–140, 162.
by Jefferson, 15, 138.
by Latrobe, 138–139.
Dinwiddie's gift of arms for portico of, 138.
doors of, 137.
doorways of, 137, 140.
foundations of, 134, 136, 137, 138, 198, 207, 208.
acquired by the A.P.V.A., 198, 208.
excavated, 138.
laid (1751), 136, 138.
old foundations reused, 134, 137, 207–208.
furniture in, 137, 139, 140.
galleries in, 139, 140.
gate of, 137, 139, 140.
General Court Room in, 137, 139, 140.
grammar school in (1784), 189–190.
H form of, 139.
hall of, 139.
hospital in (1781), 189.
King's arms on, 138, 139.
lead on cupola of, 140, 189.
lobby of, 139, 140
materials from sold, 190.
militia quartered in, 189.
piazza of, 138, 140, 157, 168.
pictures of, 138.
portico of, 137, 138, 139.
portraits in, 139, 140.
repairs to, 152, 189, 190.
roof of, 137, 138.
rooms in, 139, 140.
    See also Burgesses Room in; General Court Room in.
sash-work in, 137, 142.
    See also windows of.
seats, new model for, 137, 139.
site of, 191, 196, 198, 208.
acquired by A.P.V.A., 198.
acquired by Colonial Williamsburg, 208.
speaker's chair in, 139.
stairs of, 137.
statue in see Botetourt statute in.
steps of, 137

stone for, 137, 138.
stove in, 139.
timber for, 137.
undertaker for building of, 134, 135, 136.
wall around, 139.
walls of, 137, 138, 190, 191.
old walls reused, 137.
windows of, 136.
wings of, 137, 139, 190, 191.
workmen for, 79, 134, 135, 136.
The Capitol . . . 1704 to 1779, 221.
Capitol Landing, 218.
Capitol Square, 11, 189, 205.
Captain Roger Jones of London & Virginia, 213.
Cardinal paper, 179, 220.
Caroline, Queen, 140.
Caroline County Courthouse (Virginia), 50.
Carpenters, 12, 15, 21, 32, 41, 42, 46, 77, 79, 97, 121, 134, 136, 137, 141, 142, 162, 164, 182, 217, 218, 220, 231.
for Bruton Parish Church, 77, 79.
for Capitol, 41, 42, 46, 79, 134, 136, 137.
for Palace, 141, 142.
for Public Hospital, 164, 231.
for William & Mary College, 21, 97, 121, 182, 220.
from England, 41.
in England, 15, 32.
measuring rod of, 12.
tools of, 46, 218.
    See also Workmen.
Carpenters' Company, 70.
Carpenters' Hall (Philadelphia), 162.
"Carpenters' Hall" (Peterson), 219.
Carter, Charles, 217.
James, 154.
John, 154.
Carter-Saunders House (Williamsburg), 142.
Carter's Grove (James City County, Va.), 133, 135, 136, 217.
account book of (ms.), 217.
doorway of (illus.), 135.
Carts, 55.
Cary, Henry, 40, 41, 42, 44, 45, 46, 47, 48, 51–52, 55, 56, 57, 58, 61, 65, 66, 79, 84–89, 214.
overseer of Capitol, 40, 41,

42, 44, 45, 46, 47, 48, 56, 84.
overseer of Gaol, 51–52.
overseer of Palace, 55, 56, 57, 58, 65, 84, 89.
Henry, Jr., 84, 88, 93, 107, 112, 120, 121, 123, 125, 147.
Brafferton built by, 107–108, 112.
churches built by, 84.
magazine fence built by, 88, 147.
Palace worked on by, 93.
undertaker for President's House, 123, 125.
William & Mary College chapel built by, 120–121.
Miles, 21, 40, 44.
Miles, Sr., 40.
family, 212.
Casement windows, 42, 210.
    See also Windows.
Catesby, Mark, 212.
"Cato" (play), 215.
Cavendish, Earl of, 95.
"Celtic Highlights" (Lancaster), 211.
Chair-rails, 133.
Chairs, 65, 104, 106, 218.
Chamberlayne, C. G., 214, 217, 218.
Chancellors of William & Mary College, 23, 32, 216, 217.
Changeable Scenery: its Origin & Development in the British Theatre, 216.
Chapels, 121, 123, 183, 184, 185–187, 233.
at English universities, 121, 123.
at William & Mary College see William & Mary College, Main Building.
Jefferson's design for octagonal chapel, 183, 184, 185–187, 233.
design (illus.), 183.
notes for, 184, 233.
Morris's plan for octagonal chapel (illus.), 185.
octagonal chapels see Jefferson's design for; Morris's plan for.
Charles I, 127.
Charles II, 48.
Charles City (City Point), 2.
Charles City County (Virginia), 50, 65, 139, 157.
Charles City Courthouse, 50, 157.
Charleston (South Carolina), 8, 86, 116, 139, 152, 171.
magazine at, 86, 214.

statue of Pitt at, 171.
theatre at, 116.
Charlottesville (Virginia), 187.
Charter for college see William &
 Mary College, charter for.
*The Charter & Statutes of the Col-
 lege of William and Mary
 in Virginia*, 215.
Cheere, John, 94.
Chelsea College, 48.
Chelsea Hospital (London), 30,
 102, 123.
Cherokee Indians, 142.
Chevening House (Kent, Eng-
 land), 61.
Chickahominy Indians, 52, 107.
Chimmey glasses, 65.
Chimney pieces, 168.
Chimneys, 65, 134.
 end, 65.
 T-plan, 134.
 See also under buildings by
 name.
Chiswell, John, 147.
Chiswell House (Williamsburg),
 112.
Chowan County Courthouse
 (North Carolina), 50, 157.
Christ Church, (Lancaster County,
 Va.), 84.
Christ Church (Philadelphia),
 162.
Christ Church Parish (Middlesex
 County, Va.), 218.
Chumbley, G. L., 213.
Church of England, 212.
*Church Review & Ecclesiastical
 Register*, 214, 218, 219.
Churches, 6, 15, 36, 42, 75–85, 86,
 123, 133, 136, 157, 162,
 187, 212, 214, 218.
 apses of, 36, 42.
 buttresses of, 75, 77, 214.
 cruciform plans of, 15, 82–84,
 136, 157.
 doorways of, 84, 133.
 in England, 36, 83, 77, 187.
 in Maryland, 36, 83, 214.
 in Pennsylvania, 83, 162, 214.
 in Philadelphia, 162, 214.
 in Rhode Island, 123.
 in Virginia, 6, 15, 36, 42, 75–
 85, 86, 123, 133, 136, 157,
 212, 218.
 interiors of, 123.
 octagonal, 187.
 tarring of roofs, 212.
 See also Bruton Parish Church;
 and other churches by
 name.

Cicogna, 177.
Citadel (Parma), 31.
*The City and Countrey Purchaser,
 and Builder's Dictionary*,
 213.
City Point (Virginia), 2.
Civil War, 190, 193, 195–196,
 199, 216, 218.
Clarke, Mr., 20.
Clayton, John, 74.
Cleverdon, Varney & Pike, 207.
Cliveden (Buckinghamshire), 64.
Clocks, on Capitol, 128, 140, 189,
 227.
Closen, Baron Louis Von, 220.
Cloud machines, 115.
Coal sheds, 192.
Coalter, Mrs. Frances Bland, 218.
Cocke, James, 154.
Cockle-shell lime, 210.
 See also Lime.
Codrington College (Barbados),
 102, 103, 104, 105, 182,
 215.
 engraving of (*illus.*), 104.
 plan of (*illus.*), 105.
Codrington Chronicle, 215.
Coffee women, 116.
Coffin plates, 216.
Coffins, 121, 216, 217.
Coleman, Mrs. Cynthia B. T., 221.
 Mrs. George P., 221.
Coleshill (Berkshire, England), 61.
Colleges proposed for Virginia, 1,
 2, 4.
 See also William & Mary Col-
 lege.
Collinson, Peter, 212.
*Colonial Capitals of the Dominion
 of Virginia*, 221.
*Colonial Churches of Tidewater
 Virginia*, 214, 217.
"The Colonial Courthouses of
 York County, Virginia,"
 (Riley), 210, 212, 219.
Colonial Justice in Virginia, 213.
Colonial Williamsburg, 208.
 architects of, 208.
 research department of, 211.
 See also Williamsburg Restora-
 tion.
Colonial Williamsburg Archives,
 209, 210, 215, 217, 218,
 220, 221.
Columns, 14, 138, 139, 155, 157,
 179, 199, 233.
 Doric, 138, 199.
 Ionic, 138, 157.
 Jefferson's use of, 14, 179, 233.
 of Capitol (second building),
 138, 139.

of courthouses, 155, 157, 199.
of houses, 139.
Colvin, H. M., 77, 210, 212, 214,
 215, 217.
 letter of quoted, 217.
Commons, House of, 36.
Communion tables, 79, 123.
The Compleat Gard'ner, 95.
A Complete Body of Architecture,
 143.
Compton, Henry, 4.
 See also London, Bishop of.
Confederate army, 195, 196.
Contractors, 15, 16, 75, 79, 164.
 See also Builders; Undertakers.
Contracts see Building contracts.
*Contributions to the Ecclesiastical
 History of the United
 States of America*, 221.
Coolidge Collection (Massachu-
 setts Historical Society),
 220.
Copland, Rev. Patrick, 2, 4.
Copperplates see Bodleian Plate.
Corinthian order, 186.
Corn, 41.
Cornices, 28, 31, 230, 231.
 See also under individual buildings.
Coscohunk, 52.
Council, Virginia, 5, 6, 18, 19, 20,
 21, 23, 33, 34, 35, 38, 42,
 45, 51, 53, 54, 55–56, 57,
 58, 64, 67, 77, 89, 90, 93,
 96, 130, 131, 134, 141,
 142, 215, 217, 228.
 activities of, concerning Capitol,
 34, 38, 42, 54.
 concerning Gaol, 51.
 concerning Palace, 53, 54, 55,
 56, 57, 58, 64, 89, 90,
 215.
 concerning Secretary's Office,
 130, 131.
 concerning William & Mary
 College, 5, 6, 18, 20, 21,
 96.
 Blair suspended from, 19–20.
 journals of, 218, 219.
 meets in Capitol (1703), 45.
 meets at William & Mary College (1700–04), 23, 33.
 members of, 19, 20, 21.
 pews for in Bruton Parish
 Church, 77.
 presidents of, 89, 93, 134, 141,
 157, 167, 217.
 room for in Capitol, 35, 228.
 See also Capitol, Council
 Chamber in.
Council Papers, 212.

Councillors, 67, 114.
  See also Council, members of.
Country Life, 219.
Coursey (Courcey), Colonel, 20.
Court of Admiralty, 189.
Court of Chancery, 190.
Courthouse of 1770, 15, 150, 152–
  161, 198–199, 208, 212.
  burned (gutted) in 1911, 198–
    199.
  chimneys of, 160.
  columns intended for, 155, 157.
    added (1911), 199.
  cupola of, 160.
  dimensions of, 157, 158, 160.
  doorway of, 160.
  elevation of (illus.), 159.
  furnishings of, 161, 198–199.
  land for, 154–155.
  museum in, 212.
  photograph of (illus.), 156.
  plan of, 154, 158.
    (illus.), 158.
  portico of, 155, 160, 199.
  rebuilt on old walls (1911), 199.
  restoration of (1932), 208.
  rooms in, 157.
  steps of from England, 157.
  walls of, 198, 199.
  weathervane on, 158.
  windows of, 160.
Courthouses, 15, 50, 116–117,
    127, 137, 152, 157, 161,
    212, 219.
  apsidal ends of, 50.
  arcaded porches of, 50.
  directions for interiors of, 161.
  furnishings for, 161.
  in Williamsburg, 116–117, 127,
    152.
    See also Courthouse of 1770.
  porticoes of, 15, 155, 160, 199.
  T-plan of, 157.
"Courthouses of Lancaster
    County" (Peirce), 212,
    219.
Courts, ecclesiastical, 36.
  English, 36.
    See also Court of Admiralty;
    Court of Chancery; Gen-
    eral Court; Hustings Court.
Covent Garden (London), 179,
    211.
Cramps, 137.
Cranston, L. J., 148, 190, 194,
    195, 221.
  watercolor of Magazine by
    (illus.), 191.
  watercolor of Palace outbuilding
    by (illus.), 194.
Crawford, Hugh, 217.

Creeks near Williamsburg, 10, 12.
Crew, Nehemiah, 72.
Criss Cross (New Kent County,
    Va.), 103.
Crowfield (South Carolina), 213.
Cruciform churches, 82, 83, 84,
    136, 157.
    See also Bruton Parish Church.
Cryer, George, 22.
"A Cubist Folk Art" (Piper), 211.
Cumberland Parish (Lunenberg
    County, Va.), 217.
Cupolas, 26, 29, 35, 63, 139, 140,
    160, 166, 189, 227.
  on Capitol, 35, 63, 139, 140,
    189, 227.
  on Courthouse of 1770, 160.
  on Palace, 63.
  on Public Hospital, 166.
  on William & Mary College, 26,
    (illus.) 27, 63.
Currituck Inlet, 212.
Custis, John II, 217.
  John III, 95.
Custis-Maupin House (Williams-
    burg), 136.
Cutts, A. B., 209.
Cypress shingles see Shingles.

D

Dale, Sir Thomas, 2.
Dancing schools, 103, 112, 113,
    191.
Davenport, F. G., 205.
  Matthew, 181.
Davis, N. M., 214.
Dawson, Mr., 123,
  William, 120, 125, 215, 217.
Dean, C. G. T., 217.
Dearstyne, Howard, 163, 218, 220.
Debtors, punishment of, 51.
Debtors Prison, 68–74.
  added to Gaol, 70.
  dimensions of, 70.
  flat roof of, 17, 74.
  Spotswood and design of, 68,
    70, 73, 74.
Debutts, Hunter, 217.
de la Force, Piganiol, 94.
de la Quintinie, Jean, 95.
Delegates, Virginia House of, 188,
    220, 226.
Delony, Lewis, 79, 137.
Department of Research, Colonial
    Williamsburg, 211.
Department of Research and Rec-
    ord, Perry Shaw & Hep-
    burn, 205.
Derbyshire (England), 220.

Description des Châteaux et Parcs
    de Versailles, de Trianon et
    de Marly, 94.
Dialect Notes, 211.
Dictionary of American Biography,
    19, 209.
The Dictionary of Architecture,
    214.
Dictionary of British Sculptors,
    219.
Dictionary of National Biography,
    215.
Dill, A. T., 219.
Dinwiddie, Robert, 134, 138, 142,
    172, 213, 226.
  arrival of, 134, 142.
  gift of King's arms for Capitol
    portico, 138.
  governor of Virginia, (1751–
    1758), 226.
  house rented for, 142, 213.
  Palace described by, 213.
"Discovery of Foundations for
    Jefferson's Addition to the
    Wren Building" (Kocher
    & Dearstyne), 220.
"Dr. Johnson's Lichfield Forbears
    and Dr. Johnson's Acad-
    emy" (Laithwaite), 213.
Doctors' Commons (London), 36,
    211.
Dodson, L., 214.
Doorways, brickwork of, 133,
    (illus.) 135.
    See also under individual build-
    ings.
Dorchester County (Maryland),
    36.
Doric Building, Public Hospital,
    193.
Doric columns, 138, 199.
Dorset (England), 61.
Dorsey, S. P., 214.
Drayton Hall (South Carolina),
    139.
"Drunken Peasant" (play), 215.
Drysdale, Hugh, 68, 119, 225.
  governor of Virginia (1722–
    1726), 225.
Duell, P., 210, 211.
Duke of Gloucester Street (Wil-
    liamsburg), 10, 11, 12, 49,
    50, 125, 126, 136, 192, 193.
  building restrictions for, 12, 51.
  college buildings in relation to,
    125–126.
  name of, 11, 12.
  watercolor of (illus.), 192.
Dunmore, John Murray, Earl of,
    86, 99, 179, 180, 181, 220,
    226.

governor of Virginia (1771–1775), 226.

plan for college addition requested by, 99, 181, 220.

powder removed by order of, 86.

Dutch influence on building, 63.

Dutch stoves, 218.

Dutch tiles, 176.

E

E-plan for houses, 28.

Early American Architecture, 211, 212.

The Early Architecture of North Carolina, 212.

Early English Churches in America, 214.

East India Company, 2.

East India School, 2.

Eastern Lunatic Asylum, 193.

See also Public Hospital.

Eastern State Hospital, 219, 221.

See also Public Hospital.

Easton Neston (Northamptonshire), 64, 65–66.

Eaton, William, 150.

Ecole des Beaux Arts (Paris), 203, 204.

Eddings, William, 33.

Edenton (North Carolina), 50, 157.

Edial Hall (Staffordshire), 62, 213.

watercolor of (*illus.*), 62.

Edinburgh (Scotland), 28, 29, 219.

Edinburgh, University of, 4, 29.

"Educational Influence of Aberdeen in Seventeenth Century Virginia" (Cutts), 209.

Effingham, Lord Howard of, 53, 225.

Elevations of buildings (*illustrations*):

Brafferton–north, 109.

Bruton Church–south, 155.

Courthouse of 1770–south, 159.

The Magazine–north, 87.

Octagonal chapel design, 186.

President's House–south, 126.

Secretary's Office–south, 132.

William & Mary main building–east, 102.

Elizabeth, Queen, 48, 212.

Elizabeth City County (Virginia), 212.

Elizabethan architecture, 28, 36, 50, 61.

Eltham Lodge (Kent, England), 177.

Emmanuel College (Cambridge University), 212.

Engineers, 207.

England, 2, 4, 5, 6, 7, 12, 14, 15, 16, 17, 18, 19, 20, 21, 22, 29, 30, 31, 32, 34, 36, 41, 43, 44, 45, 49, 50, 53, 55, 57, 58, 61–63, 64, 65, 68, 73, 79, 83, 84, 91, 92, 93, 94, 97, 102, 103, 106, 107, 113, 114–115, 118, 120, 121, 123, 135, 140, 143, 145, 146, 149, 157, 160–161, 164, 167, 168, 171, 179, 187, 210, 213, 217, 231.

actors and musicians from, 113.

architects in see Architects, English, and also under individual names.

architecture of, 14, 29–32, 34, 36, 49, 50, 58, 61–63, 64, 65–66, 68, 83, 84, 102, 103, 114, 118–119, 121, 143, 160–161, 179, 210, 211.

See also under names of houses and buildings.

building materials from, 41, 44–45, 55, 58, 97, 120, 121, 135, 157, 164, 231.

building methods in, 15, 16, 17, 210.

building terms used in, 41, 211, 212, 217.

buildings in, 36, 50, 83, 84, 102, 114, 165, 179, 211.

See also churches in; houses in; and under house and building names.

chapels in, 121, 123, 185.

church of see Church of England.

churches in, 83, 84, 168, 179, 187, 210, 214, 217.

See also under names of churches.

fire engine from, 97.

furniture from, 104.

gardening in, 94–95.

glass from, 55, 97, 120.

houses in, 36, 61–63, 64, 65–66, 143, 177, 213, 214.

See also under houses by name.

ironwork from, 55, 94, 164, 231.

lead from, 55.

lime in, 210.

market halls in, 50.

octagonal churches in, 187.

organ from, 146.

sculptors in, 167, 168.

slate from, 55, 57, 58.

statues from, 167, 168, 171.

stone from, 55, 120, 121, 157, 164.

theatres in, 114–115, 216.

tombs from, 145.

tombs in, 218.

town halls in, 50.

town planning in, 12, 14.

universities in, 2, 103, 121, 123, 182.

See also Cambridge University; Oxford University.

workmen from, 2, 19, 21, 22, 44, 79.

See also London.

England Street (Williamsburg), 10, 152.

English bond, 121, 210.

English Homes, 213, 220.

English pattern books, 84.

English warships, 25.

Enthoven, E. J., 210.

Essex (England), 64, 218.

Essex County (Virginia), 133.

Euston (Suffolk, England), 83, 214.

Evelyn, John, 9, 95, 215.

Exall, Henry, 194, 195.

Executive Journals of the Council, 218, 219.

F

Farley (Wiltshire), 83, 214.

Farrar's Island (James River), 1.

Fauquier, Francis, 161, 162, 166, 172, 174.

governor of Virginia (1758–1768), 226.

promotes Public Hospital, 161–162, 166.

Faxon, Eben, 194, 195.

Female Academy (Williamsburg), 191, 196.

Fenwick Hall (South Carolina), 213.

Finch, Philip, 215.

Fire engines, 97.

Fireplaces, 32–33, 48, 49, 63, 65, 112, 125, 131, 134, (*illus.*) 176, 215.

corner, 65, 112, 125, 215.

See also Chimneys.

Fireworks, 25, 26.

Firewood, 95.

"First Architectural School . . ." (Hall), 210.

The First Book of Architecture by Andrea Palladio, 70, 71.

illustration from, 71.

"The First Williamsburg Theatre" (Land), 215, 216.
Fitsherbert, John, 41.
Fitzhugh, W., 134.
Flagstone, 35, 228.
See also Paving stone.
Flanders, 5, 67.
Flemish bond, 121, 133, 210.
Floor plans see Plans.
See also under names of buildings.
Flooring, pine, 41, 231.
Floors see under names of individual buildings.
Fontaine, John, 214.
Footlacing, 214.
The Forest (Warwick County, Va.), 40.
Forman, H. C., 211, 213, 214.
Forms, 121, 233.
Fort, Alexander, 214.
Fort Christanna (Brunswick County, Va.), 215.
Foster, M. L., 221.
The Founding of Harvard College, 211.
Fox, Mr., 123.
Framing, oak or poplar, 231.
See also Building Materials.
France, 14, 62.
architectural influence of, 62.
town planning in, 14.
Francis I (King of France), 9.
"Francis Fauquier and an English Architect" (Little), 220.
Francis Street (Williamsburg), 152.
Fredericksburg (Virginia), 116.
Free schools, 20.
See also Grammar School, William & Mary College; Indian Schools.
French and Indian War, 172.
French architectural books, 84.
French army, 189, 195.
French army map (1781), 12, 13, 218–219.
See also Frenchman's Map.
French frigates, 25.
French hospital, 189.
French paper, 179, 220.
French privateers, 56, 225.
Frenchman's Map (1782), end-papers, 148, 218–219.
Friezes, 31.
Fry, Mr., 123.
Fulham Mss. (Lambeth Palace Library), 210, 211, 216.
Furniture, 104, 106.
See also under individual building names.

G

Galleries, 33, 35, 37, 38, 39, 75, 79, 82, 83, 227, 228, 233.
in Capitol, 35, 37, 38, 39, 227, 228.
See also Capitol, cross-gallery in.
in churches and chapels, 75, 79, 82, 83, 233.
in William & Mary College Main Building, 33.
Gaol, Public, 14, 42, 44, 45, 50–52, 70–74, 93, 150, 162, 189, 195, 203, 204, 208, 221, 228.
acts of General Assembly concerning, 42, 51, 70, 74, 228.
additions to, 51, 70, 74.
alterations to, 74.
brick from reused, 195.
cells in, 51, 74.
completion of building (1704), 51–52.
conveyed to Colonial Williamsburg, 221.
debtors prison in, 68–74.
See also Debtors Prison.
description of (1705), 14.
dimensions of, 51, 70, 74.
flat roof of, 70–74.
gaoler's room in, 51.
inspection of work on, 93.
keeper of, 130–131.
See also Gaolers.
keeper's house added to, 74.
lunatics in, 162.
"modell" of mentioned, 51.
overseer or superintendent of building, 51.
See also Henry Cary.
photograph of (illus.), 203, 204.
plan of (illus.), 74.
portion of destroyed (1862), 195.
prisoners in, 51, 52.
repairs to, 150.
restoration and reconstruction of (1935–36), 208.
roof of, 44, 45, 51, 52, 70, 74.
tarred, 45.
rooms in, 51, 74.
shingles for, 44, 51, 74.
Spotswood and addition to, 68, 70, 73, 74.
timber for, 51.
used by city and county (1784), 189.
walled yard of, 51.
walls of, 51–52, 70, 74.
yard of, 70.

Gaolers, 51, 74, 130.
Gaols, at Yorktown (Virginia), 21.
in Lunenburg County (Virginia), 137.
See also Gaol, Public.
Gardeners, 93.
Gardening, books on, 94, 95.
Gardens, English, 94–95.
See also Palace, gardens of.
Garland (H.M.S.), 152.
Garvan, A. N. B., 209.
Gates, Sir Thomas, 53.
Gates, 88, 94, 137, 140, 227.
at Capitol, 137, 140, 227.
at Palace, 88, 94.
The General Armory of England, Scotland, Ireland and Wales, 212.
General Assembly of Virginia, 1, 4, 5, 7–8, 12, 18, 23, 34, 35, 36, 37, 38, 42, 43, 45, 46, 48, 53, 54, 56, 57, 70, 74, 77, 85, 86, 88, 128, 129, 130, 138, 144, 146, 147, 154–155, 167, 171, 188, 190, 218, 226.
acts of, concerning Bruton Parish Church, 77, 146.
concerning Capitol, 7–8, 12, 35, 37, 38, 42, 130, 134, 190, 211, 227–228.
concerning Courthouse of 1770, 154, 155.
concerning Debtor's Prison, 70, 74.
concerning Gaol, 42, 51.
concerning James City & York counties, 154–155.
concerning Magazine, 85, 86, 147.
concerning Palace, 53–56, 88, 89, 93.
concerning Public Hospital, 162, 164.
concerning Secretary's Office, 130.
concerning William & Mary College, 18.
concerning Williamsburg, 7–8, 10, 12, 35, 227.
for rebuilding Capitol in Williamsburg, 130.
for removal of capital to Richmond, 188.
address of to King (1691), 5.
Capitol built for meetings of, 7–8.
college for Virginia requested by (1619), 1–2; (1691) 4–5.
See also William & Mary College.

governor elected by (1776), 226.
meets at Capitol (1704), 45.
   at second Capitol (1753),
    138.
meets at Jamestown, 36.
meets at Richmond (1780), 188.
meets at William & Mary College (1700–04), 23;
   (1752), 138.
records of, 128, 130, 131, 188.
removal of capital considered by
   (1747), 129–130.
removal of capital enacted by
   (1779), 188.
statue of Botetourt erected by,
   167, 171.
   See also Botetourt Statue.
tomb for Gov. Nott voted by,
   144.
town built for meetings of, 7–8.
   See also Burgesses, House of;
   Council.
General Court, 8, 35, 37, 43, 44,
   45, 50, 51, 70, 129, 130,
   216, 228.
   Capitol erected for, 8, 37, 129,
    130, 228.
    See also Capitol.
   debtors tried in, 70.
   defendants in, 50, 51.
   jail for, 50–51, 70.
    See also Gaol, Public.
   meets at Capitol (1703), 43, 44.
   room for in Capitol, 35, 37, 43,
    44, 45, 137, 139, 140, 227,
    228.
   See also Capitol.
   time of meeting, 216.
   town for, 8, 129.
Genoa, 29, 30.
Gentleman's Magazine, 88, 214.
George II, 118–119.
George III, 140, 149, 218.
   arms of on Capitol, 139.
   portraits of, 140, 218.
Georgian architecture, 140.
Georgian London, 210.
The Georgian Playhouse, 216.
Gerbier, Sir Balthazar, 58, 62.
Gibbs, James, 16, 119, 174.
Gilmer, Dr. George, 116, 216.
Gilmore, Mr., 216.
Glass, window, 45, 55, 97, 210,
   229.
   from England, 45, 55, 97.
   See also Windows.
Glass lustres, 218.
Glazier's tools, 218.
Glebe houses, 134, 218.
Gloria Dei Church (Philadelphia),
   83, 214.

Gloucester County (Virginia), 6,
   79, 133, 135, 136, 217.
   churches in, 133, 135, 136, 217,
    (illus.), 135.
   considered as site for college, 6.
Gloucestershire (England), 62, 63,
   64.
Golden Section ratio, 24, 80, 82,
   86, 100.
Gooch, Lady, 213.
   Sir William, 116, 119, 128, 129,
    130, 131, 134, 140, 146,
    213, 226.
    governor of Virginia (1727–
     1749), 226.
    letter of quoted (1728), 119.
    London house of, 213.
    organ for church requested
     by, 146.
    rebuilding of Capitol urged by
     (1747), 129, 130.
    removal of capitol urged by,
     129, 140.
    return of to England, 134,
     140.
    speech of quoted, 128.
    subscriber to theatre, 116.
Gooch Papers (Virginia Historical
   Society), 218.
Goochland County, Virginia, 50,
   136.
Goochland Courthouse, 50.
Goodwin, Mary F., 205.
   T. R., 221.
   Rev. William A. R., 200, 201,
    202, 203, 204, 205, 208,
    211, 221.
Gordon, Lord Adam, 14.
Gordon's Hospital (Aberdeen,
   Scotland), 219.
Gosset, Isaac, 167, 168, 171.
Gothic Building, Public Hospital,
   193.
Gottesman, R. S., 210.
Governor Tryon and his Palace,
   219.
Governor's Palace (Williamsburg)
   see Palace.
Governors of Virginia, 6, 53, 54,
   55, 226–227.
   house for, 53, 54, 55.
    See also Palace.
   house-rent allowed, 53.
   Latin verses delivered to, 6.
   list of (1690–1781), 226–227.
    See also under names.
Grammar Schools, 4, 5, 20, 23,
   24, 26, 33, 107, 189–190.
   at William & Mary College, 4,
    5, 20, 23, 24, 26, 33, 107.

   school-house for, 96, 107.
   schoolroom of, 24, 26, 33.
   in Capitol, 189, 190.
Grates, 32, 106.
Great Halls, 63, 64.
   See also Halls; and under build-
    ings by name.
Greek town planning, 9.
Green Spring (James City County,
   Va.), 53, 61.
Greenhow, John, 146.
Greenwich, Queen's House at, 215.
Gridiron plan for towns, 8, 9.
Grigsby, Hugh Blair, 216, 217.
Guard House (Williamsburg),
   147–148.
   foundations of, 148.
   on Frenchman's Map (1782),
    148.
   picture of mentioned, 148,
    (illus.), 202.
   reconstruction of (1949), 148,
    208.
   workmen for, 147.
Guide to Manuscript Material for
   the History of the United
   States, 205.
Guildhalls, 36.
Gunnis, R., 168, 219.
Gunther, R. T., 213.
Gutters, 24.
   lead from, 33.

H

H-plan buildings mentioned, 37,
   50, 139, 211.
   See also Capitol.
Hadley, Dionysia, 22.
   Thomas, 21, 22, 30, 41.
Hair, for upholstery, 43.
Halfpenny, William, 152.
Hall, L., 210.
Halls, 24, 33, 63, 64, 50, 177.
   great, 63, 64.
   octagon, 177.
   See also Market halls; Town
    halls; and under buildings
    by name.
Hamlin, T., 214, 218.
Hampton (Virginia), 84, 212.
Hanover (Virginia), 88.
Hanover County (Virginia), 112,
   134, 136, 217.
Hanover County Courthouse, 50,
   157.
Harden House (Scotland), 219.
Hardenbrook, Theophilus, 210.
Hardware from England, 45.
   See also Ironwork.
Harmonic Architecture, 160.

Harrison, Mr., 57.
  Benjamin, 220.
  Nathaniel, 217.
  Peter, 179.
  Robert, 21.
  Mrs. Robert, 221.
Hartwell (Buckinghamshire), 220.
Harvard College, 28, 105, 210.
  studies at, 105.
Harvard Hall, 28.
Harvard in the Seventeenth Century, 211.
Harwood, Humphrey, 122, 189, 210, 215, 216.
  Ledger of (Ms. Colonial Williamsburg Archives), 210, 215.
  Thomas, 213.
Havard, Mr. see Hayward, Richard.
Hawks, F. L., 221.
  John, 172.
Hawksmoor, Nicholas, 16, 64.
Hawtrey, Edward, 215.
  Stephen, 215.
Hay, Mr. [Anthony], 154.
  G., 214.
Hayes, Elizabeth, 221.
  J., 221.
Haymarket (London), 94.
Hayward, Richard, 139, 140, 167, 168, 171.
Hazard, Ebenezer, 138, 139–140, 162, 182.
  description of Capitol by, 138, 139–140.
  description of proposed college addition by, 182.
Headlam, C., 213.
Heawood, E., 220.
Hemphill, John, 217.
Hening, William Waller, 211, 228.
Henrico (Virginia), 1–2, 4, 29, 106.
  Blair rector at, 4.
  college planned for, 1–2, 4, 29, 106.
"Henrico and its College" (Land), 209.
Henrico County (Virginia), 50, 188.
Henry, Patrick, 226.
Hepburn, Andrew, 204.
Heriot's Hospital (Edinburgh, Scotland), 28, 29, 30.
  plan of (illus.), 28.
Hertfordshire (England), 83.
Higham, Walter R., 198.
Highmeadow (Gloucestershire), 64.
Hill, Colonel, 33.

Hinke, W. J., 211.
Hippodamus of Miletus, 9.
Hirst, John, 168.
Historical Collections relating to the American Colonial Church, 209, 210, 215.
Histoire des Moulins à Papier du Sud-Ouest de la France, 220.
The History and Antiquities of the Church and City of Lichfield, 213.
The History and Present State of Virginia, 209, 213, 214.
History of the British Plantations in America, 68.
The History of the College of William & Mary in Virginia, 215, 221.
History of the Dividing Line, 212.
"The History of the Founding of the Eastern State Hospital" (Jones), 219.
The History of South Carolina under the Royal Government, 219.
Holloway, John, 74.
Hooke, Robert, 165, 166.
Hoppus, Edward, 211.
Horrocks, Mr., 168.
Horses, 25, 55.
Hospitals, 189, 219.
  in Williamsburg, 189.
    See also Public Hospital.
  Scottish, 219.
    See also under their names.
Hostilius, Marcus, 11, 129.
House of Burgesses see Burgesses, House of.
House of Commons see Commons, House of.
House of Delegates see Delegates, House of.
Houses, in England, 36, 61–63, 64, 65–66, 143, 177, 213, 214.
  in South Carolina, 213.
  in Virginia, 58, 131, 211, 214.
  plans of, 131, 211, 214.
    See also under individual names.
Hughes, Emery, 145.
  James, 119–120.
Huguenots, 167.
Hunter, Robert, 56, 225.
Huntington Library (California), 216, 220, 233.
Huntington Library Quarterly, 220.
Hussey, C., 219.
Hustings Court (Williamsburg), 116–117, 154.

Hygeia Hotel (Old Point Comfort, Va.), 217.
Hyland, Anthony D. C., 186.

I

Ichnographia Rustica, 94.
Indentured servants, 16, 21, 46.
Indian massacre (1622), 1, 2, 106.
Indian schoolmasters, 107, 109.
Indian schools, 1, 4, 106, 107.
  See also The Brafferton; William & Mary College.
Indians in Virginia, 1, 2, 4, 26, 52, 106, 107, 109, 142.
  at the Palace, 142.
  attend William & Mary College, 106, 107, 109, 112.
  attend William & Mary commencement, 23.
  education of, 1–2, 4, 106, 107, 109, 112.
    See also The Brafferton; William & Mary College.
  in the Gaol, 52.
  shooting match for, 26.
  visit Williamsburg, 23, 142.
Ingles, Mungo, 24, 33, 96.
Insane, care of, 161–162.
  hospitals for, 161–166.
    See also Public Hospital.
Insurance policies, 219, 221.
Ionic columns, 138, 157.
Ireland, 2, 31.
Iron balconies, 35, 43–44, 227.
Iron bedsteads, 97.
Iron gates, 94, 139.
Iron rails, 167.
Iron window grates, 229, 230, 231.
Ironwork from England, 55, 94, 167, 231.
Ironworks (Spotsylvania County, Va.), 68, 73.
Isle of Wight County (Virginia), 75.
Isle of Wight Courthouse, 50, 157.
Italian architecture, 31, 103, 118, 211.
Italian books on architecture, 84.
Italy, 9, 16, 31, 211.
  piazzas in, 211.
  rustication used in, 31.

J

Jackson, Christopher, 209.
Jacobean architecture, 28, 61.
Jailers see Gaolers.
Jails see Gaols.
Jamaica, 8, 215.
Jamaican Historical Review, 215.

James I, 1.
James II, 25, 48.
James, John, 94.
James City, 40, 228.
    See also Jamestown (Virginia).
James City County (Virginia), 22,
        74, 79, 133, 135, 137, 141,
        152, 154–155.
    burgesses for, 74, 137.
    courthouse land annexed to,
        154–155.
    courthouses for, 152, 154, 155.
        See also Courthouse of 1770.
James River, 1, 10, 12, 129.
    creeks from, 10, 12.
Jamestown (Virginia), 4, 7, 8, 11,
        34, 36, 39, 40, 41, 48, 50,
        53, 75, 86, 157, 228.
    capital moved from (1699), 7, 8,
        34.
    churches at, 36, 75.
    convention of clergy at (1690),
        4.
    courthouse at, 157.
    first General Assembly in Amer-
        ica at, 36.
    governors' houses at, 53.
    houses at, 41, 53.
    magazine at, 86.
    statehouse (fourth) at, 7, 8, 34,
        36, 39, 48, 50, 157, 211.
        bricks from reused, 157.
        burned, 7, 8, 34, 48.
        Capitol compared to, 36, 39,
            50.
        cruciform building, 39.
        dimensions of, 211.
        hall of, 36.
        plan of, 36, 39, 50.
*Jamestown and St. Mary's, Buried
    Cities of Romance,* 211,
        213, 214.
Japan, 2.
Jefferson, Thomas, 14, 15, 24, 38,
        60, 63, 65, 98, 99, 103,
        118, 132, 136, 138, 143,
        149, 150, 161, 172–173,
        174, 177–181, 181–185,
        185–187, 189, 210, 211,
        217, 218, 220, 226, 233.
    architectural designs by, 63, 149,
        150.
        See also plans by.
    at Palace, 149.
    "Cardinal" paper used by, 179,
        220.
    columns admired by, 14, 179,
        233.
    criticism of Williamsburg build-
        ings by, 14–15.
    criticism of workmen by, 15.

description of Capitol (second)
    by, 15, 138.
description of Palace by, 177,
    181.
governor of Virginia (1779–
    1781), 149, 226.
instructions concerning Capitol
    clock, 189.
letters of, 179, 218, 220.
manuscripts of, 38.
plan by for addition to William
    & Mary College, 24, 98,
    99, 103, 181–182, 185,
    211.
    illustration, 99.
plan of and notes for octagonal
    chapel, 182–183, 184, 186,
    187, 233.
    illustrations, 183, 184.
    text of notes, 233.
plan of Palace by, 60, 63, 65,
    143, 174.
    illustration, 60.
plans for remodelling of Palace
    by, 177–181, 220.
    illustrations, 178, 180.
portrait of (*illus.*), 173.
student at William & Mary Col-
    lege, 103, 149.
sweating of bricks explained by,
    132.
wife of, 136, 217.
"Jefferson and the Arts" (Kim-
    ball), 220.
"Jefferson and the Public Build-
    ings of Virginia" (Kim-
    ball), 220.
Jefferson Collection (Library of
    Congress), 211, 227.
*The Jefferson Papers of the Univer-
    sity of Virginia,* 220.
Jenings (Jennings), Edmund, 21,
        56, 79, 89, 93, 96, 212.
    bricks for church from, 79.
    letter of, 212.
    Palace building begun under, 93.
    president of the Council, 56, 89,
        93, 96.
Jennings, Captain John, 5.
Jeoffreys, Mr., 5.
Jerdone, Francis, 217.
*John Norton & Sons, Merchants
    of London & Virginia,* 219.
Johnson, Dr. Samuel, 213.
Joiners, 46, 121, 214.
    See also Carpenters.
Jones, Daniel, 97.
    Granville L., 166, 219.
    Hugh, 9, 14, 30, 31, 32, 73, 98,
        102, 107, 119, 209, 212,
        215.

description of Bruton Parish
    Church by, 14.
description of Palace by, 14.
description of William &
    Mary College by, 30, 32,
    98, 102.
description of Williamsburg
    houses by, 212.
description of Williamsburg
    streets by, 9.
Indian school mentioned by,
    107.
professor at William & Mary
    College, 73.
quoted, 9, 14, 30, 32, 98, 102,
    107, 119, 212.
suggestions of for college
    chapel, 119.
Inigo, 30, 61, 211, 215.
L. H., 213.
Thomas, 79, 216.
Jones Papers (Library of Con-
    gress), 79, 214.
*Journal of the American Institute
    of Architects,* 210.
"The Journal of Ebenezer Hazard"
    (Shelley), 218, 220.
The Journal of Latrobe, 221.
*A Journal of the Life of Thomas
    Story,* 216.
"Journal of an Officer in the West
    Indies," 209.
*Journal of the Society of Architec-
    tural Historians,* 214, 220.
*Journal of the Warburg and Cour-
    tauld Institutes,* 212.
Journals of the House of Burgesses,
    209, 214.
Journals of the Meetings of the
    President and Masters of
    William & Mary College
    (Ms.), 217, 218, 220.
"A Journey on Horseback from
    Philadelphia to Charles-
    ton, S. C." (Ms.), 221.
Journeymen, 15.
Julius Caesar, 9.
Jupiter (planet), 48.

K

Kedleston (Derbyshire), 168.
Keene, Henry, 220.
Keith, Sir William, 68, 73, 86, 88.
Kendall, Joshua, 121, 122.
Kendrew, A. Edwin, 205, 208.
Kennett, Basil, 11.
Kennon, Elizabeth B., 216.
Kent (England), 61, 177.
Kidd, J., 220.

Kimball, Fiske, 63, 179, 181, 186, 213, 220.
　S. F. *see* Fiske Kimball.
King and Queen County (Virginia), 133.
King William County (Virginia), 133.
King William Courthouse, 50, 157.
King's arms, 139.
King's birthday celebrations, 113–114, 142, 144.
Ye Kingdome of Accawmacke, 216.
Kingston (Jamaica), 8, 215.
Kingston Lacy (Dorset), 61, 213.
Kitchens, 55, 57, 63, 103.
　at Palace, 55, 57, 63.
　at William and Mary College, 7, 97, 103.
　basement, 103.
　in England, 62–63.
Klingberg, Frank J., 215.
Knox, John, 67.
Kocher, A. Lawrence, 163, 211, 218, 220.
Krumbhaar, E. B., 219.

L

Labaree, W., 209.
Lafayette-Le Clerq Papers (Colonial Williamsburg Archives), 220.
Laithwaite, P., 213.
Lambeth Manuscripts (Bodleian Library, Oxford), 210.
Lambeth Palace (London), 5, 20, 22, 210.
Lancaster, O., 211.
Lancaster County (Virginia), 84.
Lancaster County Court Records, 219.
Lancaster County Courthouse, 50, 161, 212.
　furnishings of, 161.
Land, R. H., 209, 215, 216.
Latin verses, 6.
Latrobe, Benjamin Henry, 16, 138–139, 190.
　Capitol described by, 138–139, 190.
　pupils taken by, 16.
　J. H. B., 221.
Lavedan, Pierre, 12.
Lead, 24, 33, 55, 57, 58, 140, 189, 214.
　for roof of Palace, 57, 58, 214.
　from England, 55.
　gutters of, 24, 33.
　on Capitol cupola, 140, 189.
　use of sand with, 214.
Leather, gilt, 65, 176.

Le Blond, A. J. B., 94.
Lectures on Architecture, 160.
Lee, Philip, 217.
　Richard Henry, 179.
　Thomas, 217.
Lee Papers, 220.
Lees-Milne, J., 213.
Leicestershire (England), 32.
Leigh, Thomas, 50, 212.
Leoni, Giacomo (James), 118, 209.
A Letter, to the Rev. Jedidiah Morse, 221.
Levingston, William, 103, 112, 113, 116, 216.
　dancing school of, 103, 112–113.
　house of, 116.
　theatre built by, 112, 113, 116.
　　See also Playhouse.
　widow of, 116.
Libraries, 104, 109, 174.
　at the Brafferton, 109.
　at the Palace, 174.
　at William & Mary College, 104, 109.
Library of Congress, 38, 79, 211, 214, 220, 221, 227.
Lichfield (Staffordshire), 213.
The Life and Works of James Gibbs, 210, 220.
Life and Works of Sir Christopher Wren, 210.
Lightfoot, Mr., 33.
Lilly, Christian, 102, 103, 215.
Lime, 21, 97, 164, 210, 214, 216.
　cockle-shell, 210.
　cost of, 216.
　methods of burning, 210.
　oyster shell, 21, 41, 210.
"Lime Preparation at Jamestown in the Seventeenth Century" (Bailey), 210.
Limestone, 210.
Lincolnshire (England), 62.
Liquor and Slaves, duty on, 54, 56, 70, 77, 86, 90.
Little, B., 210, 220.
Livery stables, 197.
Log Cabin Myth, 205.
Loggias, 211.
London, 1, 4, 5, 9, 12, 14, 25, 36, 58, 83, 114, 123, 135, 139, 145, 165, 167, 209, 210, 211, 213, 214.
　arcaded loggias in, 211.
　architects in, 174.
　　See also by names.
　building materials from, 135.
　　See also England, building materials from.

buildings in, 36.
　See also under names of buildings.
carpenter's measures in, 12.
churches in, 14, 83.
　See also under names of churches.
fire of (1666), 9, 36, 83.
Gooch's house in, 213.
halls in, 36.
hospital for insane in, 165.
　See also Bedlam; Bethlehem Hospital.
houses in, 213.
　See also under names of houses.
masons in, 123.
merchants in, 167.
mode of followed in Virginia, 114.
monuments from, 123, 145.
plans for by Wren, 9, 12.
roof-coverings in, 58.
sculptors in, 167.
statues from, 139, 167.
　See also Botetourt Statue.
statues in, 1.
tombstones from, 145.
tools from, 135.
See also England.
London, Bishop of, 4, 5, 20, 22, 23, 32, 36, 106, 109, 120, 210, 215, 217.
　chancellor of William & Mary College, 23, 32.
　commissary for in Virginia, 4.
　　See also James Blair.
　letters to, 20, 22, 109, 120, 210, 215, 217.
　See also Henry Compton.
London, George, 95.
London Gazette, 210.
London Magazine, 209.
London Post Boy, 22.
Londonderry (Ulster), 10.
Longnor Hall (Shropshire), 61.
Looking glasses, 65.
Lossing, Benson J., 190.
Loudoun, Earl of, 213, 226.
Louis XIV, 14.
Lowell, Guy, 204.
Ludwell, Philip I, 18, 19, 21, 79.
　Philip II, 18, 95.
　family, 75.
Ludwell Papers (Ms. Virginia Historical Society), 214.
Lumley, John, 212.
Lunatic asylums, 161–166.
　See also Public Hospital.

Lunenberg County (Virginia), 137, 217.
  courthouse and gaol in, 137.

M

McCabe, J. C., 150, 214, 218.
McCrady, E., 219.
McIlwaine, H. R., 220.
Macomber, Walter, 205.
Madeira wine, 174.
Madison, Rev. James, 190, 216, 217.
Magazine (Williamsburg), 15, 68, 85, 86, 88, 93, 146, 147, 148, 187, 190, 191, 197, 198, 207, 208.
  act of General Assembly to build, 85, 86.
  Baptist meeting house in, 191.
  brick wall for, 147.
  bricks from reused, 191.
  cannon balls at, 191.
  damage to, 191, 197.
  dancing school in, 191.
  design of, 68, 86, 88.
  engraving of (illus.), 190.
  fence of, 88, 147.
  guard house built for see Guard House.
  inspection of, 93.
  keeper of, 86.
  livery stable in, 197.
  market house in, 191.
  museum in, 198.
  overseer for building, 86.
  photograph of (illus.), 202.
  powder removed from, 86.
  preservation of by A.P.V.A., 197–198.
  restoration of (1889), 197–198.
  restoration of (1934–35), 208.
  roof of burned, 197.
  Spotswood's design for, 68, 86, 88.
  used for arms (1861), 197.
  wall around, 88, 147.
  watercolor of (illus.), 191.
Magazines, 85, 86, 88, 214.
  at Annapolis (Maryland), 86, 214.
  at Charleston (South Carolina), 86, 214.
  at Hanover (Virginia), 88.
  at Middle Plantation (Virginia), 85.
  described in Gentleman's Magazine, 88, 214.
  See also Magazine (Williamsburg).
Manor houses, 28.

The Mansions of Virginia, 212, 213, 214, 215, 219.
Mantelpieces, 168, 176, 177.
  illustration, 176.
Maps of Williamsburg, 12, 13.
  See also Frenchman's Map.
Marable, George, 75.
Marble mantelpieces, 177.
Marble statues, 168, 221.
  See also Botetourt Statue.
Marbleizing of woodwork, 45.
Marcus Hostilius, 11, 129.
Marischal College (Aberdeen University), 2, 4.
Market-halls, 50.
Market-houses, 191.
Market Square (Williamsburg), 10, 85, 146, 154–155, 158.
Marot, John, 33.
Mary, Queen, 5.
Maryland, 6, 8, 10, 18, 36, 83, 86, 214.
  capitals of, 8, 10.
  churches in, 36, 83.
  governors of, 8, 18.
  magazine in, 86, 214.
  Nicholson, governor of, 8, 18.
  tobacco exported from, 6.
  See also Annapolis; St. Mary's City.
Mash, James, 52.
Mason, F. N., 219.
  G. C., 214, 217.
Masons, 29, 32, 168.
  See also Master masons.
Massachusets Historical Society, 220.
Massachusetts Institute of Technology, 203, 204.
Massacre of 1622, 1, 2, 106.
Master builders, 16, 162, 210.
  methods of in England, 210.
Master joiners, 214.
Master masons, 29.
Mattapony Church (King & Queen County, Va.), 84, 133.
Matthews, A., 209, 211.
Maury, A., 215.
  Walker, 189.
May Day celebration (1699), 7, 22.
Mayors of Williamsburg, 74, 117, 152.
Mazzei, Philip, 220.
Measuring rods, 12, 209.
  for bricklayers, 209.
  for carpenters, 12.
Mechanica, 72.
Mechanick Exercises: or the Doctrine of Handiworks, 209, 210.

Memoirs of a Huguenot Family, 215.
Menetree, David see Minitree.
Meriwether, Thomas, 130.
  William, 130.
Michael Rysbrack, Sculptor, 219.
Michel, Franz Ludwig, 25, 26, 27, 28, 31, 49, 75, 78, 85, 211.
  description of celebration in Williamsburg (1702) by, 25, 26.
  diary of quoted, 25, 26.
  described, 211.
  drawing of Bruton Parish Church (first) by, 75, (illus.) 78.
  drawing of William & Mary College (first building) by, 26, (illus.) 27, 28, 31, 49, 75.
  in London, 25.
  in Williamsburg, 25–26.
  magazine mentioned by, 85.
  Johan, 26, 211.
The Microcosm of London, 211.
Middle Plantation (Virginia), 6, 7, 8, 10, 22, 34, 75, 85, 209.
  advantages of for capital, 7, 10, 209.
  capital moved from Jamestown to, 7, 8, 10, 34.
  church at, 6, 75.
    See also Bruton Parish Church.
  city of Williamsburg built at, 7, 8, 10.
    See also Williamsburg.
  college of William & Mary at, 6, 7, 8, 22.
    See also William & Mary College.
  magazine at, 85.
  springs at, 10.
  statehouse at, 34.
    See also Capitol.
Middleton, A. Pierce, 213.
Millington, Thomas Charles, 193, 195.
  drawing by (illus.), 192.
Mills, Peter, 62.
Minge, James, 46, 48.
Minitree, David, 84, 133, 218.
Minsterley (Shropshire), 77.
Monticello (Albemarle County, Va.), 139.
Monuments, 122, 123, 168.
  See also Statues; Tombs.
Moore, Sir John, 32.
Moorehead, Singleton P., 205, 208, 213, 216.

Moorfields (London), 165.
Mordecai, Samuel, 216.
Morgan, Dr. John, 174.
    M. H., 209.
Morison, S. E., 211.
Morris, James, 79, 137.
    Owen, 46.
    Robert, 160, 186.
Morrison, H. S., 211, 212.
    Robert J., 216, 217.
Morse, Rev. Jedidiah, 221.
Mortar, 230, 231.
Mosquitoes, 209.
Mount Airy (Richmond County, Va.), 118.
Moxon, Joseph, 209, 210.
Mulberry (South Carolina), 213.
Murray, C. A., 221.
    John see Dunmore, John Murray, Earl of.
Museum Regalis Societatis, 72.
Museums, 198, 212.
Musicians, 25, 113.
Muter, George, 218.
Mutual Assurance Society, 219, 221.
Mylne, Robert, 29.

N

Nails, 43, 182, 185.
    burnished, 43.
Nassau Hall (Princeton), 162.
Nassau Street (Williamsburg), 141.
Nation, 209.
Natural History of Oxfordshire, 70.
Necessary houses, 94.
    See also Privies.
Negroes, 44, 46, 56, 57.
    See also Slaves.
Nelson, Robert, 216, 217.
    Thomas, 130.
    William, 130, 157, 167, 219.
        letterbook of, 219.
Neo-classicism in architecture, 15, 146, 179, 187.
Nether Lypiatt Manor (Gloucestershire), 62, 63.
Neve, T., 213.
New Bern (North Carolina), 172, 219.
New England, 106, 204.
    See also Boston; New Haven; Newport.
New Haven (Connecticut), 10.
New Kent County (Virginia), 79, 103, 134, 136, 217.
New York City, 42, 50, 171, 200, 201, 202, 225.
    city hall of, 42, 50.
    statue of William Pitt in, 171.

New York Mercury, 210.
Newbold Hall (Warwickshire), 64.
Newcastle (Virginia), 130, 134.
Newman, John, 46.
Newport (Rhode Island), 123, 179.
Newspapers, architects' advertisements in, 17.
Nicholas, Abraham, 216.
    Robert Carter, 122, 123, 150, 167, 168, 181.
Nicholson, Francis, 4–5, 7, 8, 9, 11, 12, 14, 18, 19, 20, 21, 22, 24, 25, 32–33, 34, 39, 40, 43, 47, 48, 53–54, 67, 107, 129, 210, 212, 215, 225.
    accession of Anne proclaimed by (1702), 25, 48.
    Capitol building promoted by, 34, 40, 43, 48.
    character of, 8.
    coat-of-arms of, 48, 212.
    criticism of by J. Blair, 47–48.
    education of Indians promoted by, 107.
    faults in William & Mary College building noted by, 32–33.
    governor of Maryland, 8, 18, 20, 39.
    governor of Nova Scotia, 8.
    governor of South Carolina, 8.
    governor of Virginia (1690–1692 and 1698–1705), 4, 5, 7, 8, 18, 22, 25, 47, 225.
    governor's house urged by, 53–54.
    letters to, 18, 19, 21, 24, 210, 215.
    motto on arms of, 48, 212.
    plans of for Williamsburg, 7, 9, 11, 12, 14.
    promoter of new capitals, 7–8.
    promoter of William & Mary College, 5, 8.
    promoter of Williamsburg, 7, 8, 9, 11, 12, 14.
        See also Williamsburg.
    recalled as Virginia governor, 5, 47.
Nicholson Papers (Colonial Williamsburg Archives), 209, 211, 215.
Nicolaï, A., 220.
Nomini Hall (Westmoreland County, Va.), 65, 118, 214.
"Norborne Berkeley: Gloucestershire Magnate" (Little), 220.

Norfolk (Virginia), 84, 128.
North Carolina, 50, 152, 172, 212.
    courthouse in, 50.
        See also Chowan County Courthouse.
    dividing line between Virginia and, 212.
    governor of, 172.
    palace in, 172.
        See also Tryon's Palace.
North Staffordshire Field Club Transactions, 213.
Northamptonshire (England), 64.
Northern Neck Historical Magazine, 212, 219.
Norton, John, 167, 168, 182, 219.
Norton Papers (Colonial Williamsburg Archives), 219.
"Notes on Jamestown, Williamsburg and Yorktown" (Campbell), 214, 221.
"Notes on Robert Smith" (Peterson), 219.
Notes on the State of Virginia, 161, 177, 181, 210, 217, 218.
    quoted, 161, 177, 181.
Nott, Edward, 47, 54, 55, 56, 93, 144–145, 225.
    act to build governor's house urged by, 54–55, 93.
    death of, 56.
    governor of Virginia (1705–1706), 47, 54, 225.
    letter of quoted, 55.
    tomb of, 144–145.
        (illus.), 144.
Nova Scotia, 8.

O

Oak, 41, 231.
Oboes, 25.
"Observations in Several Voyages and Travels in America . . . 1736," 209.
Octagonal chapels, 183, 184, 185–187, 233.
    Jefferson's design and notes for, 183, 184, 185–187, 233.
        (illus.), 183.
    Morris's plan for (illus.), 185.
Octagonal churches, 187.
"Of Powder Magazines" (Belidor), 214.
Office of Works (London), 16.
The Official Letters of Alexander Spotswood, 216, 219.
Official Letters of the Governors of the State of Virginia, 220.
The Official Records of Robert Dinwiddie, 213.

Old Point Comfort (Virginia), 217.

Old Rectory (Sutton Coldfield, Warwickshire), 111, 112. (*illus.*), 111.

Old Salpia (Apulia), 11.

The Old South: the Founding of American Civilization, 211.

Oldmixon, John, 70, 210.

Opechancanough, 1.

Orange County (Virginia), 189.

Ordinary-keepers, 22, 33, 41.

Organists, 192.

Organs, 146, 192.

Orkney, Earl of, 225, 226.

Orphan's Hospital (Edinburgh), 219.

Oudenarde, battle of, 67.

Outbuildings *see* under building names.
    See also Kitchens; Privies; Stables.

Overseers (building), 21, 40, 41, 42, 55, 79, 86, 89, 90, 212.
    English use of word, 41, 212.
    for Bruton transept, 79, 86.
    for Capitol, 40, 41, 42.
    See also Henry Cary.
    for Gaol, 51.
    for Magazine, 86.
    for Palace, 55, 89, 90.
    See also Henry Cary.
    for William & Mary College, 21.

Overwharton Church (Stafford County, Va.), 135.

Overwharton Parish, 218.

Oxen, 12.

Oxford, Bishop of, 210.

Oxford English Dictionary, 121.

Oxford University, 29, 31, 72, 103, 121, 123, 182.
    chapels at, 121, 123.
    "flat floors" at, 70, 72.
    professors at, 72.
    quadrangular colleges at, 29, 31.
    schools at, 70, 72.
    students' rooms at, 103, 182.

Oxfordshire, 70.

Oyster-shell lime, 210.
    See also Lime.

Oyster shells, 21, 41.

Oysters, 210.

Oznabrig, 220.

P

Page, Francis, 75, 77.
    Gregory, 218.

Paine, James, 220.

Paint from England, 45.

Paint colors, 45, 64.

"Painted Rustics" (Whiffen), 211.

Painters, 33, 216.

Palace, 12, 14, 15, 16, 47, 53–66, 68, 80, 84, 88–95, 134, 136, 140–144, 172, 174, 175, 176, 177-181, 187, 188, 189, 194, 195, 201, 205, 208, 213, 214, 215, 218, 220.
    act of Assembly for building, 55, 56, 57.
    act of Assembly for finishing, 88.
    additions to, 143, 144.
      See also ballroom of.
    alterations to, 64, 65, 93.
    archaeological investigation at site, 59, 63, 65.
      plan of foundation (*illus.*), 59.
    architectural influence of, 65–66, 84.
    architectural style of, 14, 15, 61–63, 65, 66.
    avenue to planted, 215.
    balcony of, 93.
    ballroom of, 143–144, 174, 176, 177, 213, 218, 220.
    ballroom wing of, 174, 177, 181.
    balls at, 142, 144.
    bannio of, 94.
    barn at, 89.
    basement of, 63.
      See also cellars of.
    bedchambers of, 174.
    billiard room of, 94.
    Botetourt's bedchamber in, 174.
    Botetourt's furnishings in, *see* Botetourt.
    boxwood at, 94.
    brick wall around, 88, 93.
    bricks for, 89.
    bricks from reused, 189, 195.
    brickwork of, 63.
    building materials for, 55, 56, 57, 58, 89.
      from England, 55, 57.
    burning of (1781), 181, 189.
    cellars of, 55, 56, 63, 174.
    chairs in, 65, 218.
    chimney glasses in, 65.
    chimneys of, 64, 65, 177, 178.
    closets in, 174, 220.
    compared to English houses, 61–64.
    completion of building, 88–95.
    contract for repairs to, 142.
    contracted for by piece-work, 16.
    court-yard of, 88, 93, 94.
    cupola of, 63.
    curtains in, 220.
    descriptions of, 14, 15, 213.
    designer of, 56.
    dimensions of, 55, 60, 80.
      on Jefferson's plan of (*illus.*), 60.
    dining room of, 64, 174.
    dinners at, 174.
    Dinwiddie describes (1756), 213.
    directions for building, 55, 56, 57, 58, 64.
    "draft" of, 53, 54, 56.
    dressing room in, 213.
    east flanking building of, 194, 195.
      watercolor of (*illus.*), 194.
    entrance hall of, 63–65, 174, 213.
      See also hall of.
    excavations at site of, 59, 63, 65.
      plan of (*illus.*), 59.
    falling gardens of, 92, 94.
    fences of, 88.
    firearms in, 94.
    fireplaces in, 63, 65, 177.
    fish-pond at, 92, 94.
    flanking buildings of, 57, 189, 194, 195.
    flat roof of, 57, 214.
    floor plan of (*illus.*), 175.
    flower beds at, 94.
    flower pots at, 94.
    forecourt of, 88, 93, 94, 189.
    foundations of, 56, 59, 63, 65, 214.
      excavated, 59, 63, 65.
      plan of (*illus.*), 59.
      laid, 56.
    funds for building, 54, 55, 56, 57.
      for finishing, 88, 89–90, 91, 92, 93.
    furniture in, 65, 143, 144, 213, 218.
    garden front mentioned, 178.
    gardens of, 68, 88, 91, 92, 93, 94, 95.
    garret rooms of, 174, 213.
    gates of, 88, 94.
    glass for, 55.
    glass lustres in, 218.
    great hall in, 63, 64, 65.
    hall of, 63, 64, 65, 174, 178, 213.
    hospital in (1781), 189.
    influence of *see* architectural influence of.
    inspection of work on, 93.
    Jefferson a guest at, 174.
    Jefferson's opinion of, 15.

Palace (continued)
Jefferson's plan of, 60, 61, **63**, 64, 65, 142, 143, 174, 220.
(*illus.*), 60.
Jefferson's plans for remodelling, 177–181, 187, 220.
(*illus.*), 178, 180.
Jefferson's removal from (1780), 188.
kitchen of, 55, 57, 63, 92, 140, 174.
new, 57, 140.
kitchen garden of, 88.
land for, 54, 92, 189.
sold, 189.
lead on roof of, 57–58.
leather hangings for, 65.
library in, 174.
little middle room of, 174, 178, 213.
looking glasses for, 65.
mantelpieces in, 176, 177.
(*illus.*), 176.
muskets arranged in, 94.
name "Palace" used first by Council, 90.
necessary houses at, 94.
offices of, 213.
on Bodleian plate, 58, 61, 93, 94, 205.
(*illus.*), 58.
orchards of, 88, 92.
outbuildings at, 55, 57, 63, 89, 92, 94, 140, 189, 194, 195, 213.
overseer for building, 55, 56, 57, 58, 65, 84, 89, 90, 92.
See also Henry Cary.
paint colors in, 64.
pantry in, 174.
parlor in, 64, 65, 174, 176.
pasture at, 88–89.
plan of by Jefferson *see* Jefferson's plan of.
plan of foundations (*illus.*), 59.
plan of ground floor (*illus.*), 175.
plans for remodelling *see* Jefferson's plans for remodelling.
plaster in, 94.
porch of, 144.
portraits of King and Queen in, 218.
powder room in, 174.
reconstructed building (*illus.*), 201.
reconstruction of (1931–34), 208.
remodelling planned for, 177–181.

See also Jefferson's plan for remodelling.
repairs to, 56, 140–143, 172, 174.
cost of, 140, 141, 142, 143.
roof of, 55, 57–58, 63, 144, 174, 179, 214.
rooms in, 63, 64, 65, 94, 143, 144, 174, 176, 178, 213, 218.
ruins of, 189.
sconces in, 65.
shingles for, 58.
slate for, 55, 57, 58.
smokehouse at, 140.
Spotswood's influence on, 58, 65, 68, 88, 89, 90, 91, 92, 93, 94, 95.
stable at, 55, 57, 63, 92.
staircases of, 177, 178.
standing furniture in, 65, 88, 94, 143, 174, 213, 218.
See also furniture in.
store-rooms in, 144, **174**.
stoves (Dutch) in, 218.
study in, 174.
supper room in, 143, 176, 213, 218, 220.
tables in, 65, 218.
timber for, 57, 89.
upper middle room of, 65.
vaults of, 55, 56.
Venetian blinds in, 218.
view of on Bodleian plate, 61, 93, 94, 205.
(*illus.*), 58.
Virginia arms at, 65.
vista at, 95.
walks of, 94.
wall around, 88, 93.
wallpaper in, 176, 220.
walls of, 57, 63.
windows of, 55, 56, 60, 61.
workmen on, 55, 56, 57, 58, 89, 90, 91, 136, 141, 142.
Palace Green, 15, 64, 141, 205, 215.
planted, 215.
width of, 64.
Palace Street, 60, 113, 116, 117.
Palazzi di Genova, 29, 30.
Palazzo Antonio Doria (Genoa), (*illus.*) 29, 30.
Palazzo Bevilacqua (Bologna), 31.
Palazzo Pesaro (Venice), 31.
Palladio, Andrea, 29, 70, 71, 139, 177, 185, 186, 219.
Palladio Londinensis, 73, 82, 211, 219.
Palmer, W. P., 214.

Pamunkey Indians, 107.
Pamunkey Neck (Virginia), 6.
Pamunkey River, 129, 130, 134.
Panchouque's Encyclopaedia, 220.
Paper, watermarks on, 179, 220.
The Papers of Thomas Jefferson, 220.
Papers Relating to an Affidavit made by his Reverence James Blair . . ., 210.
Parentalia, 72, 210.
Paris, 203.
Parke, Daniel, 19, 21.
Parliament, British, 5.
Parma, 31.
Pavilions, 62–63.
Paving stone, 43, 44, 45, 120, 121, 132, 138, 228.
Peas, 41.
Peden, W., 210.
Pediments, 100, 166, 179, 231.
Peirce, E. C., 212, 219.
Pendleton, Edmund, 88.
Penn, William, 12.
Pennsylvania, 83, 162, 204.
buildings in, 162.
churches in, 83, 162.
See also Philadelphia.
Pennsylvania Cavalry, 195.
Pennsylvania Gazette, 127, 139, 217.
quoted, 127–128.
Pennsylvania Hospital, 162, 163, 165–166.
"The Pennsylvania Hospital" (Krumbhaar), 219.
Pericles, 9.
Perry, W. S., 209, 210. 215.
William Graves, 203, 204, 205.
Perry, Shaw, & Hepburn, 203, 204, 205, 208.
Peterson, C. E., 219.
Petersburg (Virginia), 200.
Pevsner, N., 214.
Pews, 77, 79, 83, 121, 122, 123, 192.
Peyton Randolph House, 112.
Phi Beta Kappa Memorial Hall, 201, 202.
Philadelphia, 8, 12, 162, 166, 174, 214, 230.
architects in, 162.
buildings in, 162, 166.
churches in, 162, 214.
prison in, 166.
town plan of, 8, 12.
Philadelphia Bettering House, 162.
Philadelphia Inquirer, 195.
Physic Garden, Chelsea, 171.
Physicians, 161, 162, 166.
"Piaches," 211.

Piazzas, 35, 37, 50, 104, 157, 168, 182, 211, 227.
  at Capitol, 35, 37, 50, 168, 227.
  at William & Mary College, 104, 182.
  in England, 50, 211.
  in Italy, 211.
  on courthouses, 50, 157.
Piccadilly (London), 167.
Pickford, Joseph, 220.
Pierce, John, 150.
Pine plank, 41, 231.
Piper, J., 211.
Piranesi, G. B., 171.
Pitch, 214.
Pitt, William, 171.
Planks, 41, 214.
Plans (illustrations):
  Brafferton, 108.
  Bruton Parish Church (first brick) foundations, 76.
  Bruton Parish Church (built 1711–15), 154.
    diagrammatic plans of, 81.
  Capitol, foundations, 47.
    floor plans, 44, 45.
    from Bland survey, 39.
  Chapels, octagonal, 183, 185.
  City house (Serlio), 29.
  Codrington College, 105.
  Courthouse of 1770, 158.
  Gaol, 74.
  Heriot's Hospital, 28.
  Magazine, 85.
  Palace, foundations, 59.
    ground plan, 175.
    Jefferson's plan, 60.
    Jefferson's plans for remodelling, 178, 180.
  Palazzo Antonio Doria, 29.
  Playhouse foundations, 115.
  President's House, William & Mary College, 127.
  Public Hospital, 163.
  Secretary's Office, 131.
  William & Mary College, Main Building, 101.
    Jefferson's plan for addition, 99.
Plantation houses, 15.
  See also under names.
Plantations of the Carolina Low Country, 213.
Planters, Virginia, 16.
Plasterers, 189.
Playhouse, 15, 68, 112–117, 127, 154, 208, 216.
  actors in, 113, 114, 216.
  altered for Hustings Courthouse, 116–117, 127, 154.

archaeological investigation at site of, 114, 115.
  plan of foundations (illus.), 115.
balconies in, 115.
boxes in, 114, 115.
builder of, 112–114.
  See also William Levingston.
colors used in England, 114–115.
Court of Hustings in see altered for Hustings Courthouse.
curtain of, 115.
dimensions of, 114
doors of, 114, 115, 117.
English precedent followed in, 114–115.
first in American colonies, 117.
foundations of, 114, 115.
  plan of (illus.), 115.
gallery of, 114, 115.
lots for, 113, 216.
musicians for, 113.
orchestra of, 115.
performances in, 113, 114, 116, 216.
pit of, 114, 115.
plastering in, 117.
scenery for, 115.
shingles for, 117.
stage of, 115.
weatherboards of, 114, 117.
windows of, 117.
Plays, 113, 114, 116, 117, 215, 216.
  in Accomac, 117.
  in Williamsburg, 113, 114, 116, 215, 216.
Playwrights, 68.
Plot, Robert, 70.
Pocahontas, 1.
Pocock, Mr., 19, 21–22.
Point Comfort (Virginia), 136, 217.
Pongoteague Church (Accomac County, Va.), 42, 84.
Pope, William, 70, 74.
Poplar Spring (Gloucester County, Va.), 136, 217.
Porches, 144, 211, 214, 227, 228.
Pork, 41.
Porta Camollia (Siena), 31.
Porticos, 15, 50, 138, 139, 160, 161, 179, 180, 187, 199, 221, 233.
  on Capitol, 15, 138, 139.
  on courthouses, 15, 50, 160, 161.
  on octagonal chapel, 233.
  on Public Hospital, 199, 221.
  on Virginia houses, 139.

proposed for Palace, 179, 180, 187.
Portraits, 3, 69, 109, 139, 140, 173, 218.
  at Capitol, 139–140.
  at Palace, 218.
  of Queen Anne, 139.
  of James Blair (illus.), 3.
  of Robert Boyle, 109.
  of George III and Caroline, 140.
  of Jefferson (illus.), 173.
  of King and Queen, 218.
  of Spotswood (illus.), 69.
Post Masters General, 68.
Potter, Dr., 216.
"Powder Horn," 197. See Magazine.
Powell, Benjamin, 150, 152, 163, 164, 165, 231.
  agreement with for Public Hospital, 231.
  contractor for Bruton Parish Church steeple, 150, 152.
  contractor for Public Hospital, 150, 163, 164, 165, 231.
  Seymour, 164.
Power, James, 147.
Powhatan (James City County, Va.), 141, 218.
The Practical Exemplar of Architecture, 218.
Pratt, Sir Roger, 61, 213.
Preparatory schools, 2, 4.
  See also Grammar Schools.
The Present State of Virginia, 30, 209, 215.
  See also Hugh Jones.
President's House (William & Mary College), 104, 123–127, 141, 181, 189, 196, 205, 212, 220.
  accounts for rebuilding, 220.
  bricklayers for, 123.
  building of, 123–127.
  burned (1781), 189.
  chimneys of, 125.
  compared to Brafferton, 125–126.
  damage to (1862), 196.
  dimensions of, 125.
  doors of, 125.
  elevations of, 125, 126.
    south (illus.), 126.
  floor plan of (illus.), 127.
  foundations laid, 123.
  French occupy (1781), 189.
  funds for building, 123.
    for rebuilding, 189.
  garden of, 123.
  rebuilding of (1782–83), 189, 220.

President's House (William & Mary College) (continued)
repairs to, 141.
restoration of (1931), 205.
rooms in, 125.
undertaker for, 123.
   See also Henry Cary, Jr.
views of, 97, 124, 212.
   on Bodleian Plate (*illus.*), 97.
windows of, 125.
Presidents, William & Mary College *see* Rev. James Blair; William & Mary College, presidents of.
Preston, Rev. William, 215.
Prince George Street (Williamsburg), 141, 218.
Princeton University, 162.
Printing-Office (Williamsburg), 219.
Prisons, 15, 51, 166.
first model, 15.
in Philadelphia, 166.
in Williamsburg *see* Gaol, Public.
Privies, 46.
   See also Necessary Houses.
Proceedings of the American Philosophical Society, 220.
"A Progress to the Mines in the Year 1732" (Byrd), 214.
Professors *see* William & Mary College, professors at.
Public Gaol *see* Gaol, Public.
Public Hospital, 14, 15, 150, 161–166, 190, 193, 196, 208, 219, 221, 229, 230, 231.
act of Assembly establishing, 164.
additions to, 193, 219, 221.
agreement for building *see* building contract for.
architect for, 162, 163, 166, 229–230.
   See also Robert Smith.
Botetourt statue at, 190.
brickwork of, 164, 229, 230, 231.
building contract for, 164, 165, 166, 231.
building materials for, 163, 164, 229, 230, 231.
building of (1770–73), 161–166.
burned (1885), 196.
cellars of, 229.
chimneys of, 230.
completion of, 164–165.
contractor for, 150, 164, 231.
   See also Benjamin Powell

cornice of, 230, 231.
cupola of, 166.
dimensions of rooms in, 229, 230.
directors for, 162, 163, 164, 165, 229, 231.
doors of, 229, 230, 231.
Doric Building at, 193.
eaves of, 230.
Fauquier promotes, 161–162.
floors of, 229, 231.
funds for, 164.
Gothic Building at, 193.
grates for windows of, 164, 229, 230, 231.
hall of, 229.
ironwork for, 229, 230.
   See also grates for.
keeper and matron of, 164.
keeper's apartment in, 229, 230.
land purchased for, 231.
partition walls of, 229.
passages in, 230.
pediment of, 231.
plan of, 163, 164, 166.
   (*illus.*), 163.
portico of, 221.
roof of, 230, 231.
rooms in, 229, 230, 231.
scantling for, 230, 231.
shingles for, 231.
specifications for, 229–230.
staircase in, 229.
stone for, 229.
stone steps of, 164.
stoves for, 230.
undertaker for, 164, 165.
   See also Benjamin Powell.
views of (*illus.*), 165, 193.
walls of, 164, 229, 230, 231.
windows of, 229, 230, 231.
   See also grates for.
woodwork of, 230, 231.
workmen on, 164.
yard of, 164.
Public Prison, 42, 228. *See* Gaol, Public.
"Public Powder Magazines at Charleston" (Davis), 214.
Public Record Office (London), 12, 209, 210, 212, 213, 214, 217, 218, 219.
Public Records Office (Williamsburg), 131. *See* Secretary's Office.
Pugin, A. C., 211.
Pulpits, 79, 122, 123, 233.
Purbeck stone, 121, 138.
Purdie, Alexander, 88.

Q

Quadrangular buildings, 22, 28–29, 31, 36, 99, 102, 105, 181–182.
at Cambridge University, 31.
at Oxford University, 29, 31.
intended for Codrington College, 102.
   plan of (*illus.*), 105.
intended for William & Mary College, 22, 28–29, 31, 102, 181–182.
Jefferson's plan for addition to complete, (*illus.*) 99, 181–182.
Quakers, 119.
"Queen Elizabeth as Astraea," (Yates), 212.
Queen's Arms at Capitol, 43.
   See also Anne, Queen.
Queen's Creek (near Williamsburg), 41.
Queen's House (Greenwich), 215.
Quit-rents, 96, 97, 212.

R

Radoff, M. R. 209, 211, 214.
Rainham Hall (Essex, England), 64.
Raleigh Tavern (Williamsburg), 154.
Randolph, Harry, 33.
   Sir John, 122, 123, 216.
   Peyton, 112, 147, 150, 181.
   house of, 112.
   William, 96.
Ravenscroft, Dionysia (Savage), 22.
Record Book of William & Mary College (Ms.), 221.
"The Recruiting Officer" (play), 216.
Rectors, William & Mary College, 21, 23, 40.
Redwood Library (Newport, R. I.), 179.
Reedwood, Mr., 33.
Registrars, William & Mary College, 23.
Research and Record, Department of (Perry, Shaw & Hepburn), 205.
Research Department (Colonial Williamsburg), 211.
Revolution, American, 11, 189, 191, 193.
Reynolds, Sir Joshua, 171.
Rhoads, Samuel, 162.
Rhode Island, 220.
   See also Newport.

Richards, Godfrey, 70, 71, 73.
  Mourning, 141, 142, 218.
Richardson, H. H., 203.
  John, 217.
Richmond (Virginia), 161, 181, 188, 195, 196, 198, 220.
  capital removed to, 181, 188.
  Capitol at, 161, 181, 220.
Richmond (Yorkshire), 216.
Richmond County (Virginia), 50, 118–119.
Richmond County Courthouse, 50.
Richmond Enquirer, 221.
Rifles, 25.
Riley, E. M., 210, 212, 219.
Rives, Alfred L., 196, 197.
Robertson, Captain, 167.
Robinson, John, Jr., 130.
Rochambeau, General, 220.
Rochambeau Papers, 220.
Rochester (New York), 201.
Rockefeller, John D., Jr., 201, 202, 212.
Rockets, 26.
Roehampton House, (Surrey, England), 66.
Romae Antiquae Notitia, 11.
Roman Antiquities, 11.
Roman architecture, 64.
Roman camps, 86.
Roman Catholics, 8, 83.
Roman town plans, 9, 10, 11.
Rome, 11, 168, 171.
Roofs, 57, 58, 63, 70, 71, 72, 73, 74, 75, 84, 100, 214, 227, 231.
  flat, 57, 70, 71, 72, 73, 74, 214. (*illus.*) 71, 72, 73.
  hip, 84, 100, 227, 231.
  lead on, 57, 58, 214.
  painting of, 214.
  pantiles for, 58.
  platforms on, 63.
  shingles for *see* Shingles.
  slate for *see* Slate.
  tarred, 45, 46, 75, 212, 214.
  See also under buildings by name.
Rose, Rev. Robert, 134, 135, 217.
Rosewell (Gloucester County, Va.), 65, 214.
Rotterdam, 25.
Rowlandson, T., 211.
Royal family, pictures of, 128.
  See also Anne; George III; King and Queen.
The Royal Hospital, Chelsea, 217.
Royal Infirmary (Edinburgh), 219.
Royal Society, 72.
Rubens, P. P., 29, 30.
Rum, 25.

Rustication, 31.
A Ryght Frutefull Mater . . . the Booke of Surveying, 212.
Rykwert, J., 209.
Rysbrack, Michael, 171.

S

Saddles, 33.
St. Andrews, Archbishop of, 67.
St. Anne's Church (Annapolis, Md.), 83, 214.
St. Anne's Parish (Albemarle County, Va.), 134.
St. Asaph, Bishop of, 5.
St. John's Church (Hampton, Va.), 84.
St. John's Church (King William County, Va.), 133.
St. John's Church (Petersburg, Va.), 200.
St. Luke's Church (Isle of Wight County, Va.), 75.
St. Martin-in-the-Fields (London), 179.
St. Mary's Chapel (Birmingham), 220.
St. Mary's City (Maryland), 8, 83.
St. Michael's Church (Charleston, S. C.), 152.
St. Paul's Cathedral (London), 30, 32, 36, 83, 179, 210.
St. Paul's Church (Norfolk, Va.), 84.
St. Paul's Church (Rochester, N. Y.), 201.
St. Paul's Parish (Hanover County, Va.), 134, 217.
St. Paul's Parish (Stafford County, Va.), 134.
St. Peter's Church (New Kent County, Va.), 134, 136.
St. Peter's Church (Philadelphia), 162.
St. Peter's Parish (New Kent County, Va.), 79, 217.
St. Stephen's Chapel (Westminster), 36.
Salisbury, Bishop of, 5.
Salmon, William, 72–73, 211, 219.
Salzman, L. F., 214.
San Marino (California), 233.
Sand, 214.
Sash glass, 97.
Sash windows, 23, 42, 55, 210.
  earliest use of, 210.
  See also Windows.
Saunders, Mrs. Frances Bland Coalter, 218.
  John, 182, 220.
Savage, Dionysia, 22.

Sawyers, 21.
Scaffolding, 41.
Scandinavia, 212.
Scantling, 79, 182, 230, 231.
Schoolhouses (Williamsburg), 96, 107.
Schools, 2, 4, 16–17, 20, 212.
  architectural, 16–17.
  free, 20.
  preparatory, 2, 4, 20, 212.
  See also Grammar schools; Indian school; William & Mary College, grammar school at.
Sconces, 65.
Scotchtown (Hanover County, Va.), 112.
Scotland, 2, 29, 67, 83–84, 219.
  cruciform churches in, 83–84.
  Secretary for, 67.
  Surveyor General for, 29.
  universities in, 2.
  See also Aberdeen University, Edinburgh University.
Scots, 2.
Scottish architecture, 29–30, 83–84, 219.
Scottish influence on American colonial architecture, 219.
  on William & Mary College, 29.
Sculptors, 167, 168, 171.
Seats, 43, 161.
The Secret Diary of William Byrd of Westover, 1709–1712, 215.
Secretary of Virginia, 25, 32.
Secretary's Office, 130–134, 189, 190, 191.
  alterations to (1785–86), 189–190.
  bill for erecting (1747), 130.
  bookcases for, 133.
  brick walls of, 132.
  brickwork of, 133.
  chair-rails in, 133.
  chimneys of, 134.
  Clerk's Office in, 191.
  completed (1748), 130.
  cornice of, 134.
  designer of, 131.
  doorway of, 133.
  eaves of, 133–134.
  elevation (south) of, (*illus.*), 132.
  fireplaces in, 131, 134.
  floors of, 132.
  photograph of (*illus.*), 133.
  plan of (*illus.*), 131.
  presses for, 133.
  records in, 130, 132, 133.

Secretary's Office (continued)
  roof of, 132.
  rooms in, 131, 133.
  shingles of, 132.
  stone paving in, 132.
  walls of, 132, 133.
  workmen for, 130.
Select Architecture, 186.
Serge, green, 43.
Serlio, Sebastiano, 29, 30, 31, 61, 65, 71, 72, 73, 213, 214.
Servants, 16, 21, 46, 93.
  indentured, 16, 21, 46
Shadows in Silver: a Record of Virginia 1850–1900, 218.
Shaftesbury, Earl of, 94.
Shaw, Thomas Mott, 204.
Sheldonian Theatre (Oxford), 72.
Shells, 21, 210.
  See also Cockle-shell lime; Oyster-shell lime.
Shelly, F., 218. 220.
Shepley, Rutan and Coolidge, 203.
Shingles, 21, 44, 46, 58, 70, 74, 132, 212, 214, 227, 231.
  cedar, 212.
  cypress, 212, 227, 231.
  heart-pine, 212.
  painted, 214,
  round-butt, 132.
  tarred, 45–46, 212, 214.
  See also Roofs.
Shirley (Charles City County, Va.), 139.
Shortess, J., 160.
Shrewsbury, Duke of, 19.
Shrewsbury stone, 121, 138.
Shropshire (England), 61, 77.
Shurtleff, Harold R., 205.
Siena, 31.
"The Sims and Eaton Schools and their Successor" (Campbell), 212.
Skelton, Bathurst, 217.
  James, 136, 137, 138.
  Martha (Wayles), 217.
Skins and furs, duty on, 18.
Slate, 55, 57, 58, 195.
  from England, 55, 57.
  on palaces, 58.
  See also Roofs.
Slaves, 16, 21, 44, 46, 55, 56, 57.
  See also Negroes.
Slaves and Liquors, duty on, 54, 56, 70, 77, 86, 90.
Sloane, Sir Hans, 171.
Smallpox, 127, 129.
Smith, Christopher, 107.
  Francis, 64.

Robert, 162, 163, 164, 166, 219, 229, 230.
  description of Public Hospital by, 229–230.
  William, 111, 112, 217.
Smyth, Robert, 2.
Snead, Mr., 42.
  John, 42.
  Robert, 42.
Society for the Propagation of the Gospel, 103, 104, 105.
"Some Virginian House Plans Reconsidered" (Whiffen), 214.
Somerset (England), 75.
Somerset House (London), 168.
South Carolina, 8, 64.
  See also Charleston (South Carolina).
Southampton, Earl of, 209.
Southern, Richard, 115, 216.
The Southern Argus, 217.
Southern Literary Messenger, 214.
Spanish Succession, War of, 67.
Speakers of House of Burgesses *see* Burgesses, House of.
Spotswood, Alexander, 9, 14, 30, 56, 58, 65, 67, 68, 69, 70, 73, 74, 77, 79, 80, 82, 83, 84, 86, 88, 89, 90, 91, 92, 93, 94, 95, 97, 98, 100, 102, 103, 107, 113–114, 152, 192, 214, 225.
  architectural ability of, 68.
  architectural activities of at Bruton Parish Church, 68, 77, 79–80, 82, 83, 84, 100, 102.
    at Debtor's Prison, 68, 70, 73, 74.
    at Magazine, 68, 86, 88.
    at Palace, 58, 65, 68, 88, 89, 90, 91, 92, 93, 94, 95.
    at William & Mary College, 30, 68, 97, 98, 100, 102, 103.
  arms arranged in Palace by, 94.
  avenue laid out by, 214–215.
  bell given to Bruton Church by, 152.
  biographical notes on, 67–68.
  books of, 94.
  Byrd visits, 214.
  character of, 67–68, 73.
  complaints against, 91, 92, 93, 95.
  deputy post-master general, 68.
  education of Indians promoted by, 107.
  governor of Virginia (1710–1722), 9, 56, 67, 225.

iron-works of, 68, 73.
  invitation to play refused by Council, 114.
  King's birthday celebration by, 113–114.
  letters of quoted, 90, 91, 92, 93, 113–114.
  mathematical ability of, 68, 73, 80, 82, 100.
  pew of in Bruton Parish Church, 77, 83, 192.
  portrait of (*illus.*), 69.
  servants of, 93.
  theatre patronized by, 68, 114.
  town plan of Williamsburg influenced by, 9, 14.
Spotsylvania County (Virginia), 68, 73, 116.
Spurr, Samuel, 145, 164.
Stables, 55, 57, 63, 183.
Stadtbibliothek at Berne (Switzerland), 211.
Stafford County (Virginia), 134, 217.
Staffordshire (England), 62, 217.
Stagg, Charles, 112, 113, 116.
  Mary, 112, 113.
Staircases *see* under buildings by name.
Stamp Act, 171.
Statehouses, 7, 8, 34, 36, 39, 211.
  at Annapolis, 39.
  at Jamestown *see* Jamestown (Virginia), statehouse at.
  at Williamsburg *see* Capitol (Williamsburg).
  meaning of term, 211.
Statues, 166–171
  in American colonies, 171.
  See also Botetourt Statue.
Steeples, 150, 152.
Steps, stone, 44, 137, 157, 164.
  See also under buildings by name.
Stith, Mr., 123.
Stoddert, James, 209.
Stone, 43, 44, 45, 55, 103, 120, 121, 132, 137, 138, 157, 163, 164, 228, 229.
  from England, 45, 55, 120, 157, 164.
  in Barbados, 103.
  paving *see* Paving stone.
  Purbeck, 121, 138.
  Shrewsbury, 121, 138.
Stoney, S. G., 213.
Stony Middleton (Derbyshire), 220.
Story, Thomas, 216.
Stoughton Hall (Harvard College), 28, 210.

Stoves, 139, 192, 218, 230.
  at Bruton Parish Church, 192.
  at Capitol, 139.
  at Palace, 218.
  at Public Hospital, 230.
  Dutch, 218.
Stratford (Westmoreland County, Va.), 50, 65, 214.
Stuart and Georgian Churches outside London, 214.
Suffolk (England), 83.
Summerson, J., 31, 210, 219.
Sundials, 46.
Surry County (Virginia), 103.
Surveyors-General, 6, 31.
Surveyors of buildings, 16, 17, 21, 22, 41.
  use of term, 16, 41.
Surveyors of land, 12, 16, 46.
Surveys, 12, 19, 25, 37, 39, 212.
  See also Bland Survey of Williamsburg.
Sutton Coldfield (Warwickshire), 111, 112.
  rectory at, (*illus.*) 111, 112.
Swedish Lutheran Church (Pennsylvania), 83.
Swiss travellers, 23, 25.
  See also Michel, Franz Ludwig.
Switzer, Stephen, 94.

T

T-plan houses, 211.
Tables, 65, 106, 218.
Taliaferro, Elizabeth, 218.
  Richard, 137, 140, 141, 142, 218.
Tallmadge, Thomas E., 204.
Tangier, 67.
Tankards, silver, 33.
Tape, red, 9, 43.
Tar, 75, 212.
  See also Roofs, tarred.
Tayloe, John, 217.
Taylor, Mr., 142.
  Sir Robert, 16.
Tazewell, John, 154, 216.
Tedington (Charles City County, Va.), 139.
The Ten Books of Architecture, 209.
Tents, 25.
Thacker, Mr., 24, 33.
Theatres, 15, 68, 112–117, 216.
  first in American colonies, 15, 68, 112.
    See also Playhouse
  in Charleston, S. C., 116.
  in England, 114–115, 216.
  in Europe, 115.
  in Richmond, Yorkshire, 216.

in Williamsburg, 15, 68, 112–117, 216.
  second in Williamsburg, 117.
  See also Playhouse.
  subscriptions to, 216.
Theological Seminary of Virginia, 201.
Theorike and Practike of Moderne Warres, 9.
Theory and Practice of Gardening, 94.
Third Presbyterian Church (Philadelphia), 162.
Thomas Jefferson, Architect, 213, 220.
Thorne, Thomas E., 212.
Thorpe, George, 1.
Thorpe Hall (Lincolnshire), 61–62, 64.
Thurii, 9.
Thurlow, C. E., 220.
Tiles, Dutch, 176.
Timber, 21, 42, 95, 103.
  See also Scantling.
Timson House (Williamsburg), 141.
Tinling, M., 215.
Tipping, H. A., 213, 220.
Tobacco, 6, 7, 56, 57, 75, 77, 218.
  levies paid in, 75, 77.
  staple in Virginia, 7.
  tax on, 6, 56, 57.
Toll bridges, 134.
Tombs, Braintree, Essex, 218.
Tombs, Bruton Parish Churchyard, 144, 145, 146, 147. (*illus.*), 144, 145, 147.
Town halls, 50.
Town plans, 8, 9, 10, 11, 12, 14.
  axial, 12, 14.
  for Annapolis (Maryland), 8–9, 10.
  for Charleston (South Carolina), 8.
  for London, 9, 12.
  for Londonderry (Ulster), 10.
  for New Haven (Connecticut), 10.
  for Philadelphia, 8.
  for Williamsburg, 8–14.
  French, 14.
  Greek, 9.
  gridiron, 8, 9.
  Roman, 9, 10, 11.
  Vitruvius quoted on, 10–11.
Town squares, 211.
Transactions of the American Philosophical Society, 219.
Travels in North America during the Years 1834–36, 221.
Travels through the States of North

America . . . 1795–97, 221.
Treasurer of Virginia, 56, 57, 92, 137, 167.
Trinity Church (Maryland), 36.
Trinity Church (Newport, R. I.), 123.
Trinity College (Oxford University), 31, 211.
Tryon, William, 172.
Tryon's Palace (North Carolina), 172–173.
Tuckahoe (Henrico County, Va.), 50, 177.
Tucker, Henry St. George, 221.
  Mrs. Lelia, 218.
  St. George, 221.
Tullett, John, 41, 79, 96, 97, 98.
  undertaker for rebuilding William & Mary College, 96, 97, 98.
Tuscan order, 186, 233.
Tyler, John, 79, 86, 89.
  President John, 216.
  L. G., 215, 217.
Tyler's Quarterly Historical Magazine, 216.

U

Ulster, 10.
Undertakers for buildings, 15, 16, 18, 19, 21, 35, 40, 41, 42, 75, 120, 123, 134–135, 164, 165, 182, 217.
  for Bruton Parish Church, 75.
  for Capitol, 35, 40, 41, 42, 134, 135.
  for President's House, 123.
  for Public Hospital, 164, 165.
  for William & Mary College, 18, 19, 20.
    addition to, 182.
    chapel, 120.
  in England, 15–16, 217
Upholsterers, 220.
Union troops, 195, 196, 216.
University of Edinburgh, 4, 29.
University of Virginia, 179, 220.
University planned for Virginia, 1–2, 4.
Ushers for Grammar School, 4, 23.

V

Vanbrugh, Sir John, 16, 68, 211.
Van Dyke, Sir Anthony, 139.
Varina (Henrico County, Va.), 4.
Vaughan, Samuel, 221.
Vauter's Church (Essex County, Va.), 133.
Venetian blinds, 218.

Venice, 31.

Vesta, temple of, 184, 185, 233.

The Vestry Book and Register of St. Peter's Parish, 214, 217, 218.

Vestry Book of Bruton Parish (Ms.), 1827–1889, 221; 1899–1912, 221.

The Vestry Book of Christ Church Parish, 218.

The Vestry Book of Petsworth Parish, 217.

The Vestry Book of St. Paul's Parish, 217.

Villa Thieni (Cicogna), 177.

Virginia, 1, 2, 4, 6, 7, 10, 11, 15, 16, 65, 94–95, 118–119, 160, 219, 225–226.
  arms of, 65.
  books in (titles), 11, 94–95, 160, 186, 219.
  building methods in, 15–16.
  capitals of, 6, 7, 8.
    See also Jamestown; Richmond; Williamsburg.
  colleges for, 1, 2, 4.
    See also William & Mary College.
  courthouses in, 15.
    See also Courthouses; and under names of counties.
  dividing line between Carolina and, 212.
  governors of listed, 1690–1781, 225–226.
  Indians in *see* Indians.
  plantation houses in, 15, 65, 118–119.
    See also under names of plantations.
  public records of, 128, 130, 131.
  schools planned for, 1, 2, 4.
    See also Grammar Schools; Indian School; William & Mary College.
  tobacco staple of, 7.
  towns in, 7, 8, 10.
    See also under names of towns.
  waterways in, 7, 10.

Virginia Company, 1, 2, 4.

Virginia Gazette, 88, 114, 116, 117, 138, 146, 147, 150, 152, 154, 155, 160, 164, 167, 180, 182, 216, 217, 218, 219, 220.

Virginia Gazette or American Advertiser, 221.

Virginia Historical Society, 210, 214, 218.

Virginia Indian Company, 86.

Virginia Magazine of History and Biography, 210, 211, 212, 213, 215, 216, 217, 218, 219, 220.

Virginia State Archives, 212, 213, 216, 217, 218, 219, 221.

Virginia's Eastern Shore: A History of Northampton and Accomac Counties, 212.

Vistas, 95.

Vitruvius, Marcus, 10–11, 72, 209.

Vitruvius Britannicus, 61, 66, 213.

Vitruvius Scoticus, 28, 160, 219.

Vitry-le-François, 9.

W

Wainscoting, 43, 45, 128, 133, 161, 182.
  marbleized, 45.

Wales, 5.

Walker, Thomas, 231.
  William, 134–135, 136, 137, 217.

Waller, Benjamin, 137, 147, 217.

Wallis, John, 72, 73.

Wallpaper, 176, 220.

Walnut Street Prison (Philadelphia), 166.

Ware, Isaac, 143, 219.

Ware Church (Gloucester County, Va.), 133.

Warsaw (Virginia), 50.

Warwick County (Virginia), 40.

Warwickshire (England), 64, 111, 112, 168.

Washington, General, 220.

Washington (D. C.), 214.

Waterman, Thomas T., 50, 63, 64, 205, 209, 212, 213, 214, 215, 219.

Watermarks, 179, 220.

Watermarks, 220.

Watertables, 35, 214, 227, 229, 230.

Watson's Hospital (Edinburgh), 219.

Wayles, Martha, 217.

Webb, John, 215.
  M. I., 219.

Weekly Gazette and Eastern Virginia Advertiser, 221.

Weld, Isaac, 221.

Wertenbaker, T. J., 211.

Wesley, John, 187.

Westertoun, Daniel, 46.

Westminster Abbey (London), 168.

Westminster Hall (London), 36.

Westmoreland, Earl of, 212.

Westmoreland County (Virginia), 50, 65.

Westover (Charles City County, Va.), 65, 96.

Wheatley, Mr., 33.
  John, 136, 137, 142.

Wheelwrights, 150.

Whiffen, Marcus, 211, 214.

Whitby, Thomas, 46.

Whitchurch Church (Shropshire), 217.

Whitehall Palace (London), 210.

Whitelaw, R. T., 212.

Whiting, John, 220.

"Who Planned Kingston?" (Young), 215.

Wicaco (Pennsylvania), 83.

William III, 5, 9, 48, 112, 211.
  address of General Assembly of Virginia to, 5.
  death of proclaimed in Williamsburg, 25.
  Williamsburg named for, 9.

William & Mary College in Virginia, 1, 2, 4–6, 7, 8, 12, 14, 15, 16, 18–33, 40, 41, 63, 68, 73, 96, 97–112, 119–126, 141, 210.
  accounts of, 21, 210.
  archaeological report on main building, 23, 210, 211.
  architectural style of, 14, 15.
    See also Main Building of.
  at Middle Plantation, 6–7, 8.
  Botetourt Statue at, 168–169, 190.
    See also Botetourt Statue.
  buildings of *see* Main Building of.
    See also Brafferton; President's House.
  chancellors of, 23, 32, 216, 217.
  chapel of *see* Main Building of, chapel.
  charter of, 4, 5, 6, 18, 32, 215.
  commencement exercises at, 23.
  divinity school at, 119.
  education of Indians at, 106–112.
    See also Brafferton.
  faculty at, 182.
    See also masters at; presidents of; professors at.
  fire at (1705), 23, 24, 32–33.
  fire at (1859), 193, 195, 196.
  fire at (1862), 195–196, 216.
  founder of, 2, 4–6.
  founding of, 4–6.
  French hospital at, 189.
  funds for, 5, 6, 18, 20, 22.

governors of, 20, 21, 23, 96, 97, 107, 181.
See also visitors and governors of.
grammar school in, 4, 23, 24, 26, 33, 107.
hospital at (1781), 189.
house for president of *see* President's House.
Indian school at, 106–112.
Latin verses by scholars at, 6.
Main Building of (first form, 1695–1705), 18–33, 42, 49, 96, 98, 100, 103, 107, 119, 128, 210, 211, 212.
  archaeological evidences of, 23, 24, 25, 26, 210–211.
  balconies on (1702), 25, (*illus.*) 27.
  basement of, 24, 26, 28, 31, 100, 210, 211.
  brickwork of, 24–25, 210.
    See also walls of.
  builders for, 21, 22.
  building accounts of, 21, 22.
  building materials for (1694–1697), 19, 20, 21, 22.
  burning of, 23, 24, 28, 30, 32–33, 96, 103, 107, 128, 211.
  chapel for mentioned, 20–21, 119.
  chapel held in hall, 119.
  chimneys of, 32, 33.
  compared to Heriot's Hospital, 29, 30.
  completion of building, 7, 22–23.
  cornice of, 28, 31.
  Council Chamber in, 33.
  cupola of, 26, (*illus.*) 27, 49, 102.
  descriptions of (1702–1705), 14, 25–27.
  design of, 18, 19, 24, 25, 26, 27, 28, 29, 30, 31, 32.
    attributed to Christopher Wren, 6, 28, 30, 31, 32, 33.
  dimensions of, 24, 28, 98, 100.
  doorways in, 26.
  eaves of, 28, 31.
  entrance to, 26, (*illus.*) 27, 100.
  faults in building noted by Nicholson, 32–33.
  fire at (1705) *see* burning of.
  fireplaces in, 32–33.
  floors in, 32.

foundations laid (1695), 18, 20, 41.
  excavated, 210, 211.
  rebuilt on, 24, 25.
frieze, ornamentation of, 31.
gallery in, 24, 33.
girders in, 33.
grammer school in *see* William & Mary College, grammar school of.
grates in, 32.
gutters on, 24. *See also* lead on.
hall of, 33, 100, 103, 119, 210.
illustration of *see* Michel drawing of.
interior plan of, 24, 26.
joists in, 33.
kitchen of, 103.
lantern of, 26.
lead on, 24, 33.
Michel drawing of, 23, 25, 26, 27, 28, 31, 49. (*illus.*), 27.
number of stories in, 26, (*illus.*) 27, 28.
overseer for building, 21.
platted on Bland survey (1699), 19, 25.
quadrangle planned for, 22, 28, 29.
roof of, 21, 26, (*illus.*) 27, 100, 212.
rooms in, 23, 24, 26, 32, 33.
schoolroom (grammar school) in, 24, 26, 33.
Scottish influence on, 28, 29, 30.
shingles for, 21.
stair-hall in, 24, 26, 33.
stairs in, 24, 26, 33.
steps of, 210.
surveyor for building, 21, 22.
undertaker for building, 18, 19, 21.
walls of, 21, 24, 25, 26, 28.
  rebuilt on, 24, 25, 96, 98, 195, 196.
windows of, 23, 26, (*illus.*) 27, 31, 33, 100, 210, 211.
wood fires in, 32.
workmen on, 19, 21, 22.
Wren attribution discussed, 6, 28–32.
Main Building of (second form, 1709–1859), 14, 23, 24, 25, 26, 28, 96–106, 107, 119–123, 181–185, 205, 210–211, 215.
  addition proposed for, 99, 103, 181–185, 211.

archaeological evidences of, 23, 24–25, 26, 182, 185, 210–211.
banisters for, 97.
basement of, 100, 103.
bedsteads in, 97.
bell for, 97.
"Blue Room" of, 104.
brew house for, 97.
brickwork of, 24–25, 121, 210, 216.
building materials for, 96, 97, 103.
burning of (1859), 193, 195, 196.
chapel added to (1729–32), 100, 119–123, 182, 210.
  aisle of, 121, 122, 123.
  bids for, 119–120.
  builder for, 120.
  burials in, 121–123, 216–217.
  communion table in, 123.
  completion of, 120, 123.
  design of, 121-122.
  dimensions of, 121.
  forms in, 121.
  foundations laid, 120.
  furnishings of, 121, 122.
  monuments in, 122, 123.
  on Jefferson's plan, (*illus.*) 99, 182.
  pulpit in, 122, 123.
  undertaker for, 120.
  vaults under, 121, 122, 216, 217.
  walls of, 120, 210.
  windows of, 216, 217.
classrooms in, 103, 107.
  on Jefferson's plan (*illus.*), 99.
closets in, 215.
common room in, 104.
compared to Chelsea Hospital, 30, 102.
compared to Codrington College, 102, 103.
cost of rebuilding, 96, 97.
cupola of, 102.
description of, 14.
design of, 23, 24, 25, 26, 102.
dimensions of, 24, 28, 98–100, 102.
dormer windows in, 98.
  See also windows of.
dormitories in, 104–105, 215.
east elevation of (*illus.*), 102.
eaves of, 28.
entrance to, 100.
foundations for proposed addition to, 182, 184.

William & Mary College
  Main Building—second form
    (continued)
    French hospital in (1781),
      189.
    funds for building, 96, 97.
    furniture for, 97, 104, 106.
    gallery (or passage) of, 104.
    garrett in, 215.
    grammar school-room in, 103,
      107.
    grates in, 106.
    hall of, 97, 100, 103, 105,
      119, 120, 182.
    hospital in (1781), 189.
    illustrations of, 3, 97, 98, 192,
      198, 199.
    interior plan of, 24.
    Jefferson's plan for addition to,
      24, 98, 99, 103, 181–185,
      211.
      (illus.), 99.
    kitchen of, 97, 103.
    laundry for, 97.
    library in, 104.
    new building for, 182.
      See also addition proposed
        for; Jefferson's plan for ad-
        dition to.
    number of stories, 28.
    outbuildings for, 97.
    passages in, 104, 215.
    pavilions of, 100, 101.
    pediment of, 100.
    piazza of, 50, 104, 182.
    plan for addition to see Jeffer-
      son's plan for addition to.
    plan of (illus.), 101.
    plastering in, 215.
    president's room in, 104.
    professors' rooms in, 104, 106,
      109.
    quadrangular plan for, 22, 28–
      29, 102–103, 181–182.
    repairs to, 193, 215, 220.
    restored to second form, 205,
      207.
    roof of, 100, 205.
    rooms of, 103–104, 105, 106,
      182, 185, 215.
      on Jefferson's plan (illus.),
        99.
    Spotswood and design of, 30,
      68, 97, 98, 100, 102, 103.
    stairhall in, 2, 4, 26.
    stairs in, 24, 26, 103, 105,
      182, 185, 215.
    students' lodgings in, 103–
      104, 105.
    undertaker for building, 96.

    view of on Bodleian plate, (il-
      lus.) 97, 205.
    walls of first building reused,
      24, 25, 26, 28, 96, 98, 100,
      121, 195, 196, 207.
    whitewashing in, 215.
    windows of, 97, 98, 100, 182,
      216, 217.
    workmen on, 97.
  Main Building of (third form,
      1859–1862), 194, 195,
      196.
    architects for, 194, 195.
    burned (1862), 195–196,
      216.
    classrooms of, 195.
    engraving of (illus.), 194.
    Italian style of, 195, 196.
    roof of, 195.
    stairway of, 195.
    towers of, 195, 196.
    walls of, 195, 196.
  Main Building of (fourth form,
      1865–1928), 196, 197,
      205.
    architects for, 196.
    photograph of (illus.), 197.
    walls of, 197.
  masters at, 4, 5, 7, 23, 24, 120,
      190.
  May Day celebration (1699) at,
      7, 22.
  palace lands conveyed to, 189.
  presidents of, 2, 4, 6, 23, 120,
      123, 182, 190, 215, 221.
    house for see President's
      House.
    salary of, 123.
    transfer of college to, 120.
    See also James Blair.
  professors at, 4, 5, 7, 30, 120,
      123, 182, 190, 201, 215.
  rectors of, 21, 23, 40.
  restoration of buildings at, 205,
      207.
  Scottish influence on, 29–30.
  seal of, 6.
  servants at, 7.
  site selected, 6–7, 8.
  sites for considered, 6.
  Spotswood's books left to, 94.
  statutes of, 123, 215.
  students at, 7, 22, 23, 33.
  transfer of to president and mas-
      ters, 120, 215.
  trustees of, 23, 120.
  visitors and governors of, 96, 97,
      107, 181, 215, 221.
    See also governors of.

  "Wren Building" of see Main
      Building of.
  yard of, 141.
William and Mary College Ar-
    chives, 210, 215, 216, 218,
    220, 221.
William and Mary College Quar-
    terly Historical Magazine,
    209, 210, 211, 212, 214,
    215, 216, 217, 218, 219,
    220, 221.
William Byrd's Histories of the
    Dividing Line . . . , 212.
Williamsburg, 6, 7, 8, 9, 10, 11,
    12, 13, 14, 15, 22, 23, 25–
    26, 33, 35, 39, 41, 51, 61,
    68, 74, 85, 96, 103, 107,
    112, 114, 116, 117, 126,
    128, 129, 130, 136, 141,
    142, 146, 152, 154, 158,
    160, 164, 188, 189, 190,
    191, 193, 194, 195, 196,
    198, 199, 200, 204, 205–
    208, 209, 215, 216, 218,
    219.
  access to rivers from, 10, 12.
  acreage of (1699), 11–12.
  act of General Assembly to build
      city of (1699), 7–8, 12, 35.
  architectural importance of, 15.
  asylum in see Public Hospital.
  axial plan of, 10, 12, 14, 126.
  battle of, 195.
  Bland survey of see Bland Sur-
      vey (1699).
  books sold in, 160, 219.
  building restrictions in, 12, 51.
  buildings of described, 14–15.
    See also under buildings by
      name.
  capital of Virginia moved to
      (1699), 7, 8.
  capital removed from (1779–
      80), 188.
  capitol built at see Capitol.
  capitol rebuilt at (1747–53),
      130, 140.
  celebration at (1702), 25–26.
  churches in see Bruton Parish
      Church.
  council of, 199.
  Civil War in, 190, 193, 195–
      196, 199.
  college at see William & Mary
      College.
  college exercises at (1700), 23.
  Common Hall of, 116, 117, 154.
  Corporation of, 116, 189.
  Court of Hustings of, 116, 117,
      154.
    See also Hustings Court.

courthouses for, 150, 154.
  See also Courthouse of 1770.
directors for building, 12.
Governor's Palace at *see* Palace.
hospital in *see* Public Hospital.
hospitals in (1781), 189.
houses in, 12, 51, 103, 112, 136, 141, 142, 164, 204.
  dimensions of, 51.
  regulations concerning, 12, 51.
incorporation of city (1722), 152.
Indians visit, 23, 26, 142.
  See also Indian schools.
jail at *see* Gaol, Public.
land set aside for (1699), 11–12.
lots laid off in (1699), 12.
lunatic hospital in *see* Public Hospital.
maps of, 12, 13, 218–219. (*illus.*), 13.
  See also Frenchman's Map.
Market Square in, 10, 85, 146, 154–155, 158.
mayors of, 74, 117, 152.
named for William III, 9.
Nicholson and plan of, 8–12.
ordinaries in, 22, 33, 41.
Palace at *see* Palace.
plat of (1699) *see* Bland Survey.
plays in, 114, 116, 215, 216.
  See also Playhouse; Theatre.
population of, 12.
ports for, 12, 209.
printing office in, 219.
prisons in *see* Gaol, Public.
public buildings in *see* Bruton Parish Church; Capitol; Courthouse of 1770; Gaol, Public; Magazine; Palace; Playhouse; Public Hospital; William & Mary College.
public times in, 114.
removal of capital from considered, 128–130.
removal of capital to Richmond from (1780), 188.
restoration of buildings in, 198, 200, 204, 205–207.
Revolutionary War in, 11, 189, 191, 193.
roads to, 152, 209.
schoolhouse in, 96, 107.
schools in, 189, 190, 191.
  See also Grammar schools; Indian school; William & Mary College, grammar school of.

site for, 6–7, 8, 10.
  See also Middle Plantation.
size of, 12.
smallpox in, 129.
Spotswood and plan of, 9, 68.
springs at, 10.
statehouse at called "Capitol," 11.
  See also Capitol.
streets in, 9, 10, 11, 12, 141, 152.
  in form of cypher, 9.
theatre in *see* Playhouse; Theatres.
town plan of, 8–15, 68.
Williamsburg Holding Corporation, 203.
Williamsburg Restoration, 199–208.
Wilson, Sir William, 32.
Wilton, Joseph, 171.
Wiltshire (England), 83.
Windows, arched, 42, 228.
  arrangement of, 61.
  bow, 36.
  casement, 42, 210.
  dormer, 44, 98, 227.
  sash, 23, 42, 97, 210, 227, 230.
  Venetian, 118.
  See also under buildings by name.
Wise, Henry, 94, 95.
  J. C., 216.
Wittkower, R., 219.
Woburn Abbey (Bedfordshire), 168.
"Woburn Abbey, Bedfordshire—II. Some Georgian Craftsmen" (Hussey), 219.
Woodstock, Thomas, 32.
Workmen, 2, 15, 16, 18, 19, 21, 22, 32, 41, 42, 44, 46, 49, 56, 57, 79, 89, 90, 91, 130, 134, 135, 146, 147, 164.
  drinking by prohibited, 41.
  food for, 41, 46.
  from England, 2, 21, 41, 44.
  houses for, 41, 46.
  in England, 32.
  shortage of, 18, 19.
  See also Bricklayers; Carpenters; Joiners; Masons, etc.; and under buildings by name.
Wormley, Ralph, 210.
Wray, James, 140–141, 218.
Wren, Sir Christopher, 6, 9, 12, 15, 28–32, 72, 73, 82, 83, 98, 102, 214.
  architectural style of, 31, 32.
  buildings designed by, 30, 32, 72, 83, 214.

churches designed by, 83.
  See also St. Paul's Cathedral.
comments of on quadrangles, 31.
design of William & Mary College Main Building attributed to, 6, 30–32, 98, 102.
  attribution questioned, 30–32.
funeral of, 30.
plan by for London, 9, 12.
professor of astronomy, 72.
quoted as to building methods, 15.
Surveyor-General of the King's Works, 6, 31–32.
"Wren Building," 32.
  See William & Mary College, Main Building of.
Wren Society Publications, 30, 210, 211, 214.
Wright, L. B., 209, 214.
The Writings of Col. William Byrd of Westover . . . , 212, 214, 216.
Wythe, Elizabeth (Taliaferro), 218.
  George, 141, 150–151.
Wythe House (Williamsburg), 141, 204, 205, 218.

XYZ

Yates, Frances A., 212.
Year Book of the A.P.V.A., 1896–1897, 221.
The Year Book of the City of Charleston, 214.
Yeardley, George, 1.
York County (Virginia), 42, 79, 155, 161, 219.
  courthouses of, 161, 219.
  land in annexed, 155.
York County Courthouse, 161, 219.
  furnishings of, 161.
York County Records (Clerk's Office, Yorktown), 42, 210, 212, 215–216, 218, 219.
York River, 6, 10, 12, 41, 130.
  creeks from, 10, 12, 41.
Yorkshire (England), 106, 216.
Yorktown (Virginia), 6, 21, 25, 41, 164, 167, 217.
  considered as site for college, 6.
  courthouse at, 41.
    See also York County Courthouse.
  fort at, 41.
  gaol at, 21.
Young, J. G., 215.
  John, 33.
Zion Lutheran Church (Philadelphia), 162.

THE PUBLIC BUILDINGS OF WILLIAMSBURG
was composed, printed, and bound by
The Lakeside Press, R. R. Donnelley & Sons Company,
of Chicago, Illinois, and Crawfordsville, Indiana,
for Colonial Williamsburg, Williamsburg, Virginia.
The types used are Fairfield and Centaur.
The paper is Curtis Vellum, made by Curtis Paper Company.
The book was designed by John J. Walklet, Jr.
Plans and elevations of the public buildings are by
Singleton P. Moorehead.

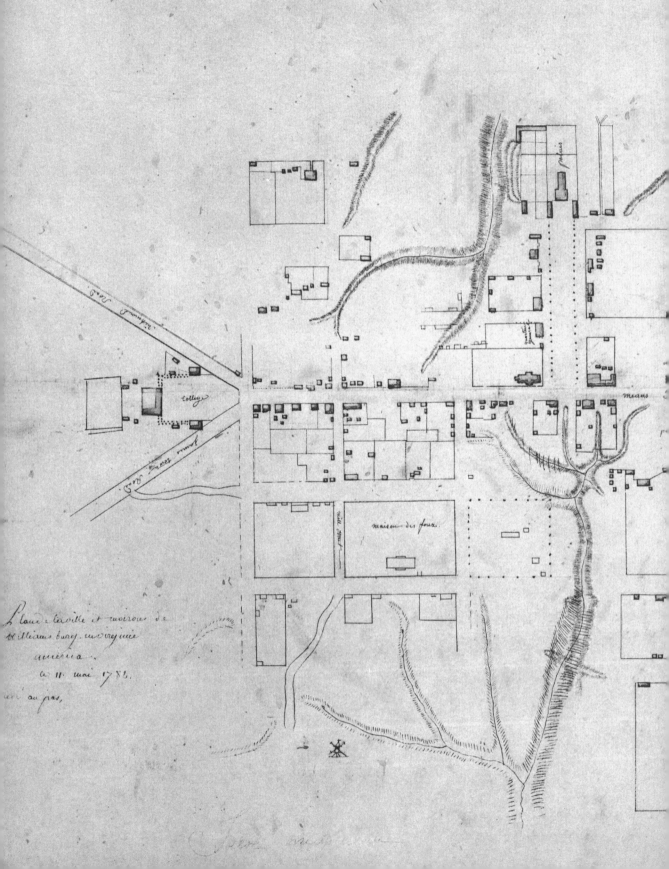

Plan de la ville et environs de
Williamsburg en virginie
amérique.
le 11 mai 1782.

levé au pas.